CONTEMPORARY ECONOMIC GEOGRAPHIES

Inspiring, Critical and Plural Perspectives

Edited by
Jennifer Johns and Sarah Marie Hall

BRISTOL
UNIVERSITY
PRESS

First published in Great Britain in 2024 by

Bristol University Press
University of Bristol
1–9 Old Park Hill
Bristol
BS2 8BB
UK
t: +44(0)117 374 6645
e: bup-info@bristol.ac.uk

Details of international sales and distribution partners are available at bristoluniversitypress.co.uk

British Library Cataloguing in Publication Data
A catalogue record for this book is available from the British Library

ISBN 978-1-5292-2056-8 hardcover
ISBN 978-1-5292-2058-2 ePub
ISBN 978-1-5292-2059-9 ePdf

The right of Jennifer Johns and Sarah Marie Hall to be identified as editors of this work has been asserted by them in accordance with the Copyright, Designs and Patents Act 1988.

Every reasonable effort has been made to obtain permission to reproduce copyrighted material. If, however, anyone knows of an oversight, please contact the publisher.

The statements and opinions contained within this publication are solely those of the editors and contributors and not of the University of Bristol or Bristol University Press. The University of Bristol and Bristol University Press disclaim responsibility for any injury to persons or property resulting from any material published in this publication.

Bristol University Press works to counter discrimination on grounds of gender, race, disability, age and sexuality.

Cover design: Liam Roberts Design
Front cover image: © Laura Johns
Bristol University Press use environmentally responsible print partners.
Printed and bound in Great Britain by CPI Group (UK) Ltd, Croydon, CR0 4YY

FSC
www.fsc.org
MIX
Paper | Supporting
responsible forestry
FSC® C013604

Contents

CONTENTS

List of Figures

Notes on Contributors

Zara Babakordi is a Human Geography PhD candidate in the School of Geography, Politics, and Sociology at Newcastle University in the UK. Her research examines articulations of ethics in consumption with a particular focus on wine.

Taylor Brydges is Research Principal at the Institute for Sustainable Futures (University of Technology Sydney, Australia). Her research explores dynamics of labour and entrepreneurship in the creative industries with a focus on the fashion industry.

Chantel Carr is ARC DECRA Fellow in the School of Geography and Sustainable Communities, University of Wollongong, Australia. Her research examines the socio-economic dimensions of energy transitions, with a focus on carbon-intensive sectors and regions.

Karenjit Clare has a Lectureship in Human Geography at Trinity College, University of Cambridge. Her research interests lie in economic geography with a particular focus on work, employment and labour, stratification, global cities, youth austerity and gender divisions within the contemporary labour market.

Jennifer Clark is Professor and Head of City and Regional Planning at the Knowlton School in the College of Engineering at The Ohio State University. She is also a Visiting Professor at the University of Stavanger, Norway. She specializes in urban and regional economic development theory, analysis and planning.

Julie Ann de los Reyes is Assistant Professor at the Center for Southeast Asian Studies at Kyoto University. Her research examines the intersection of finance and extractive industries and the dynamics of energy transition in East and South-East Asia.

Sabine Dörry is Senior Research Fellow at the Luxembourg Institute of Socio-Economic Research. Her work focuses on developing alternative ways of analysing the global financial system and development of financial centres. This includes questions about how shifts towards sustainable finance and technological immersion affect financial activities and urban development.

Mara Ferreri is Assistant Professor in Economic and Political Geography, Senior Researcher on the ERC Inhabiting Radical Housing project and Core Team Member of the Beyond Inhabitation Lab at DIST, Polytechnic of Turin, Italy. Her research focuses on precarity, temporary and platform urbanism, and struggles for housing commons.

Wenying Fu is Senior Lecturer at the Department of Geography and Environmental Sciences, Northumbria University, UK. Her research focuses on regional innovation and entrepreneurship, global production networks and informal economies.

Amy Greer Murphy is a freelance social researcher and Early Years educator in Ireland. Her research interests include intergenerational solidarity, caring relationships, early childhood education, the social determinants of health and welfare states.

Sara González is Professor of Critical Geography in the School of Geography and Associate Director of the Global Food and Environment Institute at the University of Leeds. Her work focuses on the political and economic transformation of cities, neoliberal urban policies, gentrification and contestation

Sarah Hall is 1931 Chair in Geography, University of Cambridge in the UK. Her research focuses on the implications of finance-led economic development.

Sarah Marie Hall is Professor of Human Geography at the University of Manchester, UK. Her research contributes to geographical feminist political economy, with a focus on how economic change and crises are experienced in everyday life, using ethnographic and creative methods.

Heidi Østbø Haugen holds a PhD in Human Geography and is Professor of China Studies at the University of Oslo, Norway. She has done research on logistics, migration and the social organization of trade between South China and West Africa, and regional development in the Pearl River Delta.

Caitlin Henry is Lecturer in Human Geography at the Department of Geography, University of Manchester, UK. Her feminist political economic research focuses on how economic, social and political crises and restructuring impact social reproduction, labour, welfare states and healthcare systems.

Alex Hughes is Professor of Economic Geography at Newcastle University in the UK. Her research focuses on global supply chains, corporate responsibility, and sustainable production and consumption.

Jennifer Johns is Professor of Management at the University of Bristol Business School UK. Her global political economy research is concerned with global value chains, digital technologies and the future of work.

Janelle Knox-Hayes is Associate Professor of Economic Geography and Planning in the Department of Urban Studies and Planning, MIT, US. She directs the Resilient Communities Lab. Her research focuses on the governance of climate mitigation and adaptation and systems to build socio-economic, cultural and environmental resilience for communities.

Karen P.Y. Lai is Associate Professor in Economic Geography at Durham University, UK. Her research interests include geographies of money and finance, global cities, FinTech, business services and market formation, focusing particularly on issues of financialization, knowledge networks and financial centre development.

Natasha Larkin is a PhD candidate in the School of Geography and Sustainable Communities, University of Wollongong, Australia. Her research explores the lived experiences and employment conditions of renewable energy workers.

Emma Mawdsley is Professor of Geography at Cambridge University in the UK. Her research is broadly in 'development' geographies, with a focus on South–South, and on the UK.

Sharlene Mollett is Associate Professor in the Departments of Human Geography and Global Development Studies at the University of Toronto Scarborough. She holds a Distinguished Professor Award in Feminist Cultural Geography, Nature and Society at the University of Toronto, Canada.

Rhiannon Pugh is Senior Lecturer in Innovation Studies at CIRCLE: The Centre for Innovation Research at Lund University. She researches regional economic development and the geography of innovation.

Kavita Ramakrishnan is Associate Professor in Geography and International Development at the University of East Anglia, UK. Her research broadly focuses on the lived experiences of informal housing and livelihoods on the urban margins.

Lizzie Richardson is Junior Professor in the Department of Human Geography at Goethe University, Germany. Her research examines geographies of work with digital technologies.

Luiza Sarayed-Din is a postdoc researcher at the Federal University of Rio de Janeiro, in Brazil. Her research interest includes postcolonial urban studies, informality and Global South Cities.

Suntje Schmidt is head of the Research Area 'Economy and Civil Society' at the Leibniz Institute for Research on Society and Space (IRS) and Junior Professor for Applied Economic Geography at the Humboldt-Universität zu Berlin. Her research focuses on spatial dimensions of knowledge dynamics, volatile labour markets and collaborative workspaces.

Gemma Sou is Lecturer at the Humanitarian and Conflict Response Institute, University of Manchester, UK and a Vice Chancellors Fellow at RMIT University, Australia. She adopts a postcolonial approach to explore everyday experiences of disasters, development aid micropolitics and creative research translation.

Kendra Strauss is Director of the Labour Studies Program at Simon Fraser University and a Professor in the Department of Sociology and Anthropology. She is a feminist economic and labour geographer with research interests that include precarity, care labour, social reproduction and labour-market regulation.

Lama Tawakkol is Lecturer in International Relations at the University of Manchester, UK. Her research explores capitalism and the global political economy, with particular focus on the power and politics of development aid, the social inequalities it produces and its impacts on states and marginalized populations in the Middle East.

Faith MacNeil Taylor is an artist, writer and community member. They have held teaching and research posts at Royal Holloway University of London and the Green Group at the London Assembly. Faith's writing and research explores precarity and reproduction in London's rental market. Their current focus is practically defending and nurturing children-led play spaces in the city.

Myfanwy Taylor is Leverhulme Early Career Research Fellow at The Bartlett School of Planning, University College London. Her research spans urban economic development, planning and politics, with a particular focus on collaborative research with grassroots groups, market traders, industrial firms and other small businesses.

Elena Trubina is Fellow of the Center for Slavic, Eurasian and East European Studies at the University of North Carolina at Chapel Hill and Director of the Center for Global Urbanism at Ural Federal University. Her research focuses on the hybrids of neoliberalism and authoritarianism in the cities and cultures of the Global East.

Vida Vanchan is Professor of Geography and Planning and Political Science and Public Administration at the State University of New York (SUNY) Buffalo State. Her research focuses on development, manufacturing, firm competitiveness, international trade and investments, cross-cultural management and negotiation, South-East Asia, and emerging economies.

Nancy Worth is Associate Professor in the Department of Geography and Environmental Management, University of Waterloo, Canada. Her feminist economic geography research centres on the lived experience of the economic in the contexts of work and housing.

Charlotte Wrigley-Asante is Associate Professor with the Department of Geography and Resource Development, University of Ghana. Her research focuses on how gender intersects with poverty and empowerment issues within rural and urban Ghana, gender and climate change, and women in cross-border trading activities in the West Africa subregion.

Mariama Zaami is Senior Lecturer at the Department of Geography and Resource Development, University of Ghana. Her research focuses on the gendered migration patterns from rural to urban locations and the implications of these movements for household livelihoods.

Acknowledgements

Jennifer and Sarah begin by thanking each other. The ethos of this collection has been to be supportive and patient, acknowledging the different pace at which others work, the constraints and challenges we face, and the importance of having respect for others. Since meeting in Liverpool many years ago, Sarah and Jennifer have been friends more than they have been academic collaborators. The idea and motivation for this edited collection emerged from social interactions rather than research-specific, structured meetings. Our friendship has made the editorial process easier in many ways, but we'll also look forward to returning to socialising, unfettered by chapter updates and decision making. Jennifer and Sarah would also like to thank the publishing team at Bristol University Press for the support, enthusiasm and patience they have provided for this project, from inception to delivery.

Jennifer would like to thank her family, particularly her two daughters Elea and Natalie, who give this collection extra meaning and relevance. She would also like to especially thank her mother, Laura, for her creative input into the book. When we struggled to find the right image for the book cover, Jennifer and Laura spent a wonderful afternoon crafting. Building on an idea to have weaving colours – black and white to represent the existing literatures, and bright colours to illustrate the contemporary ideas in this book – Laura used repurposed materials to create the image you see on the book cover. This fun and collaborative act between mother and daughter echoes the philosophy of the book as a whole.

Sarah thanks her family, friends and colleagues for supporting the ethos and creation of this editorial collection. Care, mutuality and compassion have been at the heart of this project, and being in generous receipt of all these things has made this work possible. Thanks is also extended to UKRI funding which provided time to develop this project (MR/T043261/1).

Introducing Contemporary Economic Geographies: An Inspiring, Critical and Plural Collection

Jennifer Johns and Sarah Marie Hall

A collective agenda

What *could* economic geographies be? What *should* economic geographies be? Who might be included in this project, what might they contribute, and how can we ensure that this work is valued? These are not new questions, and yet they remain as pertinent as ever.

This collection adopts a fresh perspective to these debates, and to economic geographies more broadly, with a focus on *plurality*. We show how contemporary economic geographies are already plural, as they are critical and inspiring. However, this remains to be widely recognized and celebrated. Such pluralism is, we argue, essential. It includes building upon economic geographies that acknowledge the deeply ingrained racial, gendered and classed power differentials inherent within the economy across space, scale and time; and that propose ways to address these problems. It involves expanding upon the areas that are considered the 'heartlands' of economic geography (such as a focus on regional and national scales, agglomeration and clustering, financial processes and industrial sectors), and advancing the theoretical devices deployed to understand these worlds. Pluralism likewise extends to empirical and methodological imagination, in terms of how, where and with whom economic geographies engage, include and empower. This involves wider engagements across international fields of study, going beyond Anglocentric sites, writings and perspectives, and broadening methodological expertise to encourage innovation and creativity.

Working towards more plural economic geographies also means tackling and addressing long-standing concerns about the overbearing heteronormativity of who 'does' and who is 'recognized' within the subdiscipline (Christopherson, 1989; McDowell, 1992). By this we refer to historical over-representation of White, male, Western, middle-class, able-bodied, older scholars, which is both an aesthetic problem and an epistemic one, and which requires constant maintenance. We are not asking for space to be made or given. This is not the economic geography we seek to expand. To our mind, there is no singular 'project', no 'one' economic geography, no particular set of gatekeepers. Rather it is a collective agenda, with varied voices, positions and approaches, and this collection celebrates this in all its diversity.

A pluralistic project is never complete; by our approach, it is a means of embracing what has been, what is to come, and what could be. To think and act plurally is to work with and for variation, alterity and difference – encompassing concepts, methods, and author identities and positionalities alike – not as the margins but as the motivation. Rather than being controversial or performative, starting from pluralistic accounts makes for an obvious but no less meaningful project and approach to doing economic geographies (note: we also write of geograph*ies* rather than geography). Plurality is for us a virtue, an asset of contemporary economic geographies, and is a collective project in which this collection can play a modest role (also see Werner et al, 2017; Rosenman et al, 2020).

Bringing together established and emerging debates, the 30 chapters in this collection chart an exciting interdisciplinary and empirically rich topography for contemporary economic geographies. We challenge traditional, more conservative ideas about what and who makes economic geography as a subdiscipline: typically acknowledged as an overtly White, Western, masculine and heteronormative space of ideas and world views alike (for more on this, see Christopherson, 1989; McDowell, 1992, 2016; Pollard et al, 2009; MacLeavy et al, 2016; Johns, 2018; Pugh, 2018). We likewise take heed calls from Rosenman et al (2020: 511), who explain that: 'engaged pluralism is an aspirational call for lively and respectful engagement across epistemologies, methodologies, and theoretical traditions, challenging scholars to open themselves up to unfamiliar perspectives and literatures'.

Readers will soon discover that this collection draws upon plural ways of understanding and approaching economic geographies across a range of ontological and epistemological positions, supported by deep empirical and globally informed engagements (see Werner et al, 2017; Gray and Pollard, 2018).

One objective of curating this collection is to engender greater consideration and insight on how scholars and students engage with economic geographies. Tracing the influence of key ideas and scholars, to contemporary areas of interest, and onto future agendas, readers are given a taste of what taking a plural approach to economic geographies can achieve. In doing so, we do not seek to claim theoretical ownership or unfettered originality. Rather, a collective project such as this, developed over time and with deep, meaningful engagement with a wide range of people, communities and experiences, is aimed to be open-ended and purposefully generative.

With the remainder of this introductory chapter, we further explore the motivations and aims of the collection, provide insights as to the praxis of pluralizing contemporary economic geographers via developing this collection, and outline the framework and contents for the rest of the book. Through this, we hope that the reader can gain a greater appreciation of the plurality of perspectives offered by contemporary economic geographies and what such plurality can achieve. This will, we intend, inspire current and future generations of economic geographers to create a more engaging, inclusive and pluralistic subdiscipline.

Towards plural economic geographies

By our definition, the study of economic geographies encompasses all manner of spatial and social relationships as they relate to the economy. With this, we include a diverse array of spatial and institutional arrangements including nation states, international organizations, local economies, cities and regions, communities and neighbourhoods, families and households, firms and corporations, workplaces, homes, third sector, the body and so on, and relations within and between. We see this in contrast to the narrower view of self-identified economic geographers who label themselves as such, with emphasis historically placed on 'core' themes such as regional economic development, financial governance and global production networks (see Nagar et al, 2002; McDowell, 2016). Economic geography has often looked to other disciplines to inform ideas and concepts and has in turn contributed to the development of other subdisciplines in geography and other disciplines. This requires deeper engagement, as chapters in this collection attest, with theories of racial capitalism, indigenous knowledge, feminist political economy and more – that have usually been marginalized, as well as engaging with those considered to be in the 'core'. Drawing a line around where the subdiscipline begins and ends is rather difficult given this ongoing dialogue. Many of the scholars we approached as part of this collection were dubious as to their identity as an economic geographer despite having significantly contributed to key debates in this field.

These dialogues help to cement how we approach economic geographies in this collection. We re-emphasized our view of economic geographies as open, not predefined, and our vision to pluralize them further. The ethos of this project was appealing to potential contributors. Our discussions with contributors have challenged us to think further about what constitutes economic geographies and the ways in which they can be pluralized. This two-way dialogue is essential in a project that seeks to avoid the imposition of ideas about who belongs in which academic communities, and how and by whom this is defined.

It was these critical discussions that also led us to reflect on our personal motivations for proposing this collection. We met at the University of Liverpool. Sarah was working on her PhD on everyday consumption practices, Jennifer was a Lecturer in Economic Geography, having completed a PhD on clustering and global production networks. Since this time many conversations have been shared, involving much tea and mulling over the state of economic geography. Central to these musings have been our views on both the direction of the subdiscipline and our own feelings of being central or peripheral (most often the latter). As Sarah's career evolved in geography and Jennifer moved to work in management, our conversations became more fraught with concerns over how the subdiscipline was developing. We were – and still are – frustrated with the inward-looking nature of much of the discussion. We also question who constitutes an 'economic geographer' and how much such labels matter anyway.

We have shared several years working on the Economic Geography Research Group (EGRG) committee and in 2018 Jennifer became Chair of the committee. During this time we both worked – with Sarah in a new dedicated Diversity and Equality role – on opening up the EGRG to new people and new perspectives. This involved holding meetings about how to pluralize economic geographies in terms of research, teaching and impact. The proceeds of this book will be donated to the Royal Geographical Society's Economic Geography Research Group, of which both editors are long-serving committee members. The funds will be used to support the ongoing activities of the EGRG, with particular focus on boosting postgraduate and early-career researcher support and opportunities through mentorship and travel grants, and on inclusion and diversity within economic geography (supporting female, BAME, LGBTQ+, disabled and working-class scholars). Thus, we hope that this edited collection becomes an important instigator of, and support for, an ongoing project aimed at increasing plurality in economic geography.

As noted, our edited collection takes plurality and difference as the starting point. It identifies themes across economic geographies that are often overlooked in mainstream overview texts and allow the voices of often marginalized scholars and marginalized research areas (in economic geography) to be heard. It has two unique qualities. First, it showcases the plurality of contemporary economic geographies via a wide range of themes, cross-cutting into various interdisciplinary terrain. Second, it highlights the importance of interdisciplinary analyses to understand economic geographies, attuned to geographical inequalities produced in and by the economy.

Economic geography remains a stalwart feature of the geographical discipline, with a range of international academic conferences organized annually, included on the curriculum of most undergraduate degrees globally, and, not least, the large academic community. And yet, economic geography as a subdiscipline with strong links outside geography – to business and management, economic sociology, economic anthropology, political economy, economics and more – is commonly noted for a distinct lack of plurality in regard to *who* and *what* it values and promotes. By this, we refer to gendered and racialized exclusions in particular, though with further intersectional effects, not limited to class, disability, faith and sexuality.

More specifically, female scholars in particular, both past and present, have made significant interventions in shaping economic geography as a subdiscipline, regarding theory, method and praxis (for example, Massey, 1984; McDowell, 1992; Gibson-Graham, 1996; Nagar et al, 2002). Thinkers, voices and experiences beyond those of White men have often struggled to be heard within economic geography. This is a well-versed debate (Christopherson, 1989) but has been reignited given a distinct lack of change or improvement within the research community. Contemporary calls (including those of McDowell, 2016; Werner et al, 2017; Johns, 2018; Pugh, 2018; Hall, 2019) all highlight the issue, but with this collection we take strides in actively addressing the problem. This edited collection gives space for a plurality of voices and experiences to come to the fore.

The lack of representation in many parts of economic geography translates to the topics deemed suitable/palatable within the subdiscipline, and thus connects to a broader problem related to plurality within the economic geography community – which is a large and significant project to which we wish to start to contribute. Those outside economic geography – including within the broader geographical community – tend to view the subdiscipline as highly masculine and narrowly focused on regional economic development, financial governance and global production networks (see Christopherson, 1989; McDowell, 2016). And yet, economic geography as defined from the margins is, and always has been, much more dynamic, plural and open to plurality in theoretical and empirical approaches and contexts. This volume will showcase both contemporary reflections on past significant contributions and cutting-edge research.

Putting together the collection

The planning of this edited collection has involved taking a fresh perspective on the ways in which contributors are identified and approached, and the role of the editors. We have not drawn on any specific events or conferences for several reasons. First, relying on pre-existing networks of researchers can privilege those able to pay for and/or attend the events. Second, it can create inequalities in terms of the geographies of author locations and backgrounds and the geographies of the research conducted. Third, overemphasis on existing networks can concentrate the representation of particular perspectives, undermining plurality. Our approach was to identify the vibrant and exciting research topics across economic geographies. We then listed potential contributors to those topics based on a range of factors, including recent published work in the field, variety in empirical contexts and seeking a diverse range of authors. Contributors have been selected based on the strength of their work in these areas rather than due to their participation in any particular networks or circles of association. We are delighted that through editing this collection we have been working with many contributors who we did not know before planning this book. We see these as just some of the ways in which plurality can become part of the praxis of economic geographies.

This book project was conceived before the COVID-19 global pandemic outbreak in 2020, with publisher approval and invitations to contribute taking place shortly after. We were acutely aware that many of our contributors were disproportionally impacted by the pandemic in their working and home lives, whether according to gender, race and ethnicity, class, disability, age, sexuality and so on, and intersections thereof. Our approach to editing the collection involved making sure that the practices we are hoping to inspire in others were also reflected in the ways in which we communicated with contributors. This involved allowing time to contributors (and ourselves!) who often understandably struggled to find space and time to concentrate on writing tasks among illness, caring responsibilities and the anxiety and uncertainty of the pandemic. For us, it echoed and magnified the processes and circumstances that can prevent more pluralistic work from being published.

The process of drawing together an edited collection such as this is rich with possibility and offers a way of bringing together views and enabling dialogue between those perspectives. It marks the beginning of a longer, larger project. An edited collection is a specific way of creating and sharing dialogue and is created across different academic and geographical contexts. This means contributors are negotiating the demands of their employers (who may have other preferred types of academic writing). Contributors in less-privileged contexts can be constrained in the time and opportunities for research. This highlights the structural constraints on attempts to start projects such as this and reflects the commitment of our contributors who have dedicated time and much thought to their chapters.

In terms of the geographical scope of the book, we have taken an international approach. We do not claim, or want to claim, global representation, for this would be unrealistic. We have especially sought to attract authors from the Global South and contributors from a range of different geographical backgrounds. We have selected authors who have expertise in various contexts (geographical, social and cultural). One of the unique characteristics of the book is around plurality – as and of itself – rather than a global perspective. Nonetheless, we acknowledge that our own backgrounds will result in a (sometimes unconscious) Anglo-Saxon approach and world view on discussions and practices within economic geographies. A collective, critically informed and inclusive project such as this is, we propose, one way to challenge and address these matters.

Overview of the collection

To demonstrate the plurality of work across economic geographies we have structured the edited collection into three interconnected parts. While the parts take a temporal approach – broadly divided into the past, present and future – there is a high degree of interaction between the individual chapters and sections. The first section focuses on the contributions of leading economic geographers, the second on contemporary economic geographies and the third on future research agendas. But this book, and the project it seeks to support, is more than a review of what has been, what exists and what will come. It also highlights connections between ideas, the accumulation of knowledge and areas of debate, and how these represent diverse and plural economic geographies.

Part 1, 'Inspirational Thought Leaders', reviews the contributions of leading economic geographers to the development of ideas in economic geographies (and often beyond). We selected ten key thinkers based on their contributions and to ensure coverage of many aspects of economic geographies, beyond the 'usual suspects' to embrace outward-facing, interdisciplinary approaches. We based our decision on the key ideas and concepts we felt have advanced the field as a plural and exciting space, and encouraged chapter contributors to think about how the work is still contributing to ongoing debates. We encouraged authors to reflect on the work of these thought leaders and how they have referenced this work in their own research, thus creating a dialogue between established and new scholars in these fields of research rather than a static picture of previous scholarship. The chapters draw together past and contemporary approaches to many facets of economic geographies, charting the evolution of the discipline through the contribution of scholars sometimes worthy of greater acknowledgement.

Part 1 begins by reviewing the contributions of Doreen Massey in which Faith MacNeil Taylor explores Doreen's theorization of space as relationally constituted, in many ways framing the discussion of subsequent thought leaders. Expanding on Massey's 'power-geometries', Caitlin Henry outlines how Bev Mullings's work has contributed to our understanding of the politics of praxis and the intimate forms of neoliberal governmentality particularly in social reproduction. Jennifer Clark then summarizes Susan Christopherson's work, focusing on how she challenged our ideas of what economic geography is, or can be, and the methodologies we use to pose and answer our research questions. Focus then turns to another interdisciplinary scholar, J.K. Gibson-Graham. Zara Babakordi reflects on their reimagination of the 'economic' beyond its conceptualization via normative centring of capitalist-oriented practices. The emphasis on the plurality of non-capitalist economic practices is echoed throughout this collection.

Karen P.Y. Lai takes our attention to international trade as she reviews the work of Jessie Poon. She traces the ways in which Poon connects economic geography with urban studies, economics and development to examine the organizational geographies of transnational corporations and finance centres. In her review of the work of Linda McDowell, Karenjit Clare discusses intersectionality in labour regulation and employment opportunities. Heidi Østbø Haugen charts for us the development of Yuko Aoyama's career in which she expands beyond the traditional confines of economic geography to examine topics such as e-commerce, video games and energy transitions, forming pathways of dialogue beyond the Anglophone sphere that other scholars have been able to follow, transcending disciplinary boundaries. Lama Tawakkol reviews the work of Susanne Soederberg who challenges orthodox and mainstream understandings of the global economy, complicating classic Marxist approaches by accounting for different structures of power, including imperialism, gender and race.

The part then turns to the work of Simona Iammarino and her contributions to economic geography and management. Alongside her academic work, Rhiannon Pugh uses interviews with Simona's collaborators and PhD students to paint a picture of not only how Simona contributes to economic geography, but to the social fabric of the discipline. Finally, we turn our focus to the work of Susan Strange on the geographies of money and finance. Sarah Hall emphasizes two main areas of Susan's work – the political economy of monetary relations and the centrality of risk and uncertainty within the international financial system.

Part 2, 'Critical Debates in Contemporary Economic Geographies', takes themes within economic geographies that reflect both the existing and potential plurality of the subdiscipline. Chapter contributors offer their insights into the work conducted across economic geographies on these themes and their methodologies. They provide contemporary review of the topics and draw out the implications of this work for developing plural ideas, approaches, authorships and audiences across economic geographies. While these chapters are important contributions in their own right – providing excellent reference points for the current state of the discipline – they also link together the insights offered in Part 1 with the future research agenda outlined in Part 3.

Part 2 begins with discussion on informal economies, taking us immediately away from the 'traditional' foci of economic geography to more pluralistic and embodied analyses of work. Kavita Ramakrishnan and Emma Mawdsley examine everyday understandings of work and new modes of urban survival, moving beyond dominant binaries of formal and informal and particularly focusing on the Global South. Vida Vanchan then discusses the global economy, contextualizing geographies of production. She evaluates the contribution of economic geographers to understanding supply chain disruption and economic life, suggesting key areas in which more resilient approaches can extend our research. Extending discussion on contemporary capitalism, Wenying Fu examines spatial peripherality and social marginality in the process of innovation–driven capitalism. Her argument draws on empirical evidence from China and informal sector entrepreneurship in the Global South to highlight the contested power struggles of everyday practices of innovation.

Moving along the continuum between production and consumption, Luiza Sarayed-Din and Alex Hughes examine consumption by acknowledging the contributions of economic geographers, while pushing us to challenge dominant narratives of consumption. They draw on food consumption in Brazil to illustrate the utility of researching postcolonial economies to better foreground inclusive and diverse economies of consumption. Janelle Knox-Hayes discusses the governance of sustainable economies in the context of climate change, calling for a focus on the socio–economic and cultural interdependencies of human and natural systems. Next, Suntje Schmidt addresses creativity in economic geography, focusing on creative work and processes, taking a critical perspective that can help us to examine inclusion and exclusion in creative sectors. Chantel Carr and Natasha Larkin discuss industrial landscapes in the context of decarbonization, revealing invisible labour and workers beyond the paid workplace in the steel and coal sectors.

The part next turns to understanding the economic geographies of labour. Nancy Worth reviews the multiple ways in which labour and work have been researched by economic geographers to then take a lens of inequality, arguing that economic geographers need to be more attentive to new developments as well as acknowledging the endurance of inequalities within labour under capitalism. Using the concept of postcolonial intersectionality, Sharlene Mollett builds on Black feminist and postcolonial thinking to research how Black women in Latin America operationalize particular knowledges and their racialized gendered subjectivities to challenge regional imaginaries that limit livelihoods and access to natural resources. Finally, in this part, Amy Greer Murphy provides an analysis of austerity policies in the Global North. She examines invisible care work and the extensive gendered risks associated with poverty, inequality and deprivation, drawing on empirical work conducted in the North of England.

In Part 3, 'Charting Future Research Agendas for Economic Geographies', contributors provide insights on the possible future directions that could (or should) be encompassed within economic geographies. They review the contemporary research position and, building on the previous parts, the chapters explicitly chart future directions. They highlight areas of neglect and indicate where economic geographers can contribute to research futures that are more inclusive. The chapters are grounded in empirical work around the struggles of marginalized groups in a diverse range of contexts, including the Global South. Many of the contributors are early career scholars who passionately articulate their vision of the pluralistic directions their research areas could take in the future.

Part 3 begins with Mara Ferreri's chapter on housing and social movements in which she discusses the impact of two global crises. Drawing on empirical research in two European cities, she reveals how dwelling practices are key to understanding control, resistance and reconfiguration in urban spaces. We then continue to focus on the urban in Elena Trubina's chapter on urban economies. In this chapter she discusses urban development, highlighting that marginalized places tend to be neglected in past studies. Elena uses the empirical context of post-Soviet spaces to outline the commonalities and specificities of urbanization processes. The part then turns to the Global South where Charlotte Wrigley-Asante and Mariama Zaami take a feminist perspective on migration and cross-border trade. They draw together work on gender, migration and cross-border trading to reveal the lived experiences of women in Ghana.

Returning to a core theme of labour, Kendra Strauss explores the resurgence of interest in social reproduction and its limited uptake in economic geography. She calls for economic geography to more seriously consider the domains of reproduction and care and highlights how racialized, gendered and classes reproductive labour is. Taylor Brydges mirrors this inclusive and intersectional approach in her analysis of existing research on creative economies, before charting the ways in which economic geography can pay greater attention to the reproduction of entrenched inequalities. The part next concentrates on the future of finance. Sabine Dörry charts the transformational shifts that finance has undergone, before proposing new directions for geographical research that focus on the social and economic potential of finance.

The part next takes us to Puerto Rico to consider the impact of a recent hurricane. Gemma Sou situates her analysis within postcolonial theory, calling for a historicization of disasters contexts and the need to acknowledge and understand the adaptation and resilience among marginalized peoples. Our focus remains on those who are marginalized in research as Myfanwy Taylor and Sara González reveal how particular groups are obscured in retailing research, including within economic geography. They call for greater engagement with feminist and postcolonial perspectives, and collaborative research methods to develop a renewed focus on marginal retail spaces and practices to inform a more socially just and inclusive policy agenda on retailing. We then return to consideration of the future challenges facing the global economy, in particular how we can realize a low-carbon energy system in response to climate emergency. Julie Ann de los Reyes, in her chapter on resources and extraction, outlines how economic geography could benefit from greater engagement with economies outside the Global North. Using examples from the Asia Pacific, Julie identifies a future research agenda based on the material economy of renewable sources and the role of finance. The final chapter in the section is by Lizzie Richardson on workplaces of the future. She questions the definition of 'the workplace' and proposes three themes for future research based on an understanding of the contingency to spatial form, or the absence of a fixed relation between function and location. With this chapter, Richardson brings us back where the collection starts, of thinking of space relationally.

Completing the book is a postscript from us, as co-editors. We reflect on how we envisage the collection being used, both in terms of as a teaching resource and as an intellectually generous project, and where the project of pluralizing economic geographies may go next. We stress, as we began this chapter, that this whole collection is a cause for celebration and engagement across economic and human geographies more broadly. As a shared agenda, we consider ourselves, as editors, to be part of the discussion as we drive forward collective knowledge of contemporary economic geographies for all.

References

Christopherson, S. (1989) 'On being outside "the project"', *Antipode*, 21(2): 83–9.

Gibson-Graham, J.K. (1996) *The End of Capitalism (As We Knew It): A Feminist Critique of Political Economy*, Oxford: Blackwell.

Gray, M. and Pollard, J. (2018) 'Flourishing or floundering? Policing the boundaries of economic geography', *Environment and Planning A: Economy and Space*, 50(7): 1541–5.

Hall, S.M. (2019) 'Everyday austerity: towards relational geographies of family, friendship and intimacy', *Progress in Human Geography*, 43(5): 769–89.

Johns, J. (2018) 'Creating a vibrant and sustainable economic geography?', *Environment and Planning A: Economy and Space*, 50(7): 1536–40.

MacLeavy, J., Roberts, S. and Strauss, K. (2016) 'Feminist inclusions in economic geography: what difference does difference make?', *Environment and Planning A: Economy and Space*, 48(10): 2067–71.

Massey, D.B. (1984) *Spatial Divisions of Labour: Social Structures and the Geography of Production*, New York: Methuen.

McDowell, L. (1992) 'Doing gender: feminism, feminists and research methods in human geography', *Transactions of the Institute of British Geographers*, 17(4): 399–416.

McDowell, L. (2016) 'Reflections on feminist economic geography: talking to ourselves?', *Environment and Planning A: Economy and Space*, 48(10): 2093–9.

Nagar, R., Lawson, V., McDowell, L. and Hanson, S. (2002) 'Locating globalization: feminist (re)readings of the subjects and spaces of globalization', *Economic Geography*, 78(3): 257–84.

Pollard, J., McEwan, C., Laurie, N. and Stenning, A. (2009) 'Economic geography under postcolonial scrutiny', *Transactions of the Institute of British Geographers*, 34(2): 137–42.

Pugh, R. (2018) 'Who speaks for economic geography?', *Environment and Planning A: Economy and Space*, 50(7): 1525–31.

Rosenman, E., Loomis, J. and Kay, K. (2020) 'Diversity, representation, and the limits of engaged pluralism in (economic) geography', *Progress in Human Geography*, 44(3): 510–33.

Werner, M., Strauss, K., Parker, B., Orzeck, R., Derickson, K. and Bonds, A. (2017) 'Feminist political economy in geography: why now, what is different, and what for?', *Geoforum*, 79: 1–4.

PART I

Inspirational Thought Leaders

1

Doreen Massey: For Political Praxis, Relationality and Contingency

Faith MacNeil Taylor

Introduction

On 3 April 2021, thousands marched from Speaker's Corner to Parliament Square in London to protest the new Police, Crime, Sentencing and Courts Bill. The bill extends British police powers to shut down protests and introduces legislation to change 'trespass' from a civil to a criminal offence – an attack on the rights of Gypsies, Travellers and Roma communities (Kirkby, 2021). After a year of seemingly perpetual lockdowns in pandemic Britain, the march felt uncanny but euphoric. Here we all were in masks, together again, fleetingly. At the Square, we gathered to listen to the speakers, one of whom was former Labour leader Jeremy Corbyn. I had last heard Corbyn speak in Parliament Square in June 2016, when the Parliamentary Labour Party was attempting to oust him. Ten thousand people turned out for Corbyn amid the coup that day, when there was a collective sense, suddenly, that integrity did matter. Doreen Massey knew about this, too. In her last editorial in 2015, Massey observed the emergence of a 'new common sense' on the back of Corbynism; 'seeds are being sown', she wrote. 'There is somehow a feeling of possibility' (2016a: 5). Connecting Corbyn's rise to anti-capitalist movements in Latin America, Greece and Spain, Massey saw left energy as a 'magma erupting beneath the carapace of neoliberalism in place after place' (2016a: 12). Yet she cautioned: '[If] the party returns to the comfort zone of pale imitation of the Tories … the Labour Party may well face extinction as any kind of progressive force. We must do everything we can to keep this initiative growing' (2016a: 12–13).

It is fitting that Massey's final published words were angled on collective responsibility for the future – although her faith in the 'progressive force' of an historically imperialist party should be critiqued. Still, it is fitting that someone with so much intellectual influence on economic geography and beyond was driven, right to the end of her life, by *praxis*: by an unwavering understanding of her place in the world as a political subject. Massey famously argued, after Althusser, that there is 'no point of departure', no pre-given subject (1995: 351) – and yet this political subjectivity of Massey's is the ideal point of departure for what follows in this chapter. Because Massey's influence on economic geography was borne from the skin she had in the game; the political and ethical investments she had in challenging monolithic thinking and interrogating understandings of space as a surface upon which the economy is merely inscribed. From her beginnings in Manchester to her endings in Kilburn, Massey was a political participant. That participation continues to breathe life into economic geographies. It is therefore to the praxis-driven political engagement Massey demonstrated throughout her career that this chapter primarily attends.

Doreen Massey was an immensely prolific scholar and commentator throughout her half-century career. To address her influence on economic geography in a handful of pages would defeat even the most concise. I have therefore chosen to approach this task by focusing on one broad yet crucial concept that Massey advanced throughout her work, and one that has altered the course of economic geography as a result – that is, *the relational constitution of space*. The discussion is structured as follows: in the first section, I outline the genealogy and diverse application of Massey's approach to relationality, focusing on four areas of her scholarship: (1) her critique of industrial locations theory, (2) her work on gendered spatial divisions of labour, (3) her analysis of capitalist landownership and (4) her advancement of 'power-geometries' as a critique of globalization theories. All of these four areas, I argue, can be read as part of an overarching commitment to discerning the political and social *relationality* of space. The second section of the chapter outlines some of the ways in which these intellectual and political advancements have shown up in feminist political economy's application within economic geography, with emphasis on recent shifts towards a 'praxis'-focused approach to 'conjuncture' (Werner et al, 2017).

Throughout the chapter, I also reflect on the influence of Massey's work on my own research on intimacy and reproduction among millennial renters in Hackney. Massey does not strike me as a thinker who subscribed to concepts as stifling as linear time (2016b), and as such I'm sure she would forgive me for only retrospectively discovering the usefulness of her work for my own; in other words, I did not fully alight upon her scholarship until I had completed the research I describe later on. And yet, of course, Massey's work remains an influence upon that study, since her ideas shaped the work of authors that inspired my thinking from proposal to viva and after. Indeed, the intellectual space Massey curated throughout her life was future-making; in her own words, spatial form 'can alter the future course of the very histories that have produced it' (2016b: 284). This was clear to me that day in Parliament Square in April 2021. As resistance to the removal of our relational capacity to make and hold public space – to assemble, grieve and dissent – gathers momentum, Massey's boundary-breaking interventions continue to reverberate.

Producing space through relations

Massey's career did not begin in academia. Following a brief spell in the private sector, she began professional research in a thinktank, the Centre for Environmental Studies (CES). Her work here bore her first article, 'Towards a critique of industrial location theory', published in 1973 in the newly founded journal *Antipode*. This article challenged the 'aspatial' and apolitical nature of prevailing theories of industrial location, interrogating the ideological underpinnings of perspectives that take as given 'the nature of economic organisation … but ignores the historical context' (1973: 33). At its core, Massey's critique was epistemological; it called forth plural knowledges to contextualize and 'know' space beyond abstraction and 'distance'.

From this point, Massey's scholarship would deal with the *production of space through relations*, weaving an epistemology grounded in situated solidarities with an altogether new ontology of economic space. As Christophers et al note (2018: 6), Massey was 'anticipating an entirely different ontology of the economic, together with an understanding of its constitutive spatiality'. This intervention in industrial geography would be fully realized over a decade later with the publication of *Spatial Divisions of Labour: Social Structures and the Geography of Production* (1984), an influential book that elaborated on her critique of industrial geography's 'economism' and its reliance on positivist conceptions of pre-fixed space. In her words, 'what is often thought of as the economic level of society is itself formed and shaped through social processes, and economic behaviour is influenced by wider social characteristics' (1984: 28). The crux of *Spatial Divisions of Labour* is the contingency of regional uneven development, and undergirding this specificity, for Massey, were *social relations*.

Massey's analysis did not end with the assertion of space as socially constructed – the ideological, too, was fundamental to her analysis. As she explains, 'The wider social relations of society also influence the internal structure of production itself. Once again, the ideological and the economic are integral to the construction of each other' (1984: 42). This conceptualization is substantiated through a wealth of case studies in the book. For example, Massey demonstrates that Northampton's mid-Victorian urbanization was a result of the relationship between gendered divisions of labour and spatial divisions of labour in the shoe industry. Massey notes that, with expansions in industrial capital's direct employment of women and children in factories, immigration to Northampton swelled, with nearly half of resident families dependent on shoe manufacturing (1984: 93). The sexual division of labour in the shoe industry – whereby men cut and women 'close' shoes – therefore shaped, in turn, the industry's spatial structure (1984: 95).

Massey continued to pursue such lines of inquiry in *Geography Matters!* (Massey and Allen, 1984), a collection published in the same year as *Spatial Divisions of Labour*. Writing with Linda McDowell, the authors employ a socialist-feminist lens to guide readers through four historical geographies of gendered labour divisions (McDowell and Massey, 1984: 129). With this, McDowell and Massey embark from the premise that capitalism 'presented patriarchy with different challenges in different parts of the country' (1984: 97), arguing that 'contrasting forms of economic development in different parts of the country presented distinct conditions of the maintenance of male dominance' (1984: 128; see also Chapter 6 in this volume). As in *Spatial Divisions of Labour*, the chapter is concerned with the *interrelationality* of sexual ideology and geographical space. For example, the authors' focus on Hackney – of interest to me as a researcher and resident of the area – explores the effects of 'sweated labour' being carried out by Victorian women in the home. Since this form of wage labour was 'individualised, isolated from other workers' (1984: 134), the 'immediate threat' to patriarchy was significantly less than in, for example, Lancashire, where women and children worked looms while men were laid off.

Beyond gender, McDowell and Massey also point out that labour costs for home-working in Hackney were kept down by the absorption of overheads by the family household, alongside employers' exploitation of migrant labour. With low-paid, irregular employment dominating the labour market for men, Hackney women also *needed* to do waged work (1984: 134). The authors moreover point to the persistence of these relations in what was their present-day Hackney, where women continued to be employed by extended family, often spelling a 'double subordination' (1984: 145). Again, the theoretical current developed by Massey a decade earlier is palpable: that place and space are in relational process and require historical contextualization. My research into disrupted intimacies among Hackney renters from 2017 to 2019 reiterated the relational 'process' of Hackney's economic spaces. Like McDowell and Massey, I found that poorly compensated wage-work in homes persisted among women marginalized by citizenship precarity and the prerogative to carry out often-unassisted childcare (Taylor, 2024).

Massey's emphasis on the social relations of capitalism as constitutive of geographical space was not limited to labour. Indeed, her most notable work at CES, in partnership with Alejandrino Catalano, was a monograph critiquing the political economy of British landownership (1978). This was preceded by a lesser known paper, 'The analysis of capitalist landownership: an investigation of the case of Great Britain', published in the *International Journal of Urban and Regional Research* in 1977. Here, Massey's co-theorization of the ideological, social and political relations shaping the uneven character of British land ownership in the 1970s alerted readers to the distinctiveness of landed property, industrial landownership and financial landownership. Anticipating later assertions regarding the mutual constitution of the ideological and economic, Massey outlined key political differences between these forms of landownership; whereas industrial landownership was a condition of production, financial landownership was 'just another sector to invest in' (cited in Christophers et al, 2018: 70), with implications for the political conflicts that flourish in regions where financial ownership was extending its reach. For example, Massey pointed out that, while financial landownership in cities was still 'small' at the time, it 'dominates the shape of the land market', since it accumulates rents not only from 'locational advantage' but also from industrial surplus value (Christophers et al, 2018: 74–5). Banking and industrial capital, in Massey's analysis, were therefore in tension – a prescient consideration at a time when neoliberalism was yet to take full hold of the organs of government, and one that has been central to my own consideration of housing financialization as a cornerstone of urban injustice and precarity in London (Fields, 2017; Taylor, 2024).

This attention to the geographical and ideological variability of capital reiterated in *Spatial Divisions of Labour*:

> 'Capital' in the United Kingdom is not the same as in the United States. In each country too the historical relations within capital, such as between banking and industry, have been different … While an abstract model of capitalism, by providing the necessary concepts, is an aid to analysis, it cannot substitute for the analysis itself. (1984: 16)

This commitment to contingency *as fundamental* to an authentic critique of capitalist political economy would land Massey in unjust trouble with Marxist contemporaries such as David Harvey, who ultimately misread *Spatial Divisions* as empiricism (Featherstone and Painter, 2013: 9) – despite Massey's insistence in the book that the 'need to confront empirical variety should in no way be seen as licence to retreat into unsituated descriptive empiricism' (Massey, 1984: 67)! Indeed, Massey's attention to contingency was explicitly tied to a broader project of situating specificity 'within the grander historical movements of capitalist societies' (1984: 68; see also Massey, 1991). Hers was an internationalism, therefore, that could not honestly do away with the fragmentation of the subject attendant upon movements for women's, gay, Black and postcolonial liberation, all of which unleashed challenges to the centrality of 'capital' – at least, where the latter is understood to mean monetary profit – and to the linearity of historical materialism.

Undergirding this commitment to specificity was Massey's distinctively relational thinking, and nowhere was this thinking more clearly applied to the complexity of capitalist relations than in Massey's critique of time-space compression. Always several steps ahead, Massey's 1993 essay 'Power-geometry and a progressive sense of place' challenged the notion of accelerated time-space compression on the basis that 'there is a lot more determining how we experience space than what "capital" gets up to' (1993: 61). Here, 'power-geometry' is a conceptual tool with which differentiated mobility amid globalized capitalism can be *relationally* discerned, with 'different social groups and different individuals' placed in 'very distinct ways in relation to (the new) flows and interconnections of postmodernity (1993: 62). Massey was not content to limit her critique of globalized capitalism to the injuries inflicted by a unitary logic of accumulation. Critiquing Harvey for his perspective that 'time space and money ... make the world go round, and us go round (or not) the world' (1993: 61), Massey's work on power-geometry brought localized – and yes, even individualized – practices of consumption within the field of political accountability. Why? Not because Massey sought to apportion liberal blame to the individual for the violences of globalized capitalism, but because she was invested in forging political subjectivities and international solidarities. This attention to fostering *accountable* social relations amid capitalism resonates with my own approach to the uneasy solidarities that are constructed – or abandoned – within Hackney's uneven rental terrain. Here, private market renters often endure poor conditions and unaffordability but are also frequently entangled in the dispossession of local social housing tenants (Taylor, 2021). Massey's approach to power-geometries makes room, in this empirical context, for discerning contours of solidarity alongside ridges of oppression.

In this way, her thinking also anticipates Cindi Katz's notion of 'counter-topography' (2001). In Massey's own words: 'Every time you drive to that out-of-town shopping centre you contribute to the rising prices, even hasten the demise, of the corner shop ... We need to ask, in other words, whether our relative mobility and power over mobility and communication entrenches the spatial imprisonment of other groups' (1991: 26).

Massey's attention to relationality was, therefore, an attention to critical solidarity, to transnational connection and to the political *compassion* of context in mapping economic phenomena. This was not a relationality born out of longing for intellectual currency; it was a theoretical device forged through pragmatically political necessity – a tool for relating, visibilizing, holding accountable, and liberating. Massey's attention to spatial relationality as a means of forging connection was thus grounded, too, in making the mundanities of everyday life politically legible, especially amid a tide of writing that tended to gratuitously reify the monolithic power of Western globalization. Famously, she critiqued time-space compression on the basis that '(much) of life for many people, even in the heart of the First World, still consists of waiting in a bus-shelter with your shopping for a bus that never comes' (1994: 163). Little wonder, then, that her work has been drawn upon so heavily by economic geographers interested in the spatial politics of everyday life, for whom traversing experiential scales – from bodies to bus stops to boroughs and beyond – is so vital to the project of relating micro to macro (Hall, 2019b; Reid-Musson et al, 2020).

Feminist political economy: towards praxis

Developing some of these ideas, my own research explores the role of economic precarity in shaping experiences of reproduction and intimacy among millennial renters living in the London Borough of Hackney. Interrogating the idea of a generational disenfranchisement locking millennials into long-term renting, I seek to discern contours of commonality as well as hierarchy between millennials living in a gentrified, yet deprived, area of a financialized city. My work can be contextualized within a surge in studies by feminist economic geographers exploring the effects of intensified neoliberal regimes on household composition and relationships in the wake of the 2008 financial crisis. The foundations for much of this theorizing were, of course, also laid by Doreen Massey's work.

Neoliberal state responses to the financial crisis incorporated intensified fiscal retrenchment and, in turn, the 'downloading' of intensified unpaid labour predominantly onto the backs of women (Meehan and Strauss, 2015; Dowling, 2021). In Britain, this reprivatization of social reproduction has been deeply ideological. Austerity measures, initially introduced through the Welfare Reform Act 2012, deliberately attacked the poor and disabled, resulting in 120,000 preventable deaths. Such a severe loss of life is largely attributable to successive Conservative governments' erosion of social security payments, which have especially harmed disabled people and single mothers. For example, the disastrous introduction of Universal Credit (UC) replaced benefits with a means-tested social security payment 'incentivising work' by tapering support as earnings rise (DWP, 2010). The work that UC 'incentivizes' is increasingly casualized and poorly compensated, with zero-hours contracts common (Armstrong, 2018: 93). Facilitating this neoliberal violence, as Massey pointed out (2015: 26), are 'social practices', and 'prevailing names and descriptions' that crystallize the 'mandatory exercise of "free choice"'. For Massey, the entire vocabulary of the economy needed switching up, lest an 'internalisation of "the system" … corrode our ability to imagine that things could be otherwise' (2015: 26).

Again, Massey's critique reminded readers of the ongoing relevance of her earlier Althusserian interventions – that economic life, including economic ideology, is constituted and practised through social relations.

Our current era of British politics in the early 2020s is characterized by the pairing of populist buffoonery and the necropolitical designation of communities as 'the herd'. In this landscape, the state has not simply economically retreated from 'care'; it has both recentralized its powers to detain, deport and kill, and delegated these powers to civil society through mandating intercommunity surveillance and monitoring, often on the basis of conditional 'rights' to economic participation (see Leahy et al, 2018). As Bhattacharyya et al point out in *Empire's Endgame* (2021), this era of governmentalization has been aimed at criminalizing poor people of colour, at least partly to reproduce a racist electorate invested in the British nation state. Once again, then, the *relations* of economic life have emerged as a key concern among economic geographers seeking to understand the cultural and political ramifications of neoliberalism. Conceptualizing shifts in boundaries between waged work and social reproduction thus remains a central task for understanding the cultural politics of the family as an institution (Wilkinson and Ortega-Alcázar, 2018; Hall, 2019a; Stenning, 2020); the sexual division of labour has returned as a central concern among feminist economic geographers. With it, nonetheless, the threat of 'economic determinism' has loomed (Werner et al, 2017); that is to say, the idea that the latest iteration of capitalist crisis is the deciding factor in the ways that people live their lives. Alongside contemporary theorizations of racial capitalism (Gilmore and Gilmore, 2016; Bhattacharyya, 2018; Shilliam, 2018), and expanded conceptualizations of social reproduction (Mullings, 2009; Bhattacharya, 2017), Massey's emphasis on the *social relations* of the economy has stewarded feminist political economy in the direction of political, economic and cultural *conjuncture*, wherein '*praxis* is foundational' (Werner et al, 2017: 4, emphasis in original). Crucial to these contemporary shifts in feminist political economy is Massey's conceptual calling card: that economic determinism should not only be critiqued owing to its masculinist erasure of subjective difference, but also that feminist politics – the 'driving force' behind relational interventions in economic geography – should not be 'evacuated' from scholarship that seeks to repair this determinism (2016a: 2).

What is meant by invoking 'conjuncture' and 'praxis'? In a nutshell, reaching beyond economic determinism requires a theorization of capitalism that conjoins subjective and locational specificity with a structural analysis of political economy. This combined approach is vital for political praxis – that is, agitating to transform the conditions of oppression – but it is also produced by it. As Bhattacharyya highlights, ours is a capitalism that can 'extract additional value from people who are deemed to be lesser' (Bhattacharyya, 2018: 22). Given that accumulation relies on the devaluation of subjects, racial hierarchies are intensified, shifting greater numbers of racialized people to the 'edge' lands of the labour market or excluding them completely. The result is that they must work harder to reproduce their lives (Bhattacharyya, 2018: 43; see also Sassen, 2014: 29). The role that individuals and communities – the role that *relations* – therefore play in reproducing this system must foreground discussions of social reproduction, around which a 'crisis' can only be understood with reference to differentiated value and labour (Bhattacharyya, 2018). These conversations matter for contemporary economic geographies, because attention must be paid to demystifying the nuanced ways in which the means of life – in other words, *the creative outputs of labour* – are contained through the imaginary borders of private ownership, nation, gender and race, and are themselves financialized and repackaged to populations as products we have the privilege of 'choosing' to purchase (Massey, 2015). The task before economic geographers is, to use Massey's words, a 'question of recognition, of the way we think of the economy as a part of society, and of valuing what it takes for a society to be reproduced' (2015: 31).

Conclusion

Doreen Massey wrote warmly and accessibly. She hid not behind excessive citational practices nor jargon. Picking up *Spatial Divisions of Labour* today, other than the conceptual anachronisms of a regional 'branch plant' economy, is as if she had written it in the present. While Massey's writing is clear, however, her theorizations are often astonishingly complex. Massey's *political* ambitiousness breathes through this complexity; simply put, it was not enough for her to turn one or two stones over. Massey wanted to not only uncover all the stones, but discern the pattern of their distribution, their proximities, their historical development and their futures. Her reasons for this were pedagogical and intergenerational – up until her death, Massey assembled a relational understanding of economic life that was necessarily complex because it was required for nuanced, effective political transformation.

I have sought in this chapter to outline some of Massey's key scholarly contributions in her relatively early career, all of which are braided by one common thread: the production of space through social and political relations. From her initial insistence on historical context in her critique of industrial locations theory, to her elaboration on the social constitution of economic life in *Spatial Divisions of Labour*, these early interventions carved out Massey's corner in geography as both astute and disruptive. This disruptive quality was linked, of course, to her affiliations with liberatory movements throughout her career, with her feminism, in particular, inflecting her work on the co-constitution of gendered divisions of labour and space. And yet, it was not only labour that captured Massey's theoretical imagination when considering the ideological relations of the economic geographies. Massey was concerned, too, with the specificity of capitals – in particular, the political differences between forms of British landownership – and with the specificity of mobilities in an increasingly globalized capitalist economy. The latter saw her make yet-more field-defining interventions through her work on 'power-geometry', an idea that was so transnationally influential that it was implemented by Hugo Chavez's socialist government in Venezuela in 2007.

Massey did not live to see the outcome of her last published desires for a collective rallying-around the 'new common sense' of Corbynism. And yet, her influence on geography and on politics far exceeds any party-political instrumentalization. Indeed, it is in the absence of any 'point of departure' that Massey's influence is so paradoxically salient: her work was forged in the fires of her own and other's related struggles; it was situated within a political context of 1970s decline, International Monetary Fund bailouts, runaway Thatcherism, the neoliberal authoritarianism of New Labour, coalition austerity, and the fleeting, momentary possibility of socialism; and it gives rise to the ongoing 'power-geometrical' engagements of our present and future, arming and armouring readers and students for battles ahead.

References

Armstrong, S. (2018) *The New Poverty*, London: Verso.

Bhattacharya, T. (ed) (2017) *Social Reproduction Theory: Remapping Class, Recentering Oppression*, London: Pluto Press.

Bhattacharyya, G. (2018) *Rethinking Racial Capitalism: Questions of Reproduction and Survival*, London: Rowman & Littlefield International.

Bhattacharyya, G., Elliot-Cooper, A., Balani, S., Nişancıoğlu, K., Koram, K., Gebrieal, D. et al (2021) *Empire's Endgame: Racism and the British State*, London: Pluto Press.

Christophers, B., Lave, R., Peck, J. and Werner, M. (eds) (2018) *The Doreen Massey Reader*, Newcastle upon Tyne: Agenda.

DWP (Department for Work and Pensions) (2010) *Universal Credit: Welfare That Works*, Cm 7957. Available from: https://assets.publishing.service.gov.uk/government/uploads/system/uploads/attachment_data/file/48897/universal-credit-full-document.pdf [Accessed 23 September 2019].

Dowling, E. (2021) *The Care Crisis: What Caused It and How We Can End It*, London: Verso.

Featherstone, D. and Painter, J. (eds) (2013) *Spatial Politics: Essays for Doreen Massey*, Oxford: Wiley.

Fields, D. (2017) 'Urban struggles with financialization', *Geography Compass*, 11(11): art e12334. Available from: https://doi.org/10.1111/gec3.12334 [Accessed 6 June 2023].

Gilmore, R.W. and Gilmore, C. (2016) 'Beyond Bratton', in J.T. Camp and C. Heatherton (eds) *Policing the Planet: Why the Policing Crisis Led to Black Lives Matter*, London: Verso, pp 173–99.

Hall, S.M. (2019a) 'A very personal crisis: family fragilities and everyday conjunctures within lived experiences of austerity', *Transactions of the Institute of British Geographers*, 44(3): 479–92.

Hall, S.M. (2019b) 'Everyday austerity: towards relational geographies of family, friendship and intimacy', *Progress in Human Geography*, 43(5): 769–89.

Katz, C. (2001) On the grounds of engagement: A topography for feminist political engagement. *Signs* 26(4): 1213-34.

Kirkby, A. (2021) 'Briefing on new police powers for encampments in Police, Crime, Sentencing and Courts Bill: Part 4', Brighton: Friends, Families and Travellers, March. Available from: https://www.gypsy-traveller.org/wp-content/uploads/2021/03/Briefing-on-new-police-powers-PCSCB ill-and-CJPOA-002.pdf [Accessed 6 June 2023].

Leahy, S., McKee, K. and Crawford, J. (2018) 'Generating confusion, concern, and precarity through the Right to Rent scheme in Scotland', *Antipode*, 50(3): 604–20.

Massey, D. (1973) 'Towards a critique of industrial location theory', *Antipode*, 5(3): 33–9.

Massey, D. (1977) 'The analysis of capitalist landownership: an investigation of the case of Great Britain', *International Journal of Urban and Regional Research*, 1(1/3): 404–24.

Massey, D. (1984) *Spatial Divisions of Labour: Social Structures and the Geography of Production*, Basingstoke: Palgrave Macmillan.

Massey, D. (1991) 'A global sense of place', *Marxism Today*, 38: 24–9.

Massey, D. (1993) 'Power-geometry and a progressive sense of place', in J. Bird, B. Curtis, T. Putnam, G. Robertson and L. Tickner (eds) *Mapping the Futures: Local Cultures, Global Change*, London: Routledge, pp 60–70.

Massey, D. (1994*). Space, Place and Gender,* Minneapolis: University of Minnesota Press.

Massey, D. (1995) *Spatial Divisions of Labour: Social Structures and the Geography of Production*, 2nd ed, Basingstoke: Palgrave Macmillan.

Massey, D. (2015) 'Vocabularies of the economy', in S. Hall, D. Massey and M. Rustin (eds) *After Neoliberalism? The Kilburn Manifesto*, London: Lawrence & Wishart, pp 24–36.

Massey, D. (2016a) 'Exhilarating times', *Soundings*, 61: 4–16.

Massey, D. (2016b) 'Politics and space/time (1992)', in C. Philo (ed) *Theory and Methods: Critical Essays in Human Geography*, Abingdon: Routledge, pp 269–88.

Massey, D. and Allen, J. (eds) (1984) *Geography Matters! A Reader*, Cambridge: Cambridge University Press.

Massey, D. and Catalano, A. (1978) *Capital and Land: Landownership by Capital in Great Britain*, London: E. Arnold.

McDowell, L. and Massey, D. (1984) 'A woman's place?', in D. Massey and J. Allen (eds) *Geography Matters! A Reader*, Cambridge: Cambridge University Press, pp 128–47.

Meehan, K. and Stauss, K. (eds) (2015) *Precarious Worlds: Contested Geographies of Social Reproduction*, Athens: University of Georgia Press.

Mullings, B. (2009) 'Neoliberalization, social reproduction and the limits to labour in Jamaica', *Singapore Journal of Tropical Geography*, 30(2): 174–88.

Reid-Musson, E., Cockayne, D., Frederiksen, L. and Worth, N. (2020) 'Feminist economic geography and the future of work', *Environment and Planning A: Economy and Space*, 52(7): 1457–68.

Sassen, S. (2014) *Expulsions: Brutality and Complexity in the Global Economy*, Cambridge, MA: Belknap Press.

Shilliam, R. (2018) *Race and the Undeserving Poor: From Abolition to Brexit*, Newcastle upon Tyne: Agenda.

Stenning, A. (2020) 'Feeling the squeeze: towards a psychosocial geography of austerity in low-to-middle income families', *Geoforum*, 110: 200–10.

Taylor, F.M. (2021) 'Cumulative precarity: millennial experience and multigenerational cohabitation in Hackney, London', *Antipode*, 53(2): 587–606.

Taylor, F.M. (2024) *Precarious Intimacies: Generation, Rent and Reproducing Relationships in London*, Bristol: Bristol University Press.

Werner, M., Strauss, K., Parker, B., Orzeck, R., Derickson, K. and Bonds, A. (2017) 'Feminist political economy in geography: why now, what is different, and what for?', *Geoforum*, 79: 1–4.

Wilkinson, E. and Ortega-Alcázar, I. (2018) 'The right to be weary? Endurance and exhaustion in austere times', *Transactions of the Institute of British Geographers*, 44(1): 155–67.

2

Beverley Mullings: Social Transformations, Social Reproduction and Social Justice

Caitlin Henry

Introduction

As a feminist political economic geographer, Beverley Mullings brings to economic geography a much-needed focus on global and intimate forms of neoliberal governmentality through an intersectional, multi-scalar analysis. Committed to feminist political economy, she has been a leader in pushing the discipline to centre the multiple systems of oppression that shape people's lives. Importantly, she has done this by focusing on the relationship between diaspora, home and spheres of social reproduction – areas of essential economic activity but not always considered important in the subdiscipline. As well, she has been preoccupied with the politics of knowledge production, including the politics of research methods, questioning dominant modes of inquiry and challenging the neoliberalizing of the academy.

In this chapter, I highlight three themes that are currents throughout Mullings' career. First is a deep commitment to feminist, anti-racist and decolonial futures. This manifests in an attention to context and history, as well as intersectionality, and a foregrounding of something so universal: work. Next, the politics and essentialness of everyday life, particularly social reproductive work and spaces to the economy animates much of her research. She demonstrates not only the usefulness and importance of social reproduction for understanding the world, but how social reproduction opens new avenues for research, understanding and ways of living. Finally, the politics of praxis is a central concern. Mullings addresses how geographers produce knowledge in myriad ways, from Geography's history to economic geography's methods to the impacts of neoliberalism on the academy.

These are, of course, economic concerns. Mullings writes, that 'economic geographers who seek to do more than 'add women and stir' must also examine how the questions that are asked, interpreted and presented may conflict with the dominant modes of representation within either feminist or economic geography' (1999a: 343). This requires a deep interrogation of and sustained engagement with the politics of knowledge production at all stages. Throughout her work, Mullings has been deeply committed to the reproduction of a different world, which includes geographers' role in that process, as well as the politics and possibilities of reproducing a different academy.

Beverley has also been a mentor, colleague and comrade to me and has shaped my development as a scholar. I first met Beverley in 2015, when Lisa Freeman and I invited her to join a panel at the American Association of Geographers Annual Meeting on the history of feminist geography. It felt like such a coup having her reflect on her experiences with her colleagues. Listening to Bev and her colleagues in conversation with each other, responding to our questions on how the subdiscipline developed, what issues they saw as most pressing at the time, and the potential of feminist geography, is a moment I treasure. Since then, I have been lucky to find myself on panels and in spaces of collaboration, as well as sharing meals and laughter with Beverley. It is a pleasure to critically review and reflect on her body of scholarship.

As I outline here, Mullings's work contributes to what and how economic geographers know, providing rich insights on diaspora-led development, new approaches to labour geographies, and the intimacies of neoliberalism in the Caribbean. Moreover, her work contends with profound existential questions for geographers, offering a different everyday praxis in the economy, geographical research and the academy.

Knowledge production

Feminist geographers have long worked to 'make the topographies of power visible within research and take active steps to redistributive power within the research process itself' (Mullings 2005: 278). Mullings repeatedly argues for and shows the importance of paying attention to how knowledge is produced, who knowledge serves, and how 'uneven geographies of power, access, and voice' shape knowledge about the Caribbean and beyond. Mullings explains:

> Researchers tend to think of 'the field' as those spaces where data is collected, but if we consider the concept of 'the field' to include those spaces where knowledge is produced, then we must begin to think of ways to destabilize the uneven landscape of research training, research publication and dissemination. (2005: 278)

Thus, she asks, what do these destabilized research relations look like? What are reciprocal research relations? How are they built?

Drawing on Fanon, Mullings (2005: 279) argues that the 'most destabilizing weapons may be [the] efforts to liberate the spaces of geographic knowledge production', rather than adapting to a colonized space, by engaging with a broader range of researchers, knowledge producers and knowledge holders. This is part of a deep commitment to feminist, anti-racist and decolonial futures that is foundational to Mullings's research and political economic analysis. These commitments shape her method and the iterative process she has engaged in over her career, showing that how geographers think, research and query, shapes knowledge and the economy (Mullings, 2017). For example, in her powerful account of the history of the racialization of work and labour markets, Mullings shows how this is also the history of Geography. Geographers played an essential role in documenting and shaping, even driving, colonial and racialized labour markets over the 18th, 19th and 20th centuries. Over its history, 'geography offered a knowledge of the world that made it possible for the knower to pragmatically engage it' and managing the labour market was key to this powerful geographic knowledge (Mullings, 2017: 2). Geography – and importantly for readers here, economic geography – has yet to meaningfully reckon with these histories and politics of knowledge production.

Work and workers are a central preoccupation of Mullings. Due not only to economic geographers' historical role, labour is also a useful starting point for feminist economic geographical analysis because of work's centrality in securing livelihoods and its role in global political economy. For Mullings, a critical and progressive labour geography accounts for formal and informal work along with worker agency, as 'there is much to be gained from juxtaposing how people have worked to maintain themselves as social, emotional, and intellectual humans in conditions of extreme uncertainty and precarity across different historical periods' (2021: 151).

Any labour analysis requires an intersectional analysis. Intersectionality demonstrates the ways that oppressions layer onto each other in a tangled web (Crenshaw, 1990), while privileges offer safety nets (Ahmed, 2014). Mullings reminds us, however, that careful attention to context and the histories of exploitation mean race and gender need disentangling. Mullings's attention to the specifics of anti-Black racism and colonialism in Jamacia, intersecting with global racial capitalism, pushes economic scholarship to grapple with agents who economic geography often ignores, such as the unfree woman and her role in the development and history of capitalism. In kinship with other histories of the gendered division of labour in feminist economics and economic geography, such as Evelyn Nakano Glenn (1992) and Marion Werner (2016), throughout her career, Mullings has contextualized her research in global and local histories of slavery and colonialism and their legacies and contemporary forms.

I hesitate to use the descriptor that scholars so often rely upon – that such work 'adds nuance'. I think this description is inaccurate, a bit trite, sells work short. The nuance is the political ground of struggle; it is where politics lives. Tidy stories simply do not capture the world accurately, whatever 'accurately' might mean. Life is complex, whether everyone (read: White privileged, mostly male people) realizes it or not. As Cindi Katz (2006: 240) asked, ' "race" is not class and class is not gender; but neither is gender gender without class, class class without gender, nor "race" race without class, to say nothing of class gender race. Is that so hard?' And that is to say nothing of sexuality, nationality, religion, migration status and on and on and on. If researchers do not live with the mess, then what worlds does knowledge production reflect? Intersectionality is not a quick label to add to research or perfect overarching theory of oppression (see Mollett and Faria, 2018; Bilge, 2020). Rather, it is a specific and political tool that eschews overly simple and thus inaccurate explanations of the world that would therefore default to the privileged and invisibilize marked bodies.

Mullings brings together intersectional, anti-colonial, feminist analysis tools in ways that reveal new geographies. For example, Mullings complicates the 'diaspora option' of development, where countries increase ties with citizens and members of the national community who live, work and have connections abroad. A popular strategy for development, Mullings cautions against uncritical analyses of diaspora strategies. Even though states celebrate attempts to capture the skills and wealth in the diaspora, Mullings warns that these strategies often obscure other issues, as states turn to them in the face of market failures (Mullings, 2012). Imaginaries and aspirations of development and the diaspora in such programmes commonly have a neoliberal orientation, shifting risk and responsibility onto migrants in the diaspora (Pellerin and Mullings, 2013; Trotz and Mullings, 2013). Furthermore, these programmes do not always consider social relations that shape local labour markets on the ground, meaning government ideas are out of step with everyday realities in potentially myriad ways (Mullings, 2011). Overall, careful attention to the diaspora option in the Caribbean leverages underused scales of analysis – the combination of local and transnational, as well as the global and the intimate. The boundaries between centre and periphery are blurred and new geographies and relations of space and place and scale emerge.

Centring social reproduction

This attention to everyday life is central to Mullings's contributions to economic geography. Her work centred in Jamaica and the Caribbean takes a place rendered to the margins and makes it the centre through the focus on diaspora. Through a political economic analysis of global economic shifts of intimate life – everyday working conditions of people around the world – she shows that analyses must centre the so-called margins.

Social reproduction refers to the means and relations by which people secure their everyday existence and the capitalist economic system is perpetuated. As Mullings (2009: 176) explains, social reproduction is 'an important frame for examining the long-term developmental impact of neoliberal restructuring because it explicitly links' the changes in social conditions to changes in structures of government and economic production. 'Examining the limits to labour's ability to secure a collective means of existence makes it possible to challenge directly the continued desirability and legitimacy of neoliberal restructuring processes'.

Despite its naturalization as 'women's work', social reproduction happens in myriad spaces and everyone contributes to its completion. In an effort to avoid associating particular people and places with certain work and to centre the life-sustaining work itself, as well as the immense diversity of work that social reproduction encompasses, Mullings utilizes the concept 'life-work' (2021). Drawing on Mitchell et al's (2004) description of social reproduction as life's work, life-work focuses on attention on the effort involved in 'producing people, communities, and economies' (2021: 152), freeing the imagination from historical binaries of home versus work or feminized and masculinized. Rather than being aspatial, life-work asks people to avoid common assumptions about space, gender and work, focusing instead on whether or not the work of life can and is being accomplished and what those conditions are that enable or prevent it.

Related, in developing the idea of life-work, Mullings has encouraged stretching the boundaries of economic and labour geography, particularly in its approach to what labour produced value, what labour is valued, and different forms of labourer agency. In response to a provocation from myself and colleagues in a *Society and Space* forum (Andrucki et al, 2017), asking if privileging the dialectical relationship between social reproduction and production may indeed privilege capitalist social relations and obscure others, Mullings takes up this challenge. Her attention to the 'mode of social reproduction' (2009) contends with the challenge of social reproduction: that both life and capitalism depend on it. Yet, social reproduction offers an aspiration for alterative, more just modes of reproducing everyday life (Hashimoto and Henry, 2017). Mullings's histories of Maroon communities shows these spaces have long existed; these stories and relations just need highlighting and fostering. There are 'labour geographies steeped in marronage, community, mutual aid and modes of survival that relied on creative practices, traces of which can be seen today in the efforts of the poorest to maintain communities and economies even under the most hostile conditions' (Mullings, 2021: 154). A focus on social reproduction or life-work is all the more important, Mullings has shown, as 'forms of economic insecurity and uncertainty that have been oppressive forces throughout the [Caribbean] region's history, resemble the forms of precarity that are now becoming a standard feature of work in much of the global North' (2021: 152). Thus, economic and labour geographers would be well-served to pay attention to 'places and historical moments that offer new ways of thinking about work and capitalism that is crucial to sustaining life in the future'.

Mullings's sustained research in the Caribbean and specifically in Jamaica gives economic geographers a rich history of the impacts of neoliberal processes over time on communities, households, labour markets, workers and the region. Her work shows how, together, these elements form a multi-scalar geography. Mullings's (1999b) study on data-entry workers is an early powerful contribution to breaking down binaries between public and private spaces, and also showing how home and work are intimately intertwined in ways that more typical social reproduction analyses may not always capture. Specifically, her work shows how the homespace facilitates resistance in the workplace, enabling employees to keep one foot out of the door, so to speak. Not being so dependent upon exploitative work, having a supportive network based in the homespace, protects workers from the brutality of the neoliberal worksite. The homespace does not 'openly contest dominant forms of law, custom, and deference … therefore remains invisible because it is a function that tends to be viewed as part of a woman's natural or biological nurturing role in the domestic domain' (1999b: 293). Yet, Mullings argues that approaching these acts collectively is important, as it is here that we can understand them as resistance, even if fleeting. This is a spatialization of what Sara Ahmed (2014) would describe as 'selfcare is warfare' as strategies 'have the capacity to create spaces of resistance insofar as household members are provided with the emotional or financial support to resist forms of domination in other sectors … [T]hese practices play a central role in creating the conditions for resisting domination and exploitative social relations' (Mullings, 1999b: 293).

The specificities of racial capitalism, neoliberalism and Jamaica are essential for understanding the universal and the particular and are, as Mullings's rich research shows, complicated notions of space and scale. Attention to detail enables seeing and developing transnational alliances and connections 'across and through the interrogation of difference' (Mollett and Faria, 2018: 574). Mullings's decades of work has complicated research on women in factories in Asia and mainland North and Central America, the early of which tended to argue that poverty and family obligation often forces women to acquiesce to employer demands (for example, Ong, 1987). Employers and governments globally have long situated women as an ideal workforce, calling them docile, dexterous and suited for tedious work; in Jamaica, Mullings explains, the government has promoted the women's workforce as dedicated, English-speaking and cheap. Yet, culturally specific notions of injustice and redress, paired with strong domestic and transnational support networks, mean a compliant workforce does not exist, as women rely on support in the homespace and community. Similarly, the neoliberalization of Jamaica's economy transnationalizes the homespace and household. The Jamaican and Caribbean diaspora is stretched around the globe and is not only a powerful economic force for development that the state hopes to capture (Mullings, 2009), but also provides essential support for households through remittances. Social reproduction is transnational. As the household is stretched across borders, Mullings argues that the community is 'narrowed' through the knock-on effects of state decline and gang welfare which fills the gaps in the social safety net. This reworking of space, scale and welfare resulting from poverty and violence are symptoms, not causes, of broader issues that show the 'erosion of the ability of households and communities to carry out the work of social reproduction' (2009: 184). The household, community and social reproduction more broadly, therefore, are simultaneously hyperlocal and transnational.

Centring praxis

Mullings's research demonstrates the power and efficacy of an intersectional feminist approach to the geographic study of the economy. In this final section, I highlight two important contributions Mullings continues to make to how economic geographic knowledge is produced: research methods and the social reproduction of the discipline of geography.

Knowledge production and research methods

Positionality is a key contribution of feminist social theory, and feminist geographers were early contributors to this idea. Attention to positionality helps to '[identify] the researcher's role in the construction of knowledge' (Browne et al, 2010: 587) and helps to 'dismantle the smokescreen surrounding the canons of neopositivist research – impartiality and objectivist neutrality' (England, 1994: 81). Faria and Mollett (2016: 79) argue that while feminist geographers continue to build intersectional theories of power, 'assumptions that researchers are always and everywhere in authority, while those we study are inherently marginalized, continue to naturalize difference in our field sites'. In other words, there is an assumption of Whiteness and thus power on the part of the researcher, which does not always hold for racialized researchers.

Mullings recommends also considering positionality as an encounter that focuses on situated knowledges and backgrounds of both interviewee and interviewer. Recognizing that positionality is relational and contextual, Mullings's concept 'positional spaces' holds race, gender, class, education, employment all together. 'Positional spaces' refers to 'spaces of communication where the situated knowledges of both parties in the research encounter generates a certain level of trust and co-operation' (2005: 277). This involves going beyond considering the impacts of researcher positionality on the research process, but also the impacts of the researcher's positionality on rapport, access and dynamics in interviews with differently positioned research participants (higher or lower status compared to the researcher) *in the moment*. Positional spaces focuses attention on situated knowledges of both interviewee and interviewer and how the situatedness of each's knowledge enables trust and cooperation. Positionality is less static and instead highly contingent, in relation to the position of both participant and researcher (and stage of research), and based on multiple visible and invisible factors. Positional spaces helps explain why and how Whiteness and/or affiliation with Global North universities can open access to researchers (Mullings, 2005; Faria and Mollett, 2016), political solidarities between researcher and participant can foster trust (Mullings, 1999a), and context may prevent White men from creating positional spaces in places like Jamaica because of the history and symbolism they carry there (Mullings, 2005).

Knowledge production and the reproduction of geography

Mullings has been a leader in applying the skills of economic geography inward, bringing not just a feminist political economic analysis to the academy, but centring new practices of social reproduction. Outside of feminist economic analyses, there is a 'tendency to view the crises of social reproduction as somehow separate from the policies associated with neoliberal restructuring' (2009: 177), but when communities and households can no longer reproduce themselves, a comprehensive analysis is necessary to understand the links between economic production and social reproduction. Myriad people, spaces and labours constitute 'academic housework' (Henry, 2018: 1369) or the university's life-work, but all have been put under the squeeze of austerity politics. Mullings collaborates widely across the discipline to bring into the light the ravages of neoliberalism on workers in the academy – a growing mental health crisis, employment insecurity, increased pressure to publish, and more – and fostering the reproduction of different social relations. As Mullings et al (2021: 6) explain:

> if geography is to remain committed to deepening human understanding, and to the production of citizens who can interpret and make sense of

the world around them, it is imperative that understanding how minds and bodies are reacting to shifts and changes in the places in which they work is accorded the highest level of importance.

Mullings's work with collaborators aims to create – to socially reproduce – a new culture of mental health and labour in geography. This work is an essential aspect of the politics and economics of knowledge production. For example, with Kate Parizeau and Linda Peake, Beverley has organized annual sessions at the American Association of Geographers (AAG) meetings on mental health in the academy and geography since at least 2015. These are both panel discussions and open forums for people to share experiences and insights. While these sessions at an annual conference are a small step, they are a rather big feat. These sessions create a designated and safe space for people to collectively share experiences and support each other and works to destigmatize mental health concerns. The sessions confront the lived realities of the political economy of geography and the contemporary academy. Importantly, Mullings is one of a group of feminist geographers who helped create the AAG Task Force on Mental Health, which led to the Standing Committee on Mental Health in Geography and the Mental Health Code of Ethics (Mullings et al, 2021). These structures help to foster a new culture of mental health in the profession, with mental-health first aid training offered as part of professional development at AAG events, as well as the data collection and subsequent advocacy on members' mental health concerns in the workplace. Additionally, mentoring is essential social reproductive work in knowledge production (Mullings and Mukherjee, 2018), but for racialized scholars, must be grounded in a decolonial transnational feminist approach that strives for transparency around power, is committed to collaboration, and continually builds trust.

With Peake and Parizeau, Mullings et al (2016: 164) question the burdens of proof that a 'reliance on numbers' puts on those who are struggling. Instead, they argue, there are myriad sources of proof of the strains on mental wellness, as 'we can gather a sense of the challenge facing universities from testimonies that detail the pervasiveness of organizational cultures, and knowledge practices that erode the capacity to maintain active states of mental healthiness'. Their efforts over the past almost-decade highlights the 'emotional and physical toll that a neoliberalizing academy is placing on specific individuals and groups' (see special issue in *Canadian Geographer*). This is especially important, Parizeau et al (2016: 197) explain as 'the academy is a site where mental, physical, and emotional struggles and illnesses proliferate' with particular impact and violence on racialized people.

While the social reproduction of geographers/y may be a feminist preoccupation, this is not a concern exclusive to women or feminists. The health and reproduction of the discipline is an existential question. This is work focused on the economics – and more – of Geography and the academy. As with general social reproduction, everyone can do life-work, everyone needs life-work and, indeed, everyone has at some point done life-work. So what life do economic geographers want to be contributing towards? What geography – one that, following Mullings's body of work, is feminist, caring, anti-racist, anti-colonial and just – could economic geographers help to reproduce?

Conclusion

The world faces considerable challenges and – reflecting on COVID-19, efforts to challenge anti-Black and other racism, the climate crisis, settler colonialism and other no-less-important and very pressing concerns – Mullings offers optimism. Considering how geographers can help foster an 'ontological shift' to meet these challenges, Mullings reminds geographers of their role as teachers. As public educators, 'we can seize the opportunity to make a more effective contribution' to raising awareness of the urgency and importance of the realities of racial capitalism and the necessary steps for meeting the Paris Agreement goals (Mullings, 2022: 140). As Mullings explains, 'the logic of coloniality that animated the creation of racial orders, even before the emergence of capitalism, also animated the distinction between nature and culture and the subordination of the former to the latter … it is only through a commitment to holding sight of the link between capitalism and coloniality, that we can build foundations that challenge and go beyond the demands of the Paris Agreement' (2022: 140). Such a commitment requires doing the everyday work of making a different world and investigating different economies. Economic geography and economic geographers are poised to be leaders in making those contributions. And as Mullings instructs, it requires seeing openings for and already existing spaces of alternatives. It requires always making clear the link between the colonizing ontologies embedded in concepts such as modernity and progress and their destructive impacts (2022). It needs a centring, prioritizing and wholesale valuing of life-work.

References

Ahmed, S. (2014) 'Selfcare as warfare', Feministkilljoys, 25 August. Available from: https://feministkilljoys.com/2014/08/25/selfcare-as-warfare/ [Accessed 6 June 2023].

Andrucki, M., Henry, C., Mckeithen, W. and Stinard-kiel, S. (2017) 'Beyond binaries and boundaries in "social reproduction"', Society & Space, 31 October. Available from: https://www.societyandspace.org/for ums/beyond-binaries-and-boundaries-in-social-reproduction [Accessed 6 June 2023].

Bilge, S. (2020) 'The fungibility of intersectionality: an Afropessimist reading', Ethnic and Racial Studies, 43(13): 2298–326.

Browne, K., Bakshi, L. and Law, A. (2010) 'Positionalities: it's not about them and us, it's about us', in S. Smith, R. Pain, S. Marston and J.P. Jones III (eds) *The SAGE Handbook of Social Geographies*, London: Sage, pp 586–604.

Crenshaw, K. (1990) 'Mapping the margins: intersectionality, identity politics, and violence against women of color', *Stanford Law Review*, 43(6): 1241–99.

England, K.V.L. (1994) 'Getting personal: reflexivity, positionality, and feminist research', *Professional Geographer*, 46(1): 80–9.

Faria, C. and Mollett, S. (2016) 'Critical feminist reflexivity and the politics of Whiteness in the "field"', *Gender, Place & Culture*, 23(1): 79–93.

Glenn, E.N. (1992) 'From servitude to service work: historical continuities in the racial division of paid reproductive labor', *Signs*, 18(1): 1–43.

Hashimoto, Y. and Henry, C. (2017) 'Unionizing for the necessity of social reproduction', Society & Space, 7 November. Available from: https://www.societyandspace.org/articles/unionizing-for-the-necessity-of-social-reproduction [Accessed 6 June 2023].

Henry, C. (2018) 'Three reflections on *Revolution at Point Zero* for (re) producing an alternative academy', *Gender, Place & Culture*, 25(9): 1365–78.

Katz, C. (2006) 'Messing with "the project"', in N. Castree and De. Gregory (eds) *David Harvey: A Critical Reader*, Oxford: Blackwell, pp 234–46.

Mitchell, K., Marston, S.A. and Katz, C. (eds) (2004) *Life's Work: Geographies of Social Reproduction*, Malden, MA: Blackwell.

Mollett, S. and Faria, C. (2018) 'The spatialities of intersectional thinking: fashioning feminist geographic futures', *Gender, Place & Culture*, 25(4): 565–77.

Mullings, B. (1999a) 'Insider or outsider, both or neither: some dilemmas of interviewing in a cross-cultural setting', *Geoforum*, 30(4): 337–50.

Mullings, B. (1999b) 'Sides of the same coin? Coping and resistance among Jamaican data-entry operators', *Annals of the Association of American Geographers*, 89(2): 290–311.

Mullings, B. (2005) 'Commentary: post-colonial encounters of the methodological kind', *Southeastern Geographer*, 45(2): 274–80.

Mullings, B. (2009) 'Neoliberalization, social reproduction and the limits to labour in Jamaica', *Singapore Journal of Tropical Geography*, 30(2): 174–88.

Mullings, B. (2011) 'Diaspora strategies, skilled migrants and human capital enhancement in Jamaica', *Global Networks*, 11(1): 24–42.

Mullings, B. (2012) 'Governmentality, diaspora assemblages and the ongoing challenge of "development"', *Antipode*, 44(2): 406–27.

Mullings, B. (2017) 'Race, work, and employment', in D. Richardson, N. Castree, M.F. Goodchild, A. Kobayashi, W. Liu, and R.A. Marston (eds) *International Encyclopedia of Geography: People, the Earth, Environment and Technology*, Oxford: Wiley. Available from: https://doi.org/10.1002/9781118786352.wbieg0660 [Accessed 6 June 2023].

Mullings, B. (2021) 'Caliban, social reproduction and our future yet to come', *Geoforum*, 118: 150–8.

Mullings, B. (2022) 'COVID-19's cracks, climate crisis, and academia's role in bringing about an ontological shift', *Professional Geographer*, 74(1): 139–40.

Mullings, B. and Mukherjee, S. (2018) 'Reflections on mentoring as decolonial, transnational, feminist praxis', *Gender, Place & Culture*, 25(10): 1405–22.

Mullings, B., Parizeau, K. and Peake, L. (2021) 'Mental health, geography, and the academy', in D. Richardson, N. Castree, M.F. Goodchild, A. Kobayashi, W. Liu and R.A. Marston (eds) *International Encyclopedia of Geography: People, the Earth, Environment and Technology*, Oxford: Wiley. Available from: https://doi.org/10.1002/9781118786352.wbieg2013 [Accessed 6 June 2023].

Mullings, B., Peake, L. and Parizeau, K. (2016) 'Cultivating an ethic of wellness in Geography', *Canadian Geographer/Le Géographe Canadien*, 60(2): 161–7.

Ong, A. (1987) *Spirits of Resistance and Capitalist Discipline: Factory Women in Malaysia*, Albany: State University of New York Press.

Parizeau, K., Shillington, L., Hawkins, R., Sultana, F., Mountz, A., Mullings, B. and Peake, L. (2016) 'Breaking the silence: a feminist call to action', *Canadian Geographer/Le Géographe Canadien*, 60(2): 192–204.

Pellerin, H. and Mullings, B. (2013) 'The "Diaspora option", migration and the changing political economy of development', *Review of International Political Economy*, 20(1): 89–120.

Trotz, D.A. and Mullings, B. (2013) 'Transnational migration, the state, and development: reflecting on the "diaspora option"', *Small Axe*, 17(2): 154–71.

Werner, M. (2016) *Global Displacements: The Making of Uneven Development in the Caribbean*, Chichester: Wiley-Blackwell.

3

Susan Christopherson: On (Still) Being Outside the Project

Jennifer Clark

Introduction

To say that any one person changed the way we think about the way we operationalize economic geography obfuscates the collaborative and iterative ways in which change *actually happens* in academic disciplines. Considering the contribution of any individual to an academic discipline involves asserting a deterministic role that almost certainly overstates the causality between the individual work and the collective change. Indeed, change is a both a process and a project involving many hands. Thus, naming Susan Christopherson's unique and specific contribution to economic geography must reflect a core argument in her work itself: economic geography is a team sport and further to note that Christopherson played it that way.

That said, Christopherson made a substantial individual contribution to economic geography. This contribution was especially remarkable given that she participated in economic geography from a position literally 'outside the project' as a Professor of City and Regional Planning rather than within a Geography department. For most of her faculty career Christopherson sat beyond the formal boundaries of the Geography discipline or its academic departments. And this liminal status has particular significance because it was not unusual for women in US economic geography at the time (and nor is it now) to hold positions in departments of public policy or urban planning rather than geography. Economic geography has closely guarded its membership rolls – and continues to – creating hard boundaries between insiders and outsiders.

Susan Christopherson's contribution to the discipline of economic geography involved expanding the field to include a broader set of epistemologies, methodologies and sites of inquiry. In other words, Christopherson challenged both what counts as an *economic geography question* and what is considered an *economic geography explanation*. Christopherson was part of a cohort of academics who pushed the analytical focus beyond the formal functions of traditional economic actors to unpack how institutions and intermediaries operate within regional and national economies to produce different spatial outcomes. And her work exhibited a sustained concern for labour.

Christopherson's work brought contingent and precarious labour into focus before it was a central concern of the discipline. And her work sustained that focus on labour and labour markets across a variety of sectors and industries, including film and new media, energy, high technology, and manufacturing. In many ways, tracing Christopherson's contribution to economic geography highlights the empirical challenges faced by economic geography during the rise of neoliberalism as regional policy sought to meet devolution, privatization and deregulation with third-sector intermediaries and industry-driven partnerships rather than formal forms of governance.

This chapter traces this theme of work across the four decades of Christopherson's career, from her early career research on the Ciudad Juárez–El Paso region documenting the rise of the maquiladoras (branch plant assembly factories) as key component of the export-oriented manufacturing strategy through to the focus on the growth of the shale gas industry and the communities confronted with its boom–and–bust market cycles and environmental consequences.

The city as studio: flexible specialization and the film industry

Susan Christopherson is perhaps best known for her early career research on flexible specialization. This work focused on the Los Angeles film industry and largely launched her career in the mid-1980s. What was so compelling about this work (a partnership with Michael Storper) was not only the selection of an industry that was of political and popular interest to the Los Angeles region and to California. The work was also relevant for a set of other regions (New York City, Vancouver) seeking to develop a high-value industry specialization with a rare combination of quality jobs, cultural cachet and the ability to project 'popularity' even before the idea of urban entrepreneurship and 'place branding' was fully integrated into local and regional economic developments schemes. This work also successfully brought flexible specialization, a thesis largely understood to apply to manufacturing and to high-value creative work (sometimes called knowledge work or advanced services).

The application of the flexible specialization thesis to film, an industry that relied on project-based work from its inception, revealed new fissures in the post-Fordist transition. And many of these points of tension and transition were located within the institutional infrastructure and sat within the boundaries of the intermediaries that had previously held the industry together, *in situ* (Christopherson and Storper, 1989). Thus, the focus on the film industry revealed the spatial implications of flexible specialization in ways that the study of manufacturing industries had not (Storper and Christopherson, 1987).

In many ways the film industry research connected Christopherson to economic geography's 'LA School' led by scholars such as Allen Scott, Michael Storper and Ed Soja (Curry and Kenney, 1999; Scott, 1999). But more accurately, Christopherson was deeply influenced by her training at the University of Minnesota. And, from Minnesota, she moved to the University of California–Berkeley to continue her studies, joining a cohort of graduate students in planning and geography that would shape theory in the field for the next 40 years. She received her doctorate in 1983 (with adviser Alan Pred) and won the American Association of Geographers' Urban Specialty Group Annual Dissertation Award. This cohort of early career scholars at Berkeley in the mid-1980s met Piore and Sabel's 'flexible specialization' thesis with a wave of theoretically informed empirical work that shaped 'industrial geography' or the 'new industrial geography' (Markusen, 1985, 1987; Glasmeier, 1986, 1991; Schoenberger, 1990; Saxenian, 1994; Peck and Barnes, 2019).

Christopherson often returned to the film industry throughout her career, revisiting theories and hypotheses about flexible specialization, the role of the state, labour-market intermediaries and project-based work that surfaced in those first path-breaking studies (Christopherson and Storper, 1986). She would return to the film industry as its spatial organization changed over time. Several scholars documented the 'runaway production' trends as movie making moved to multiple sites beyond the industry's financing and pre-production 'home base' in Los Angeles. Christopherson continued to analyse the institutional context facilitating the rise of new media and the growing emphasis on the film and media production as a tool in local and regional economic development (Christopherson, 2004, 2006, 2013; Christopherson and Rightor, 2010).

Globalization and borderlands: gender, work and extraction as development

Before the work on the film industry in Los Angeles (and beyond) Christopherson's research took her to another site where globalizing production networks, agglomeration economies and labour-market restructuring were on a collision course with neoliberalism's drive towards deregulation. In the late 1970s and early 1980s the Mexican government's strategy to build an export-oriented manufacturing zone along its northern border met with a series of currency crises. Christopherson took her research there.

The maquiladoras were intended to drive the development path of the US/Mexico borderlands and attract foreign direct investment to Mexico. These factories also attracted workers to regions like Ciudad Juárez-El Paso (Christopherson, 1983b). And, increasingly, these workers were women entering the formal labour market for the first time (Christopherson, 1983a). Notably, the feminist epistemologies evident in this early research continued to inform the research design, analysis and the selection of research questions throughout her career. Beyond the study of formal policies and regulatory regimes, Christopherson's early career fieldwork initiated a research programme that documented the practices of firms, labour-market intermediaries and public sector actors that shaped the spatial distribution of economic activities. In other words, her methodological approach both included and emphasized contingency and informality, and institutions and networks, in addition to formal governance structures so often at the centre of explanations of economic conditions.

A theme in Christopherson's work is the emphasis on how places make investment choices and choose development strategies seemingly without consideration for the cascading trade-offs that subsequently result for places and people. Economic geographers have long debated whether to hold policy implications at arm's length or directly engage in debates about how the research in the discipline reveals and confronts economic and political power and inequalities (Markusen, 1999; Martin, 2001). Christopherson stood firmly with the second camp and chose her research projects accordingly.

In response to the rise of shale gas drilling in the rural US during the early 2000s, Christopherson shifted focus to this emerging form of energy extraction and its impacts on communities and local economies. By approaching shale gas drilling through the lens of an industrial geographer, Christopherson analysed the safety of crude oil transport by rail and the economic consequences of Marcellus shale natural gas drilling (Christopherson, 2015). Christopherson recognized that this boom-and-bust industry cycle would have profound implications for rural communities and related and supporting industries.

Christopherson's research on shale gas drilling provided evidence that the economic benefits of this extractive industry (good rural jobs and increased incomes) were far less economically positive for the rural communities affected. Instead, many communities found themselves caught in yet another vicious development and disinvestment cycle. Although much of the public attention on shale gas drilling focused on the clearly negative environmental consequences of another carbon-intensive extractive energy strategy, Christopherson's research challenged the economic argument as well, underscoring the need for policies to support affected communities (Christopherson, 2017) (see also Chapter 29 in this volume).

Rules for regions: variations in regulation and restructuring

Christopherson's interest in the role of the state in setting the stage for industrial restructuring and regional variation informed a thread in her work that became prominent in the mid-1990s.

Emblematic of this approach was her 1993 article, 'Market rules and territorial outcomes', which argued for a returned emphasis on national regulatory regimes to better understand the strategic choices of both local and transnational firms. Christopherson argued that both variation in firm behaviour and market institutions mattered. The 'rules' developed through and within market institutions were iterative and influenced by firm strategies. In other words, the world wasn't flat and it was dynamic besides.

Christopherson held a strong interest in how and in what ways the divergence of market rules under the devolving processes of deregulation and privatization were changing the circumstances for firms and regions. Following specifically the divergence in labour-market rules across places, Christopherson's research fed into a growing conversation in labour geography about labour-market institutions and labour-market regulation as neoliberalism continued to reshape regional regulatory regimes (Christopherson, 2002; McDowell and Christopherson, 2009). Subsequently, Christopherson turned her attention to the international retailers as emblematic examples of this variation in both labour market and investment strategies for transnational firms across national contexts (Christopherson and Lillie, 2005; Christopherson, 2007).

Regional restructuring, technology and work

In the early 2000s Christopherson paired her theoretical interests on market rules with empirical research on the role of technological change in regional industrial restructuring. That body of work (a partnership with Jennifer Clark) uncovered implications for the strategic choices available to firms (in terms or organization and production) in the face of globalization and resulting regional restructuring. This research surfaced a crack in the 'industry clusters' literature in which power asymmetries, particularly between large and small firms in the same regional clusters, led to labour-market distortions and the co-optation of regional institutions and intermediaries (Christopherson and Clark, 2007a, 2007c, 2010).

The 'power in firm networks' approach that emerged from the study of the small and medium-sized firms in the optics and photonics industry analysed the variation in the ways knowledge-intensive industries were experiencing rapid transformations. By mapping the evolution (both conceptually and geographically) of enabling industries – their technological origins, their network organizations, their products, their processes and, ultimately, the ways in which power was constructed and exercised in these networks and by whom – the work uncovered policy implications key to understanding the construction of political and economic power (Christopherson and Clark, 2007b).

Much of Christopherson's research addressed the connections between labour, privilege and power. *Remaking Regional Economies: Power, Labor, and Firm Strategies in the Knowledge Economy*, explicitly spoke about placing the analysis of power at the centre of economic geography:

> Networks of all kinds, including firm networks, are constructed around power relations. Networks encompass hierarchies of power or they wouldn't be networks. There would be no incentive for the more powerful members to remain in the network if they didn't disproportionately gain the benefits of network participation. Just as individuals 'network' in order to promote their individual interests (rather than those of the network as a whole), so do firms. Networks can and frequently do take the form of hierarchies, with marginal benefit to the less powerful members. (Christopherson and Clark, 2007b: 7)

Conclusion

Through the course of her career the dominant mode of scholarly production within economic geography followed a 'great man' or 'great men' model. Despite the occasional long-established collaboration, most careers were established by 'big ideas' produced by a path-breaking or disruptive individual contribution to scholarship, examples like 'creative class' or 'untraded interdependencies'. 'Thought leadership' was attributed to scholars who championed yet another *turn* in the discipline from new regionalism to evolutionary economic geography.

Much of the empirical work that Christopherson is best known for resulted from collaboration in the research and the writing that resulted from it. That work required working as a team. Whether it was the film and new media industries, or advanced manufacturing and optics, or shale gas, Christopherson worked with colleagues on sustained studies of industries undergoing significant change. In many ways she never lost her core interest in restructuring as a negotiated process involving a broader set of actors in regional economies than traditional economic geography typically accepted. This centring of intermediaries and institutions (trade associations, labour-market intermediaries, economic development agencies) moved the focus away from firms as operating in a static environment but rather in a dynamic and constantly renegotiated network of market rules and territorial outcomes that were influenced by firm strategies and simultaneously the context of firm strategies (see also Chapter 13 in this volume).

Christopherson approached the development of theory differently, instigated by empirical work and embedded in an interdisciplinary reading of the landscape allied with feminist epistemologies. That is to say, Christopherson's contribution to economic geography is best understood not just as *what* she produced but *how* she chose to produce it.

Christopherson made contributions to economic geography not simply as a scholar in the discipline but as a participant in the project of constructing a discipline relevant to academics and the wider world. Among the unusual aspects of Christopherson's portfolio is how much time she spent on the very types of writings so many mentors advise against. She invested significant time and energy in book chapters, book reviews and applied policy reports. Christopherson often chose venues like book chapters and book reviews that amplified the work of economic geographers to an interdisciplinary audience and set their work (and her work) in the context of other research. She also worked with institutional partners ranging from community-based organizations to labour unions to trade associations to produce policy reports and recommendations. For Christopherson this work was crucial because it allowed her to engage the dominant power discourse and position her work, her voice squarely in the context of the real world and the existing disciplinary project.

There is a methodological orthodoxy to the approaches to theory-building and empirical analysis in economic geography. The construction of 'high theory' sits atop the hierarchy of approved activities with empirical work sitting someplace further down the ladder and qualitative and case study work lingering beneath an array of econometric techniques and quantitative tools. And within all this is a parallel set of preferred approaches to and accepted understandings of collaboration and the representation of the work produced by those partnerships.

The march of 'progressive' theory across urban and economic geography – and particularly that branch of economic geography once intertwined with industrial geography and regional science – has been both slow and episodic. The publication of Christopherson's 'On Being Outside "the Project"' (1989) marked an increase in the rate of change. An actual subfield of economic geography began as 'feminist geography' although it was never clear (and remains unclear) whether the feminist is the subject or the object of this geography or whether feminism is some distinct methodological lens through which the analysis occurs – thus implying that other approaches view geography from a non-feminist lens – an alternative reality with an alternative interpretation (McDowell, 1992).

In retrospect it seems odd that an academic project that focused on economic change and the growth and decline of places was so – and remains so – resistant to the notion that gender and race are relational – constructed and dynamic (Katz, 2017; Weber, 2017). This is the same field that has named a current theoretical turn, 'evolutionary economic geography', to better identify how innovation changes industries – and subsequently places – over time. So it is not change that is the conceptual challenge. It is the idea of agency that lies beyond stylized economic actions.

By the end of her career, Christopherson had received significant recognition for her body of work and its influence on the discipline. In December 2015, the American Association of Geographers awarded her its Lifetime Achievement award, stating:

> The AAG Honors Committee chose to recognize Susan Christopherson for her considerable and long-standing contributions to economic geography research, public engagement, teaching, and service. Her work on media, optics, agriculture, renewable energy, and manufacturing has included deep engagement with local economic development authorities to produce research that contributes to spatially and socially balanced economic growth. (AAG, 2015)

Christopherson's research as well as her approach influenced subsequent generations of scholars as well as her contemporaries. She trained numerous graduate students in city and regional planning; still others found her research through economic geography. She directly influenced her Cornell doctoral students who went on to faculty roles including Katherine Rankin (University of Toronto), Rachel Weber (University of Illinois, Chicago), Jennifer Clark (The Ohio State University), Maria Teresa Vasquez Castillo (Universidad Autónoma de Ciudad Juárez), and Harley Etienne (The Ohio State University). Additionally, scholars such as Norma Rantisi, Deborah Leslie, Betsy Donald, Jennifer Johns, Taylor Brydges and Suntje Schmidt also found Christopherson's work, particularly on creative industries, and went on to build and expand on it.

Despite the recognition she received, Christopherson retained the view the academy was not insulated from the construction of hierarchies intended to differentially assign opportunities to some participants rather than others. In 'On Being Outside "the Project"', she argued that by marginalizing questions about 'real world' work, geographers misunderstood the labour markets essential to understanding production systems. Relegating difference – variation – to the outskirts of theory results in incomplete theories (Clark, 2017).

Christopherson highlighted how a relentless formalism in economic geography runs up against the messy contingency of the real world. She spoke about the 'the emotional labor of the nurse or flight attendant' (Christopherson, 1989: 86) as indicative of that which is difficult to measure, quantify, model and compare across cases and observations but is deeply important to understanding those moments of anxiety evident within the lived experience of the participants in the systems we describe in theory. In the context of the COVID-19 pandemic, it now seems so obvious that the 'emotional labour' of healthcare workers (or flight attendants) reveals something important about the stability- and resilience-critical organizational and industrial systems (see also Chapters 11 and 18 in this volume).

However, in 1989 economic geography remained committed to formalism. not as a conservative approach to questions of political economy or politics, but rather the field remains formal in its own construction (and presentation) of self (Pugh, 2018). Economic geography retains a predilection for formal (quantitative) models and affection for categories and typologies. In short, it has an overarching affinity for fitting actors and processes into tidy, comparable boxes to better serve the construction of our grand theories: new regionalism, the new economic geography, evolutionary economic geography. Christopherson's work implicitly, and occasionally explicitly, challenged that construction. As it turned out, Christopherson's research on labour markets, work and changing industrial structures from the 1980s proved prescient. In the subsequent decades work only became more flexible, more contingent and more project-based. Those work practices and firm strategies that initially appeared marginal became central.

The contingency that once existed at the lower rungs of the career ladder crept steadily upwards, concurrently operationalizing a whole new coded vocabulary about entrepreneurship, freelancing, co-working and making. Everyone from economic geographers to technology commentators now argues that firm strategies (including locational choices) are largely determined by labour-market characteristics (a theme in *Remaking Regional Economies*). Today, the reorganization of work is rapidly reshaping the spatial organization of cities – inside buildings through co-working and makerspaces, and in central business districts through innovation neighbourhoods and technology districts. It is worth noting that the attention to difference, to variation and to power in the empirical research provided an accurate analysis of what was coming next as well as a theory that explained it. So, upon reflection, perhaps there is a transformation of geography happening after all.

References

AAG (Association of American Geographers) (2015) 'AAG Lifetime Achievement Honors: Susan Christopherson, George Malanson', AAG, 9 December. Available from: https://www.aag.org/aag-lifetime-achievement-honors-susan-christopherson-george-malanson/ [Accessed 9 June 2023].

Christopherson, S. (1983a) 'Female labor force participation and urban structure: the case of Ciudad Juarez, México', *Revista Geográfica*, 97: 83–5.

Christopherson, S. (1983b) 'The household and class formation: determinants of residential location in Ciudad Juaréz', *Environment and Planning D: Society and Space*, 1(3): 323–38.

Christopherson, S. (1989) 'On being outside "the project"', *Antipode*, 21(2): 83–9.

Christopherson, S. (1993) 'Market rules and territorial outcomes: the case of the United States', *International Journal of Urban and Regional Research*, 17(2): 274–88.

Christopherson, S. (2002) 'Why do national labor market practices continue to diverge in the global economy? The "missing link" of investment rules', *Economic Geography*, 78(1): 1–20.

Christopherson, S. (2004) 'The divergent worlds of new media: how policy shapes work in the creative economy', *Review of Policy Research*, 21(4): 543–58.

Christopherson, S. (2006) 'Behind the scenes: how transnational firms are constructing a new international division of labor in media work', *Geoforum*, 37(5): 739–51.

Christopherson, S. (2007) 'Barriers to "US style" lean retailing: the case of Wal-Mart's failure in Germany', *Journal of Economic Geography*, 7(4): 451–69.

Christopherson, S. (2013) 'Hollywood in decline? US film and television producers beyond the era of fiscal crisis', *Cambridge Journal of Regions, Economy and Society*, 6(1): 141–57.

Christopherson, S. (2015) 'Risks beyond the well pad: the economic footprint of shale gas development in the US', in M.L. Finkel (ed) *The Human and Environmental Impact of Fracking: How Fracturing Shale for Gas Affects Us and Our World*, Santa Barbara, CA: Praeger, pp 115–30.

Christopherson, S. (2017) 'Re-framing the shale decision: how do we evaluate regional costs and benefits?', in S. Bouzarovski, M.J. Pasqualetti and V. Castán Broto (eds) *The Routledge Research Companion to Energy Geographies*, Abingdon: Routledge, pp 153–66.

Christopherson, S. and Clark, J. (2007a) 'Power in firm networks: what it means for regional innovation systems', *Regional Studies*, 41(9): 1223–36.

Christopherson, S. and Clark, J. (2007b) *Remaking Regional Economies: Power, Labor, and Firm Strategies in the Knowledge Economy*, Abingdon: Routledge.

Christopherson, S. and Clark, J. (2007c) 'The politics of firm networks: how large firm power limits small firm innovation', *Geoforum*, 38(1): 1–3.

Christopherson, S. and Clark, J. (2010) 'Limits to "the learning region": what university-centered economic development can (and cannot) do to create knowledge-based regional economies', *Local Economy*, 25(2): 120–30.

Christopherson, S. and Lillie, N. (2005) 'Neither global nor standard: corporate strategies in the new era of labor standards', *Environment and Planning A: Economy and Space*, 37(11): 1919–38.

Christopherson, S. and Rightor, N. (2010) 'The creative economy as "big business": evaluating state strategies to lure filmmakers', *Journal of Planning Education and Research*, 29(3): 336–52.

Christopherson, S. and Storper, M. (1986) 'The city as studio; the world as back lot: the impact of vertical disintegration on the location of the motion picture industry', *Environment and Planning D: Society and Space*, 4(3): 305–20.

Christopherson, S. and Storper, M. (1989) 'The effects of flexible specialization on industrial politics and the labor market: the motion picture industry', *ILR Review*, 42(3): 331–47.

Clark, J. (2017) 'The construction of work, privilege, and power in economic geography: the view from inside the project', On Being Outside 'the Project': A Symposium in Honor of Susan Christopherson, Antipode Online, 23 October. Available from: https://antipodeonline.org/wp-cont ent/uploads/2017/10/3-jennifer-clark.pdf [Accessed 6 June 2023].

Curry, J. and Kenney, M. (1999) 'The paradigmatic city: postindustrial illusion and the Los Angeles School', *Antipode*, 31(1): 1–28.

Glasmeier, A. (1986) 'High-tech industries and the regional division of labor', *Industrial Relations*, 25(2): 197–211.

Glasmeier, A. (1991) 'Technological discontinuities and flexible production networks: the case of Switzerland and the world watch industry', *Research Policy*, 20(5): 469–85.

Katz, C. (2017) 'On rocking "the project": the beat goes on', On Being Outside 'the Project': A Symposium in Honor of Susan Christopherson, Antipode Online, 23 October. Available from: https://antipodeonline.org/ wp-content/uploads/2017/10/1-cindi-katz.pdf [Accessed 6 June 2023].

Markusen, A. (1985) *Profit Cycles, Oligopoly, and Regional Development*, Cambridge, MA: MIT Press.

Markusen, A. (1987) *Regions: The Economics and Politics of Territory*, Lanham, MD: Rowman & Littlefield.

Markusen, A. (1999) 'Fuzzy concepts, scanty evidence, policy distance: the case for rigour and policy relevance in critical regional studies', *Regional Studies*, 33(9): 869–84.

Martin, R. (2001) 'Geography and public policy: the case of the missing agenda', *Progress in Human Geography*, 25(2): 189–210.

McDowell, L. (1992) 'Multiple voices: speaking from inside and outside "the project"', *Antipode*, 24(1): 56–72.

McDowell, L. and Christopherson, S. (2009) 'Transforming work: new forms of employment and their regulation', *Cambridge Journal of Regions, Economy and Society*, 2(3): 335–42.

Peck, J. and Barnes, T.J. (2019) 'Berkeley in-between: radicalizing economic geography', in T.J. Barnes and E. Sheppard (eds) *Spatial Histories of Radical Geography: North America and Beyond*, Hoboken, NJ: Wiley, pp 211–46.

Pugh, R. (2018) 'Who speaks for economic geography?', *Environment and Planning A: Economy and Space*, 50(7): 1525–31.

Saxenian, A. (1994) *Regional Advantage: Culture and Competition in Silicon Valley and Route 128*, Cambridge, MA: Harvard University Press.

Schoenberger, E. (1990) 'U.S. manufacturing investments in Western Europe: markets, corporate strategy, and the competitive environment', *Annals of the Association of American Geographers*, 80(3): 379–93.

Scott, A.J. (1999) 'Los Angeles and the LA School: a response to Curry and Kenney', *Antipode*, 31(1): 29–36.

Storper, M. and Christopherson, S. (1987) 'Flexible specialization and regional industrial agglomerations: the case of the U.S. motion picture industry', *Annals of the Association of American Geographers*, 77(1): 104–17.

Weber, R. (2017) 'On Susan Christopherson's "On Being Outside 'the Project'"', On Being Outside 'the Project': A Symposium in Honor of Susan Christopherson, Antipode Online, 23 October. Available from: https://antipodeonline.org/wp-content/uploads/2017/10/4-rac hel-weber.pdf [Accessed 6 June 2023].

4

J.K. Gibson-Graham: Feminist Geographies and Diverse Economies

Zara Babakordi

Introduction

A 'Rainbow Nation' party of five, two adults and three children, sit around a kitchen table. Before them sits the board game, Mzansipoli (see Figure 4.1). Taking turns to roll the dice, the players move their tokens around the Monopoly-inspired board. Unlike Monopoly, however, Mzansipoli contains an entirely different set of rules. Wielding a 'White privilege' card, one player narrowly avoids jail. Another player receives 100 Rand in celebration of their 'racist neighbour' moving to Orania. The youngest player lands on the 'Black Tax' tile and sighs. As the players continue, a voiceover is heard. 'Mzansipoli!' it enthuses. 'Beat the game that's been playing you!'

Introducing the feminist economic geographer, J.K. Gibson-Graham, via Mzansipoli – the fictitious game of 'survival, corruption and confusion' (Nando's South Africa, 2019) – might be considered atypical. This speaks to the relative unusualness of Gibson-Graham amid the neoliberal structures of the Northern university that so often encourage an individualized and hypercompetitive approach to academic writing and publishing (Riding et al, 2019). J.K. Gibson-Graham, 'conceived in 1992 and born in published form in 1993' (Gibson-Graham and Dombroski, 2020: 20), is the shared authorial persona of Katherine Gibson and the late Julie Graham (Gibson, 2014). First meeting as graduate students at Clark University in the 1970s, Gibson and Graham worked together for 30 years until Julie's passing in 2010. Today, the continued use of this shared pen name speaks to Gibson-Graham's feminist vision of knowledge production as a space in which an ethics of relationships, connections and collaborations are centred.

Figure 4.1: The fictitious boardgame Mzansipoli

Source: Produced for Nando's South Africa by M&C Saatchi Abel. Copyright © Nando's South Africa (reproduced with permission)

For more than three decades, Gibson-Graham has imagined and enacted a feminist and ethical vision of economic geography with epistemologies and methodologies that are collective, reflexive and community-led. This is seen in her contributions towards the establishment of international research communities (for example, the Community Economies Collective), her advocacy of participatory action-based methodological approaches, and the publication of tools and materials that share knowledges, languages and ideas (Gibson-Graham et al, 2013; Community Economies, 2023). Within this shared feminist project is a determination to work ethically, with humility (Fisker, 2021), candour, transparency and hope (Gibson-Graham, 2006b).

I was first introduced to J.K. Gibson-Graham when I returned to university as a postgraduate student in human geography. Reading the work of scholars such as Gibson-Graham and engaging in inspiring discussions with my peers opened the door to an expanded understanding of feminist philosophies, epistemologies and methodologies. Gibson-Graham's arguments helped me to articulate the ways in which I had internalized the messages of a neoliberal feminism that encouraged an individualized ethos of aspiration, responsibility and resilience (Rottenberg, 2018, Banet-Weiser et al, 2020). Graduating into the 2007/8 Great Recession, the internalization of these created feelings of shame that were connected to my perceived inability to achieve within narrowly defined middle-class conceptualizations of success.

Hence my initial feelings of connection to Gibson-Graham came from a personal space of healing. This was connected to an articulation of feminist epistemologies that paid attention to the inherent messiness, subjectiveness and unevenness of the economy, beyond that valorized in a neoliberal context (Johnson, 2011). Within economic geography, Gibson-Graham has helped to push against the theoretical boundaries of the discipline, arguing for epistemologies, ontologies and methodologies that focus on 'difference, embodiment, and performativity' (Reid-Musson et al, 2020: 1459) as applied to the examination of economic relations. As Gibson-Graham (2006a: xi) notes, her contributions are grounded in economic thought 'spearheaded by feminist activists and economists, who point to the significant amount of labour … expended on unpaid and non-market-oriented activities'. In the 1970s and 1980s, for example, feminist economic geographers called attention to gendered economic relations in spaces conceptualized as 'private' (for example, the home), drawing attention to forms of (unpaid) labour that were previously unrecognized in conceptualizations of the economy (Sheppard, 2006; McDowell, 2006; Johnson, 2011; see also Chapters 17 and 18 in this volume). In time, feminist economic geographers have broadened their theoretical remit to consider the ways in which social locations connected to race, class, age, disability and sexuality complement, conflict and influence the possibilities of labour, livelihoods and the economy (Sheppard, 2006; Brown, 2009). McDowell (2011), for example, focusing on labour in the service sector, demonstrated how embodied performances of gender and conceptualizations of 'gendered and sexualized identities and idealized bodies' (2011: 342) created spaces of inclusion and exclusion for potential employees, while also regulating the 'acceptability' of performances in the workplace.

Through feminist theorizations, extensive and reflexive insights have been generated around the messiness and complexity of economic relations. However, at the centre of such theorizations is an understanding of capitalism as universal and unified. In *The End of Capitalism (As We Knew It): A Feminist Critique of the Political Economy*, Gibson-Graham (1996) sought to challenge this convention – and it is this long-standing challenge that represents one of Gibson-Graham's most important contributions to the discipline of economic geography.

Theorizing diverse economies

A core facet of Gibson-Graham's theoretical contributions to economic geography is the concept of 'diverse economies' (Gibson-Graham, 2006b). Gibson-Graham (2009: 33) argues that the ways in which capitalism has been imagined in Marxist critiques results in a near impossibility to imagine 'its supersession'. Gibson-Graham (2009: 33) interrogates 'the virtually unquestioned dominance of capitalism' within conceptualizations of the economy by its decentring, drawing attention to a plurality of non-capitalist, non-market-focused economic practices and relations that exist, that have an integral role the functioning of societies, but whose contributions to the economy are neglected (Gibson-Graham and Dombroski, 2020).

Creating the possibilities of a post-capitalist world, Gibson-Graham argues, first requires that attention be paid to these non-capitalist and diverse economic practices. Gibson-Graham (2009: 38) implores us to see and speak differently to 'make visible the hidden and alternative activities that everywhere abound, and to connect them through a language of economic difference'. Such conceptualizations do not in themselves discount the very real impact of capitalism on generations of lives; nonetheless, Gibson-Graham (2009) argues that these understandings help to unleash an anti-capitalist imagination that, for so long, has been stifled by the centring of capitalism in the economy. It is through this unleashing, Reid-Musson et al (2020: 1459) suggest, that Gibson-Graham has worked to provide a 'rich epistemology for conceptualizing difference as not necessarily – or not solely – capitalist in nature, but rather as intersecting with capitalist social relations in complex, ambiguous, and non-deterministic ways'. These practices are ubiquitous, multi-scalar and powerful (Gibson-Graham and Dombroski, 2020). Paying attention to this variety, its unequalness and unevenness (and at times, its unwantedness) makes visible a heterogeneity of economic practices with fluid and unstable connections (Sheppard, 2006; Gibson-Graham and Dombroski, 2020). In finance, for example, diverse economies recognize both normative market-focused operations (for example, banking) and the importance of other types of market operations (such as credit unions) and non-market practices (remittances, for instance) (Gibson-Graham and Dombroski, 2020; and see Figure 4.2).

As Gibson-Graham (2006a) states, her work is not without critique. This includes, for example, the provenance of concepts (such as class) as applied to her research (a category drawn from Marx) and concerns surrounding its applicability 'into times and places where they did not originate from and where they may have colonizing effects' (Gibson-Graham, 2006a: xix). Further, is resistance to the theorization of capitalism as having a constitutive 'outside' – partly addressed, according to Gibson-Graham (2006a), by 'cutting capitalism down to size (theoretically) and refusing to endow it with excessive power' (2006a: xxiv). Finally, is the push to theorize the limitations of community economies, and to 'observe their failures (and not just their successes) on the ground' (Gibson-Graham, 2006a: xxv). Here, Brown (2009: 1502) notes that criticism of the exploration of diverse economies centres its 'being framed too much through an emancipatory lens, advocating new forms of postcapitalist social justice, without stopping to acknowledge or analyse the ways power continues to be exercised in the

Figure 4.2: The diverse economies iceberg

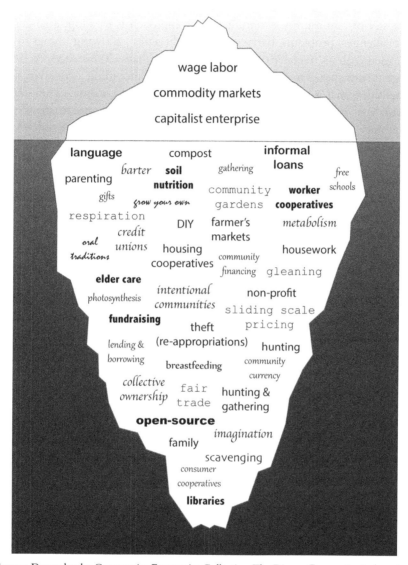

Source: Drawn by the Community Economies Collective. The Diverse Economies Iceberg is licensed under a Creative Commons Attribution–ShareAlike 4.0 International Licence

spaces' of community economies. Within the context of Gibson–Graham's work in the Philippines, for example, Kelly (2005: 41) argues that community economies could help to improve people's quality of life, but suggests there are 'limits to their potential to create, capture, and circulate value' including a 'context of highly inequitable wealth distribution, the power of private wealth to overcome the public good and the situation of the Philippines in the global economy'. Gibson-Graham suggests that, rather than theorizing through a language of limits (which may pre-emptively hinder the potential successes of community economies), her approach is to adopt a language of 'challenges, problems, barriers, [and] difficulties', allowing 'things to be struggled with' as 'tractable obstacles' (Gibson-Graham, 2006a: xxv). As Kelly suggests, this speaks to Gibson-Graham's goal of 'providing a creativity and hopefulness that is often lacking in endless rounds of critique' (2005: 39).

Much of the critique detailed by Kelly (2005) is contextualized via remittances. In 2020, the World Bank valued official remittance flows to low- and middle-income countries as US$540 billion (Ratha et al, 2021). As noted by Khanal and Todorova (2019), worldwide remittance flows are estimated to exceed total development aid and often represent the largest financial flow after foreign direct investment. Importantly, official statistics are likely to represent the 'tip of the iceberg' given they do not account for unrecorded remittances (Safri and Graham, 2010: 109; see Chapters 2 and 23 in this volume).

Remittances are often framed as catalysts for the reduction of poverty and improved health and education outcomes (Smyth, 2017). Khanal and Todorova (2019) observe that an institutional focus on remittance flows is consistent with neoliberal policies advocating for reduced public spending and individualized responsibilities. What is missing, however, are the motivations behind such practices. For Safri and Madra (2020), remittances are understood through the concept of gifting; one in which funds/goods are distributed without (it is implied) the navigation of debt. Gifting, they argue, is ubiquitous and multi-scalar, transcending social locations mediated by wealth or income. Importantly, they continue, gifting often means the difference between life and death for recipients. Despite this, the value of such practices remains hidden below the iceberg.

The importance of remittances is explored by Safri and Graham (2010) in their conceptualization of the 'global household', a financial institution that comprises those who migrate, those who are incorporated into the migrant household and those who reside in the country of origin. Focusing on remittances sent between migrants and their friends/family, Safri and Graham (2010) demonstrate the ways in which remittances are used to support the living standards of kin. Elsewhere, Gibson et al (2001) show the extent to which remittances demonstrate a fluidity in social locations of class, as navigated by contract workers migrating from the Philippines. Outsourced domestic labour, including child care, cleaning and housekeeping, is largely gendered, with labour performed by women most often from majority world nations (McKinnon, 2020). However, Gibson et al (2001) seek to challenge representations of migrant labourers as either heroes of development or victims of a global capitalist economy. Utilizing a fluid theory of class, they explore how contract domestic workers are involved in multiple class processes that allow them to produce, appropriate and distribute surplus labour. Sato and Tufuor (2020) explore similar dynamics when researching the practices of migrant women and girls in the informal sector in Accra. While remittances are in-country, and centred around urban economic centres and rural spaces, they show the ways in which financial transactions not only have material importance, funding education, food and farming costs, but also speak to moral obligations migrant women have towards their families.

Beyond the conceptualization of 'diverse economies', a key ambition of Gibson-Graham is to theorize the economy as 'a site of ethical actions' (Gibson-Graham and Dombroski, 2020: 2). Gibson-Graham (2009) argues that making diverse economies prevalent and visible encourages communities to build and transform local economies. Focusing on the collective context, Smyth (2017) explores how Mexican hometown associations in New York City practise solidarity to support transnational communities, infrastructure, and community projects. Smyth (2017) argues how the building of volunteer networks comes from a sense of shared economic responsibilities and mutual support, with the hometown association rendered as a space in which economic solidarity can be practised.

Scholars have problematized the ways in which 'diverse economies' fails to fully account for race in its conceptualization of capitalism (Bledsoe et al, 2019; Ferreira, 2021; Hossein, 2021; Naylor and Thayer, 2022; see also Chapter 19 in this volume). Hossein (2021) calls for the incorporation of an anti-racist feminism within social enterprises practising economic solidarity. Bledsoe et al (2019: 281) argue that while the concept pays attention to non-capitalist economic formations, such conversations do not sufficiently pay attention to the ways in which 'establishing non-capitalist economies entails attending explicitly to the question of race'. They argue that discussions of racial capitalism – the ways in which racialization underlies capitalism – is not sufficiently theorized in understanding how diverse economic practices, often representing survival mechanisms in response to capitalism, arise. Further, they argue:

> Economic relations need to be interpreted within the context of racial formations that configure the opportunities available to different groups of people. Black or Indigenous people must contend with specific regimes of power that define their position in society. In this context, alternative economic practices are part of a struggle to survive. (Bledsoe et al, 2019: 282)

Continuing, they argue that the creation of alternatives to capitalism requires the analysis of racial capitalism (Bledsoe et al, 2019). Paying attention to colonialism, settler colonialism and their implications for the present-day realities, Bledsoe et al (2019) state, is a necessity in understanding how capitalism remains dependent on racialized conquest and displacement. As Naylor and Thayer (2022: 793) argue, there is need to recognize the ways in which 'the theft and occupation of land that unfolded over the previous centuries of colonialism' has 'fundamentally changed people's relationships to the land', recognizing that the 'European experience of capitalism is not universal'.

Diverse economies, racial capitalism and the case of 'Black Tax'

When #Mzansipoli was released in November 2019, I had been living in Cape Town for a mere eight weeks. Through reference to 'Black Tax', it affiliated itself with an increasing number of writers, musicians, comedians and performers who had incorporated the term into their work. From around 2015 onwards, the term 'Black Tax' has been used in a South African context to refer to the systems, experiences and practices of remittances that involve the redistribution of income from young, Black, middle-income South Africans towards relatives and friends. While post-apartheid South Africa has seen an increasing number of people with improved incomes, employment and educational attainments, inequality and poverty remain high. Living standards may have improved for a minority of individuals, but these trends are often not reflected within extended kin networks. As Fongwa (2019: 2) states, 'Black Tax' 'is not limited to caring for ageing parents' and includes siblings, extended families and wider communities. Practices of distribution are multifaceted and can include payment of school fees, groceries and bills, purchasing and/or building homes, and paying church tithes (Mhlongo, 2019).

Scholars have demonstrated that remittances are critical in shaping the lives of people and communities around the world. In this regard, the practices associated with 'Black Tax' are not dissimilar to those enacted elsewhere. Additionally, the transfer of money and goods is not a post-apartheid phenomenon; as Webb (2021) details, there is extensive research demonstrating the importance of redistributive practices in southern Africa, including the sharing of income and remittances between urban migrant workers and rural households. Such practices were in part shaped by colonial- and apartheid policies that forcibly restricted Black South African people to rural 'homelands' and urban townships at a distance from economically advantageous areas classified as 'White'.

Remittances are not unique to the experiences of younger, Black, middle-income South African people (Mangoma and Wilson-Prangley, 2019). And yet, as Hunter (2019: 175) suggests, the principle behind 'Black Tax' resonates strongly, showing how 'capitalism and apartheid simultaneously divided Black family members and yet made them interdependent' in a post-apartheid setting. 'Black Tax', therefore, can only be understood as an 'intersectional term, showing that race and class must always be thought of together' (Hunter, 2019: 204). As several South African scholars and writers articulate, the concept must be understood in a national context of extreme inequality that has roots in racial capitalism, mediated via colonial- and apartheid-era systems of control (Mhlongo, 2019). This speaks to the work of Bledsoe et al (2019), who state that practices within diverse economies often represent a mechanism of survival in response to racial capitalism and colonialism. Bledsoe et al (2019: 2) argue that 'racialization and colonization are necessary for both the historic development and continued enactment of capitalist relations' and, as a result, are necessary for understanding the ways in which diverse economic practices, often operating as acts of survival, must operate.

Importantly, 'Black Tax' is recognized in mainstream South African discourses (Sibanyoni, 2015; HuffPost SA, 2017). Here, we see how a non-capitalist practice can be shaped by class locations – rather than a liberatory, non-capitalist practice, 'Black Tax' is framed by some institutional actors as a burden, a reflection on those who have insufficiently planned for their financial futures (Mwandiambira, 2015). The implication of the 'tax' in 'Black Tax' is to be burdensome – it is not a celebration of redistributive practices to ensure a more even and equal society. Such a position is challenged by Manqoyi (2018: 207) who argues that 'Black Tax' is weaponized by neoliberal ideologies that are vehemently opposed to taxation: 'Ultimately, the very reality that Black Tax highlights – historical disadvantage, inequality between "middle classes" so to speak, precarity and lack of a safety net – is employed ideologically by the system to undermine the building of a solid welfare state that would provide a safety net to all'. Manqoyi (2018: 205) rejects an understanding of the concept as one of 'cannibalising obligations ... to family and extended networks'; instead 'Black Tax' must be understood within the 'systems of racialized inequality [that] exact pressure on black professionals and graduates'. By framing the concept as a pejorative, a burden, 'Black Tax' individualizes a societal issue that must be best understood within the context of broader social and economic inequalities (Mangoma and Wilson-Prangley, 2019).

Expanding on the temporal dimensions of the concept of diverse economies, and reflecting on the systemic implications behind the construction of 'Black Tax', several scholars argue that its application must be understood within the precarity felt by a generation of South Africans born from 1994 onwards (the so-called 'born frees'). This generation represents the first cohort to access and navigate spaces of higher education that were previously prohibited to people of colour. Many Black South African people, possibly the first in their families to attend university, must navigate debt owed to state institutions and financial obligations to relatives, and contend with the precarious promise of social mobility that higher education is seen to bestow (Webb, 2021). Indeed, several South African scholars situate 'Black Tax' as an underlying factor in the 2015 #FeesMustFall student protest movement. #FeesMustFall, the largest student movement in post-apartheid South Africa, captured the frustrations of the first generation of Black students entering university with limited resources, financial commitments, rising debt and annually increasing tuition fees (Chikane, 2018; Ndinga-Kanga, 2019). In this way, the concept of 'Black Tax' pays attention to the heterogeneity and precarity of the Black middle-class experience in South Africa which has been typically ignored in favour of mainstream discourses that positions people within negatively framed ideas of conspicuous consumption and materialism (de Coninck, 2018; Dimitris Kitis et al, 2018).

'Black Tax' adds complexity to the ways in which people view their societal obligations and commitments. Challenging perceptions of burden, Ndinga-Kanga (2019) examines the experiences of self-identified Black middle-class people in South Africa, including their financial obligations to relatives. While many send remittances for a variety of reasons, most do so because of the importance of supporting others without sufficient income. In doing so, they perceive themselves to contribute to a reduction in inequality in South Africa.

Beyond a 'Tax', however, Bledsoe et al (2019) understand that redistributive practices must be comprehended beyond Eurocentric conceptualizations of economies that fail to pay attention to connected cultural specificities. Here, we can understand 'Black Tax' to act not only as a mechanism of survival and upliftment for generations of Black South African families and communities, but also as a means of maintaining networks of kinship and connection. Mangoma and Wilson–Prangley (2019) suggest that consolidating the complexity and nuance of distributive practices within a Eurocentric 'Tax' fails to pay attention to the ways in which remittances can act as bonds that tie people together, and act as expressions of gratitude, care and upliftment. Manqoyi (2018: 197) further voices frustration with the Eurocentric framing of redistributive practices that suggest that to be both inclusive and a member of the Black middle classes is to be 'an anathema'. Continuing, Manqoyi (2018: 197) argues that to promote an individualized framing of the Black middle classes:

> Is to cultivate insensitivity to the lives of fellow South Africans wasting away in neglected villages, townships and informal settlements. It is, in other words, to make a meal of the humanity of others by blaming them for not being creative, innovative or hardworking enough to make it in life.

Thus, Manqoyi (2018) recognizes an inherent problematic within the concept of 'Black Tax', with the conceptualization of practices of kinship, that may in part be guided by cultural practices and philosophies, instead being framed within a Eurocentric position of neoliberal individuality. Nonetheless, Manqoyi (2018: 197–8) also sees resistance to such discourses of individuality among Black South Africans themselves who 'tend to insist more on flexible, negotiated, relational and realistic ideas of belonging based more on conviviality and a shared humanity than on the essence of class, geography and biology'.

While the core act is ubiquitous and explored within diverse economies, the contestation of 'Black Tax' demonstrates the need to understand such concepts from an intersectional perspective. As a concept, 'Black Tax' is a symptom of the system of racial capitalism, colonialism and exploitation that has real implications for the survival of millions of South Africans. Understanding this is key to exploring the concept further as a non-capitalist economic practice. However, beyond Eurocentric understandings of transactions below the iceberg, the nuances of redistributive practices within different cultures must be recognized including, in southern Africa for example, the philosophy of Ubuntu. While diverse economies helps to imagine the complexity of the 'iceberg', it is through continued expansion of its concepts, including a focus on racialized capitalism, that we may further examine its spatial, temporal and cultural specificities.

Conclusion

Through her work on diverse economies, the feminist economic geographer, J.K. Gibson-Graham, has helped to make visible a diversity of economic practices beyond those that are capitalist-oriented and centred in conceptualizations of the economy. This is seen in work on financial remittances, with local and global implications. Yet, some argue that such conceptualizations fail to account for the ways in which such diverse practices are not purely liberatory, but are grounded in practices of survival, often for people and communities of colour, mediated by racial capitalism. Through the intersectional concept of 'Black Tax' we see this in action, examining the ways in which the concept is contested and resisted, while simultaneously recognized within culturally specific philosophies and practices of sharing, kinship and care.

References
Banet-Weiser, S., Gill, R. and Rottenberg, C. (2020) 'Postfeminism, popular feminism and neoliberal feminism? Sarah Banet-Weiser, Rosalind Gill and Catherine Rottenberg in conversation', *Feminist Theory*, 21(1): 3–24.
Bledsoe, A., McCreary, T. and Wright, W. (2019) 'Theorizing diverse economies in the context of racial capitalism', *Geoforum*, 132: 281–90.
Brown, G. (2009) 'Thinking beyond homonormativity: performative explorations of diverse gay economies', *Environment and Planning A: Economy and Space*, 41(6): 1496–510.

Chikane, R. (2018) 'Young people and the #hashtags that broke the Rainbow Nation', in S. Pickard and J. Bessant (eds) *Young People Regenerating Politics in Times of Crises*, Cham: Palgrave Macmillan, pp 19–40.

Community Economies (2023) '"About": take back the economy'. Available from: https://www.communityeconomies.org/index.php/take-back-economy/about [Accessed 1 March 2023].

de Coninck, L. (2018) 'The uneasy boundary work of "coconuts" and "black diamonds": middle-class labelling in post-apartheid South Africa', *Critical African Studies*, 10(2): 155–72.

Dimitris Kitis, E., Milani, T.M. and Levon, E. (2018) '"Black diamonds", "clever Blacks" and other metaphors: constructing the Black middle class in contemporary South African print media', *Discourse & Communication*, 12(2): 149–70.

Ferreira, P. (2021) 'Racial capitalism and epistemic injustice: blindspots in the theory and practice of solidarity economy in Brazil', *Geoforum*, 132: 229–37.

Fisker, J.K. (2021) 'Encountering post-foundationalism in J.K. Gibson-Graham's space of pregnant negativity: or, ungrounding the ground itself', in F. Landau, L. Pohl and N. Roskamm (eds) *[Un]Grounding: Post-Foundational Geographies*, Bielefeld: transcript, pp 63–80.

Fongwa, S.N. (2019) 'Interrogating the public good versus private good dichotomy: "Black tax" as a higher education public good', *Compare: A Journal of Comparative and International Education*, ahead of print. Available from: https://doi.org/10.1080/03057925.2019.1651194 [Accessed 6 June 2023].

Gibson, K. (2014) 'Thinking around what a radical geography "must be"', *Dialogues in Human Geography*, 4(3): 283–7.

Gibson, K., Law, L. and McKay, D. (2001) 'Beyond heroes and victims: Filipina contract migrants, economic activism and class transformations', *International Feminist Journal of Politics*, 3(3): 365–86.

Gibson-Graham, J.K. (1996) *The End of Capitalism (As We Knew It): A Feminist Critique of Political Economy*, Cambridge, MA: Blackwell.

Gibson-Graham, J.K. (2006a) *The End of Capitalism (As We Knew It): A Feminist Critique of Political Economy*, Minneapolis: University of Minnesota Press.

Gibson-Graham, J.K. (2006b) *A Postcapitalist Politics*, Minneapolis: University of Minnesota Press.

Gibson-Graham, J.K. (2009) 'Economic imaginaries', in S. Browne (ed) *Irish Pavilion Catalogue, 53rd International Art Biennale*, Venice Carrick-on-Sharron: The Dock, pp 33–41.

Gibson-Graham, J.K. and Dombroski, K. (2020) 'Introduction to *The Handbook of Diverse Economies*: inventory as ethical intervention', in J.K. Gibson-Graham and K. Dombroski (eds) *The Handbook of Diverse Economies*, Cheltenham: Edward Elgar, pp 1–24.

Gibson-Graham, J.K., Cameron, J. and Healy, S. (2013) *Take Back the Economy: An Ethical Guide for Transforming Our Communities*, Minneapolis: University of Minnesota Press.

Hossein, C.S. (2021) 'Racialized people, women, and social enterprises: politicized economic solidarity in Toronto', *Feminist Economics*, 27(3): 21–50.

HuffPost SA (2017) 'Special report: Black Tax', Huffington Post, 12 July (updated 14 July 2017). Available from: https://www.huffingtonpost.co.uk/entry/special-report-black-tax_uk_5c7e86dde4b048b41e38d6a4 [Accessed 6 June 2023].

Hunter, M. (2019) *Race for Education: Gender, White Tone, and Schooling in South Africa*, Cambridge: Cambridge University Press.

Johnson, L. (2011) 'Feminist economic geographies', in A. Leyshon, R. Lee, L. McDowell and P. Sunley (eds) *The SAGE Handbook of Economic Geography*, London: Sage, pp 353–67.

Kelly, P. (2005) 'Scale, power, and the limits to possibilities: a commentary on J.K. Gibson-Graham's "Surplus Possibilities: Postdevelopment and Community Economies"', *Singapore Journal of Tropical Geography*, 26(1): 39–43.

Khanal, K. and Todorova, Z. (2019) 'Remittances and households in the age of neoliberal uncertainty', *Journal of Economic Issues*, 53(2): 515–22.

Mangoma, A. and Wilson-Prangley, A. (2019) 'Black Tax: understanding the financial transfers of the emerging Black middle class', *Development Southern Africa*, 36(4): 443–60.

Manqoyi, A. (2018) 'Researching cannibalising obligations in post-apartheid South Africa', in F.B. Nyamnjoh (ed) *Eating and Being Eaten: Cannibalism as Food for Thought*, Bamenda: Langaa Research and Publishing, pp 197–222.

McDowell, L. (2006) 'Feminist economic geographies: gendered identities, cultural economies and economic change', in S. Bagchi-Sen and H. Lawton Smith (eds) *Economic Geography: Past, Present and Future*, Abingdon: Routledge, pp 34–46.

McDowell, L. (2011) 'Doing gender, performing work', in A. Leyshon, R. Lee, L. McDowell and P. Sunley (eds) *The SAGE Handbook of Economic Geography*, London: Sage, pp 338–50.

McKinnon, K. (2020) 'Framing essay: the diversity of labour', in J.K. Gibson-Graham and K. Dombroski (eds) *The Handbook of Diverse Economies*, Cheltenham: Edward Elgar, pp 116–28.

Mhlongo, N. (ed) (2019) *Black Tax: Burden or Ubuntu?*, Johannesburg: Jonathan Ball.

Mwandiambira, G. (2015) 'Planning ahead the solution for saving the sandwich generation', Bizcommunity, 21 July. Available from: https://www.bizcommunity.com/Article/196/357/131786.html [Accessed 1 March 2021].

Nando's South Africa (2019) '#*Mzansipoli*', YouTube. Available from: https://www.youtube.com/watch?v=jJyRFyusfWk [Accessed 1 March 2021].

Naylor, L. and Thayer, N. (2022) 'Between paranoia and possibility: diverse economies and the decolonial imperative', *Transactions of the Institute of British Geographers*, 47(3): 791–805.

Ndinga-Kanga, M. (2019) 'Triple jeopardy: race, class and gender among the Black middle class in South Africa', YouTube, 10 October. Available from: https://www.youtube.com/watch?v=0EgXM2FvuM0&ab_channel=MasanaNdinga [Accessed 6 June 2023].

Ratha, D., Kim, E.J., Plaza, S. and Seshan, G. (2021) *Resilience: COVID-19 crisis Through a Migration Lens*, Migration and Development Brief 34, May, Washington, DC: KNOMAD–World Bank.

Reid-Musson, E., Cockayne, D., Frederiksen, L. and Worth, N. (2020) 'Feminist economic geography and the future of work', *Environment and Planning A: Economy and Space*, 52(7): 1457–68.

Riding, J., Kallio, K., Behroozi, P., Berg, L.D., Brackebusch, A., Derksen, M., et al (2019) 'Collective editorial on the neoliberal university', *Fennia: International Journal of Geography*, 197(2): 171–82.

Rottenberg, C. (2018) *The Rise of Neoliberal Feminism*, New York: Oxford University Press.

Safri, M. and Graham, J. (2010) 'The global household: toward a feminist postcapitalist international political economy', *Signs*, 36(1): 99–125.

Safri, M. and Madra, Y.M. (2020) 'Framing essay: the diversity of finance', in J.K. Gibson-Graham and K. Dombroski (eds) *The Handbook of Diverse Economies*, Cheltenham: Edward Elgar, pp 332–45.

Sato, C. and Tufuor, T. (2020) 'Migrant women's labour: sustaining livelihoods through diverse economic practices in Accra, Ghana', in J.K. Gibson-Graham and K. Dombroski (eds) *The Handbook of Diverse Economies*, Cheltenham: Edward Elgar, pp 186–93.

Sheppard, E. (2006) 'The economic geography project', in S. Bagchi-Sen and H. Lawton Smith (eds) *Economic Geography: Past, Present and Future*, Abingdon: Routledge, pp 11–23.

Sibanyoni, M. (2015) 'Credit given far too easily', Sowetan (South Africa), 6 July. Available from: https://www.sowetanlive.co.za/business/2015-07-11-credit-given-far-too-easily-/ [Accessed 6 June 2023].

Smyth, A. (2017) 'Re-reading remittances through solidarity: Mexican hometown associations in New York City', *Geoforum*, 85: 12–19.

Webb, C. (2021) 'Liberating the family: debt, education and racial capitalism in South Africa', *EPD: Society and Space*, 39(1): 85–102.

5

Jessie Poon: International Trade and Geographies of Finance

Karen P.Y. Lai

Introduction

Jessie Poon is a pioneering economic geographer whose early research into international trade and regional agreements in Asia plays a vital role in shaping economic geography research on Asia. Her research on trade, foreign direct investment (FDI), transnational corporations (TNCs), and Asia's innovation and technological shifts has shaped debates on state–firm relationships, capital markets, technological innovation and regional development for almost three decades. The influence of her work has been felt beyond economic geography in diverse fields such as international political economy, economics and regional science. Drawing from her quantitative training and research experience, Poon also contributed to significant debates on the changing roles and potential of quantitative methods in geography. Other than international trade and corporate geographies, a major strand of Poon's research focuses on geographies of finance, particularly on the governance of capital markets, Islamic finance and offshore jurisdictions. Through archival research and interviews with finance workers, lawyers, religious bodies, policy makers and regulators, she unpacked the complex ways in which new forms of financial and legal spaces are carved out for Islamic finance and special purpose vehicles in offshore jurisdictions. These have important implications for how we study new forms and spatialities of knowledge production and regulatory power in economic geography, as well as legal geography and postcolonial debates.

This chapter highlights four strands of Poon's contributions to economic geographical analysis and the ways in which they have advanced the field and shaped contemporary debates. These are (1) international trade and regionalism, (2) TNCs and regional development, (3) economic geographies of finance and (4) quantitative methods. The final section concludes with some reflections on the impacts of her research and wider scholarly engagements on the development of economic geography.

Geographies of international trade and regionalism

Poon's early research on international trade and regional agreements played a vital role in shaping economic geography research on Asia during a period of rapid economic expansion in the 1990s and early 2000s. In studying how the flows of goods and services shape economic growth and development, and shifting power dynamics between firms and state actors, these contributed to empirical understandings of the growing role of Asia in interregional and intra-regional trade, as well as conceptual debates regarding regionalism. Insights from these studies went on to inform her subsequent research on FDI flows, the roles of TNCs and Asia's innovation and technological shifts.

In analysing global trade linkages and flows, Poon focused on examining the relationship between export growth, world demand and competitiveness. She argued that favourable trade environment alone could not ensure higher export-led growth, but also required domestic conditions such as entrepreneurship, labour skills, resources and institutions in order for a country to be competitive (Poon, 1994). These have important implications for understanding development pathways and potential for developing economies (Poon, 1997a). These studies on international trade are significant in the context of wider economic change and growing academic research on the rise of TNCs in the global economy. Through data analysis of global trade interactions, Poon's research showed that while there is increased intra-regional trade, there is also strong extra-regional activities largely driven by TNC activities (Poon, 1997a) (see Chapter 12 in this volume).

In studying international trade flows, Poon also developed particular geographical and economic understandings of regional formations and governance (Poon and Pandit, 1996; Poon, 2001). Her conceptual arguments critiqued Western universal principles of liberalism and democracy in regional initiatives and highlighted the significance of Asian culture in developing a distinctive form of regionalism (Poon, 2001). This interrogation of spatial organizations of economic power continued in Poon's critique of the global 'triad' of economic regions (centred on North America, Europe and Japan) by demonstrating that this conceptualization of a global triad was a normative assertion rather than demonstrated through empirical evidence (Poon et al, 2000). By analysing international trade and FDI flows between 1985 and 1995 and the changing shape of trade and investment blocs globally, Poon and colleagues found that investment and trade flow patterns were more globally diffused rather than a straightforward triad. These provided political impetus for new bloc formations and evolution, which resulted in a much more messy pattern of overlapping accords and agreements. Such studies provided important empirical evidence to show that trade and FDI patterns were better articulated in the form of 'network regions' rather than contiguous, continental regions. These played an important role in foregrounding later theorization of relational economic geographies, and the interaction of firms, states and other institutional actors in processes of governance and regional development outcomes (Bathelt and Glückler, 2003).

Transnational corporations and regional development

An important strand of Poon's work addressed the increasingly important role of TNCs in shaping economic processes in local, regional and global contexts, how they shaped learning and innovation, and their impacts on regional development. In doing so, she was a notable contributor to an emerging body of work from economic geographers who were becoming interested in using the firm as a conceptual lens to examine the intersections of local and global processes in shaping firm behaviour and their impacts on consumption, labour markets, state policies and developmental strategies. With detailed empirical studies based on quantitative analyses of government data, questionnaire surveys of firms, and qualitative interviews with firm managers, Poon examined the roles and impacts of foreign TNCs in Asian economies as well as the strategies and experience of Asian TNCs in their internationalization drive into US and European markets.

The long-standing rivalry between Singapore and Hong Kong regarding their roles as international financial centres (IFCs) and strategic locations for regional headquarters (RHQs) of TNCs has featured in scholarly, industry and policy debates for decades. While it is now commonly recognized that they have specific 'divisions of labour' in terms of geographical coverage, research by Poon and colleagues in the late 1990s was among the earliest studies that established the distinctive and complementary roles of Hong Kong and Singapore in terms of their territorial specialization as RHQs (Perry et al, 1998a, 1998b). Despite speculation and political uncertainty in Hong Kong following the 1997 handover from the UK to China, their findings showed that there was limited impact on relocation consideration among firms surveyed or in government data. Hong Kong remained the dominant location of regional offices for East Asian markets while Singapore was the preferred RHQ location for TNCs focusing on South-East Asia. They concluded that the two centres performed complementary functions rather than as competing regional office locations for the Asia Pacific region – an argument that continued to inform further studies in geographies of financial centres and global cities (Lai, 2012; Pan et al, 2020). They also noted the growth in Hong Kong's role as a regional management base for

China even from that early stage, which continues to shape debates regarding Hong Kong's current positioning and advantage as a gateway financial centre for China's inward and outward FDI (Gemici and Lai, 2020).

In response to traditional depiction of regional offices as mainly a coordinator of regional affiliates, Poon's research developed more nuanced conceptualization of RHQ functions within complex corporate structures and how they shaped knowledge flows and investment patterns across space (Poon and Thompson, 2003). With the deepening of foreign investment across Asia and the multiplication of regional offices, RHQs took on increasing responsibilities for logistics and distribution, with investment in information systems and physical infrastructures leading to stronger embeddedness in local and regional economies. These findings also pointed to the importance of government incentives for attracting RHQs (Perry et al, 1998a,b). In studying TNC behaviour in Asia Pacific markets, Poon's research highlighted the significance of national differences in strategic corporate functions among TNCs, such as enduring business structures and practices of American and Japanese TNCs across different host country environments (Poon and Thompson, 2004). Such findings addressed debates regarding cultural and economic homogenization and contributed to the theorization of corporate economic geography and economic globalization, which were important research areas in the social sciences in the 1990s and early 2000s.

The role of TNCs in shaping learning and innovation processes was another important dimension of Poon's research. Much of this literature focused overwhelmingly on the regional competences of firms in European and North American regions, with analyses and explanations of knowledge exchanges, especially regarding tacit knowledge, tending to have a spatial bias that focused on *local contexts* and insider communities. Poon's research underscored the importance of studying international knowledge production and transmission, that is, *extra-local* technological learning and acquisition among foreign firms, especially those from industrializing countries (Poon et al, 2006; Hsu et al, 2008).

In moving away from the local scale for investigating technological innovation and knowledge acquisition, Poon developed a multi-scalar perspective to examine the intertwining of local, trans-regional and extra-local international spaces in the organization and coordination of technology and knowledge flows. In addition to regional systems of domestic learning, Taiwanese and Korean firms were particularly active in broadening their knowledge acquisition base through outward FDI, including R&D (research and development) investment, in the US (Poon et al, 2006; Hsu et al, 2008; Poon et al, 2013). Poon's work on the R&D operations of Asian firms informed subsequent studies of later waves of industrializing Asian economies, such as Thailand and China, in terms of their strategies and approaches to learning, and for innovation and developmental outcomes for particular cities and regions (Sajarattanachote and Poon, 2009; Poon and Sajarattanachote, 2010; Shang et al, 2012).

Spatialities of finance

Since the early 2000s, Poon's research took a distinctive turn towards spatialities of finance, reflecting the growing impact of the finance industry on other industry sectors and the wider economy. A key research theme was on Islamic finance with particular focus on developmental implications for Malaysia in emerging circuits of financial knowledge and networks, and the growth and decline of financial centres more broadly. Investigations into issues of legitimacy and standards setting in Islamic finance later evolved into further studies on offshore finance in conceptualizing power and governance in global financial networks. This research on Islamic finance and offshore finance provided significant momentum in pushing economic geography research beyond its traditional focus on developed economies, the global 'triad' economies and large international financial centres.

The shift from international trade and corporate geographies to finance was unsurprising given the deep impacts of the Asian financial crisis on the region. In an early intervention piece, Poon and Perry (1999) critiqued conventional commentaries that presented Asian economies as being drawn into the financial crisis like collapsing dominoes. Using macroeconomic analysis, they showed that nationally differentiated strategies in production, currency reserves and national debt produced a more spatially nuanced account of the crisis on Asian economies. Poon's work also drew attention to different forms of capital and their impacts on economic strategies and regional development (Poon and Thompson, 2001). Unlike the highly mobile portfolio investment ('hot money') that swiftly exited Asia during the Asian financial crisis, FDI from firms, especially in electronics sector, was significantly embedded in Asia and displayed low levels of spatial mobility due to sunk costs in the form of production and sales operations and embedded subcontracting and logistical networks. With the expected changes in political economic organization and financial practices in Asia following post-crisis reforms, TNCs from Japan, Europe and North America with operations in Asia focused on the long-term economic potential of the region, resulting in *greater* embedding of transnational capital in the region, rather than dis-embedding from the region post–financial crisis. These early studies into the importance of finance in shaping firm behaviour and global flows of investments inspired my own foray into financial geography by tracing impacts of the Asian financial crisis on firm activities and response to government discourse and policies (Lai and Yeung, 2003). The assertion that 'the economic crisis in Asia highlights the importance of money as a subject for further geographic research' (Poon and Perry, 1999: 194) was certainly a timely intervention during a period when financial geography was emerging as a subfield within economic geography.

While much of the literature on world cities and financial centres at the time focused on banking or advanced producer services (for example, Sassen, 2001; Beaverstock et al. 1999), Poon (2003a) focused on capital markets in explaining the roles of financial centres in global networks, especially since the growing securitization of financial markets in the 2000s had been driven by institutional investors and the increased cross-border activities of TNCs (see also Chapters 10 and 26 in this volume). Poon also extended the boundaries of world cities research through her work on the development of Islamic finance in Malaysia and the Middle East, addressing how world cities control knowledge, norms and resources among firms and workers. Her research on the emergence of Islamic financial expertise and knowledge in Malaysia showed how Kuala Lumpur, as a financial centre, was able to develop particular 'frontier' advantages (Poon et al, 2017) by bridging the financial knowledge of Western world cities and shariah authority claimed by Gulf cities. This focus on Islamic finance was a distinctive contribution to financial geography in examining the roles of world cities in global financial accumulation outside the top tier of conventional financial centres (see also Pollard and Samers, 2007).

Poon's work on knowledge production in Islamic finance generated new theoretical insights into issues of legitimacy and institutional foundations of legal and regulatory practice (Poon et al, 2018; Ewers et al, 2018). Focusing on the roles of lawyers, judges, shariah scholars and regulatory institutions, Poon and colleagues studied the ways in which legal experts, documentation and structures institutionalized the (re)production of Islamic values in Islamic financial markets, which produced and legitimized capital in different forms and spaces. In Malaysia, these involved the rescaling and consolidation of legal spaces and institutions – including the central bank, juridical system, Islamic universities, research think tanks and their shariah bureaucrats and professionals – in order to facilitate the geographical mobility of Malaysian shariah expertise transnationally (Poon et al, 2018). In the case of Bahrain, its competitive advantage relies on it being home to 'gatekeepers' of the industry, such as the Accounting and Auditing Organization for Islamic Financial Institutions and the Islamic International Rating Agency, which govern Islamic financial industry worldwide (Ewers et al, 2018).

These studies presented novel findings and arguments regarding market formation, financial centre development and governance of economic processes. Rather than interpreting these developments in Islamic financial markets as a retreat from neoliberal influence, Poon argued that these constitute a reordering of market values and norms that combined moral risks and market risks in a form that others have called 'ordo-liberalism' (Lai and Samers, 2017; see also Rethel, 2018). Such conceptual interventions contributed to critical discussions in economic geography as well as heterodox economics on varieties of capitalism, variegated capitalism, comparative capitalisms and neoliberal morality (Peck and Zhang, 2013; Sheppard and Leitner, 2010). This approach highlighted the importance of examining the political economy of markets as a juridical project while attending to plural conception of values – in this case, Islamic values in financial market formation. Greater analytical attention and theorization of state and quasi-state actors is now taken up by financial geographers in examining the ways in which they shape financial processes and as vital constituents of the global economic system, whether in the form of sovereign wealth funds (Dixon and Ashby, 2012), state-led financialization (Lai and Daniels, 2017; Pan et al, 2021) or the state–finance nexus (Töpfer and Hall, 2018; Dal Maso, 2020). This strand of research on Islamic finance and Islamic financial centres also contributed to a growing body of work that was shifting attention away from upper echelons of the global economy in conventional global cities research, which had been criticized for reproducing a Western-centric view of globalization and marginalizing cities in developing regions (Robinson, 2006).

'Doing' economic geography: quantitative methods and digital futures

Poon's methodological expertise in quantitative analysis is a distinctive feature of her scholarship. This is especially notable when the disciplinary training and research culture in economic geography have moved steadily away from quantitative to qualitative research since the 1990s, such that it is now uncommon to find journal articles based on quantitative analysis published in leading economic geography and related journals. Although Poon makes use of interviewing as a method, it is usually deployed alongside her core competencies in the quantitative analysis of large datasets. Her skilful use of statistical analysis and social network analysis sets her apart from the qualitative research usually associated with contemporary economic geographers. Through her critical reflections in *Progress in Human Geography* (Poon, 2003b, 2004, 2005) as well as her own research practice, Poon has contributed to wider disciplinary efforts at addressing criticisms of quantitative methods in geography research (see also Abreu et al, 2021). Criticized for their emphasis on generalization and simplification, quantitative methods have been on the decline in many areas of human geography scholarship since the 1990s. Paradoxically, other fields such as sociology, new economic geography and regional science have been stepping up on their use of quantitative methods. One might argue that it is precisely her expertise in quantitative methods and economic geographical analysis that enable her research to travel well beyond economic geography into other fields that value quantitative research, as seen in her regular publications in economics and regional science journals, and the citation of her work by trade economists and regional scientists.

In her progress reports, Poon (2003b, 2004, 2005) was critical about the false caricature of quantitative methods and argued that it was a misnomer to treat the literature as a collection of unequivocal modernist narratives. Instead, she highlighted the key objective of methodological legislation and statistical governance in data analysis, rather than a fixation on the discovery of laws and universal truths. Moreover, increased computational power and complexity now allow forms of analysis that reflect heterogeneous positions and experiences, such that quantitative analysis is no longer just about producing metanarratives. With a greater emphasis on situated rather than objective knowledge, Poon (2005) pointed to abduction reasoning as a mode of geospatial knowledge production that could potentially provide richer explanations and a more pluralistic view of quantitative geography.

Beyond methodological debates, Poon's intervention raised more important intellectual concerns regarding the international production of geographical knowledge, pointing out that the relative universality and communicability of mathematical and statistical language continued to perform a useful role in geography (see also Sheppard, 2001). In a survey of authors in the geography journals, Poon (2003b) found that *Antipode* and *Environment and Planning D: Society and Space*, which published largely qualitative research with strong emphasis on theoretical innovations, were overly represented by authors with Anglo-American affiliations or from English-speaking countries. *Geographical Analysis*, which welcomed more quantitative submissions, had more diverse authors including those from Asia and Africa. Papers in the latter journal were also more likely to be single-authored and not co-authored with US- or UK-based authors to overcome language barriers and fulfil the theoretical demands of many mainstream human and economic geography journals. Given that geographical education and research cultures in many parts of the world are heavily reliant on quantitative methods (see Qian and Zhang, 2021), such reflections on the role and value of quantitative methods raises important considerations for transnational communication and in bridging core–peripheral patterns in the production of geographical scholarship.

More recently, Poon's methodological arguments have engaged with digital methods and online data to consider what these data structures and social use of data might reveal about contemporary cultural economies and new economic subjects. These extend from her research interest on the production of knowledge and shifting dynamics arising from the social interactions and communication of economic agents through digital channels. Studies include how Dell's use of business Weblog (or blog) to interact directly with its customers led to changing forms of interpersonal and reciprocal knowledge construction (Poon and Cheong, 2009), and the ways in which Protestant and Buddhist organizations in Singapore utilized digital channels to convert religious performance into forms suitable for commodification and transfers (Poon et al, 2012). While they deal with very different sectors, there is a common research theme in analysing how communication in an increasingly digitized and mediatized environment is transforming the nature of transactions in the various market domains. In a new book on *Misinformation in the Digital Age* (Stephens et al, 2023), Poon and colleagues delve deeper into the ways in which online digital engagements and new media platforms are reshaping the reproduction, storage and circulation of knowledge and (mis) information, and how these have rescaled and disrupted relationships of trust and authority. These methodological interventions continue to enrich our understanding of knowledge production, social structures of authority and legitimacy, and socio-economic values in contemporary societies.

Conclusion

Jessie Poon's work has been instrumental in shaping empirical and theoretical understandings of international trade and the global activities of firms. Her focus on the economic geographies of Asian economies, firms, states and other institutional actors provided a strong foundation for further investigations into a rapidly growing region that had evolved from being a key destination for inward FDI and branch plant economies into a source region of capital and technology for other developing countries. Her research on Islamic finance and offshore finance provided valuable insights into often overlooked dimensions and spaces of global finance, and developed new geographical understandings of power and governance in financial centres and global financial networks. With her expertise and commitment to quantitative methods, she also made distinctive contributions to economic geography research and helped to bridge intellectual exchanges with other fields such as economics and regional science. Taken together, Poon's scholarly work over the years has pushed at the boundaries of the discipline and opened up new geographical, conceptual and methodological spaces for economic geographers. Her research findings and insights into economic geographies of Asia firmly established the importance of the region to globalization processes and outcomes, and paved the way for subsequent cohorts of economic geographers interested in economic development in Asia and their global networks. Her conceptual arguments on innovation networks have influenced more nuanced and multi-scalar approaches to knowledge and governance. In addition to her scholarship, Poon demonstrated exemplary intellectual citizenship through her professional roles on numerous journal editorial boards, organizing committees and advisory boards of research centres and government panels, and the mentoring of early-career researchers. Her success as an Asian female economic geographer, and her research contributions and intellectual endeavours continue to inspire future generations of economic geographers, especially in the context of growing research interest in Asian economies and societies.

References

Abreu, M., Poon, J. and Elhorst, P. (2021) 'Women in spatial economic analysis', *Spatial Economic Analysis*, 16(2): 241–6.

Bathelt, H. and Glückler, J. (2003) 'Toward a relational economic geography', *Journal of Economic Geography*, 3(2): 117–44.

Beaverstock, J., Smith, R.G. and Taylor, P.J. (1999) A roster of world cities. *Cities*, 16(6): 445–58.

Dal Maso, G. (2020) *Risky Expertise in Chinese Financialisation: Returned Labour and the State–Finance Nexus*, Singapore: Palgrave Macmillan.

Dixon, A.D. and Ashby, M.H.B. (2012) 'Rethinking the sovereign in sovereign wealth funds', *Transactions of the Institute of British Geographers*, 37(1): 104–17.

Ewers, M.C., Dicce, R., Poon, J.P.H., Chow, J. and Gengler, J. (2018) 'Creating and sustaining Islamic financial centers: Bahrain in the wake of financial and political crises', *Urban Geography*, 39(1): 3–25.

Gemici, K. and Lai, K.P.Y. (2020) 'How "global" are investment banks? An analysis of investment banking networks in Asian equity capital markets', *Regional Studies*, 54(2): 149–61.

Hsu, J.Y., Poon, J.P. and Yeung, H.W.C. (2008) 'External leveraging and technological upgrading among East Asian Firms in the United States', *European Planning Studies*, 16(1): 99–118.

Lai, K.P.Y. (2012) 'Differentiated markets: Shanghai, Beijing and Hong Kong in China's financial centre network', *Urban Studies*, 49(6): 1275–96.

Lai, K.P.Y. and Daniels, J.A. (2017) 'Financialization of Singaporean banks and the production of variegated financial capitalism', in B. Christophers, A. Leyshon and G. Mann (eds) *Money and Finance After the Crisis: Critical Thinking for Uncertain Times*, Oxford: Wiley, pp 217–44.

Lai, K.P.Y. and Samers, M. (2017) 'Conceptualizing Islamic banking and finance: a comparison of its development and governance in Malaysia and Singapore', *Pacific Review*, 30(3): 405–24.

Lai, K.P.Y. and Yeung, H.W.C. (2003) 'Contesting the state: discourses of the Asian economic crisis and mediating strategies of electronic firms in Singapore', *Environment and Planning A: Economy and Space*, 35(3): 463–88.

Pan, F., Bi, W., Liu, X. and Sigler, T. (2020) 'Exploring financial centre networks through inter-urban collaboration in high-end financial transactions in China', *Regional Studies*, 54(2): 162–72.

Pan, F., Zhang, F. and Wu, F. (2021) 'State-led financialization in China: the case of the government-guided investment fund', *The China Quarterly*, 547: 749–72.

Peck, J. and Zhang, J. (2013) 'A variety of capitalism … with Chinese characteristics?', *Journal of Economic Geography*, 13(3): 357–96.

Perry, M., Poon, J. and Yeung, H. (1998a) 'Regional offices in Singapore: spatial and strategic influences in the location of corporate control', *Review of Urban and Regional Development Studies*, 10(1): 42–59.

Perry, M., Yeung, H. and Poon, J. (1998b) 'Regional office mobility: the case of corporate control in Singapore and Hong Kong', *Geoforum*, 29(3): 237–55.

Pollard, J. and Samers, M. (2007) 'Islamic banking and finance: postcolonial political economy and the decentring of economic geography', *Transactions of the Institute of British Geographers*, 32(3): 313–30.

Poon, J.P.H. (1994) 'Effects of world demand and competitiveness on exports and economic growth', *Growth and Change*, 25(4): 3–24.

Poon, J.P.H. (1997a) 'Inter-country trade patterns between Europe and the Asia-Pacific: regional structure and extra-regional trends', *Geografiska Annaler Series B: Human Geography*, 79(1): 41–55.

Poon, J.P.H. (1997b) 'The cosmopolitanization of trade regions: global trends and implications, 1965–1990', *Economic Geography*, 73(4): 390–404.

Poon, J.P.H. (2001) 'Regionalism in the Asia Pacific: is geography destiny?', *Area*, 33(3): 252–60.

Poon, J.P.H. (2003a) 'Hierarchical tendencies of capital markets among international financial centers', *Growth and Change*, 34(2): 135–56.

Poon, J.P.H. (2003b) 'Quantitative methods: producing quantitative methods narratives', *Progress in Human Geography*, 27(6): 753–62.

Poon, J.P.H. (2004) 'Quantitative methods: past and present', *Progress in Human Geography*, 28(6): 807–14.

Poon, J.P.H. (2005) 'Quantitative methods: not positively positivist', *Progress in Human Geography*, 29(6): 766–72.

Poon, J.P.H. and Cheong, P. (2009) 'Objectivity, subjectivity, and intersubjectivity in economic geography: evidence from the internet and blogosphere', *Annals of the Association of American Geographers*, 99(3): 590–603.

Poon, J.P.H. and Pandit, K. (1996) 'Pacific trade and regionalisation, 1965–1990', *International Trade Journal*, 10(2): 199–221.

Poon, J.P.H. and Perry, M. (1999) 'The Asian economic "flu": a geography of crisis', *Professional Geographer*, 51(2): 184–96.

Poon, J.P.H. and Sajarattanachote, S. (2010) 'Asian transnational enterprises and technology transfer in Thailand', *European Planning Studies*, 18(5): 691–707.

Poon, J.P.H. and Thompson, E.R. (2001) 'Effects of the Asian financial crisis on transnational capital', *Geoforum*, 32(1): 121–31.

Poon, J.P.H. and Thompson, E.R. (2003) 'Developmental and quiescent subsidiaries in the Asia Pacific: evidence from Hong Kong, Singapore, Shanghai and Sydney', *Economic Geography*, 79(2): 195–214.

Poon, J.P.H. and Thompson, E.R. (2004) 'Convergence or differentiation? American and Japanese transnational corporations in the Asia Pacific', *Geoforum*, 35(1): 111–25.

Poon, J.P.H., Huang, S. and Cheong, P. (2012) 'Media, religion and the marketplace in the information economy: evidence from Singapore', *Environment and Planning A: Economy and Space*, 44(8): 1969–85.

Poon, J.P.H., Hsu, J. and Suh, J. (2006) 'The geography of learning and knowledge acquisition among Asian latecomers', *Journal of Economic Geography*, 6(4): 541–59.

Poon, J.P.H., Kedron, P. and Bagchi-Sen, S. (2013) 'Do foreign subsidiaries innovate and perform better in a cluster? A spatial analysis of Japanese subsidiaries in the US', *Applied Geography*, 44: 33–42.

Poon, J.P.H., Pollard, J. and Chow, Y.W. (2018) 'Resetting neoliberal values: lawmaking in Malaysia's Islamic finance', *Annals of the American Association of Geographers*, 108(5): 1442–56.

Poon, J.P.H., Pollard, J., Chow, Y.W. and Ewer, M. (2017) 'The rise of Kuala Lumpur as an Islamic financial frontier', *Regional Studies*, 51(10): 1443–53.

Poon, J.P.H., Thompson, E.R. and Kelly, P.F. (2000) 'Myth of the triad? Geography of trade and investment "blocs"', *Transactions of the Institute of British Geographers*, 25(4): 427–44.

Qian, J. and Zhang, H. (2021) 'University geography in China: history, opportunities, and challenges', *Transactions of the Institute of British Geographers*, 47(1): 28–33.

Rethel, L. (2018) 'Economic governance beyond state and market: Islamic capital markets in Southeast Asia', *Journal of Contemporary Asia*, 48(2): 301–21.

Robinson, J. (2006) *Ordinary Cities: Between Modernity and Development*, Abingdon: Routledge: London.

Sajarattanachote, S. and Poon, J.P.H. (2009) 'Multinationals, geographical spillovers, and regional development in Thailand', *Regional Studies*, 43(3): 479–94.

Sassen, S. (2001) *The Global City: New York, London, Tokyo* (2nd edn), Princeton, NJ: Princeton University Press.

Shang, Q., Poon, J.P.H. and Yue, Q. (2012) 'The role of regional knowledge spillovers in China', *China Economic Review*, 23(4): 1164–75.

Sheppard, E. (2001) 'Quantitative geography: representations, practices, and possibilities', *Environment and Planning D: Society and Space*, 19(5): 535–54.

Sheppard, E. and Leitner, H. (2010) '*Quo vadis* neoliberalism? The remaking of global capitalist governance after the Washington Consensus', *Geoforum*, 41(2): 185–94.

Stephens, M., Poon, J.P.H. and Tan, G.K.S. (2023) *Misinformation in the Digital Age: An American Infodemic*, Cheltenham: Edward Elgar.

Töpfer, L.M. and Hall, S. (2018) 'London's rise as an offshore RMB financial centre: state–finance relations and selective institutional adaptation', *Regional Studies*, 52(8): 1053–64.

6

Linda McDowell: Complex Geographies that Matter

Karenjit Clare

Introduction

Linda McDowell has been path-breaking within and beyond the discipline of geography, and particularly at the intersection of economic and feminist geography. She has been at the forefront in demonstrating how and why 'geography', 'class', 'ethnicity' and 'gender' matter in research into a more complete understanding of space, place, capital and power. She has written highly influential articles on social and economic processes underlying economic restructuring and divisions of labour in United Kingdom, the impact of migration and of women's changing lives, and how this relates to feminist methodology and theory. Her empirical trajectory has covered an extraordinary array of contexts, ranging from rethinking migrant women's voices, to examining young White unskilled men searching for employment, through to bankers in the City of London. Yet, they are all related by their focus on the significance of gender as a category of analysis (McDowell, 1997, 2003a,b, 2016a,b).

Together, these all highlight the importance of a more localized lens for understanding how geography affects opportunity and employment. Linda's ideas are communicated in path-breaking scholarly papers and pioneering books which have been translated into a number of languages, including Chinese, Spanish, Japanese, German and Korean. While documenting the changing and varied gender, ethnicity, class and employment interconnections would be a challenge to anyone, Linda has achieved this with seeming ease. Many previous studies had ignored these categories, reaching general conclusions that neglected important distinctions between economic and social subgroups. It has become clear not only that significant categories are apparent but also that they can be related in a coherent way to classifying factors of the individual or the group.

Despite the remarkable diversity of economic geographies today, there remains a fundamental tension between a disciplinary approach via practice of scholarship and one that endorses different perspectives. Instead of an engaged pluralism, economic geography has largely descended into a fragmented pluralism for reasons very much internal to the history of the field (Clare and Siemiatycki, 2014). Here, I outline the contributions that Linda McDowell has made to a fuller, more diverse economic geography that is grounded in rigorous empirical research.

Gender in economic geography

> Gender refers to '*socially created* distinctions between femininity and masculinity'
>
> McDowell and Sharpe, 1997: 20, original emphasis

Gender is essential; as McDowell compellingly conveys:

> gender is not a category distinct from class and ethnicity but is mutually constructed through a range of social relations including in the workplace and the home – both of which are sites of work; men are gendered too and the advantages and disadvantages conferred by masculinity and femininity vary across time and space, as they intersect with class relations, labour market change and the geographically specific relations of place, including forms of regulation and solidaristic struggles at different scales in different sites. (McDowell, 2016b: 2093)

She has drawn particular attention to questions regarding what gets recognized as economic, which individuals are considered in economic analyses, and what processes and organizations figure in the theorization of economic systems and change (McDowell and Sharp, 1997).

McDowell's article 'Life without father and Ford: the new gender order of post-Fordism' was especially significant in motivating investigation of interconnections between production and social reproduction, a category of analysis that includes the welfare state, the community and the family (1991). She emphasized the gendering of skills and the changing value of 'masculine attributes' in the labour market, advocating further research into the service sector and informal work. Conceptions of the shifting space-economy, McDowell contended, had been focused too narrowly on transformations in the manufacturing sector and formal factory workplace (see Chapters 2, 4 and 20 in this volume). Consequently, the significance of gender relations in post-Fordist economic restructuring had been overlooked. Placing women's labour at the centre of analysis would both reveal the increasing participation of women in paid work and the manner in which increasing flexibility of labour was impacting both sexes as irregular employment conditions were becoming more widespread.

This short chapter cannot do full justice to the radical transformation in human geography initiated by Linda's work highlighting the centrality of gender relations. Therefore, I will focus on her impact in three key areas. In the first section, I discuss (1) McDowell's research on gendered spatial divisions of labour. I will then describe the influence of her work on my own research on (2) inequalities within the 'creative' sector, and (3) the precarious lives and obstacles facing young people in the East End of London. Moreover, Linda has had an enormous influence on my academic life, as a scholar, friend and mentor.

Gender and finance

> 'Jobs are not gender neutral – rather they are created as appropriate for either men or women'
>
> McDowell, 1997: 25

Many studies of banking and finance have provided insight into the economic aspects of global capitalism. Missing from this literature have been attention to financial workplaces and the influence of gender on workers who make 'their living by moving invisible sums around the globe or by advising companies to invest, divest and take over other firms whose products and workers would never be seen' (McDowell, 1997: 159). Focusing on three investment banks in the city of London, McDowell exposed in her seminal book, *Capital Culture: Gender at Work in the City*, the social and spatial processes that foster gender segregation in these settings (1997). This formative study highlighted the various ways in which gender and power are constructed and maintained in the city of London. It generated a surge of literature and political activity now focusing on gender equality.

Capital Culture illustrated how masculinity remained an advantage in investment banking. It starts with a provoking theoretical discussion on conceptualizing the changing workplace and illuminating how 'location … affects, as well as reflects, the social construction of work and workers and the relations of power, control, and dominance that structure relations between them' (1997: 12). McDowell illustrates how business conduct is not rational and disembodied but that masculine performances are valued and women regarded as 'out of place', not 'one of the boys', and often made to feel like imposters. The book recounts the ways in which the places, spaces and cultures of the big investment banks undervalue female employees while 'male power is implicitly reinforced in many of the micro-scale interactions in organizations; in workplace talk and jokes' (1997: 27). For example, the trading floor is still regarded as a place for gentleman, as argued in 'Capital culture revisited: sex, testosterone and the city' (McDowell, 2010). Linda's research continues to have significant impacts on thinking and empirical research into the male dominance aspect as a central organizing principle of this high-status employment.

Nevertheless, she also noted increasing evidence of women/girls being more successful than in the past in obtaining educational and professional qualifications in the US, the UK and the rest of Western Europe. This led to better access to previously restricted professions, including law and medicine, and into highly paid employment in the financial services sector (McDowell, 1997, 2010). However, McDowell also argues that it is less clear whether these patterns of relative success are paralleled in newer occupational categories, for example in the creative and cultural industries that are important in a city such as London (2010).

Cool, creative and egalitarian? Gender within the creative industries

As geographers and other scholars argue, the 'production of difference' based on bodily attributes including gender and ethnicity, is a key mechanism of labour-market discrimination and a hierarchy of eligibility among groups (McDowell et al, 2016; Roediger and Esch, 2012). Intermediaries have also affected, directly and indirectly, career trajectories and local labour markets. In particular, headhunters' work, though hidden, impacts profoundly on the professional lives of many employees. Reliance of firms on these intermediaries does not necessarily reduce discrimination and, in fact, may sometimes have the opposite effect, because of the conscious or even unconscious bias by these intermediaries in fulfilling what they think are the requirements of their clients. Is this specific to these professions? Here, I illustrate that access to the benefits of social capital is unequally distributed. Importantly, as McDowell aptly writes, 'there are still surprisingly few studies ... which directly compare men and women within the same organization, even doing the same job, and which unravel the different ways in which non-hegemonic versions of femininity and masculinity are constricted and maintained as inferior' (McDowell, 1997: 30).

The introduction of machines empowered women, especially in labour-intensive occupations. However, while it reduced the male muscular advantage it did not lead to a rapid equalization of gender in those occupations. This must be then attributed to other causes, mostly social, educational and even cultural. These factors are still operational, not only in traditional labour-intensive occupations, but also in more recent occupations developed by technology and social change (Twine, 2022). These occupations include the 'creative' industries, which need not, in principle, hold gender-related barriers (see Chapters 16 and 25 in this volume).

Following McDowell, my own research has found that, despite the rhetoric of flexibility, egalitarianism and non-hierarchical structures, categorical inequalities (in particular gender) exist in the creative industries, which shape labour-market outcomes. My findings are that gender is often more important than performance in facilitating career trajectories of workers. This is particularly prominent in the newer creative industries, such as advertising, information technology and the media. An example is the process of employee recruitment. I have found that headhunters directly affect the professional paths of many employees in a hitherto hidden way, and consequently labour-market segmentation. Headhunters determine the candidate shortlists by assessing candidates based both on their professional experience and their potential fit with the firm's ethos. Thus, headhunters perpetuate, both strategically and inadvertently, labour-market inequalities by influencing the candidate–employer matching. As McDowell and other feminist analysts of the labour market have also shown, organizations are saturated with masculinist values and this is evident in patterns of gender segregation across time and space (McDowell, 2014).

The most profound influences of gender and class occur at higher level (executive/board level) appointments. I have found that headhunters select candidates with attributes similar to those already at board level. These are often: male, ethnically homogenous and often from similar class backgrounds. This narrows the talent pool and forms a visible barrier to the progression of those not fitting easily into this pattern. My study showed that both executives and the headhunters assisting them display marked biases in their selection. Moreover, focused interviews with headhunters revealed more knowledge than was originally apparent about the nature of this bias; when questioned more closely, headhunters largely agreed they were influencing their selection process with factors which were not directly related to the abilities of possible candidates but were designed to fit in with the resumed prejudices or preferences of the employer. The employers themselves are unaware of this bias to some extent, though they readily accept that they feel more comfortable working with people of ethnic, gender, class and educational similar to theirs. Thus, as feminist and, indeed, other theorists insist, gender intersects with other social characteristics, including ethnicity and class, as well as nationality, age and sexual orientations, to produce and reproduce inequality in the labour market (McDowell, 2008).

The hidden power of social networking

Linda McDowell in her book *Redundant Masculinities?* (2003b) investigates the links between the so-called 'crisis of masculinity' and contemporary changes in the labour market through the lives of young working-class men. She discusses ways in which the voices of poorly educated men might be heard, and how this might be altered in a rapidly changing labour market. One example is the focus on the difference and experience of white working-class youths stereotyped by the government, media and general public life as 'yobs' to be feared for their lack of culture and work ethic. McDowell (2003b) recognizes and defines the social construction of gender and racial identities and stereotypes, which involves dispelling some of the myths about masculinity and its supposed crisis. One of these potent factors is the role played by socialization.

Social networks have become critical, and they have been one focus of my own work (Clare, 2013). They can provide arenas of professional socialization through instrumental resources (for example, advice and sponsorship) and they have the potential to open up access to careers in project industries (Gill, 2011). A further dimension regarding their economic geographies is the pressure on individuals and firms to network strategically in order to remain competitive (Jarvis and Pratt, 2006). A good example comes from the advertising industry. Advertising is an inherently collective process, with teams and managers, and this may help explain why proximity and interaction matters so much. Personal connections are extremely important as conduits for information about jobs, projects and in general to get the latest gossip. It is vital to be part of the social scene and social networks serve as a new form of labour-market mediation. It is important to remember that social networking is certainly not unique to the advertising industry. Other sectors – media, fashion, art, IT in particular – also rely on the networks of those working within the industry. Professional workers have increased pressures to 'network' through social engagements (Gray and James, 2007; Clare, 2013). Few scholars, however, have studied in any depth the nature of the social ties within these industries. As Currid-Halkett (2009) argues, many of the conventions, access to jobs and gatekeepers within the creative industries, of which advertising is one example, tend to occur within a collective social milieu, 'the scene'. This scene is defined by the industry events, nightlife and spatial proximity to each other where business issues are also being discussed. Therefore, empirical work on the relationships between place and social ties is a key component in exploring patterns in employment and promotion in professional white-collar careers.

In a wider context, ephemeral and intense relations are becoming the norm in work and non-work situations. While networking is not new, what is new is the move to regularize these new network forms – to work them up through more formalized structures, conventions and forms. Rather than deepening relationships, sociality networks are more strategically career-oriented (Grabher and Ibert, 2010). It is now recognized that decisions in economic and social life are situated within a unique regional context defined by shared habits, routines and attitudes (see Chapter 16 in this volume). This will limit the access both by women, who may not share the cultural habits of men, and by those from a more deprived background, such as the subjects I have been studying, who may have difficulties in adapting or conforming to, or being accepted by, those in more privileged circumstances.

Progressing within a career requires learning not only the skills and roles required to perform tasks successfully in that industry, but also understanding the industry and regional culture, since these norms, values and conventions establish how careers are experienced and work is organized (James, 2014). They (1) create opportunities for career progression; (2) develop a reputation within the firm and the industry; (3) provide the chance to meet senior individuals who nurture individuals in a very informal way, leading to better career opportunities; and (4) senior individuals may act as sponsor which helps with the individual's advancement. Social networks are the main mechanism through which accounts or projects are constructed and dismantled within many 'creative' occupations. They are also important for freelance workers to establish and maintain new contacts.

Certainly, there is a darker side to compulsory networking and self-promotion, especially given how the growing instability of the flexible creative economy requires workers to take on the burdens of 'entrepreneurial labour' by shouldering more of the risks and overhead costs of developing creative careers (Neff, 2005). There is also a negative side to this emphasis on personal relationships to facilitate success, such that favouritism can exclude other equally competent workers from projects. Moreover, over time it may become difficult to reconcile family or personal life with regular or incessant socializing. Those from a background different from the mainstream, either gender or class-related, may find it difficult to join in, or even be excluded from particular social environments. But we still need more information: as McDowell and Dyson (2011: 2199) stated 'we make a plea for more empirical studies and working conditions of labour market change'. Relationships are replacing more traditional factors, such as perceived competence, as important elements in an individual's progress. Individuals must 'calculate' themselves (calculate their own career trajectories, project portfolios, links to gatekeepers and so on) and 'work upon themselves' (maintaining their profiles within the industry through networking and socializing). Social interactions are a core mechanism by which careers are developed. Networking is the now the norm in many sectors and countries; those who do not or cannot are substantially disadvantaged (Jeffrey, 2010). Pushing more individuals into insecure, precarious, irregular working patterns and network-reliant careers may be more than many are able to handle (Johnston, 2018). On the other hand, recruiting talented workers may prove difficult in sites where socializing is impeded because of a lack of facilities.

These biases seem to apply less to recruitment and acceptance of interns. Internships are often the entrée to more important employment to companies. There is greater bias, mostly unintentional and unconscious, in appointments to higher positions. Part of this change in attitude may relate to individual ability to socialize. This is not a prominent requirement for an intern but much more significant when a person becomes permanently employed and begins to take part in the social activities of the firm. This suggests that equalities which are not directly concerned with a professional or commercial ability play a considerable, but often unsuspected role in selection, particularly for higher positions.

Working Lives: Gender, Migration and Employment in Britain, 1945–2007 *(2013)*

Linda McDowell has been prominent in analysing the varied and changing interconnections between gender, class, ethnicity and employment over six decades, an intimidating task. Her aim was to rebalance a dominant concentration in the literature on male migrant workers and to focus instead on women migrants to Britain and the gendered and ethnic or racialized nature of their experiences of work. *Working Lives* (2013) covers the immediate post-war period until 2007, and McDowell skilfully weaves together the personal testimony of particular women with the much bigger historical picture of which their experience is a part; their origins, why and how they came to Britain and their subsequent work location and history. McDowell draws on interviews she conducted in a variety of research projects on the economic geography of work which detail how particular groups of migrants are prioritized for the different time periods.

Linda McDowell's captivating book recounts the experiences of exceptional ordinary women in the British labour market between 1945 and 2007 who have been born elsewhere. Its basic premise is that women, and especially migrant women, are still neglected in accounts of labour markets. It aims to provide an alternative yet complementary account of post-war economic change from a gendered perspective that places women at the centre rather than on the periphery of the analysis. This draws on a range of different research projects carried out by the author over several decades. It is this deliberate focus on women, and not on gender, that is the core strength of this book. In tracing the intersections between British labour and migration history from the perspective of women, the book ends up being much richer and more insightful than many broadly similar accounts of this period. Indeed, while this scholarly work is about economic change, work and migration, it is also about communities, motherhood, emotional labour, the body and exploitation.

The vivid testimonies of South Asian migrant workers and the activism of migrant women record their restriction to low-paid repetitive assembly work and almost total segregation from the 'native' women office workers. A more or less absolute gender segregation of work was rendered more complex and divisive by an almost equally absolute ethnic segregation between native and migrant women, resulting in minimal contact and little commonality of interest (see also Chapter 23 in this volume). Labour is not homogenous and workers with the same skills can earn very different wages. Additionally, the labour market is imperfect in that not every worker has total knowledge of job opportunities, or what others earn. This militates against the existence of one wage for a particular job or level of skills (Strauss and McGrath, 2017).

McDowell's book (2013) points out that many texts to date have ignored migrants' voices in general and in particular women migrants' voices. The rich extracts from oral histories from a diversity of women – from Latvia, Jamaica, Barbados, Ireland, Uganda, Kenya, India, South Africa and the US – bring the book alive in important ways. This approach not only captures the complex histories and geographies that influence women's lives, but also their differences, resonances and similarities in their experiences. Full of unique and compelling insights into the working lives of migrant women in the UK, McDowell draws on more than two decades of in-depth research to explore the changing nature of women's employment in post-war Britain.

Complexity and harshness: the impact of environmental and social change

The lives of groups of people are often changed radically by events outside their control or even their knowledge. McDowell (2003a) investigated the effects of rapid changes in the labour market that impacted poorly educated young men. One example is the Second Industrial Revolution of the late 19th and early 20th centuries, which had radical effects on employment, housing and wage levels. Another is the Second World War, which had dramatic effects on social boundaries and educational opportunities, as well as profound personal and geopolitical consequences, vividly described in Kazuo Ishiguro's book *The Remains of the Day*. My own empirical work on a group of social and financially deprived youths is a microcosm of this scenario. They and their families have lived for years in a run-down and neglected area of East London, a traditional area that housed the poor and recent immigrants. However, this environment was quite suddenly altered by the 2012 Olympic Games. This triggered an enormous building spree in East London, which included large housing developments to high standards for the competitors and officials. After the Games ended, this housing entered the open market. The consequence was an influx of middle-class inhabitants, and a rapid transition of the area from a deprived working-class one to a desirable and busy middle-class part of London. Shops selling pies and chips were replaced by avocados and smoked salmon sandwiches. House prices rocketed. But the previous inhabitants stayed put.

Empirical evidence remains limited regarding the everyday opportunities and working practices for young Londoners aged 16–25 who have lived in this area before it was modernized but are now disengaged from working and do not have access to the social, cultural and economic activities within the locality. They face unpreceded social and economic disadvantages during a time of intense economic urban change. In this area, the population is relatively young with over 60 per cent being under 34 and only 4 per cent over 65 (London Legacy Development Corporation, 2018). As in 2014, the peak in current population is within the 20-to-35 age band. The Legacy Corporation has a higher proportion of young adults aged 25–34 (33 per cent) than London and the rest of the country (17 per cent and 14 per cent respectively) (London Legacy Development Corporation, 2018). Therefore, a large proportion of these young people have been exposed to dramatic changes in their social environment at a critical and formative stage of their lives. The overarching emotion before the Games arrived was one of despondency.

It might be expected that these attitudes and circumstances would be radically changed by the advent of the Olympic Games and the consequent transition of their neighbourhood into a more middle-class environment. In fact, my work shows that this was not the case, and islands of deprivation continued to exist among a more prosperous society. The interesting conclusion is that injecting a deprived neighbourhood with a nucleus of different levels of prosperity and expectation does not necessarily transmit itself to those accustomed to a very different set of social circumstances, but only establishes new class divisions. There are multiple possible reasons why this should be so, but one prominent one that came out of my investigation was that when these young people applied for opportunities within the new and very different environment, they were often rejected because of their appearance, background and even their accents. Employers preferred those that more closely resembled their own social milieu. This surely is a particular example of a more general phenomenon that impedes social change and advancement and needs special attention and understanding if it is to be rectified.

Conclusion

McDowell's research has changed economic geography; it has, in the classic words of feminist scholar Christine di Stefano, 'been brought down to earth and given a pair of pants' (McDowell, 2019: 31). The insights she presents continue to resonate and are ongoing. She has an unusually wide view of the way that social and geographical factors influence the patterns of employment. This has included socialization, selection bias, class, and ethnic and gender barriers, which she has shown to be significant impediments to a more equal employment strategy. Social, economic and feminist debates will continue to animate the field and set agendas for future work, widely acknowledged to be influenced by the impressive, persuasive and powerful scholarship of Linda McDowell.

References

Clare, K. (2013) 'The essential role of place within the creative industries: boundaries, networks and play', *Cities*, 34: 52–7.

Clare, K. and Siemiatycki, E. (2014) 'Primacy or pluralism: future directions in economic geography', *Professional Geographer*, 66(1): 4–10.

Currid-Halkett, E. (2009) *The Warhol Economy*, Princeton: Princeton University Press.

Gill, R. (2011) '"Life is a pitch": managing the self in new media work', in M. Deuze (ed) *Managing Media Work*, London: Sage, pp 249–62.

Grabher, G. and Ibert, O. (2010) 'Project ecologies: a contextual view on temporary organizations', in P.W.G. Morris, J.K. Pinto and J. Söderlund (eds) *The Oxford Handbook of Project Management*, Oxford: Oxford University Press, pp 175–99.

Gray, M. and James, A. (2007) 'Connecting gender and economic competitiveness: lessons from Cambridge's high-tech regional economy', *Environment and Planning A: Economy and Space*, 39(2): 417–36.

James, A. (2014) 'Work–life "balance" and gendered (im)mobilities of knowledge and learning in high-tech regional economies', *Journal of Economic Geography*, 14(3): 483–510.

Jarvis, H. and Pratt, A.C. (2006) 'Bringing it all back home: the extensification and "overflowing" of work – the case of San Francisco's new media households', *Geoforum*, 37(3): 331–9.

Jeffrey, C. (2010) 'Timepass: Youth, class and time amoung unemployed young men in India', *American Ethnologist*, 37(3): 465–81.

Johnston, L. (2018) 'Gender and sexuality III: precarious places', *Progress in Human Geography*, 42(6): 928–36.

London Legacy Development Corporation (2018) *Spatial Portrait Background Paper*, October. Available from: https://www.queenelizabetholympicpark.co.uk/-/media/lldc/local-plan/examination-2019/technical-background-papers/tbp7-spatial-portrait-background-paper [Accessed 7 June 2023].

McDowell, L. (1991) 'Life without father and Ford: the new gender order of post-Fordism', *Transactions of the Institute of British Geographers*, 16(4): 400–19.

McDowell, L. (1997) *Capital Culture: Gender at Work in the City*, Oxford: Blackwell.

McDowell, L. (2003a) 'Masculine identities and low-paid work: young men in urban labour markets', *International Journal of Urban and Regional Research*, 27(4): 828–48.

McDowell, L. (2003b) *Redundant Masculinities? Employment Change and White Working Class Youth*, Oxford: Blackwell.

McDowell, L. (2008) 'Thinking through work: complex inequalities, constructions of difference and transnational migrants', *Progress in Human Geography*, 32(4): 491–507.

McDowell, L. (2010) 'Capital culture revisited: sex, testosterone and the city', *International Journal of Urban and Regional Research*, 34(3): 652–8.

McDowell, L. (2013) *Working Lives: Gender, Migration and Employment in Britain, 1945–2007*, Chichester: Wiley-Blackwell.

McDowell, L. (2014) 'Gender, work, employment and society: feminist reflections on continuity and change', *Work Employment and Society*, 28(5): 825–37.

McDowell, L. (2016a) *Migrant Women's Voices: Talking About Life and Work in the UK Since 1945*, New York: Bloomsbury Academic.

McDowell, L. (2016b) 'Reflections on feminist economic geography: talking to ourselves?', *Environment and Planning A: Economy and Space*, 48(10): 2093–9.

McDowell, L. (2019) 'Border crossings: geographies of class, gender, mobility and migration', *Landmark*, 7: 30–1, Cambridge: Department of Geography. Available from: https://www.geog.cam.ac.uk/files/alumni/landmark/landmark7/landmark7.pdf [Accessed 7 June 2023].

McDowell, L. and Dyson, J. (2011) 'The other side of the knowledge economy: "reproductive" employment and affective labours in Oxford', *Environment and Planning A: Economy and Space*, 43(9): 2186–201.

McDowell, L. and Sharp, J.P. (eds) (1997) *Space, Gender, Knowledge: Feminist Readings*, London: Arnold.

McDowell, L., Rootham, E. and Hardgrove, A. (2016) The production of difference and the maintenance of inequality: the place of young Goan men in a post-crisis UK labour market', *Gender, Work & Organisation*, 23(2): 108–24.

Neff, G. (2005) 'The changing place of cultural production: the location of social networks in a digital media industry', *Annals of the American Academy of Political and Social Science*, 597(1): 134–52.

Roediger, D.R. and Esch, E.D. (2012) *The Production of Difference: Race and the Management of Labor in U.S. History*, Oxford: Oxford University Press.

Strauss, K. and McGrath, S. (2017) 'Temporary migration, precarious employment and unfree labour relations: exploring the "continuum of exploitation" in Canada's Temporary Foreign Worker Program', *Geoforum*, 78: 199–208.

Twine, F.W. (2022) *Geek Girls: Inequality and Opportunity in Silicon Valley*, New York: New York University Press.

7

Yuko Aoyama: Curiosity as Method

Heidi Østbø Haugen

Introduction

When reading through Yuko Aoyama's publications in preparing this chapter, I was reminded of what a rare luxury it is to study someone's scholarship in its entirety. Our purpose for reading affects how we do it, and as academics, we often review our colleagues' writings with the aim of identifying their relevance to our own scholarly endeavours. As we cite other researchers to express how our insights build on their works, we simultaneously recirculate their intellectual contributions and validate them as relevant disciplinary knowledge. Quoting and referencing are central to academic research, and recent debates about gender and racial inequalities within the academy have drawn much-needed attention to how citation practices suppress or promote diversity. Awareness of who we read, cite and assign to our syllabi should be extended to include attentiveness to who is given the opportunity to consolidate their status through public appraisals of their entire scholarship. Academia provides occasions to publicly appraise professional careers while people are still alive and productive, for example through introductions to keynote speeches, award announcements, and honorary title ceremonies. Such events reveal how the scholar's ideas have evolved and how their intellectual and personal lives intersect. Invitations and honorifics matter, not just as endorsements but also as occasions to convey broader academic projects and appreciate intellectual contributions beyond how they prove applicable to a task we have at hand.

A review of Aoyama's body of research from the mid-1990s until today, the early 2020s, brings out themes that are less noticeable in the texts individually: a comparative lens, a strong commitment to understanding both large trends and minutiae in context, the straddling between economic geography and other disciplinary perspectives, and linguistic and disciplinary diversity in the source material. A chronological reading of Aoyama's work takes us from the US to Japan, Germany, Spain and India. It spans as widely thematically as it does geographically. In the early 1990s, she addressed traditional core questions in economic geography, concerning, for example, the nature of globalization, shifts toward a post-industrial society, and firm location strategies. She then ventured into territories that were less commonly explored by economic geographers at the time, including e-commerce, video games and cultural tourism. Her more recent work pushes the boundaries of the subdiscipline of economic geography by analysing social entrepreneurship and energy transitions. Alongside a prolific research career, Aoyama has shaped the subdiscipline of economic geography through her leadership positions. She was editor of the journal *Economic Geography* 2006–14, one of only three women (along with Amy Glasmeier and Susan Hanson) to hold this post during the journal's nearly 100-year history, the centenary falling in 2025. The editorial role was both an important indicator of esteem and a vantage point from which Aoyama exercised influence over the subdiscipline.

When I meet Aoyama online to discuss her research trajectory, she is quick to bring up what she has learned from female academic role models – Ann Markusen, Erica Schoenberger, Susan Christopherson, Amy Glasmeier and Helga Leitner – at various stages in her career. She also mentions interaction with students at Clark University's Graduate School of Geography as an important source of inspiration, especially discussions with international students and US students with an international background. Her list of publications further attests to her readiness to work with both senior and junior researchers. While she enthusiastically speaks of the role of mentorship in shaping new cohorts of scholars, she pauses a bit before commenting on how she thinks her work can be taken forward by new generations of geographers. 'What I have done is not necessarily what I tell my students to do', she says, noting that academia has become more competitive. 'But I do consistently talk about the methodological usefulness of comparative study and particularly international comparative study. And I try to encourage them to triangulate by bringing in literature, in particular non-geography literature.' Aoyama attributes her preference for comparative studies to her experiences with living in different societies in Asia, North America and Europe from a young age. She received her training in academic environments where the focus at the time was almost exclusively on the Anglo-American world, and believes she is very much a product of that. 'But', she says, 'I knew that there were other worlds out there. Having been to Malaysia, France, Japan, I always thought that there were *multiple* capitalisms. How, as economic geographers, can we look at and understand those different capitalisms?'

Aoyama's insistence on inquiring into how capitalism works in different contexts has entailed a potential to disrupt dominant understandings of the economy. Her scholarship illuminates issues from new angles and sets out from an open perspective about what she would find. She insists that she never consciously intended to be postcolonial or deconstruct the Anglo-American hegemony through the way she picked research topics or went about studying them. However, she is content if her research has worked to that effect. Her aspiration to learn as much as she can about context in her research, combined with her tendency to excitedly provide details about the technical and cultural specifics in ongoing projects, recalls discussions in feminist theory of the importance of curiosity. In the essay collection *The Curious Feminist*, Cynthia Enloe (2004) recommended that conventionally ordered and orderly understandings of international relations were disrupted through adopting a curious stand towards all women's experiences. Enloe contrasted curiosity with complacency, an attitude that denies that there are more events and relations worth investigating to figure out why things have turned out the way they are. Similarly, Aoyama uses curiosity as a method in her research through adopting an inquisitive attitude towards phenomena that are not conventionally seen as relevant to economic geography. She captures the complexity of the phenomena under study by taking in as much detail as possible rather than reducing their richness to certain predefined parameters, and she uses anomalies as a basis for theorization rather than bracketing them.

The topics from Aoyama's research discussed next – e-commerce and the video game industry – were not chosen as foci for this chapter because they are more significant than her other works, but rather because the current relevance of her studies is remarkable considering the comprehensive reorganization and fast technological advances in these fields. The sustained significance of this research is attributable to the enthusiasm with which Aoyama delved into the details of the cases under study. Where high-flying musings about technological evolution quickly become stale, reflections based in meticulous empirical analysis remain useful because they tell a more enduring story of the relationship between social and technological developments.

E-commerce

The retail industry is organized in strikingly diverse fashions around the world. While alkaline batteries, cotton buds and laundry detergent sold in Dakar, Tokyo and Houston are essentially the same, the ways through which they reach consumers differ greatly. Aoyama started researching e-commerce when the word 'Internet' was still capitalized and people marvelled at its reach. The book *Cities in the Telecommunications Age*, which Aoyama co-edited with James O. Wheeler and Barney Warf, states that the 'Internet is uncontestably the largest electronic network on the planet, connecting an estimated 100 million people' (Wheeler et al, 2000: 7). Aoyama's research on e-commerce started from the observation that retail conducted on this globally shared platform displayed as many idiosyncrasies as face-to-face retail. In the article 'Structural foundations for e-commerce adoption' (Aoyama, 2001), she inquired into why Japan and the US, two equally technologically advanced societies, exhibited fundamentally divergent paths in their adoption of e-commerce.

People in Japan rely on neighbourhood convenience stores for their day-to-day purchases. At the eve of the e-commerce revolution, Aoyama (2001) noted that the convenience stores started to serve as points of ordering, payment and collection of goods bought online. This close integration of online and in-person retailing contrasted with the emerging competition between online and brick-and-mortar stores in the US during the same period. To understand why such different patterns of collaboration and competition emerged, Aoyama used as a vantage point her empirical observations of differences in the shopping habits in the two countries before broadening the discussion to include regulatory frameworks and the spatial structures of retail. While Japanese consumers do much of their shopping in convenience stores reached by foot, US consumers buy in bulk and by car. The article offered vivid images of what retail stores were like in the two countries and the roles they played in people's lives, which the analysis showed to be a crucial background for understanding divergences in how e-commerce was organized. Societies adopt technologies in historically conditioned ways. Japan lacked the institutional foundation, social legitimacy and historical familiarity necessary for rapid proliferation of direct online retailing. However, online retailers were able to surmount these obstacles, and they turned consumer nationalism and the legal regulation of the country's retail market into resources that they harnessed to popularize e-commerce.

The study was groundbreaking in the ways it shed light on the links between technological developments, urban form and consumer behaviour, connections that now form a mainstay in geographical scholarship on retail and consumption (see also Chapter 28 in this volume). Aoyama undertook it at a time when consumption was largely neglected in academic studies of the economy, which tended to represent production in a more nuanced and empirically informed manner than consumption (Thrift, 2003: 696–9). Aoyama's knowledge of Japan made it possible for her to identify new consumption behaviours early and discuss their social and historical context. Her commitment to contextualization makes readers conscious of what they take for granted about the economy. A publication about the failing attempts of global retail giants Carrefour and Wal-Mart to establish a presence in Japan provides rich descriptions of the North American and European shopping experience, with its unwieldy carts, clunky aesthetics and focus on price over needs (Aoyama, 2007). By encouraging readers to adopt an outsider's view on mega-market shopping, she conveyed how cultural conditions combined with market structures and feedback loops to cause the multinational retail ventures' failure in Japan. Such decentralized perspectives present important correctives to exoticizing accounts of non-Western consumption habits.

Japanese convenience stores constituted a surprising vantage point for understanding how technology would shape our lives 20 years ago and exemplified how cases from diverse geographic contexts are useful to identify emerging topics in economic geography and formulate new critical agendas. Insights into how technology and the organization of retail will shape our future may not best be gained through studying the bulldozer tactics and utopian imaginings of large American corporations and the titans of Silicon Valley. An e-commerce village in China or blockchain chicken farm (compare Wang, 2020) are just as fruitful vantage points from which to understand how technology will sculpt consumption in the future.

Video games

For the generation that grew up in North America and Western Europe in the 1980s, few products were as coveted as Japanese video game systems. Their popularity sparked debates about whether video games were harmful to children's development, discussions that have continued into the present and recently led to including 'gaming disorder' in the World Health Organization's disease classification (World Health Organization, 2023). However, this industry was by and large ignored as an economic phenomenon by geographers before Aoyama and her colleague Hiro Izushi published their seminar study on the topic – 'Hardware gimmick or cultural innovation? Technological, cultural, and social foundations of the Japanese video game industry' (Aoyama and Izushi, 2003). The study contributed to establishing the thriving subfield in economic geography of research on the creative industries. It called attention to job creation in video game hardware and software, the ubiquity of video game consumption in the US and Japan, and the economic size of the industry.

Anglo-American cultural products prevailed globally in the 1980s and 1990s, and Japanese video games represented a relatively rare exception to this cultural dominance at the time. The establishment of Japan's video game industry was made possible through joining the capabilities of two pre-existing sectors in the Japanese economy: the technical capacity and expertise from Japan's consumer electronics industry and the artistic knowledge from the manga and animation film industry. The former was crucial to developing the technology-intensive consoles, including the design of the physical interface and the necessary computer chips. Previous experience with producing toys, arcade games, televisions, home computers and cars had generated skills and created a manufacturing platform from which the console industry could develop. The manga and animation industry provided talents who could draw, engineer audio, program and develop plots for video game software. The artistic creativity that had gone into cartoons and animation films for a national market became crucial to creating a global cultural product. Aoyama and Izushi explored in detail the creative and technical sides of video game development to show how Japanese video games resulted from a unique combination of circumstances and drew upon this in a comparative analysis of the evolution of the video game industry in Japan, the US and the UK (Izushi and Aoyama, 2006). Their studies of how actors and technologies came together in video game production in Japan laid the foundation for subsequent work that attended to how power was maintained and exercised in the industry (Johns, 2006; Cohendet et al, 2018). Aoyama hopes to get the chance to revisit the field. 'It's been backburnered for a while, but it's not that I have abandoned it', she says. 'It was fun work! My collaborator and I keep in touch and continue to play around with this and that idea. When the time comes, I think we may return to it.'

Innovation in base-of-the-pyramid markets

In her research on e-commerce and video games, Aoyama's curiosity was piqued by phenomena that had no immediate explanation. 'I like looking at anomalies that cannot be explained by our theoretical understanding and then thinking about what's missing', she says. In the case of e-commerce in Japan, the incongruity consisted in the symbiosis between a comprehensive network of physical stores and online shopping. The thriving video game industry was a riddle within a riddle: the Japanese software complex in the late 1990s and early 2000s was *not* thriving even though the country was a global electronics leader, but in video games, Japan was indeed a global software development leader. Her interest in how technologies and organizational approaches are developed to fit specific contexts subsequently directed her attention towards 'base-of-the-pyramid' markets (Aoyama and Parthasarathy, 2012; Parthasarathy et al, 2015; Horner et al, 2018). These studies show how services for the poor need to be designed differently to fit limited economic and infrastructural resources. Providing products and services that are appropriate for the context at hand while remaining cost effective necessitates innovation. For example, high-tech artefacts that require a constant power supply with stable voltage to work must be tweaked before they can be applied in contexts with unstable electricity. When people tweak products to environments with suboptimal infrastructural and institutional conditions, innovation and new knowledge transpire.

Recent environmental disasters and the COVID-19 epidemic have highlighted that even groups located at the top of the pyramid are vulnerable in some respects. The exposure of such vulnerabilities can diminish confidence in the ability of the state and market in combination to meet the basic needs of people and societies. 'Crises do happen, [and then] you can't rely on the infrastructure', Aoyama says, referencing the pandemic, wildfires and drought that sent many parts of the US into emergency mode in 2020–21. 'This is not an experiment: people are marginalized and vulnerable. But there are seeds of innovation and knowledge that emerge from that context.' Social entrepreneurs find ways to make do under challenging circumstances and provide services to the vulnerable where conventional solutions fail.

In her work on the hybrid domain, Aoyama, together with her colleague and long-standing collaborator Balaji Parthasarathy, charted how companies leverage local knowledge to figure out how technology was adopted to new circumstances and how social entrepreneurs in turn converted contextually grounded understandings into services for the poor (Aoyama and Parthasarathy, 2016). The hybrid domain denotes realms of state and market failures within which for-profit and non-profit actors come together to pursue common objectives and produce social innovation. Aoyama and Parthasarathy described how innovation happens when products were adapted. In doing so, they challenged the idea that societies travel along the same trajectory in adopting new technologies, demonstrating the merits of learning from the localization strategies of organizations that succeed rather than covering their success with a veil of mysticism. Their project is resolutely optimistic. In looking back at their meetings with Western social entrepreneurs in India, however, Aoyama contemplated the ways it brought up critical questions about the origins, uses and attribution of knowledge. 'They [the Western entrepreneurs] try to harvest to the local knowledge in India to turn it into some kind of a service for the poor', she says. 'But is this the right path? Or is it some kind of colonialism, however well intentioned?'

Diverse capitalisms

'Oligopoly is difficult to accomplish', wrote Aoyama in an analysis of expansion strategies among transnational retail corporations (2007: 472). She attributed the failure of retail transnational corporations (TNCs) that attempt to expand into new geographical markets to the contradictory forces of standardization and localization (see Chapters 5 and 12 in this volume). Standardization is what allows these companies to exert downward pressure on sourcing prices and achieve economies of scale, whereas localization is necessary for adaptation to new contexts. Aoyama warned against assuming that lack of innovative capacity is the reason when a regional market has not implemented a particular retail model; it may well be that the model has not been tried simply because those who know the context have concluded that it would work poorly there (Aoyama, 2007: 486). The attempts by Carrefour and the then–Wal-Mart to enter the Japanese market in the early 2000s were the cases she used to argue this point. Confident in the superiority of their corporate strategies, these retail TNCs failed to adequately consider why their models might be ineffective in Japan.

Stories about corporate giants that fail to understand local contexts when they venture overseas make for fascinating reads and have become a staple feature of mainstream business literature (see, for example, Haig, 2005). Spectacular accounts of failures in new markets serve a double purpose of warning and entertaining readers. Given the popularity of such tales, do we still need economic geographers to remind us that local contexts matter and that capitalism takes on many forms? Other accounts, equally forceful, suggest that we do. A particularly persistent narrative is that of untapped markets, typically located in the Global South, that are ready to be exploited. For example, Western consultancy firms have expressed great optimism about the prospects of rolling out North American and European-style retail in African countries. For decades, international consultants have told Western retail corporations that African markets are ripe for investments, with a young and urbanizing population, a growing middle class and an evolving preference for tidy hypermarket environments (Deloitte, 2016; KPMG, 2016). Yet, giant multinational retailers that try to establish a presence in African countries have often failed. For example, Walmart subsidiary Massmart, Africa's second-largest retailer, has been unsuccessful at establishing a substantial presence outside of South Africa (Massmart, 2021). Aoyama's study of e-commerce in Japan helps rid us of the idea that developing markets follow a trajectory where they eventually employ Western-style economic organizations. Her work on base-of-the-pyramid markets shows what alternative economic paths may look like. The relative economic decline of the US and Europe and the growth of China and India add urgency to the pursuit of understanding variations of capitalism. In the remainder of this chapter, I discuss how a Chinese electronics corporation managed to capture a sizeable share of the distribution of electronics in West Africa at the same time as Walmart was forced to scale back its ambitions in the region. What has allowed this and other Chinese companies to succeed where larger TNCs failed? How do they avoid the structural paradox due to the contradictory forces between standardization and localization described in Aoyama's (2007) work?

The Chinese founder of the trading corporation Avator (a pseudonym) first arrived in the West African trading hub of Lomé in 2000. He arrived with two assets: contacts in electronics factories in Shenzhen and a client base consisting of a group of local traders. Avator had limited capital and needed to make a profit from the outset in its overseas operations. The modest start notwithstanding, Avator now has a notable presence in all African regions except Southern Africa. The company ships containers of electronics directly from factories in China to various African end markets, and its distribution relies heavily on locally based wholesalers and retailers. I interviewed Avator's founder in 2015 when he was going to Niamey, Niger, where he was supporting a Chinese employee in setting up a new distribution office. He recalled the early days of the company's expansion into Africa with fondness, as competition had been moderate, prices high and deals could be sealed with a handshake.

Informal credit extension is essential to the organization of West African retail and wholesale. Chinese companies across sectors collaborate with local traders and retailers to extend credit to customers, and the local partners are necessary for assessing the customers' ability to repay loans and for applying social sanctions in case of non-payment (Haugen, 2017). In addition to expanding the customer base, the partnerships give Chinese suppliers information about fashion trends and how to adapt technical features to suit the local infrastructure. The founder of Avator initially imported single containerloads of electronics, distributed the contents on credit to the businessmen he worked with, and received their settlement payments by 3 pm every Saturday. The businessmen could in turn extend credit to retailers and end customers. Today, Avator's wholesale model has changed in response to the company's expansion and new regional trading patterns that bypass Lomé, but new sales models are still fitted with informal financial systems.

Avator's manufacturing was set up in ways that ran counter to global industry trends. Manufacturing has come to be regarded as a relatively less profitable segment of electronics value chains, and TNCs have handed over production responsibilities to contract manufacturers (Lüthje et al, 2013). Avator, by contrast, went from sourcing goods from the same factories in Shenzhen that sell to TNCs to setting up its own factory. This allowed for better control over delivery times and quality, and Avator went from selling unbranded or counterfeit products to establishing its own brand under which it now markets goods across Africa.

Next, Avator established a logistics branch, leveraging its experience with commissioning shipping containers and air cargo capacity to Africa. My own first encounter with the company came about in 2014 through its container logistics operations, which were marketed to the large African trading community in Guangzhou, South China. Avator tried to come across as an African rather than a Chinese company, for example by offering free office space to African university students in Guangzhou in the showroom where they brought the customers for their logistics business. Profit margins in China–Africa logistics were slim at the time (Haugen, 2019), and the logistics operations were set up to collect market information rather than to generate direct profits. The company's logistics branch later formed the basis for a fully fledged e-commerce platform through which Avator now has set up retail and wholesale solutions that reach customers throughout Africa directly.

In contrast to Walmart, Avator did not arrive in West Africa with preconceived ideas about how to achieve efficiency. Rather, the company studied and adapted to local distribution methods, found ways of harvesting information about demand, and dealt with its weaknesses as a buyer of a limited size by moving production in-house and operating a factory in Shenzhen alongside those that serve large electronics companies. As a born-transnational company, Avator did not expect capitalism to work in a certain manner in the places to which it expanded, but was set on identifying a business model that fit with its resources and conditions on the ground. The result was an efficient and resilient TNC that so far has been more successful than Walmart in retailing electronics to West African customers.

Conclusion

Understanding how different capitalisms evolve is one of the most challenging tasks facing economic geographers, and Aoyama has pioneered these efforts. This is apparent in the individual pieces of work she has published, which, like all good non-fiction writing, open up worlds to readers that they otherwise might not have known they were interested in. Aoyama's methodological and analytical contributions to economic geography become even more evident when we review her scholarship in its entirety. While transnational entrepreneurs may get further by approaching markets in an open-ended manner, we as scholars come closer to comprehending how the global economy works by following Aoyama in adopting a curious stance.

Funding
Haugen's work on this chapter has received funding from the European Research Council (ERC) under the European Union's Horizon 2020 research and innovation programme (Grant Agreement No. 802070).

References
Aoyama, Y. (2001) 'Structural foundations for e-commerce adoption: a comparative organization of retail trade between Japan and the United States', *Urban Geography*, 22(2): 130–53.

Aoyama, Y. (2007) 'Oligopoly and the structural paradox of retail TNCs: an assessment of Carrefour and Wal-Mart in Japan', *Journal of Economic Geography*, 7(4): 471–90.

Aoyama, Y. and Izushi, H. (2003) 'Hardware gimmick or cultural innovation? Technological, cultural, and social foundations of the Japanese video game industry', *Research Policy*, 32(3): 423–44.

Aoyama, Y. and Parthasarathy, B. (2012) 'Research and development facilities of multinational enterprises in India', *Eurasian Geography and Economics*, 53(6): 713–30.

Aoyama, Y. and Parthasarathy, B. (2016) *The Rise of the Hybrid Domain: Collaborative Governance for Social Innovation*, Cheltenham: Edward Elgar.

Cohendet, P., Grandadam, D., Mehouachi, C. and Laurent, S. (2018) 'The local, the global and the industry common: the case of the video game industry', *Journal of Economic Geography*, 18(5): 1045–68.

Deloitte (2016) *African Powers of Retailing: New Horizons for Growth*, London: Deloitte Touche Tohmatsu. Available from: https://www2.deloitte.com/content/dam/Deloitte/za/Documents/consumer-business/Deloitte-African-powers-of-retailing-Feb16.pdf [Accessed 10 February 2018].

Enloe, C. (2004) *The Curious Feminist: Searching for Women in a New Age of Empire*, Berkeley: University of California Press.

Haig, M. (2005) *Brand Failures: The Truth About the 100 Biggest Branding Mistakes of All Time*, London: Kogan Page.

Haugen, H.Ø. (2017) 'Petty commodities, serious business: the governance of fashion jewellery chains between China and Ghana', *Global Networks*, 18(2): 307–25.

Haugen, H.Ø. (2019) 'The social production of container space', *Environment and Planning D: Society and Space*, 37(5): 868–85.

Horner, R., Sanyal, B., Schoenberger, E., Storper, M., Aoyama, Y. and Parthasarathy, B. (2018) 'The rise of the hybrid domain: collaborative governance for social innovation', *AAG Review of Books*, 6(2): 133–40.

Izushi, H. and Aoyama, Y. (2006) 'Industry evolution and cross-sectoral skill transfers: a comparative analysis of the video game industry in Japan, the United States, and the United Kingdom', *Environment and Planning A: Economy and Space*, 38(10): 1843–61.

Johns, J. (2006) 'Video games production networks: value capture, power relations and embeddedness', *Journal of Economic Geography*, 6(2): 151–80.

KPMG (2016) The African Consumer and Retail: *Sector Report*, Johannesburg: KPMG Africa. Available from: https://assets.kpmg/content/dam/kpmg/zm/pdf/2016/10/African-Consumer-Retail-Report-2016.pdf [Accessed 3 May 2016].

Lüthje, B., Hürtgen, S., Pawlicki, P. and Sproll, M. (2013) *From Silicon Valley to Shenzhen: Global Production and Work in the IT Industry*, Lanham, MD: Rowman & Littlefield.

Massmart (2021) 'Our operating model'. Available from: https://www.massmart.co.za/our-business-model/ [Accessed 10 April 2021].

Parthasarathy B., Aoyama Y. and Menon, N. (2015) 'Innovating for the bottom of the pyramid: case studies in healthcare from India', in S. Hostettler, E. Hazboun and J.C. Bolay (eds) *Technologies for Development: What Is Essential?*, London: Springer, pp 55–69.

Thrift, N. (2003) 'Pandora's box? Cultural geographies of economies', in G.L. Clark, M.P. Feldman and M.S. Gertler (eds) *The Oxford Handbook of Economic Geography*, Oxford: Oxford University Press, pp 689–704.

Wang, X. (2020) *Blockchain Chicken Farm: And Other Stories of Tech in China's Countryside*, New York: Farrar, Straus and Giroux.

Wheeler, J.O., Aoyama Y. and Warf, B. (2000) *Cities in the Telecommunications Age: The Fracturing of Geographies*, London: Routledge.

World Health Organization (2023) *International Classification of Diseases 11*. Available from: https://icd.who.int/browse11/l-m/en [Accessed 18 January 2023].

8

Susanne Soederberg: A Critical and Multidisciplinary Global Political Economy

Lama Tawakkol

Introduction

In her works, Susanne Soederberg adopts a critical and multidisciplinary perspective to understand the global political economy's dynamic and complex nature. As per the late Robert W. Cox's (1981) distinctions, critical theory diverges from traditional problem-solving approaches in its questioning of pre-existing structures and their political agendas/ commitments. A critical understanding of the global political economy questions the bases on which its structures rest, interrogates the political relations and processes it perpetuates and reproduces and, in doing so, resists and seeks to disrupt them. Such a critical approach helps account for gaps in our existing knowledge by acknowledging how the global political economy operates on multiple levels and scales, in ways that are connected but that also unfold differently in various temporal and spatial settings (Brenner et al, 2010). It reveals underlying tensions and power relations driving these political economic relations and processes, rather than treating the status quo as set in stone. Such a multi-scalar and fundamentally relational approach expands the field and study of political economy, allowing it to converse and engage with questions of geography, development, governance, finance and others (see also Chapters 1 and 6 in this volume). It both broadens and deepens our understanding of how global political economic structures, actors and processes necessarily interact with, impact and often shape issues in various spheres and across different levels.

In this chapter, I zoom in on Soederberg's contributions to this comprehensive and multidimensional understanding of the global political economy and capitalism, and to the study of critical economic geography. Soederberg's research is diverse, both empirically and in terms of the contributions it provides. Transcending disciplinary boundaries, Soederberg takes seriously questions both within and beyond orthodox and mainstream understandings of the global economy. While she primarily employs a Marxian framework with strong emphasis on historical materialism, Soederberg complicates classic Marxist approaches by accounting for different structures of power, including imperialism, gender and race. She thus provides nuanced and more comprehensive analyses of diverse social and political phenomena that might not immediately seem connected. Soederberg's corpus encompasses five single-authored books, alongside a wide range of articles. Through them she analyses how global financial institutions responded to the economic downturns of the early 2000s and their impact on and power over Global South countries (Soederberg, 2004), and (re)situates global economic governance within broader capitalist relations, connecting it to American power and empire (Soederberg, 2006). She also investigates the politics and power of corporations, their ownership structures and emerging resistance to them (Soederberg, 2010). Focusing more on how global capitalism impacts people's lived experiences, she explores debt and money as a social and power relation, which helps both increase accumulation and discipline workers in the neoliberal era, with strong reliance on the state form (Soederberg, 2013, 2014; Roberts and Soederberg, 2014). Most recently, Soederberg analyses urban homelessness as a lens for understanding capitalism's governance of surplus product and populations, and the continuous exploitation and impoverishment of workers (Soederberg, 2018a, 2018b, 2021), situating evictions within a longer history of state austerity at the urban scale and more broadly (Soederberg, 2018b; Soederberg and Walks, 2018).

Surveying her various works and arguments, I interrogate how Soederberg's contributions are significant to the field of (global) political economy and how she adds to the understanding and formulation of (critical) economic geographies, even when some of her focuses might not immediately be thought of as questions of geography. I argue that, through her emphasis on power, analysis of benefits accrued and interests served, and historical understanding of capitalism, Soederberg provides rich, comprehensive and multidisciplinary analyses of her topics. She brings together various scholarship, making her arguments applicable to a host of questions and geographies beyond those she directly investigates, and contributes towards a more critical, global, relational, empirically grounded and fundamentally political understanding of global political economy. She thus also provides a useful framework and agenda for future research and political mobilization.

I divide the rest of the chapter into three main sections. First, I focus on some of Soederberg's key terms and specific arguments to explore their utility and impact on the field. Next, I provide a more general overview of her work, showcasing the overarching characteristics of her theoretical and methodological approaches, their analytical significance and how her contributions inform analyses of diverse topics across disciplines. I conclude by noting how the field can continue to learn from and build on Soederberg's work. I suggest avenues for future research and topics for further investigation within economic geographies that would benefit from applying Soederberg's approach and arguments. I also briefly touch on the practical relevance of Soederberg's work to our everyday political struggles and commitments.

Concepts for analysis: debtfare, monetized governance and displaced survival

In her work, three of Soederberg's ideas particularly stand out in terms of their conceptual contributions and analytical utility. First, she uses *debtfare* to make sense of the increasing pervasiveness and normalization of debt in everyday life. Second, I show that, when combined, her ideas about *monetized governance* and *displaced survival* elucidate how rising rates of rental evictions and homelessness in some of Europe's largest urban centres are part and parcel of global capitalism.

Debtfare

Soederberg's analysis of debt/credit and debtfare as a tool of (neoliberal) governance is an important contribution insofar as it is one of few studies that take seriously the need to critically theorize money as a relation in and of itself and (re)situate it within the relations and processes driving the global capitalist economy. Through her analysis, Soederberg goes to the heart of, not only credit structures, such as student loans, that displace the responsibility to survive onto workers, but also the social power and role of money underlying them, and the discourses that depoliticize and normalize them. She understands money as part of 'historical social constructions that express particular relations of class-based power in capitalist society' (Soederberg, 2014: 5). A loan thus becomes more than 'a voluntary exchange of equivalents between two consenting parties' and is instead understood as a political and class-based relation (Soederberg, 2014: 4). This understanding of money is essential for Soederberg's conceptualization of credit and debt as similarly 'part of the wider and tension-ridden processes of capital accumulation' (Soederberg, 2014: 11) and paves the road for understanding how debtfare, as a mode of governance, effectively rests on this neutralization of money and, thus, debt and the exploitation it introduces.

Against this backdrop of money as a social relation (Zelizer, 2017), Soederberg discusses debtfare as a key feature of neoliberalization and neoliberal governance. She explains debtfare as 'the societal structures and processes that have normalized, disciplined and naturalized the reality of pervasive debt' (Soederberg, 2014: 1) and 'a component of neoliberal state intervention that has emerged to mediate, normalize and discipline the monetized relations that inhabit the poverty industry' (Soederberg, 2014: 3). By invoking debtfare as a form of governance, Soederberg reveals that something as mundane as taking out a loan to supplement one's income actually serves as an additional form of worker exploitation and impoverishment outside the workplace, as workers struggle to repay these loans and associated interests and fees, alongside their other commitments.

Through debtfare, Soederberg dispels the idea that debt, and the poverty it creates and perpetuates, is natural, necessary and inescapable. She highlights how the extension of credit in various forms and under different guises in both the Global North and Global South is part of wider processes and modes of governance, that is, workfare and prisonfare, that impoverish, exploit and discipline workers and, hence, facilitate capital accumulation (Peck, 2001; Wacquant, 2010). By outlining how debtfare compels actors to continuously supplement their income through further indebtedness to meet their basic needs, Soederberg shows how it also normalizes neoliberal modes of living, where state forms of welfare are increasingly rolled back and workers bear the responsibility for surviving and maintaining a degree of self-sufficiency on their own (see Chapter 20 in this volume).

Soederberg's analysis thus reveals the twofold exploitation that underlies debtfare where workers are impoverished amid increasingly precarious working conditions and minimal social support, and then made further vulnerable by virtue of the debt they have no choice but to incur. Through this understanding, Soederberg builds on her theorization of money to lay bare the politics and interests that go into (re)producing these debt structures, the regulatory functions they serve and the role of the (neoliberal) state in promoting these structures, as well as serving as a struggle terrain.

Monetized governance and displaced survival

In her most recent book, *Urban Displacements* (2021), Soederberg continues her theorization of money by introducing the concepts of monetized governance and displaced survival to explain how it shapes and maintains neoliberal governance structures. She uses monetized governance to explain how 'capitalist states have facilitated, legitimated and normalized the expansion of credit-led accumulation across scales' (Soederberg, 2021: 4), describing how 'surpluses (money, workers, product or, what is the same thing, social surplus) generated by credit-led accumulation ... relate to emerging forms of state interventions and attempts at facilitating societal reproduction' (Soederberg, 2021: 7). Relatedly, displaced survival denotes 'the societal reproduction of impoverished workers in and through displacements over the past two decades' and the state's key role in this process (Soederberg, 2021: 5). Through this understanding of money's political role in shaping governance structures, Soederberg analyses how urban evictions and displacements are based in global capitalist relations that (re)produce both accumulation (for capital) and scarcity (for workers) (see Chapter 21 of this volume). Through rental monetary exchanges (or lack thereof with evictions), workers' survival becomes further contingent on and entangled in capitalist relations mediated by the state (in its various forms and scales), and their most basic right to shelter jeopardized.

In this sense, Soederberg shows how (lack of) access to housing and rent in the contemporary moment, and its increasing subjugation to financial terms, market logics and accumulation interests, contributes to the dual exploitation of workers much like debt does and indicates broader political modes of governance (Soederberg, 2021: 37). On a more theoretical level, Soederberg also shows the intricate links between neoliberal states and capitalist interests at this moment as state policies and practices increasingly favour accumulation interests over social support or welfare. She reveals the state's increasing reliance on the social power of money to depoliticize class-based societal struggles inherent to everyday survival, conceal and erase exploitative practices and discipline workers to the demands of global capitalism.

Soederberg's exploration of how the everyday experience of rent is fundamentally unequal and part of wider class-based relations builds on and contributes to her earlier theorizations of money, offering significant insight for future research to build on. Taken together, then, Soederberg's analyses of debtfare, evictions and money-based governance, and her earlier contributions, provide a broad and rich theoretical and methodological approach for studying the global political economy and how it operates and develops beyond debt and evictions.

A framework for analysis: theoretical contributions and commitments

Regardless of her specific focus, Soederberg approaches her topics from a global, critical and relational perspective that is based in empirical data and a firm political standpoint. She thus accounts for many aspects that could otherwise be overlooked or un(der)studied and inspires scholarship on a multidisciplinary range of questions on global capitalism.

Soederberg's approach is firmly grounded in a *critical* understanding of the global political economy, insofar as her analyses problematize existing structures, and question and unveil the power relations undergirding and driving them. Heeding Cox's (1981) insight that critical theory goes beyond the surface and exposes the political economy's underlying contradictions, Soederberg (2004: 7) debunks myths about technical institutions and neutral policies. Her historical materialist method shows how things we typically take for granted, like debt, are 'socially constructed in the wider context of the dynamics of and relations of power inherent to capital accumulation' (Soederberg, 2014: 7).

For example, rather than an apolitical multilateral body for financial governance in the wake of the 1997–98 Asian financial crisis, Soederberg situates the New International Financial Architecture and policies it promotes, like trade and financial liberalization, within global capitalism and class relations (Soederberg, 2004). She transcends dominant understandings of global economic governance as neutral, which depoliticize fundamentally capitalist and exploitative practices like austerity (Soederberg, 2006), and commonsensical understandings of debt as a necessary feature of everyday life that democratizes finance and includes marginalized people in the global economy (Soederberg, 2014). Instead, she understands debt as a private and contractual transaction between two parties to emphasize its disciplinary and predatory nature. She also highlights how rental housing is more than an immediate exchange between landlord and tenant, and actually reflects contradictions in global capitalism where housing can be either shelter (a public good) or investment (a private interest) (Aalbers and Christophers, 2014; Konings et al, 2021; Soederberg, 2021; see also Chapters 5 and 21 in this volume).

Soederberg highlights how institutions of global capitalism, and the policies they promote, are inherently political, looking at both their material benefits and role in the circuit of capital, as well as their disciplinary and ideological uses, showing how they primarily benefit transnational financial elites in the US and globally (Soederberg, 2004, 2006). By adopting this critical approach, she delves deeper into un(der)explored aspects of global capitalism, such as shareholder activism and resistance movements against corporations. She understands such activism, including calls for the Sudan divestment campaign, for example, within the broader framework of a global, uneven and exploitative capitalism instead of as apolitical or internal disputes over corporate strategies and governance (Soederberg, 2010). In doing so, she paves the road for understanding the increasing role of the private sector in other fields of capitalism, including development (Sharma and Soederberg, 2020).

In these diverse analyses, Soederberg accounts for capitalism's interconnections and transnational nature, grounding her arguments in a *global* framework. Even when her study focuses on the US, or Global North institutions like the International Monetary Fund, Soederberg highlights how their structural power necessarily impacts the Global South, both directly and indirectly (Soederberg, 2004), and understands the concrete implications of American empire on other spaces and global capitalism as a whole (Soederberg, 2006). Her interrogation of credit and debt relations in specific locations, like the US and Mexico, does not end there. It is applicable to other contexts, both in the Global North and South, and topics as diverse as financial inclusion, agricultural insurance and the relation of credit-based welfare to workers, citizenship and gendered relations (Isakson, 2015; Montgomerie and Tepe-Belfrage, 2016; Kaika, 2017; Mertens, 2017; Grover, 2018; Güngen, 2018). As she explains it, '[s]imilarities between [her] case studies emerge from their connection to global capitalism, whilst differences appear due to historically and geographically distinct configurations of power relations and struggles along gendered, class and racialized lines' (Soederberg, 2021: 7).

In the same vein, her study of urban evictions and displacements is not confined to her European cases, but is easily applicable to other spaces of capitalism (Ferreri, 2020; Bhagat, 2021; Soederberg, 2021). Soederberg's work thus goes beyond its specific, and often local, focuses, illustrating the broader processes and relations driving the global political economy, and emphasizing the dialectical and interrelated nature of its various levels and structures. For example, debt and displacement combine in the governance of refugees in Kenya (Bhagat and Roderick, 2020).

Soederberg's work also emphasizes the significance of a *relational* and *multi-scalar* approach. Her emphasis on how different scales of daily life interact and co-constitute allow for a deeper understanding of the topics at hand. By drawing on a relational understanding of global capitalism, she highlights connections that might not otherwise be immediately clear, for example between states and corporate governance structures, banks and rent relations. She explains that, because 'corporations represent *historical social relations* ... [c]orporate power, including the relations of domination and contestation, cannot be separated from the wider struggles and contradictions of capitalism' (Soederberg, 2010: 13, original emphasis). Similarly, the 'exploitative and unequal social relations inherent to debt' can manifest on various levels, such as through emerging financial technologies, or 'fintech', and aid extended to refugee host countries (Soederberg, 2010: 8; Bernards, 2019; Soederberg and Tawakkol, 2020).

By focusing on relations instead of static structures (Massey, 1995), Soederberg emphasizes the state's reliance on, and key stake in, different areas like debt and evictions (Soederberg, 2014). Her relational approach informs her understanding of the state as a power and social relation that is constantly in flux, rather than a thing. Through these relations between different scales, Soederberg lays bare the deeply complex interconnections between politics and daily life at the local levels, the state's role at the national scale, and the structures and actors of the global political economy (Soederberg, 2010, 2014). She contributes to understandings of the (neoliberal) state's role in governing money, mediating power struggles, enforcing debt relations among gendered and racialized communities, and perpetuating market modes of governance and private accumulation (Alami, 2018a, 2018b; Roberts, 2014, 2016; Wamsley, 2019). This also expands to discussions of the production of surplus workers and the spread of authoritarian forms of neoliberalism (Tansel, 2017; Bhagat and Soederberg, 2019; Bernards and Soederberg, 2020; Tawakkol, 2020). Through her emphasis on relations, particularly as they cut through and operate across multiple geographic scales, Soederberg reveals connections that are often obscure and left uncritiqued, and contributes to a more comprehensive understanding of her subject.

Alongside her strong theoretical framework and contributions, Soederberg also firmly grounds her analyses in *empirical* data that makes them timely, *relevant* and relatable. In problematizing global capitalist relations and understanding the politics, interests and power driving them, Soederberg analyses important tropes that regularly shape the everyday lives of ordinary people, such as poverty, debt, homelessness, refugee integration and displacements, in spaces as varied as Mexico, the US, Ireland and Germany, among others (Soederberg, 2006, 2010, 2014, 2018b, 2021). She also inspires similar investigations of how global capitalism plays out in various settings, including Cairo, Dhaka, Nairobi, and Paris (Bhagat, 2020a, 2020b; Tawakkol, 2020; Sharma, 2021).

Relying on data from both the Global North and Global South, Soederberg uses the empirical details of daily experiences to repoliticize and situate them within broader political economic structures. She translates her theoretical conceptualizations to applicable tools for understanding how the world works, rather than simply abstract terms. In doing so, Soederberg adopts a clear political position and agenda, which her work serves. Through her academic and scholarly contributions to our understandings of the politics and tensions of global capitalism, Soederberg helps the on–ground struggle against class-based politics. As she puts it, her analytical framework and Marxian understanding of money (and other topics) help us 'to effectively "Occupy Economics"' in resisting depoliticized and normalized forms of capitalist power and exploitation (Soederberg, 2014: 10).

Conclusion

In this chapter I have demonstrated how, through conceptualizations of *debtfare*, *monetized governance* and *displaced survival*, the analyses they inform, and her broader analytical approach, Soederberg opens and contributes to a critical research agenda on the contemporary global political economy. This is particularly the case regarding power and relations of money, the role of the state in neoliberal-led capitalism and the various ways by which the exploitation and impoverishment of workers occurs and evolves.

Through her various arguments, Soederberg also opens up new questions and avenues for future research in different aspects of the global political economy. Questions on the contemporary role of states, and debates on the states' relative strength and significance vis-à-vis private and transnational actors, could benefit from her discussions of how neoliberal states govern and (re)produce inequalities and class relations through various strategies. Her insight into American empire and its influence over global institutions relates to studies of evolving global governance structures and the geopolitics and power dynamics underlying them in fields such as development, climate change and environmental governance, and migration. Soederberg's analysis of urban evictions is also significant to studies of how local and urban dynamics fit within global capitalist processes and relations, helping problematize topics as diverse as the local integration of refugees and migrants, and urban infrastructure development and situate them in global political economic processes and labour relations and as well as how neoliberal strategies unfold at multiple scales.

Regardless of the immediate questions and topics under study, future research stands to benefit from Soederberg's holistic approach and the overall analytical framework she brings to all her scholarship. By building on her critical insight and global perspective, scholars can transcend surface appearances to unpack power relations that are not immediately apparent and understand their objects of study as necessarily part of and interlinked with global and transnational processes and relations, linking cases, geographies and topics that might otherwise seem unrelated. Along these same lines, Soederberg's work emphasizes the importance of accounting for the connections between different geographic scales and using them as a lens for analysing how political economic dynamics unfold on the ground. Together with a strong empirical grounding, this help produces relevant and relatable scholarship that contributes not only to academic knowledge, but also informs everyday political struggle against class-based inequalities and exploitation.

References

Aalbers, M.B. and Christophers, B. (2014) 'Centring housing in political economy', *Housing Theory and Society*, 31(4): 373–94.

Alami, I. (2018a) 'Money power of capital and production of "new state spaces": a view from the Global South', *New Political Economy*, 23(4): 512–29.

Alami, I. (2018b) 'On the terrorism of money and national policy-making in emerging capitalist economies', *Geoforum*, 96: 21–31.

Bernards, N. (2019) 'The poverty of fintech? Psychometrics, credit infrastructures, and the limits of financialization', *Review of International Political Economy*, 26(5): 815–38.

Bernards, N. and Soederberg, S. (2020) 'Relative surplus populations and the crises of contemporary capitalism: reviving, revisiting, recasting', *Geoforum*, 126(4): 412–19.

Bhagat, A. (2020a) 'Governing refugee disposability: neoliberalism and survival in Nairobi', *New Political Economy*, 25(3): 439–52.

Bhagat, A. (2020b) 'Governing refugees in raced markets: displacement and disposability from Europe's frontier to the streets of Paris', *Review of International Political Economy*, 29(3): 955–78.

Bhagat, A. (2021) 'Displacement in "actually existing" racial neoliberalism: refugee governance in Paris', *Urban Geography*, 42(5): 634–53.

Bhagat, A. and Roderick, L. (2020) 'Banking on refugees: racialized expropriation in the fintech era', *Environment and Planning A: Economy and Space*, 52(8): 1498–515.

Bhagat, A. and Soederberg, S. (2019) 'Placing refugees in authoritarian neoliberalism: reflections from Berlin and Paris', *South Atlantic Quarterly*, 118(2): 421–38.

Brenner, N., Peck, J. and Theodore, N. (2010) 'Variegated neoliberalization: geographies, modalities, pathways', *Global Networks*, 10(2): 182–222.

Cox, R.W. (1981) 'Social forces, states and world orders: beyond international relations theory', *Millennium: Journal of International Studies*, 10(2): 126–55.

Ferreri, M. (2020) 'Painted bullet holes and broken promises: understanding and challenging municipal dispossession in London's public housing "decanting"', *International Journal of Urban and Regional Research*, 44(6): 1007–22.

Grover, C. (2018) 'Violent proletarianization: social murder, the reserve army of labour and social security "austerity" in Britain', *Critical Social Policy*, 39(3): 335–55.

Güngen, A.R. (2018) 'Financial inclusion and policy-making: strategy, campaigns and microcredit *a la Turca*', *New Political Economy*, 23(3): 331–47.

Isakson, S.R. (2015) 'Derivatives for development? Small-farmer vulnerability and the financialization of climate risk management', *Journal of Agrarian Change*, 15(4): 569–80.

Kaika, M. (2017) 'Between compassion and racism: how the biopolitics of neoliberal welfare turns citizens into affective "idiots"', *European Planning Studies*, 25(8): 1275–91.

Konings, M., Adkins, L. and Rogers, D. (2021) 'The institutional logic of property inflation', *Environment and Planning A: Economy and Space*, 53(3): 448–56.

Massey, D. (1995) *Spatial Divisions of Labour: Social Structures and the Geography of Production* (2nd edn), Basingstoke: Palgrave Macmillan.

Mertens, D. (2017) 'Borrowing for social security? Credit, asset-based welfare and the decline of the German savings regime', *Journal of European Social Policy*, 27(5): 474–90.

Montgomerie, J. and Tepe-Belfrage, D. (2016) 'A feminist moral-political economy of uneven reform in austerity Britain: fostering financial and parental literacy', *Globalizations*, 13(6): 890–905.

Peck, J. (2001) *Workfare States*, New York: Guilford Press.

Roberts, A. (2014) 'Doing borrowed time: the state, the law and the coercive governance of "undeserving" debtors', *Critical Sociology*, 40(5): 669–87.

Roberts, A. (2016) 'Household debt and the financialization of social reproduction: theorizing the UK housing and hunger crises', *Risking Capitalism: Research in Political Economy*, 31: 135–64.

Roberts, A. and Soederberg, S. (2014) 'Politicizing debt and denaturalizing the "new normal"', *Critical Sociology*, 40(5): 657–68.

Sharma, S. (2021) 'Reactive, individualistic and disciplinary: the Urban Resilience Project in Dhaka', *New Political Economy*, 26(6): 1078–91.

Sharma, S. and Soederberg, S. (2020) 'Redesigning the business of development: the case of the World Economic Forum and global risk management', *Review of International Political Economy*, 27(4): 828–54.

Soederberg, S. (2004) *The Politics of the New International Financial Architecture: Reimposing Neoliberal Domination in the Global South*, London: Zed Books.

Soederberg, S. (2006) *Global Governance in Question: Empire, Class and the New Common Sense in Managing North–South Relations*, London: Pluto Press.

Soederberg, S. (2010) *Corporate Power and Ownership in Contemporary Capitalism: The Politics of Resistance and Domination*, Abingdon: Routledge.

Soederberg, S. (2013) 'The US debtfare state and the credit card industry: forging spaces of dispossession', *Antipode*, 45(2): 493–512.

Soederberg, S. (2014) *Debtfare States and the Poverty Industry: Money, Discipline and the Surplus Population*, Abingdon: Routledge.

Soederberg, S. (2018a) 'Evictions: a global capitalism phenomenon', *Development and Change*, 49(2): 286–301.

Soederberg, S. (2018b) 'The rental housing question: exploitation, eviction and erasures', *Geoforum*, 89: 114–23.

Soederberg, S. (2019) 'Governing global displacement in austerity urbanism: the case of Berlin's refugee housing crisis', *Development and Change*, 50(4): 923–47.

Soederberg, S. (2021) *Urban Displacements: Governing Surplus and Survival in Global Capitalism*, Abingdon: Routledge.

Soederberg, S. and Tawakkol, L. (2020) 'The humanitarian-development nexus and the Jordan Compact: tensions and trajectories in global capitalism', *Journal Für Entwicklung*, 36(4): 129–53.

Soederberg, S. and Walks, A. (2018) 'Producing and governing inequalities under planetary urbanization: from urban age to urban revolution?', *Geoforum*, 89: 107–13.

Tansel, C.B. (2017) 'Authoritarian neoliberalism: towards a new research agenda', in C.B. Tansel (ed) *States of Discipline: Authoritarian Neoliberalism and the Contested Reproduction of Capitalist Order*, London: Rowman & Littlefield, pp 1–28.

Tawakkol, L. (2020) 'Reclaiming the city's core: urban accumulation, surplus (re)production and discipline in Cairo', *Geoforum*, 126: 420–30.

Wacquant, L. (2010) 'Crafting the neoliberal state: workfare, prisonfare, and social insecurity', *Sociological Forum*, 25(2): 197–220.

Wamsley, D. (2019) 'Neoliberalism, mass incarceration, and the US debt–criminal justice complex', *Critical Social Policy*, 39(2): 248–67.

Zelizer, V.A. (2017) *The Social Meaning of Money: Pin Money, Paychecks, Poor Relief and Other Currencies*, Princeton, NJ: Princeton University Press.

9

Simona Iammarino: Interdisciplinary Approaches to the Economy

Rhiannon Pugh

Introduction

Simona Iammarino is a highly productive and well-cited scholar within the economic geography field, who has had a strong influence on the discipline as a whole, contributing to many topics and themes therein. These include, but are not limited to: the geography of innovation, multinational companies, the dark side of innovation, industrial clusters and regional development. She is also a well-known and key figure within the economic geography community, occupying central roles such as editor of flagship journals. Simona Iammarino is a multidisciplinary academic, with a background in economics but having transitioned during her career more towards the economic geography field, as evidenced by her current employment as Professor of Economic Geography at the London School of Economics.

Her research spans various disciplines including management, economics, innovation studies and political economy, whilst making a core contribution to economic geography. She combines both qualitative and quantitative approaches in her work, and most commonly works in collaboration with other researchers. This chapter is structured as follows. The first section provides some brief overview of her career and published works to date, attempting to summarize her significant canon into a short review that highlights (at least in the author's own reading) the key contributions. The second section picks out some specific theoretical advancements that Simona Iammarino has made to economic geography, broadly defined, attempting to elucidate what some of her most important and influential contributions to the field have been and why. This section will also touch on how further work in the discipline has been influenced by that of Simona Iammarino. The third section will discuss her role within the economic geography community on more of an individual level, focusing on her role as a mentor and collaborator.

Overview

While Simona Iammarino currently holds the title of Professor in Economic Geography, her PhD was in international economics. Over time, she has moved more in the direction of economic geography, to the point where she is now considered one of the leading scholars of the discipline, also confirmed by the economic geography colleagues interviewed for this piece. An albeit simplistic but illustrative Google Scholar tally confirms that Simona Iammarino's work is well read and cited: she has a total of more than 150 papers, reports, chapters and so forth which have been collectively cited more than 10,000 times. Her work has been published in a wide range of forums across the economic geography discipline but also in adjacent fields: moreover, she has written a number of reports and evaluations for different public sector bodies.

Turning the question over disciplinary 'fit' over to Simona Iammarino herself, rather than trying to prejudge this from the outside, she expressed feeling part of many academic communities, but perhaps more at home in some than others. The *Regional Studies* community has been a particular central space for her, and her long list of contributions and roles within that community bear testament to this, such as sitting on boards, editing the journals of the association, and also publishing on their blog and websites. This is a popular forum for economic geographers, but an interdisciplinary one involving colleagues from a number of different backgrounds all interested in the key themes of regional planning, governance, and development. She currently acts as editor of the *Journal of Economic Geography* at the time of writing.

The contributions of Iammarino to economic geography are multiple and varied; however, upon asking her collaborators and mentees, her work on multinational companies, trade, and regional innovation determinants stood out as those regarded as the main areas in which she has progressed the field of economic geography. More recent critical work on the 'dark sides of innovation' was given as an example of her work becoming more and more inspired by a critical economic geographic perspective (for a full discussion of this concept please see Coad et al, 2021).

Her contributions within the field of regional innovation that are significant; these help us to unpack exactly how and why some regions are leading, and others are lagging in the innovation stakes (Iammarino, 2005a). In particular, the way in which she combined an evolutionary or historical perspective with a regional focus to understand how regional cultures and trajectories influence the innovation patterns we can observe, was influential in the early phase of the development of the so-called evolutionary economic geography subfield, to be discussed at greater length in the next section.

Another element of her work, which was also among the early pioneer contributions to a now well-established research theme, is that of multinational corporations and international dimensions of innovation, which has since evolved into the contemporary rich discussions on global production networks, and the well-versed 'local buzz, global pipelines' conversation (Bathelt et al, 2004). In short, Simona Iammarino's work has been highly influential in demonstrating how we can combine analysis of different levels – localized firms, clusters, regions, nations, multinationals, to understand processes of innovation and development in a nuanced and holistic manner (Archibugi and Iammarino, 2002; Iammarino, 2005a; Iammarino and McCann, 2006).

Interestingly, when considering the whole canon of Simona Iammarino's work, trying to pinpoint those publications which are most influential based on, for example, Google Scholar citations, paints only a monotone picture of her contributions to the field overall. When asking Simona Iammarino directly about what she considered her most important contributions, she admitted that sometimes the most-cited and well-known works are not those that are necessarily of the highest importance to her, but it is hard to predict which ones will prove popular with others. Those pieces receiving the most citations are about related variety and regional growth (Boschma and Iammarino, 2009); industrial clusters (Iammarino and McCann, 2006); evolutionary economic geography (Iammarino, 2005a); innovation dynamics (D'Este et al, 2012; Archibugi and Iammarino, 2002); university–industry collaboration (D'Este et al, 2013), and regional systems of innovation (Evangelista et al, 2001, 2002). These are all hot topics within the economic geography and regional studies research community, and it is hard to imagine large parts of these disciplines today without her work as some of the seminal contributions in their development. What was interesting in our conversation was that Simona Iammarino herself does not situate herself purely as an economic geographer, but rather self-identifies as an interdisciplinary researcher with shifting or evolving identity as time passes.

Theoretical advancements

One of the main issues preoccupying the field of Economic Geography is why some places grow and other don't. Arguably, this question stretches back to the foundations of the field, such as Marshall's original contributions on industrial districts through to more recent work about clusters, regional innovation systems, and 'places that don't matter' (Rodríguez-Pose, 2018). Even with over a century's interrogation into this issue, we still do not have a definitive answer, but Simona Iammarino is one of the researchers who has made great efforts and contributions towards solving this conundrum. In the earlier stages of her career, Simona Iammarino was primarily concerned with understanding regional innovation patterns and dynamics within Italy, a very interesting case within which to explore these issues because of the vast regional inequalities but also the special nature of the Italian industrial districts that have long been of interest to economic geographers (for a broad discussion of these trends see Bianchi, 1998; Hadjimichalis, 2006). Simona Iammarino's early works were written often in Italian, and thus are not accessible to this author to read, unfortunately, but throughout her career she has published also in English: her contributions unpack the specificities of the Italian innovation scenario, but also link this to wider European and international levels (Cantwell and Iammarino, 1998; Iammarino and Santangelo, 2000).

A strong theme in Simona Iammarino's research, which emerges at the start of her career and can be seen throughout her work to the present day, is that of enhancing our understanding of the role of multinational corporations both in driving innovation generally, but more specifically in the context of regional development (for example, Cantwell and Iammarino, 1998, 2000; Iammarino, 2005b; Iammarino and McCann, 2013, 2015) (see also Chapter 12 in this volume). By drawing the linkages between regional, national and international levels of analysis, for instance through the lens of multinational corporations, Simona Iammarino has made great strides in helping us to conduct economic geography in a multilayered perspective, appreciating the linkages, overlaps and also contradictions that exist. According to colleagues interviewed for this piece, Simona Iammarino's contributions to our understanding of the economic geographies of multinationals is one of her most significant and appreciated contributions to the field.

Another of her well-known contributions has been to show how 'related variety' – as in the complementarity of competences in different economic sectors – is significant for regional growth, in addition to the importance of combining external-to-region knowledge into existing competencies (Boschma and Iammarino, 2009). This popular and well-cited piece was one of the key papers sparking an interest amongst economic geographers in how 'local knowledge' from within the region gets combined with 'external knowledge' sourced from outside, possibly internationally. For instance, researchers in the Nordics have taken this line of thinking forward and found that firms in different regions can successfully innovate by pursuing strategies to access and combine knowledge from outside their regions, especially in peripheral regions where knowledge resources and infrastructure might be quite thin (Grillitsch and Nilsson, 2015; Fitjar and Rodríquez-Pose, 2017; Grillitsch et al, 2018). While sectors with shared competencies will have a greater propensity for knowledge spillover (Frenken et al, 2007), Boschma and Iammarino (2009) find that related variety (a degree of similarity or complementarity) has stronger economic growth associations than unrelated variety, even though previous work has suggested unrelated variety could provide more resilience to sector specific shocks. We can arguably credit Iammarino for being one of pioneers to inspire this now popular line of investigation into related variety and regional growth trajectories (for example, Kuusk and Martynovich, 2021; see also Chapter 13 in this volume).

Other important contributions have attempted to disentangle the importance of proximity as a factor in innovation and technological developments, for instance examining university–industry links in the physical sciences and finding that geographical proximity does indeed make partnership more likely (D'Este et al, 2013). Again, this line of inquiry has inspired more investigation both in economic geography and management fields (for example, Alpaydın and Fitjar, 2021). Simona Iammarino (and her co-authors') contributions here have been to fully link up debates around university–industry linkages with those of proximity, one of the 'hot topics' that has long been at the heart of mainstream debates in economic geography (Boschma, 2005).

In recent work, Simona Iammarino has turned her attention to the sticky problem of regional inequality (Iammarino et al, 2019). In this work, Iammarino and her co-authors critique previous approaches to regional economic development, which have left some regions behind, and propose a new approach, which they label 'place-sensitive distributed development policy'. In essence, they call for a differentiated policy approach to regional development whereby stronger economic regions are enabled to continue on their positive growth trajectory, but new approaches are developed for declining and post-industrial regions. This is quite contrary, in some senses, to the current approach to regional development in Europe, smart specialization, which due to the rules of *ex ante* conditionality is necessarily implemented in a more or less universal fashion in all regions of Europe no matter what their innovation and economic profile.

In more recent works, new avenues are being explored by Iammarino as an expansion of her work on international trade and regional innovation in the past but taking these themes in interesting new directions. One such direction is the so-called 'dark side of innovation', whereby an alternative approach to innovation studies (one which is less celebratory and uncritical) is being taken (see also Chapter 13 in this volume). In this new area of research, rather than viewing innovation as an objectively good thing, scholars position it as both good and bad, with negative implications such as public health crises and environmental degradation (Coad et al, 2021). Simona Iammarino and her co-authors are exploring conflict minerals, as one example in this new direction (see also Chapter 29 in this volume). Another example is recent published work examining the power of the financial sector and linking this discussion to that of regional inequality (Feldman et al, 2021). Yet another interesting dimension is her recent work into Brexit effects, examining uncertainty in UK textile and apparel sectors (Casadei and Iammarino, 2021). For someone who studies innovation dynamics and processes, her work is in itself quite innovative and constantly evolving to explore new topics and approaches, and Simona Iammarino has an important role in the economic geography community of constantly pushing the field forwards in fresh and exciting new ways. As one respondent to my questions put it: her work keeps getting better and better. It is exciting to see Simona Iammarino turning her attention and expertise to new topics and issues, with recent work examining the reporting of sexual violence (Denti and Iammarino, 2021, 2022) a good example of a new path opening up in her research, and using her quantitative skills to explore issues that in the past have lacked such an analysis.

Role in the economic geography community

In addition to the discussion of Simona Iammarino's academic works, it is also important to highlight her important position as a woman economic geographer at the core of the community. Not only an active researcher and teacher, Simona Iammarino has a long history of engaging in policy debates such as through work with the Organisation for Economic Co-operation and Development and the European Commission: she is an academic who works beyond the ivory tower. She is also a popular teacher, as evidenced by the teaching awards she has won, and has supervised several PhD students, many of whom have gone on to pursue successful academic careers (and many beyond academia too). Upon interviewing some recent and current PhD students, she clearly is a popular and well-liked supervisor, appreciated for her humanistic touch to supervising the whole person as opposed to being focused only on the academic side. As one recent PhD student put it: Simona Iammarino is able to appreciate and support her students through the psychological challenges of completing a PhD as well as the purely academic side. We should celebrate those who dedicate time and effort to mentoring junior colleagues, who appreciate this so much.

Other collaborators mentioned her importance as a friend as well as a colleague, and it's clear that a lot of her collaborative work stems from a place of friendship and enjoying working together. As Simona Iammarino herself expressed it: every paper she has published tells a story of a friendship. Simona Iammarino spoke at length about her enjoyment of collaboration, the motivations it provides her in the work, and the new directions that can be explored through collaborative work. She also raised the importance of collaboration with junior colleagues and PhD students as the source of new ideas and directions; her own mentees also highlighted this as an important element of her working style.

This issue speaks beyond her academic contributions to her role in the field, and illustrates her way of being an academic. Simona Iammarino's collaborators and mentees mentioned that she is an academic who works constructively and supportively with junior colleagues and fully partakes in the partnerships, which we know is not always the case in collaborations which have large power or seniority imbalances. The issue of mentorship, female role models, caring academic environments and more have been hotly discussed in the academic geography literature recently, especially by more junior geographers (for example, Bayfield et al, 2020; Smyth et al, 2020; Webster and Caretta, 2016, 2019). It is important that we also celebrate these elements of Simona Iammarino's achievements and her legacy, beyond her publications and accolades, and appreciate her as a person who made the economic geography world a more enjoyable place to be for many people.

Simona Iammarino has made important inroads to debates about the role and status of women in economic geography: she is a clear advocate for her colleagues. Interviews with collaborators in the field cited her blog piece for the *Regional Studies Association* (written with Paula Prenzel (Iammarino and Prenzel, 2018)) as an important piece that informed the debate about the role of women within that community, which has a large representation of regional economic geographers. In summary, this piece analysed the major conferences in the economic geography and regional studies domain, exposing the deep gender bias that still exists especially when it comes to 'prestigious' positions within these conferences. Iammarino and Prenzel collected data on female keynote speakers, editorial board members and award recipients in regional science and economic geography generally. Of the seven large conferences they studied, the average share of female keynote speakers was 18.9 per cent. For instance, looking at ERSA (European Regional Science Association), a large conference for regional scientists, while 34.6 per cent of participants were female only 13.8 per cent of keynote speakers were. Similar trends can be seen in their analysis of editorial boards and prizes awarded. What this piece really highlighted was that increasing participation of women overall is not necessarily translating into prestige or positions in the higher echelons of the field, but that within regional studies and economic geography there were large variations between different conferences, journals and associations, raising the question as to why some had successfully broadened their participation of women while others have not. Iammarino and Prenzel (2018) suggest that some forums remain a 'boys club'.

This blog piece has spurred tangible changes. On the part of the *Regional Studies Association*, a group of female scholars (myself, Taylor Brydges and Ida Andersson) received funding to begin a network on the issue of gender and regional studies; Iammarino and Penzel's blog was instrumental in us making our case for why such a network was important to establish. This work also spurred others to think more critically about conference organization and even inspired one colleague to implement gender equal guidelines for a conference they were organizing which then became standard practice within their department. We thank Simona Iammarino for speaking up about these issues, also turning her quantitative approach to their discussion so that we all have some data and evidence to draw on when making the case for change.

Conclusion

While economic geography is not always a particularly friendly place for women (see Maddrell et al, 2016; McDowell, 2016; Gray and Pollard, 2018; Johns, 2018; Pugh, 2018), senior scholars such as Simona Iammarino are making great efforts to change the status quo and improve the environment for everyone. In addition to her role as a mentor, supporter and collaborator, she has made key contributions to the economic geography and regional studies communities that have stood the test of time.

In addition to the topics she has contributed to in her work, as discussed earlier, she has held key positions in the centre of the field, such as editorial roles at *Regional Studies* and *Journal of Economic Geography*. Not only by these 'prestige' measures, she is also well appreciated as a supervisor, mentor, friend and role model by those who work with her at all levels of the academic career. Also, beyond those who are in close contact with Simona Iammarino, her mere presence at the 'top table' is significant: even today it is still sometimes surprising or fresh to see a woman economic geographer in these positions, and the whole academic community benefits from her presence. No doubt, this has often been a heavy burden to carry, and Simona Iammarino's colleagues also mentioned the issue of being 'the only woman in the room' and the hard work and pressure this must entail. Those of us who come after key figures such as Simona Iammarino and the other women in this collection must be grateful for their efforts.

To sum up, Simona Iammarino is an economic geographer whose work also borders other areas such as international business and innovation studies. She places interdisciplinarity at the heart of her work, and aims to speak to several different communities, even though economic geography is her primary home these days. When questioned about the final message she would like her work to leave behind, interdisciplinarity was the core of this: that to make advancements in our thinking and understanding about the world we must embrace and interdisciplinary way of working. Surely we can all find inspiration and guidance in such a statement and apply it to our own work, following in the footsteps of Simona Iammarino, who never ceases to innovate and open new doors in her work.

Acknowledgements

Special thanks go to the following individuals for generously giving their time to help me in the writing of this chapter: Simona Iammarino, Andres Rodríguez-Pose, Elvira Uyarra and Andreas Diemer. Also, I would like to thank the editors of the collection for their support and patience throughout the process of completing the chapter.

References

Alpaydın, U.A.R. and Fitjar, R.D. (2021) 'Proximity across the distant worlds of university–industry collaborations', *Papers in Regional Science*, 100(3): 689–711.

Archibugi, D. and Iammarino, S. (2002) 'The globalization of technological innovation: definition and evidence', *Review of International Political Economy*, 9(1): 98–122.

Bathelt, H., Malmberg, A. and Maskell, P. (2004) 'Clusters and knowledge: local buzz, global pipelines and the process of knowledge creation', *Progress in Human Geography*, 28(1): 31–56.

Bayfield, H., Colebrooke, L., Pitt, H., Pugh, R. and Stutter, N. (2020) 'Awesome women and bad feminists: the role of online social networks and peer support for feminist practice in academia', *Cultural Geographies*, 27(3): 415–35.

Bianchi, G. (1998) 'Requiem for the Third Italy? Rise and fall of a too successful concept', *Entrepreneurship & Regional Development*, 10(2): 93–116.

Boschma, R. (2005) 'Proximity and innovation: a critical assessment', *Regional Studies*, 39(1): 61–74.

Boschma, R. and Iammarino, S. (2009) 'Related variety, trade linkages, and regional growth in Italy', *Economic Geography*, 85(3): 289–311.

Cantwell, J. and Iammarino, S. (1998) 'MNCs, technological innovation and regional systems in the EU: some evidence in the Italian case', *International Journal of the Economics of Business*, 5(3): 383–408.

Cantwell, J. and Iammarino, S. (2000) 'Multinational corporations and the location of technological innovation in the UK regions', *Regional Studies*, 34(4): 317–32.

Casadei, P. and Iammarino, S. (2021) 'Trade policy shocks in the UK textile and apparel value chain: firm perceptions of Brexit uncertainty', *Journal of International Business Policy*, 4(2): 262–85.

Coad, A., Nightingale, P., Stilgoe, J. and Vezzani, A. (2021) 'Editorial: the dark side of innovation', *Industry and Innovation*, 28(1): 102–12.

Denti, D. and Iammarino, S. (2021) 'The geography of Violence Against Women and Girls (VAWG): support services and the reporting of sexual crimes in England and Wales', Women, Peace and Security Forum, LSE Blog, 18 March. Available from: https://blogs.lse.ac.uk/wps/2021/03/18/the-geography-of-violence-against-women-and-girls-vawg-support-servi ces-and-the-reporting-of-sexual-crimes-in-england-and-wales/ [Accessed 7 June 2023].

Denti, D. and Iammarino, S. (2022) 'Coming out of the woods: do local support services influence the propensity to report sexual violence?', *Journal of Economic Behavior & Organization*, 193: 334–52.

D'Este, P., Guy, F. and Iammarino, S. (2013) 'Shaping the formation of university–industry research collaborations: what type of proximity does really matter?', *Journal of Economic Geography*, 13(4): 537–58.

D'Este, P., Iammarino, S., Savona, M. and von Tunzelmann, N. (2012) 'What hampers innovation? Revealed barriers versus deterring barriers', *Research Policy*, 41(2): 482–8.

Evangelista, R., Iammarino, S., Mastrostefano, V. and Silvani, A. (2001) 'Measuring the regional dimension of innovation: lessons from the Italian Innovation Survey', *Technovation*, 21(11): 733–45.

Evangelista, R., Immarino, S., Mastrostefano, V. and Silvani, A. (2002) 'Looking for regional systems of innovation: evidence from the Italian innovation survey', *Regional Studies*, 36(2): 173–86.

Feldman, M., Guy, F. and Iammarino, S. (2021) 'Regional income disparities, monopoly and finance', *Cambridge Journal of Regions, Economy and Society*, 14(1): 25–49.

Fitjar, R.D. and Rodríguez-Pose, A. (2017) 'Nothing is in the air', *Growth and Change*, 48(1): 22–39.

Frenken, K., Van Oort, F. and Verburg, T. (2007) 'Related variety, unrelated variety and regional economic growth', *Regional Studies*, 41(5): 685–97.

Gray, M. and Pollard, J. (2018) 'Flourishing or floundering? Policing the boundaries of economic geography', *Environment and Planning A: Economy and Space*, 50(7): 1541–5.

Grillitsch, M. and Nilsson, M. (2015) 'Innovation in peripheral regions: do collaborations compensate for a lack of local knowledge spillovers?', *Annals of Regional Science*, 54(1): 299–321.

Grillitsch, M., Asheim, B. and Trippl, M. (2018) 'Unrelated knowledge combinations: the unexplored potential for regional industrial path development', *Cambridge Journal of Regions, Economy and Society*, 11(2): 257–74.

Hadjimichalis, C. (2006) 'The end of Third Italy as we knew it?', *Antipode*, 38(1): 82–106.

Iammarino, S. (2005a) 'An evolutionary integrated view of Regional Systems of Innovation: concepts, measures and historical perspectives', *European Planning Studies*, 13(4): 497–519.

Iammarino, S. (2005b) 'Multinational firms in the world economy', *Transnational Corporations*, 14(3). Available from: https://go.gale.com/ps/i.do?p=AONE&u=googlescholar&id=GALE|A149769323&v=2.1&it=r&sid=googleScholar&asid=153f040e [Accessed 28 September 2021].

Iammarino, S. and McCann, P. (2006) 'The structure and evolution of industrial clusters: transactions, technology and knowledge spillovers', *Research Policy*, 35(7): 1018–36.

Iammarino, S. and McCann, P. (2013) *Multinationals and Economic Geography: Location, Technology and Innovation*, Cheltenham: Edward Elgar.

Iammarino, S. and McCann, P. (2015) 'Multinational enterprises innovation networks and the role of cities', in D. Archibugi and A. Filippetti (eds) *The Handbook of Global Science, Technology, and Innovation*, Chichester: Wiley-Blackwell, pp 290–312.

Iammarino, S. and Prenzel, P. (2018) 'Women in Regional Science – Really a Success Story? Regional Studies Association Blog'. Available from: https://regionalstudies.org/news/women-regional-science-really-success-story/ [Accessed 13 April 2022].

Iammarino, S. and Santangelo, G.D. (2000) 'Foreign direct investment and regional attractiveness in the EU integration process: some evidence for the Italian regions', *European Urban and Regional Studies*, 7(1): 5–18.

Iammarino, S., Rodríguez-Pose, A. and Storper, M. (2019) 'Regional inequality in Europe: evidence, theory and policy implications', *Journal of Economic Geography*, 19(2): 273–98.

Johns, J. (2018) 'Creating a vibrant and sustainable economic geography?', *Environment and Planning A: Economy and Space*, 50(7): 1536–40.

Kuusk, K. and Martynovich, M. (2021) 'Dynamic nature of relatedness, or what kind of related variety for long-term regional growth', *Tijdschrift voor economische en sociale geografie*, 112(1): 81–96.

Maddrell, A., Strauss, K., Thomas, N.J. and Wyse, S. (2016) 'Mind the gap: gender disparities still to be addressed in UK higher education geography', *Area*, 48(1): 48–56.

McDowell, L. (2016) 'Reflections on feminist economic geography: talking to ourselves?', *Environment and Planning A: Economy and Space*, 48(10): 2093–9.

Pugh, R. (2018) 'Who speaks for economic geography?', *Environment and Planning A: Economy and Space*, 50(7): 1525–31.

Rodríguez-Pose, A. (2018) 'The revenge of the places that don't matter (and what to do about it)', *Cambridge Journal of Regions, Economy and Society*, 11(1): 189–209.

Smyth, A., Linz, J. and Hudson, L. (2020) 'A feminist coven in the university', *Gender, Place & Culture*, 27(6): 854–80.

Webster, N.A. and Caretta, M.A. (2016) '"Women in groups can help each and learn from each other": the role of homosocial practices within women's social networks in building local gender contracts', *Multidisciplinary Journal of Gender Studies*, 5(3): 1072–97.

Webster, N.A. and Caretta, M.A. (2019) 'Early-career women in geography: practical pathways to advancement in the neoliberal university', *Geografiska Annaler Series B: Human Geography*, 101(1): 1–6.

10

Susan Strange: Trading Zones

Sarah Hall

Introduction

Susan Strange is perhaps best known across the social sciences for her work in international relations, and particularly the development of the subfield of international political economy. Strange saw this approach as critical to understanding the (il)logics of the global economy and financial markets in particular. Throughout her work, Strange emphasized the importance of a heterodox approach to the global economy. As a result, her work has several shared underpinning assumptions with economic geography. For example, Strange was critical of orthodox economics and the limitations she saw in its emphasis on understanding the global economy through abstract models. She was also critical of the ability of political scientists to analyse the operation of the global economy because of their focus on institutions and power, particularly within nation states. Indeed, given that these concerns have also been expressed by economic geographers (Pollard et al, 2009) in many ways it is surprising that Strange's work has not been picked up more widely within economic geography. In short, there appears to be a clear 'trading zone' (Peck, 2012) between her work and that of economic geographers given their shared commitment to look beyond mainstream economics and politics in order to understand the global economy.

In this chapter, I examine the trading zone between Strange's work in international political economy and that of economic geography through a focus on research into the geographies of money and finance. In the first part of the chapter, I examine how her seminal work on the emergence of cross-border financial markets in *Casino Capitalism* (Strange, 1986) and *States and Markets* (Strange, 1988) was most fully taken up by the vibrant research field of the geographies of money and finance within economic geography.

Next, I draw on recent work that documents the changing nature of financial geography itself (Gibadullina, 2021), to examine how, despite the considerable shared epistemologies between Strange's approach and that of economic geography, the trading zone that this has resulted in is best understood as being episodic in nature. In particular, I suggest that while economic geographical scholarship in the 1980s and early 1990s opened up a dialogue with Strange's work, grounded in critical international political economy, this dialogue became much more limited as economic geography turned to focus increasingly on the cultural and social dimensions of economies. I suggest that as questions of inequality have come increasingly to the fore within both real world economies and more latterly academic economic geography following widely adopted austerity policies following the 2007–08 financial crisis, there is growing scope to reignite the trading zone between Strange and economic geography. This will allow fundamental questions of who benefits and who loses within the global economy to be placed more centrally in our analyses of the global economy as some of the key tenets of recent years such as globalization are increasingly challenged.

In the final substantive section of the chapter, I suggest that as financial geography adopted an increasingly sociocultural lens in the 2010s, the engagement with Strange declined, although the same was not true of heterodox work on money and finance within international political economy. At its broadest, this meant that analyses of money and finance within economic geography developed in-depth understandings of the sociocultural and macroeconomic reproduction of financial centres and markets (although see Langley, 2008 and Loomis, 2022). At the same time, political economy and international political economy scholars were increasingly focused on the questions of politics and power within global finance through work on, for example, debt and financialization (Montgomerie and Tepe-Belfrage, 2017). I then examine how some of the most pressing questions concerning contemporary global finance, including its geopolitics and its relationship to climate change, demand a return to the wider political questions posed by Strange and outline some of the ways in which the trading zone between Strange and economic geography is currently being reinvigorated. I conclude by reflecting on both the strengths and blind spots of such an approach for wider economic geographical thinking on money and finance.

Establishing the trading zone between Strange and economic geography

When considering the trading zone between Strange's work and geographical work on money and finance, it is important to note that the latter itself is a diverse and dynamic field. As Gibadullina (2021) argues, although an overwhelmingly Anglophone, and comparatively 'young' field, over its short intellectual history from the late 1980s onwards, a range of intellectual traditions has developed in financial geography, some of which speak more closely to Strange's work than others. Importantly, a strong alignment can be found in the early writings on the geographies of money and finance and Strange's work.

The formative writing in economic and financial geography dates back to the early 1990s and focused on the relationship between state power and finance (Thrift and Leyshon, 1994). This resonates strongly with wider international political economy work concerned with the growing power of the US and the associated decline of the UK within the international financial system in the post–Second World War era (Eichengreen, 2012) including the work of Strange herself. Reflecting the institutionalization of state power and multilateral state relations during the Bretton Woods era, work examining this period emphasizes the close relationship between state power and monetary and financial relations (Agnew, 2009). For example, Leyshon and Thrift (1997) argue that the international financial system at this time can be understood as an: 'international regulated space, comprised of a constellation of nation states linked one to another through reciprocal flows of money, goods and services, complemented by a set of international institutions which existed to manage processes of adjustment within the international economy' (Leyshon and Thrift, 1997: 71).

A driving focus of this work in both economic geography and international political economy was the making and breaking of the Bretton Woods agreement in 1973. Following its collapse, the international financial system moved to floating exchange rates, a move largely seen as signalling the creation of the contemporary international financial system as we know it today. In terms of the trading zone between financial geography and international political economy, this development is important in stimulating a debate about the nature of financial globalization it ushered in. For some researchers, the move to floating exchange rates is a clear indication of the decline of the nation state in relation to global financial flows, with nation states struggling to respond to the power of money. Some authors have gone so far as to argue that this situation gives rise to the 'end of geography' in that financial networks become increasingly separated from the spaces and places in which they are (re)produced (O'Brien, 1992).

In many ways the end of the Bretton Woods era was central in Strange's own writings. In a landmark text, Strange (1986) characterized the collapse of Bretton Woods and the creation of the international financial system as a form of 'Casino Capitalism' in which critical questions need to be asked regarding the ability of states to contain and regulate global finance. The title of her book clearly signals her insistence that financial institutions, and large US investment banks in particular, have created risks within financial markets that are akin to the risks of gambling rather than a utility financial system supporting the livelihoods of individuals, households and firms. As she writes,

> As in a casino, the world of high finance today offers the players a choice of games. Instead of roulette, blackjack, or poker, there is dealing to be done – the foreign exchange market and all its variations, or in bonds, government securities or shares. In all these markets you may place bets on the future by dealing forward and by buying or selling options and all sorts of other recondite financial inventions … some of the players – banks especially – play with very large stakes. (Strange, 1986: 1)

Within economic geography, her interventions on the power of the state (or lack thereof, see also Strange, 1988) dovetailed closely with debates at the time on the changing nature of global finance and in particular the ways in which deregulated financial markets gave rise to new spatialities within the international financial system, particularly in the form of offshore financial centres. Work here focused on documenting the ways in which these places, notably in the Caribbean, used a range of regulatory and sociocultural interventions in an attempt to enhance trust within them within the financial system (Roberts, 1994, 1995; Hudson, 1998). This geographical literature can be understood as examining the spatiality and scalar formations of the state–finance relations that are central to Strange's work on Bretton Woods.

The importance of Strange's interventions extend beyond geography. Her provocations regarding the decline of state power in the face of global finance can be situated in wider debates concerning the extent to which processes of globalization mark a decline or a reworking of state power in both geography (Dicken, 2014) and in the wider social sciences. For example, some authors argue that an emphasis on the epochal shift marked by events such as the breaking of the Bretton Woods agreement overstate the decline in state power under conditions of market globalization (Hirst and Thompson, 1999). To support their argument, these authors point to what they view as commonalities between the contemporary globalized world economic and previous global economic orders. In relation to the question of financial globalization with which Strange was particularly concerned, this approach argues that rather than the development of one new international financial system, we are seeing the development of several neo-imperial trading blocs of which that dominated by the US is just one sitting alongside, for example, the growing place of China and the Chinese state within global finance (Eichengreen, 2012; Hall, 2021).

In a similar vein, other scholars, largely beyond geography, have argued that contemporary processes of globalization should not be understood as a zero-sum game in which powerful global (financial) markets increasingly eclipse the power of states. This echoes work in economic geography on global production networks that seeks to tease out the relative power of different acts, includes states, markets and regions in shaping the world economy. For instance, Cerny (2010) argues that we are witnessing the emergence of what he terms the 'competition state' in which a range of activities collectives referred to as the state (such as politicians, the media and wider interest groups) are increasingly working on 'promoting competitiveness in a work market place and multilevel political system'. In other words, the state still has a major national role to play, but that role is increasingly to expose the domestic to the transnational, to prise open the nation state to a globalizing world (Cerny, 2010: 5).

The making and breaking of Bretton Woods therefore marks something of an empirical high point in the engagement of economic and financial geographers with Susan Strange's work on casino capitalism, particularly the role of the state within international finance. What is interesting is how this dialogue has developed since then.

Susan Strange and financial geography: beyond Bretton Woods

After the initial interest in the role of the state within the international financial system, it is notable that economic and financial geographers' foci changed during the 2000s to increasingly examine the sociocultural practices underpinning global finance (Hall, 2011; Gibadullina, 2021) as well as the increasingly financialized nature of firms and households (Hall, 2012). These literatures have done much to reveal the ways in which power in financial markets emerges and the implications for individuals, households and firms of needing to rely on financial markets to secure livelihoods through the changing nature of pension provision, for example. However, it does mean that during the 2000s, Strange's work was not as widely used in economic geography as it had been done previously as questions of power largely, but by no means entirely, fell down the analytical priority list of economic geography.

Given the interdisciplinary nature of heterodox approaches to money and finance, it is important to note that the same is not true of work at this time outside of economic geography. For example, an important literature has emerged that develops out of the wider literature on financialization but retains a focus as suggested by Strange on the state by examining the ways in which developing and emerging economies (DEEs) are integrated into the international financial system. This work which comes largely out of heterodox macroeconomics and takes as its starting point the subordination of DEEs into the world economy (Palma, 1978). By taking this literature and applying it to the case of international financial markets, this literature responds to critiques of work on financialization that argues that work beyond the Global North has remained limited (French et al, 2011).

Building on work that takes the role of the state seriously in global finance, and particularly the role of the state in supporting national currencies, this work reveals the ways in which international currency hierarchies serve to differentially insert countries into the international financial system. As Kaltenbrunner and Painceira (2018: 294) write:

> Whereas the top currency is the uncontested leader of the international monetary system due to its economic attractiveness, master and negotiated currencies maintain an internationally prominent role either through direct coercion (e.g., through colonial relations) or financial and political inducements. Neutral currencies are economically attractive, but do not have the means to become top currencies.

However, while examples such as this, that take forward Strange's focus on the role of the state in shaping global financial markets did not widely develop in economic geography in the 2000s, more recently, a number of productive lines of inquiry have been opened up that appear to signal a reinvigorated trading zone between Strange's work, international political economy and economic/financial geography.

Towards a reinvigorated interdisciplinary trading zone

Geographers have much to contribute to ongoing debates concerning state power and global finance, particularly in terms of the scale at which state power operates and the geographical imaginations that underpin this. Here critical observations from geographers regarding the approaches developed within international political economy are particularly important. Most notably, Agnew (1994) has argued convincingly that in work on international relations, there is often a tendency for analysis to operate with what he terms a 'territorial trap'. This means that an implicit assumption is made regarding the nature and scale of state power such that the state is understood 'as a fixed territorial entity (even if its actual boundaries can change) operating much the same over time and irrespective of its place within the global geopolitical order' (Agnew, 1994: 54). This means that the production and use of state power within the state remains largely overlooked – an oversight that is particularly important in the case of finance given the centrality of a small number of international financial centres in shaping the nature of global finance (Hall, 2017). For Agnew (1994) this development reflects at least in part the nature of academic labour in that international relations focused largely on the relations between states while political science took as its central focus internal domestic politics.

In many ways, given the ways in which Strange emphasized the everyday risks globally open financial markets posed, her work provides an important counterpoint to this limited geographical imagination. Several productive ways of doing this are emerging, even though they do not necessarily explicitly link back to Strange's work, particularly in economic geography where she has not become embedded in the cannon to the same extent as David Harvey's writings on money and finance for example (Harvey, 1982). Indeed, there are some early examples of this approach that have developed alongside Strange's work such as cultural economy approaches that examine how everyday financial subjectivities are increasingly co-produced alongside the international financial system (see for example Langley, 2008)

One particularly productive such development is the renewed interest in state capitalism from an economic and financial geography perspective (Whiteside et al, 2023). As Alami and Dixon (2020) note, state capitalism is a broad field that extends beyond a focus on questions of money and finance. It includes analysis on policies and material changes in global finance such as the increase in the number and size of state-sponsored sovereign wealth funds (Lyons, 2007); the development of a distinctive variety of capitalism (Nolke, 2014) alongside work that emphasizes the challenge it may pose to liberal state economies (McNally, 2013). Given this breadth, Alami and Dixon (2019) argue that state capitalism is best viewed as a method that can be developed to make visible the ways in which states shape monetary and financial relations in global finance. By documenting and taking seriously the variegated nature of state capitalism it is possible to move beyond simplistic or reductive narratives about the decline of state power in the face of financial globalization. Rather, it allows us to focus on the ways in which state activities are working to reshape contemporary financial markets.

This has been developed in relation to the changing geopolitics of global finance, for example. For instance, Lim (2019) provides a detailed analysis of the nature of state restructuring in China post-1949. In terms of questions of money and finance, his work sets out how the managed nature of currency internationalization targeted by Chinese policy makers demanded a graduate process of policy experimentation dating back to the first Mao regime.

Similarly, Alami (2018: 21) has argued that processes of global financial transformation need to be understood as emerging at the intersection between monetary and financial networks mediated through states and international financial centres. He terms this the 'relational geographies of money-power'. This work has influenced a wider literature that examines how different countries and financial centres, particularly in Latin and South America are unevenly situated within a hierarchy of monetary relations in global finance (see, for example, Kaltenbrunner and Painceira, 2018). Using this approach, I have suggested elsewhere that international financial centres such as London and New York represent important places and sites in which state power within the international financial system emerges and is reproduced (Hall, 2021). In particular, financial centres emerge and are (re)produced 'through state intervention in setting the institutional and regulatory parameters of legitimate financial activity' (Hall, 2017: 490). In many ways, while not drawing explicitly on Strange, her emphasis on taking seriously the role of the state, particularly in terms of its within-state implications, resonates with this renewed interest in the state in economic and financial geography.

Conclusion

The trading zone between Susan Strange's work and research in economic, and particularly financial, geography, is characterized by its episodic nature. In many ways it is surprising that given her critical interventions on the limited ability of the state to control the power and risks of global finance, her work has not been drawn on in a more sustained manner by economic geographers as questions of power and politics have also featured episodically in economic geographical scholarship on questions of money and finance. This is particularly striking given the centrality of her work to the canon within international political economy. In this chapter, I have suggested that one reason for this is the ways in which work on the geographies of money and finance moved away from prioritizing research that explicitly focused on state–market–finance relations in the 2000s in favour of work on financialization and the cultural political economy of finance. However, more recently, as the continued crisis-prone nature of finance has continued and wider questions such as the changing geopolitics of finance and the role of finance in climate change have emerged, so work on the state has become an increasingly fruitful set of research activities. This suggests that the future may point to a more sustained engagement with Strange's work once more.

However, a further issue that may contribute, at least in part, to the episodic engagement of Strange's work in economic geography lies in the gendered nature of the subdiscipline. This was particularly true of the 1980s when Strange was working. Much has been written about the diversity, or lack thereof, within economic geography more generally (Rosenman et al, 2019). Similar patterns are at work within financial geography. For example, in Gibadullina's analysis of the 38 most-cited first authors in 440 key financial geography texts, six are women. Similarly, of the 29 most-cited texts in financial geography, six are first-authored by women. This clearly points to the need to diversify the research, writing and citational practices within financial geography, alongside wider strategies to support all researchers' career development. Given the uneven impacts felt by different researchers as a result of the COVID-19 pandemic, this task

susssésı

seems more urgent than ever. It is clear from the analysis in this chapter that Susan Strange's work has much to offer in this respect for financial and economic geographers.

References

Agnew, J. (1994) 'The territorial trap: the geographical assumptions of international relations theory', *Review of International Political Economy*, 1(1): 53–80.

Agnew, J. (2009) 'Money games: currencies and power in the contemporary world economy', *Antipode*, 41(S1): 214–38.

Alami, I. (2018) 'On the terrorism of money and national policy-making in emerging capitalist economies', *Geoforum*, 96: 21–31.

Alami, I. and Dixon, A.D. (2019) 'State capitalism(s) redux? Theories, tensions, controversies', *Competition & Change*, 24(1): 70–94.

Alami, I. and Dixon, A.D. (2020) 'The strange geographies of the "new" state capitalism', *Political Geography*, 82: art 102237. Available from: https://doi.org/10.1016/j.polgeo.2020.102237 [Accessed 7 June 2023].

Cerny, P.G. (2010) 'The competition state today: from *raison d'État* to *raison du Monde*', *Policy Studies*, 31(1): 5–21.

Dicken, P. (2014) *Global Shift: Mapping the Changing Contours of the World* (7th edn), London: Sage.

Eichengreen, B. (2012) *Exorbitant Privilege: The Rise and Fall of the Dollar*, Oxford: Oxford University Press.

French, S., Leyshon, A. and Wainwright, T. (2011) 'Financializing space, spacing financialization', *Progress in Human Geography*, 35(6): 798–819.

Gibadullina, A. (2021) 'The birth and development of Anglophone financial geography: a historical analysis of geographical studies of money and finance', *Geoforum*, 125: 150–67.

Hall, S. (2011) 'Geographies of money and finance I: cultural economy, politics and place', *Progress in Human Geography*, 35(2): 234–45.

Hall, S. (2012) 'Geographies of money and finance II: financialization and financial subjects', *Progress in Human Geography*, 36(3): 403–11.

Hall, S. (2017) 'Rethinking international financial centres through the politics of territory: renminbi internationalisation in London's financial district', *Transactions of the Institute of British Geographers*, 42(4): 489–502.

Hall, S. (2021) *Respatialising Finance: Power, Politics and Offshore Renminbi Market Making in London*, London: Wiley-Blackwell.

Harvey, D. (1982) *The Limits to Capital*, Oxford: Blackwell.

Hirst, P. and Thompson, G. (1999) *Globalization in Question* (2nd edn), Cambridge: Polity Press.

Hudson, A.C. (1998) 'Reshaping the regulatory landscape: border skirmishes around the Bahamas and Cayman offshore financial centres', *Review of International Political Economy*, 5(3): 534–64.

Kaltenbrunner, A. and Painceira, J.P. (2018) 'Subordinated financial integration and financialisation in emerging capitalist economies: the Brazilian experience', *New Political Economy*, 23(3): 290–313.

Langley, P. (2008) *The Everyday Life of Global Finance: Saving and Borrowing in Anglo-America*, Oxford: Oxford University Press.

Leyshon, A. and Thrift, N. (1997) *Money/Space: Geographies of Monetary Transformation*, London: Routledge.

Lim, K.F. (2019) *On Shifting Foundations: State Rescaling, Policy Experimentation and Economic Restructuring in Post-1949 China*, London: Wiley.

Loomis, J.M. (2022) 'Holding hope: financial coaching and the depoliticization of poverty', *Transactions of the Institute of British Geographers*, 47(4): 940–54.

Lyons, G. (2007) 'State capitalism: the rise of sovereign wealth funds', *Journal of Management Research*, 7(3): 119–46.

McNally, C.A. (2013) 'The challenge of refurbished state capitalism: implications for the global political economic order', *DMS – Der Moderne Staat: Zeitschrift für Public Policy, Recht und Management*, 6(1): 33–48.

Montgomerie, J. and Tepe-Belfrage, D. (2017) 'Caring for debts: how the household economy exposes the limits of financialisation', *Critical Sociology*, 43(4/5): 653–68.

Nolke, A. (ed) (2014) *Multinational Corporations from Emerging Markets: State Capitalism 3.0*, Basingstoke: Palgrave Macmillan.

O'Brien, R. (1992) *Global Financial Integration: The End of Geography*, London: Pinter for Royal Institute of International Affairs.

Palma, G. (1978) 'Dependency: a formal theory of underdevelopment or a methodology for the analysis of concrete situations of underdevelopment?', *World Development*, 6(7/8): 881–924.

Peck, J. (2012) 'Economic geography: island life', *Dialogues in Human Geography*, 2(2): 113–33.

Pollard, J., McEwan, C., Laurie, N. and Stenning, A. (2009) 'Economic geography under postcolonial scrutiny', *Transactions of the Institute of British Geographers*, 34(2): 137–42.

Roberts, S (1994) 'Fictitious capital, fictitious spaces: the geography of offshore financial flows', in S. Corbridge, R. Martin and N. Thrift (eds) *Money, Power and Space*, Oxford: Blackwell, pp 91–115.

Roberts, S. (1995) 'Small place, big money: the Cayman Islands and the international financial system', *Economic Geography*, 71(3): 237–56.

Rosenman, E., Loomis, J. and Kay, K. (2019) 'Diversity, representation, and the limits of engaged pluralism in (economic) geography', *Progress in Human Geography*, 44(3): 510–33.

Strange, S. (1986) *Casino Capitalism*, Oxford: Blackwell.

Strange, S. (1988) *States and Markets*, London: Pinter.

Thrift, N. and Leyshon, A. (1994) 'A phantom state? The de-traditionalization of money, the international financial system and international financial centres', *Political Geography*, 13(4): 299–327.

Whiteside, H, Alami, I., Dixon, A.D. and Peck, J. (2023) 'Making spaces for the new state capitalism, part 1: working with a troublesome category', *Environment and Planning A: Economy and Space*, 55(1): 63–71.

PART II

Critical Debates in Contemporary Economic Geographies

11

Informal Economies: Towards Plurality and Social Justice

Kavita Ramakrishnan and Emma Mawdsley

Introduction

Our starting inspiration for this chapter is the work of Mary Njeri Kinyanjui (2013, 2014, 2019), an economic geographer who has written extensively on women entrepreneurs running garment stalls in Nairobi. In *African Markets and the Utu-buntu Business Model* (2019: xiii), Kinyanjui recounts a popular song that underscores the widespread belief that 'markets sustain traders' sense of their own power as well as that of their families and communities'. Important here are two strands: that social reproduction is intimately connected to the market, and that solidarities and mutualities exist between traders and the wider community. Kinyanjui refers to this business model as *utu-buntu*, which contrasts with neoliberal logics of individuality and competition, thus pointing to what a model of economic and social justice, rooted in alternative values, may entail. Following Kinyanjui, we ask what political possibilities emerge when we read the myriad labour practices that are grouped as 'informal' alongside principles of care and solidarity? (Compare Gibson-Graham, 2008; see also Chapter 4 in this volume.) What might such practices inspired by principles of mutuality in turn say about dwelling and surviving on the urban 'margins', and urban justice more broadly? These ideas are important to contemporary economic geographies, as they acknowledge that solidarity economies are key to surviving in and actively shaping the interlinking spheres of home and work, and the city writ large.

It would be impossible to do justice to the full diversity of work on informal economies within Geography or allied fields (see, for example, Banks et al, 2019). Instead, we organize our intervention across particular spatialities where forms of *labour and dwelling* take place, and which are often part of interconnected processes. We draw on recent thinking around the dissolving boundaries between re/productive labour, and feminist economic geographers' concerns over the unrecognized labour that takes place at home (Mezzadri, 2020). Looking at housing and labour in conjunction with one another thus cuts across 'usual' urban sites and scales, namely the 'market', the 'street', the 'home', and the 'margins' to understand how working across such spatialities is mutually co-constituted, and critical to subject formation. Put differently, stories of the informal economy are as much about 'homes' as 'work', contextualized within the interconnected histories of colonial and postcolonial planning, as well as contemporary processes of urban change (Roy and AlSayyad, 2003; Watson, 2009; Potts, 2020). The chapter is informed by our commitment to critically engaging with frameworks of economic and urban 'development', from diverse sites and encounters such as eviction and resettlement in Delhi (Ramakrishnan, 2014) and infrastructural labour (Ramakrishnan et al, 2021) within and beyond the Global 'South', the latter an idea that we hold in tension and actively seek to destabilize (Mawdsley, 2018).

We start by tracing debates on informality beyond the binary opposition to formality and beyond resistance/coercion. We then turn to informal housing, and push for understandings on alliances to secure (informal) housing *and* livelihoods, and attempts to make visible shifting labour arrangements from *within* the home. We conclude by considering how (renewed) attention to embodied labour/care within economic geography can speak to a feminist, anti-racist ethics of engaging with informal work – in its broadest sense – that is attuned to plurality and social justice.

Beyond the informal/formal dichotomy: towards a broader (urban) conceptualization of informality

Keith Hart (1973) is usually credited with coining the label 'informal sector', based on his research on rural migrants in Accra.[1] He found that terms such as 'underemployment' and 'unemployment' obscured a range of activities undertaken by migrants, which instead demonstrated the importance of kin and trust networks in securing work within informal economies, as well as migrants' resourcefulness and dynamism. Furthermore, his work challenged normative assumptions that underpinned categories such as 'legal' and 'illegal'. In the late 1970s and 1980s, the International Labour Organization (ILO) adopted Hart's (1973) definition of the 'informal sector'. But this 'recognition' came at a price, reifying in the process a scholarly and policy binary, albeit one that was subsequently reproblematized in academic and policy circles (see also Chen and Carré, 2020).

Critical urban theorists have expanded on the conceptualization of the 'informal' beyond economic activities in the shadows of the state (Roy,

2009a; Goldman, 2011; McFarlane, 2012; Varley, 2013; Schindler, 2014), thus broadening a previously narrow focus on economic livelihoods to consider the role of the state in *perpetuating* informality. A vibrant theory of 'informality' has emerged from work seeking to decentre Western urban experiences as universal, pointing to specific processes at work in Southern cities that need(ed) their own vocabularies (Robinson, 2011; Parnell and Robinson, 2012; Bhan, 2019). Understandings of informality are not static, and shift depending on who holds power, the interest groups involved and the everyday subversions of ordinary people. Roy's (2009b) influential work is instructive to understanding planning regimes' shifting logics and the limitations of viewing informality as that in opposition to formal land-use regulations. Roy (2009b) defines informality as 'a state of deregulation, one where the ownership, use, and purpose of land cannot be fixed and mapped according to any prescribed set of regulations or the law' (Roy, 2009a: 80). While 'informality' may be difficult to conceptually pinpoint, its value as a theory remains, as Schindler (2014) notes, to further our understandings of the 'mechanisms' that produce informality and the 'processes' that render some land and space use deemed 'formal' and others 'informal'. Importantly, informality emerges as the *norm* in much of the world, rather than the exception (Banks et al, 2019), as demonstrated in the intersecting exclusions from housing and livelihoods (Gillespie, 2016).

Building on these ideas, an inherent disconnect emerges: inherited colonial planning concepts and tools, such as 'Master Plans' – detailed formal plans that designate current and future land use and rights – have been reproduced by municipal planners and officials, despite their inability to accommodate flexible land use and the sheer numbers of people living and working informally in Southern cities (Sundaresan, 2020). Moreover, it is important to note the role that colonial and postcolonial planning regimes have played in problematically linking the informal to that which is unruly, messy and out of place (Roy, 2009a). Spatial planning has all too often served as a disciplinary tool by the state, to determine which bodies, dwellings and livelihoods 'do not belong', especially in cities that have sought 'world-class' (Bhan, 2019; Dupont, 2011) or 'competitive' status (Watson, 2009). This is not to suggest that Master Plans or related technologies are necessarily 'rational', all-powerful or coherent in inscribing formal visions of legible cities. Ghertner (2011) has written compellingly of a 'rule by aesthetics' in Delhi, whereby certain world-class building projects are given the green light by city officials, even though they contravene Master Plan regulations.

Despite decades of progressive thinking beyond the binary, planning policy prescriptions since Keith Hart's (1973) work have often adopted a simplistic view that 'integrating' those who labour within the informal economy into formal spatial planning is always possible and desirable. In his work among youth traders in Harare and elsewhere in Southern Africa, for example,

Kamete (2018) argues that the often poorly executed integration attempts constitute a 'pernicious assimilation': mobile traders are forced to conduct business from permanent stalls and during designated trading hours, while others who traded on the sidewalks or in public plazas face relocation to the city's periphery. Premised on discourses of 'modernization' and 'legal' planning frameworks, inclusion is simply equated with expanding formality (Kamete, 2018). Similarly, Ramakrishnan's (2014) work demonstrates how the state-led eviction of residents from informal settlements in central Delhi led to a punishing erasure of former homes and informal livelihoods. Many residents previously worked as maids, auto-rickshaw drivers and traders in local markets, and had to not only rebuild homes in the far-flung resettlement, but also rebuild economic opportunities. This painfully demonstrated the paradoxes of so-called 'formalization', and the inextricable links between housing and livelihoods.

Beyond resistance/coercion

The idea that informal economic activities stand outside the purview of the state has led to much engagement and rebuttal, as scholars have sought to understand the linkages and connections between formal and informal economic spheres. Urban social anthropologists such as Caroline Moser (1978), pointed to a 'continuum' of activities that cannot be separated, but which are intrinsically linked. Her framing posited informal workers as 'subordinate' to capitalist production, in contrast to Hart (1973), who held a largely positive account of the informal economy, insofar as informal livelihoods contributed to the urban economy, and offered viable income strategies in the absence of formal waged employment (Chen, 2012). Intertwined with debates on the connections between the formal/informal economies are perspectives on the nature of agency of those who labour (see also Chapters 21, 24 and 27 in this volume). More specifically, are informal livelihoods born out of necessity – a survivalist venture on the margins given the absence of alternative wage employment; or are such livelihoods driven by voluntary decisions to choose the informal sector (Kamete, 2013, 2018)? While important to consider varying forms of exploitation, the dominant framing of agency versus coercion masks the myriad ways in which subversive and insurgent activities and everyday politics emerge, with implications for maintaining and expanding claims to urban space.

One avenue for understanding the politics of informality[2] is through Bayat's (2000) conceptualization of 'quiet encroachment', based on urbanism in the Middle East. It captures the long-term and cumulative negotiations of those marginalized within the city beyond the revolutionary/passive dichotomy, defined by Bayat as the 'silent, protracted, but pervasive advancement of the ordinary people on the propertied and powerful in order to survive and improve their lives' (Bayat, 2000: 545). And yet these struggles, while sometimes demonstrably successful through the extension of infrastructural services by the state, or the encroachment of street vendors on public space, do not always lead to collective action. Instead, the ultimate aims are for capillary rather than revolutionary social redistribution and autonomy, the latter from the quotidian disciplinary mechanisms and institutions of the state. Bayat's (2000) work has been generative, particularly in studies of informal street vending to understand what forms resistance takes, and how and when actors decide to negotiate with the state – charting out ways in which resistance can emerge in non-totalizing forms.

Kinyanjui's (2013) work on women garment traders in Nairobi's central business district (CBD), reframes quiet encroachment as one of subaltern urbanism, whereby women traders formally constrained to conduct their business activities on the peripheries of the city (or banned from them altogether), reconfigured space within the city centre for their trading needs. Despite pushback from elite planners, women traders 'through group occupancy, sharing spaces and collaboration … have initiated a new way of appropriating space in the city in a legitimate manner' (2013: 160), that transcends (new) colonialist and masculinist planning perspectives. For Gillespie (2016), looking at street hawkers in Accra, 'quiet encroachment' enables traders to appropriate space for their livelihoods, but it is the addition of 'bold encroachment' – collective organizing – against municipal-led decongestion policies and housing evictions that has seen visible gains. Finally, Crossa (2009), writing on street vendors in Mexico City, also notes a multiplicity in resistance that goes beyond encroaching, to negotiating with and even undermining the hostile elements of the state, concluding that the state does not have sole purview over exercising power.

Thus, though informality is often deployed by the state and targeted to reconfigure urban spatialities for accumulation and exclusion, many scholars still see some room for manoeuvre. For Schindler, in his study of street hawkers in Delhi:

> power is dispersed across a range of sites, and rests in varying degrees with a host of state and non-state actors, none of whom are able to unilaterally impose their vision of formality. Instead, these interest groups negotiate and struggle to define (in)formality and gain control over, or access to, urban space. (Schindler, 2014: 2597)

While we have predominantly centred Southern cities in our discussions, informality can be explored in relation to the variegated urbanity of the 'North'. In Los Angeles, for example, while we find migrant bordering and racialization permeate informal livelihoods, many of the same threads of state ambiguities vis-à-vis informality and tensions between surviving and thriving feature. *Fruteros* – predominantly undocumented Latin American migrants who run fruit salad stalls on the streets of Los Angeles – are simultaneously criminalized and legitimized by different arms of the state (Rosales, 2013). On the one hand, *fruteros* can publicly store their vending carts with the Department of Public Health, while on the other, they face penalties and even incarceration at the hands of the police, since street vending, at the time of the research, remained illegal. In the face of this fractured and uneven governance, Rosales is pessimistic about the survival opportunities for *fruteros* (in comparison to other forms of migrant labour), given the confiscations of vending supplies suffered through crackdowns, and at times, deportation. However, Muñoz (2016), finds that despite navigating a complex terrain of gangs, conflicts with neighbours and police raids, street vendors are still able to 'create viable economic strategies making informal labour a choice within fluid and temporal[ly] complex restrictive systems' (Muñoz, 2016: 339; see Villafana (2022) on recent legalization to fully decriminalize street vending).

Alford et al (2019) remind us that precarious street vendors are also embedded in global production networks, rescaling often highly localized imaginaries of 'marginal' labour. Without reifying a particular form of 'subaltern urbanism' (see Roy, 2011; Lindell, 2019), we see that agency too can be tentative and dependent on intersectional precarity determined by race, gender and (differentiated) citizenship, and the opportunities provided by state ambiguities. Amid critiques that 'choice' and 'autonomy' are curtailed for informal workers given the informal economy's imbrications with uneven capitalist structures (see Samers, 2005, for example), care must be taken in understanding agency and its inherent tensions. And yet, there is still scope for agency to reveal potential labour-worlds that ameliorate capitalism's effects, particularly in relation to new forms of organizing, and spaces of work (Strauss, 2020). As Thieme et al (2021: 9) write in relation to Kenya, the variable use of the idiom 'hustle' among youth interlocutors in the informal economy is part of an 'urban vernacular' of 'struggle' that has a 'dual significance': brimming with subjectivities and lived experiences that stubbornly resist victimization on the 'margins' of the city, even as the struggle is punctuated by wider structural inequalities.

Housing and the informal economy

We now turn to housing as a site which, from a gendered perspective, often co-constitutes, and reproduces women's informal labour (see also Chapter 21 in this volume). We consider how the 'home'[3] can simultaneously obscure women's labour and expand our understandings of the informal economy in productive ways. While we discuss ongoing invisibilizations of labour across the home–work nexus, we ultimately follow the 'diverse economies' research agenda of Gibson-Graham (2008), to think about transformative orientations within the informal economy that are replete with possibility for challenging supposedly stable and predetermined economic identities (Roelvink et al, 2015), such as provisionality.

Informality is fundamentally linked to the 'question of land fueled by formal (yet opaque) state bodies working informally to change land tenure' (Goldman, 2011: 575), resulting in shifting configurations and regulations over public space (Roy, 2009b; McFarlane, 2012). Not only are livelihoods threatened by relocation as land is seized by the state to accelerate private accumulation under the banner of entrepreneurialism, but affordable housing is scarce, and under similar threats, in many Southern cities. Rural-to-urban migrants in many contexts have had to navigate informal employment *and* construct makeshift dwellings. For Gillespie (2016), 'class-based dispossession' occurs through strategies seeking to 'decongest' Accra's city centre: removing street hawkers as well as demolishing a central informal settlement which is in close proximity to the CBD constitutes the destruction of vital connectivities between homes and labour opportunities. It can take years – even decades – for those evicted to re-establish their livelihoods (Ramakrishnan, 2014), affecting multiple generations and their social and economic mobility (Rao, 2010).

The salience and security of home-based enterprises for women in particular, has been the subject of considerable scholarship from feminist geographers (for example, Chant, 2006, 2013; Chant and McIlwaine, 2015). While it is impossible to speak about any universal experience of gender, and an intersectional approach is important to understanding how livelihoods and housing mesh with other social identities, Chant and McIlwaine (2015) remind us that everyday gendered negotiations within informal settlements are important to excavate. This includes unpaid care and domestic labour: a tendency exists to solely prioritize certain forms of labour as generative of 'value', thereby ignoring reproductive spheres (Meehan and Strauss, 2015). Thus, recent Marxist feminist interventions have argued for the 'centrality of all labour to value-generation' (Mezzadri, 2021: 1186). Writing on migrant labour in Delhi, Cowan (2021) proposes that one can explore women's migrant experiences within labour dormitories through the concept of 'rooted flexibility'. By challenging dominant narratives of 'footloose' (read: masculinized) labour, Cowan demonstrates that the material decay of and patriarchal disciplining within tenement housing map onto equally precarious labour that women must take up: a 'double-bind' emerges, whereby women's mobility and behaviour are policed in both the workplace *and* tenement.

Elsewhere, scholars have found more hopeful social and economic orientations in 'provisionality' (Simone, 2018; Simone and Pieterse, 2018; Bhan, 2019) within the urban, creating space for makeshift and temporary dwellings as valid forms within urban landscapes, that in turn, impact livelihoods. 'Provisional' housing provides opportunities for incremental transformation by residents, or what Bhan (2019) calls a 'Southern urban practice'. Writing on Nairobi, Guma (2021) starts their intervention with the story of King'ori who lives in Kibera, and whose informal shanty is adjacent to the micro-stall she runs, selling charcoal and water. Considering the shanty and stall in tandem, Guma argues 'offer viable alternatives to … neoliberal and market-oriented interventions' and insight into 'provisional urban worlds in city making' (2021: 212). Tenement shelters newly built by the state outside Kibera were often rejected by residents as they afforded little by way of sustaining small-scale livelihoods; instead, structures within Kibera, characterized by their 'temporariness', were considered critical to allowing residents to 'get by'. Provisionality in both housing and livelihoods, then, offers scope for residents to build what they need, when needed.

Perspectives that foreground housing can thus reveal the emergence of new alliances to secure (informal) housing and make visible shifting labour arrangements intricately linked to the home – whether by effecting further constraints on gendered mobility, or by offering the flexibility of provisionality. In the next section, we centre the body and care as a praxis for both uncovering difference across shifting sites of 'work', and performing economic relations less constrained by capitalist and neoliberal logics.

Towards a deepening engagement between informal economies, embodied labour and care

We now turn to embodiment, which has animated recent scholarship on precarity, labour and care (Doshi, 2017; Fredericks, 2018; Ramakrishnan et al, 2021), and as we argue, destabilizes received and dominant economic scripts in relation to informal economies. As part of the recent 'infrastructural turn' in the social sciences, these works broadly consider 'the body as a material and political site' (Doshi, 2017: 125) imbued with affect, that in turn is mapped onto shifting infrastructural arrangements (Datta and Ahmed, 2020). While much of the earlier conversations have focused on informal markets and street vendors, the provisioning, maintenance and repair of infrastructure, such as electricity, water and waste management, often demand informal labour, even if infrastructural systems themselves are formalized and municipal-led (see, for instance, Dias, 2016).

Writing on trash workers in Dakar, Fredericks conceptualizes 'vital infrastructures', whereby 'new arrangements for garbage management reconfigure everyday lives and embodied materialities of labour, and along the way communities, political subjectivities, and relationships to the city' (2018: 61). Fredericks's work holds important insights into how labouring bodies reconstitute social and political relationships, impact the meanings and values associated with such work, and ultimately challenge neoliberal logics (with some success). Extending these arguments beyond infrastructure, attention to embodiment means that the physical and emotional toll of informal labour is recuperated and plays a role in workers' articulations of exploitation and citizenship (Fredericks, 2018). These works build on earlier theorizations by feminist political geographers on the 'body' and the sites and scales it collapses when understanding power and its effects (see Mountz, 2018 for an overview). Our concern with labour here, is how embodied difference, across race, gender, caste/class and other axes, reshapes subjectivities and spaces of informal labour, with important implications for countering exploitation (Cowan, 2021; Ramakrishnan et al, 2021) that can often take place within the informal economy.

Care becomes crucial, as the interest that many feminist scholars have in 'care' as a practice of labour and as a reparative commitment beyond the immediate and localized site of labour (Martínez, 2017) points to social justice in plural forms. Similar to mutuality and solidarity economies (Kinyanjui, 2019), care and embodied labour can also activate an experimental politics, connecting the exacting and arduous work that infrastructural provisioning often demands of informal workers, to the multiple and overlapping scales of home and public space.

Conclusion

To close, we return to our earlier questions based on Kinyanjui's work (2019) on mutuality in the informal economy, and alternative economic practices that can oppose (post)colonial and capitalist logics. In terms of theory and praxis, narrow conceptualizations of the 'informal' can obscure important lifeworlds in the making (compare Simone, 2018; Guma, 2021). As illustrated in this chapter, enduring tensions remain between the ways in which planning accommodates informality, and between agency and exploitation within informal livelihoods. Foregrounding housing to understand interconnected labour struggles, and thinking through embodied labour/care may open productive avenues to imagine and chart post-capitalist economies (Gibson-Graham, 2008).

In this select review, we urge that greater attention is paid to how the economies of the informal sector interplay with those of housing, embodied labour and care. New economic subjectivities and economic transformations even on smaller scales continually emerge, as many of those labouring within the informal economy reclaim makeshift sites of dwelling, discard individualistic logics, and elide seemingly fixed categories of race and other markers of social difference – in turn, writing economic possibilities and social justice anew.

Acknowledgements

Both Kavita and Emma are indebted to Tatiana Thieme for her generous reading of an earlier version, and for the many thoughtful suggestions she made. Many thanks to Sarah Marie Hall and Jennifer Johns for their invitation to contribute to this volume. When revising this chapter, we were saddened to hear news of the passing of Professor Vanessa Watson. Her ideas loom large throughout.

Notes

[1] We do not wish to minimize Hart's contribution, but note the language of 'discovery' and 'coining' for entrepreneurial activities that predate the Western (and White, male) scholarly gaze, and which reproduce the subdiscipline, 'making certain bodies and thematics core, and others not even part' (Ahmed, 2013; and for an example that acknowledges Indigenous and precolonial forms, see Crossa, 2009). To his credit, Hart (2009) himself provides thoughtful reflections on how his ideas travelled and were coopted by the development industry to legitimize particular hierarchical economic classifications.

[2] Given the limited scope of this chapter, we only have room to chart one of these avenues, though important works by Chatterjee (2004) and Benjamin (2008) from the Indian context speak to other mechanisms through which the urban poor make claims on the city, as does the lens of 'insurgent' planning and citizenship in South Africa and Brazil, respectively (Holston, 2009; Miraftab, 2009). For a more detailed review see Bénit-Gbaffou and Oldfield (2014).

[3] It is not our intent here to conflate housing with 'home' (see Blunt, 2005), but rather to unpack the ways in which home–work (in all of its forms) is implicated in the informal economy, and how eviction and resettlement can (re)concentrate gendered labour in the home.

References

Ahmed, S. (2013) 'Making feminist points', Feministkilljoys, 11 September. Available from: https://feministkilljoys.com/2013/09/11/making-femin ist-points/ [Accessed 30 April 2021].

Alford, M., Kothari, U. and Pottinger, L. (2019) 'Re-articulating labour in global production networks: the case of street traders in Barcelona', *Environment and Planning D: Society and Space*, 37(6): 1081–99.

Banks, N., Lombard, M.B. and Mitlin, D. (2019) 'Urban informality as a site of critical analysis', *Journal of Development Studies*, 56(2): 223–38.

Bayat, A. (2000) 'From "dangerous classes" to "quiet rebels": politics of the urban subaltern in the Global South', *International Sociology*, 15(3): 533–57.

Bénit-Gbaffou, C. and Oldfield, S. (2014) 'Claiming "rights" in the African city: popular mobilization and the politics of informality', in S. Parnell and S. Oldfield (eds) *The Routledge Handbook on Cities of the Global South*, Abingdon: Routledge, pp 281–95.

Benjamin, S. (2008) 'Occupancy urbanism: radicalizing politics and economy beyond policy and programs', *International Journal of Urban and Regional Research*, 32(3): 719–29.

Bhan, G. (2019) 'Notes on a Southern urban practice', *Environment & Urbanization*, 31(2): 639–54.

Blunt, A. (2005) 'Cultural geography: cultural geographies of home', *Progress in Human Geography*, 29(4): 505–15.

Chant, S. (2006) 'Re-thinking the "feminization of poverty" in relation to aggregate gender indices', *Journal of Human Development*, 7(2): 201–220.

Chant, S. (2013) 'Cities through a "gender lens": a golden "urban age" for women in the global South?', *Environment and Urbanization*, 25(1): 9–29.

Chant, S. and McIlwaine, C. (2015) *Cities, Slums and Gender in the Global South: Towards a Feminised Urban Future*, London: Routledge.

Chatterjee, P. (2004) *The Politics of the Governed: Reflections on Popular Politics in Most of the World*, New York: Columbia University Press.

Chen, M. (2012) *The Informal Economy: Definitions, Theories and Policies*, Women in Informal Employment Globalizing and Organizing (WIEGO) Working Paper No. 1, Cambridge, MA: WIEGO.

Chen, M. and Carré, F. (2020) *The Informal Economy Revisited: Examining the Past, Envisioning the Future*, Abingdon: Routledge.

Cowan, T. (2021) 'Rooted flexibility: social reproduction, violence and gendered work in the Indian city', *Gender, Place & Culture*, 28(1): 66–87.

Crossa, V. (2009) 'Resisting the entrepreneurial city: street vendors' struggle in Mexico City's historic center', *International Journal of Urban and Regional Research*, 33(1): 43–63.

Datta, A. and Ahmed, N. (2020) 'Intimate infrastructures: the rubrics of gendered safety and urban violence in Kerala, India', *Geoforum*, 110: 67–76.

Dias, S.M. (2016) 'Waste pickers and cities', *Environment and Urbanization*, 28(2): 375–90.

Doshi, S. (2017) 'Embodied urban political ecology: five propositions', *Area*, 49(1): 125–8.

Dupont, V.D.N. (2011) 'The dream of Delhi as a global city', *International Journal of Urban and Regional Research*, 35(3): 533–54.

Fredericks, R. (2018) *Garbage Citizenship: Vital Infrastructures of Labor in Dakar, Senegal*, Durham, NC: Duke University Press.

Ghertner, D.A. (2011) 'Rule by aesthetics: world-class city making in Delhi', in A. Roy and A. Ong (eds) *Worlding Cities*, Chichester: Wiley, pp 279–306.

Gibson-Graham, J.K. (2008) 'Diverse economies: performative practices for "other worlds"', *Progress in Human Geography*, 32(5): 613–32.

Gillespie, T. (2016) 'Accumulation by urban dispossession: struggles over urban space in Accra, Ghana', *Transactions of the Institute of British Geographers*, 41(1): 66–77.

Goldman, M. (2011) 'Speculative urbanism and the making of the next world city', *International Journal of Urban and Regional Research*, 35(3): 555–81.

Guma, P.K. (2021) 'Recasting provisional urban worlds in the Global South: shacks, shanties and micro-stalls', *Planning Theory & Practice*, 22(2): 211–26.

Hart, K. (1973) 'Informal income opportunities and urban employment in Ghana', *Journal of Modern African Studies*, 11(1): 61–89.

Hart, K. (2009) *On the Informal Economy: The Political History of an Ethnographic Concept*, Working Paper CEB 09-042.RS, Brussels: Université Libre de Bruxelles.

Holston, J. (2009) 'Insurgent citizenship in an era of global urban peripheries', *City & Society*, 21(2): 245–67.

Kamete, A.Y. (2013) 'On handling urban informality in Southern Africa', *Geografiska Annaler Series B: Human Geography*, 95(1): 17–31.

Kamete, A.Y. (2018) 'Pernicious assimilation: reframing the integration of the urban informal economy in Southern Africa', *Urban Geography*, 39(2): 167–89.

Kinyanjui, M.N. (2013) 'Women informal garment traders in Taveta Road, Nairobi: from the margins to the center', *African Studies Review*, 56(3): 147–64.

Kinyanjui, M.N. (2014) *Women and the Informal Economy in Urban Africa: From the Margins to the Centre*, London: Zed Books.

Kinyanjui, M.N. (2019) *African Markets and the Utu-buntu Business Model: A Perspective on Economic Informality in Nairobi*, Cape Town: African Minds.

Lindell, I. (2019) 'Introduction: re-spatialising informality – reconsidering the spatial politics of street work in the Global South', *International Development Planning Review*, 41(1): 3–21.

Martinez, L. (2017) 'Agribusiness, peasant agriculture and labour markets: Ecuador in comparative perspective', *Journal of Agrarian Change Studies*, 17(4): 680–93.

Mawdsley, E. (2018) 'The "Southernisation" of development?', *Asia Pacific Viewpoint*, 59(2): 173–85.

McFarlane, C. (2012) 'Rethinking informality: politics, crisis, and the city', *Planning Theory & Practice*, 13(1): 89–108.

Meehan, K. and Strauss, K. (eds) (2015) *Precarious Worlds: Contested Geographies of Social Reproduction*, Athens: University of Georgia Press.

Mezzadri, A. (2021) 'A value theory of inclusion: informal labour, the homeworker, and the social reproduction of value', *Antipode*, 53(4): 1186–205.

Miraftab, F. (2009) 'Insurgent planning: situating radical planning in the Global South', *Planning Theory*, 8(1): 32–50.

Moser, C.O.N. (1978) 'Informal sector or petty commodity production: Dualism or dependence in urban development?', *World Development*, 6(9–10): 1041–64.

Mountz, A. (2018) 'Political geography III: bodies', *Progress in Human Geography*, 42(5): 759–69.

Muñoz, L. (2016) 'Agency, choice and restrictions in producing Latina/o street-vending landscapes in Los Angeles', *Area*, 48(3): 339–45.

Potts, D. (2020) *Broken Cities: Inside the Global Housing Crisis*, London: Zed Books.

Parnell, S. and Robinson, J. (2012) '(Re)theorizing cities from the Global South: looking beyond neoliberalism', *Urban Geography*, 33(4): 593–617.

Ramakrishnan, K. (2014) 'Disrupted futures: unpacking metaphors of marginalization in eviction and resettlement narratives', *Antipode*, 46(3): 754–72.

Ramakrishnan, K., O'Reilly, K. and Budds, J. (2021) 'The temporal fragility of infrastructure: theorizing decay, maintenance, and repair', *Environment and Planning E: Nature and Space*, 4(3): 674–95.

Rao, U. (2010) 'Making the global city: urban citizenship at the margins of Delhi', *Ethnos*, 75(4): 402–24.

Roelvink, G., St. Martin, K. and Gibson-Graham, J.K. (eds) (2015) *Making Other Worlds Possible: Performing Diverse Economies*, Minneapolis: University of Minnesota Press.

Rosales, R. (2013) 'Survival, economic mobility and community among Los Angeles fruit vendors', *Journal of Ethnic and Migration Studies*, 39(5): 697–717.

Roy, A. (2009a) 'Why India cannot plan its cities: informality, insurgence and the idiom of urbanization', *Planning Theory*, 8(1): 76–87.

Roy, A. (2009b) 'Strangely familiar: planning and the worlds of insurgence and informality', *Planning Theory*, 8(1): 7–11.

Roy, A. (2011) 'Slumdog cities: rethinking subaltern urbanism', *International Journal of Urban and Regional Research*, 35(2): 223–38.

Roy, A. and AlSayyad, N. (2003) *Urban Informality: Transnational Perspectives from the Middle East, Latin America, and South Asia*, Lanham, MD: Lexington Books.

Samers, M. (2005) 'The myopia of "diverse economies", or a critique of the "informal economy"', *Antipode*, 37(5): 875–86.

Schindler, S. (2014) 'Producing and contesting the formal/informal divide: regulating street hawking in Delhi, India', *Urban Studies*, 51(12): 2596–612.

Simone, A.M. (2018) 'The urban majority and provisional recompositions in Yangon', *Antipode*, 50(1): 23–40.

Simone, A.M. and Pieterse, E. (2018) *New Urban Worlds: Inhabiting Dissonant Times*, New York: Wiley.

Strauss, K. (2020) 'Labour geography III: Precarity, racial capitalisms and infrastructure', *Progress in Human Geography*, 44(6): 1212–1224.

Sundaresan, J. (2020) 'Decolonial reflections on urban pedagogy in India', *Area*, 52(4): 722–30.

Thieme, T., Ference, M.E. and van Stapele, N. (2021) 'Harnessing the "hustle": struggle, solidarities and narratives of work in Nairobi and beyond', *Africa*, 91(1): 1–15.

Varley, A. (2013) 'Postcolonialising informality?', *Environment and Planning D: Society and Space*, 31(1): 4–22.

Villafana, J. (2022) 'A new era of "legal" street vending awaits L.A's sidewalk vendors, but will they finally stop getting fined?', L.A. Taco, 23 November. Available from: https://www.lataco.com/street-vendor-legal-los-angeles-policing/ [Accessed 6 April 2023].

Watson, V. (2009) 'Seeing from the South: refocusing urban planning on the globe's central urban issues', *Urban Studies*, 46(11): 2259–75.

12

Global Economy: Geographies of Production During Crises

Vida Vanchan

Introduction

The global economic and social stresses are at their heights given the ripple effects of the COVID-19 pandemic, ongoing and emerging new variant/s, supply chains disruptions, war, rising inflations and unemployment. Economic and psychological hardships have been echoed across the globe since the start of the pandemic. These uncertain times and the changing nature of the global economy and societies require rethinking of the global production system, of trade and of livelihoods, particularly in developing a more resilient approach in economic geography to understanding the geographies of production and the state of the global economy during crises (see also Chapters 21 and 27 in this volume). This chapter, therefore, explores the state of the global economy and geographies of production during crises by examining the key actors and processes that contribute to the global economy and the work by economic geographers in understanding the geographies of production, supply chains disruptions as well as economic life. It aims to develop a more comprehensive approach to understand the changing nature of global economy, production systems, and societies by acknowledging the vulnerabilities and flexibilities of those involved. It also underscores the work of economic geographers in identifying the relationships between people and places as well as the location and distribution of economic activities and uneven development across geographic space and scale. The work of economic geographers ranges from traditional location theories/economic geography to new economic geography and economic geographies (Wood and Roberts, 2011). The field has broadened and become very diverse (see all chapters in Part I). The methodological approaches have also been mixed reflective of this plurality (Poon, 2005). This chapter utilizes the diverse approach in economic geography by offering an overview of the global economy, key actors and processes. It then discusses the evolving geographies of production and disruptions of the global supply chains. The chapter concludes with a discussion of developing a comprehensive approach to understanding and addressing the state of the global economy, geographies of production and crisis management.

The changing nature and current state of the global economy

The world has witnessed the impact of COVID-19 pandemic on both people and economy since the official start of the pandemic in early 2020. Lives, work and businesses have been altered in ways that were unprecedented, such as lockdowns, mask wearing, social distancing, virtual learning and remote working, especially for those that were not subjected to these prior to the pandemic. Despite a recent return to somewhat 'normal' lives because of declining death and increasing vaccination rates in many countries, the world is still reeling from its effects. After rebounding to an estimated 5.5 per cent in 2021, global growth is expected to decelerate markedly to 4.1 per cent in 2022, reflecting continued COVID-19 flare-ups, diminished fiscal support, and lingering supply bottlenecks (World Bank Group, 2022). Conflict in Europe further proves the vulnerability of global peace, economic stability and sustainability. It is hard for economists to predict the future costs of war but there is a consensus on its long-term effects, which will be long-lasting for those directly involved and indirectly shared by those that are not. We can all feel the pain of rising food and fuel prices, among other things. Public anger over rising costs has triggered responses from politicians, particularly those that are in danger of losing their control such as Democrats over Congress in the US. In early 2022 US President Biden's Administration pursued of the possibility of antitrust enforcement against the four companies that dominate the American meat supply because of rising costs for pork and poultry as well as record beef prices (Goodman, 2022). This demonstrates the circular and interrelated processes that explain the very nature of each economy and how economic geographers are well positioned in examining these.

The economy is the interrelated processes of production, circulation, exchange and consumption through which wealth is generated. Modes of production determine how resources are deployed, how work is organized and how wealth is distributed. Economic historians have identified various modes of production ranging from subsistence to capitalism in which each creates distinctive relationships between the main factors of production: land, labour and capital. These relationships have also been changing over time.

This alteration requires a complex understanding of the main factors and modes of production. Although the work of economic geographers and economists is overlapping and complementary, there are differences in their emphasis and general orientation (Anderson, 2012). Economic geographers are interested in how economic processes play out in differentiated space whereas economists are generally interested in developing models in an abstract, homogenous space (Anderson, 2012). Economic geographers seek explanations for the differences in economic activities rather than developing generalizations. Space, place and scale play a critical role in their analysis. Firms, state and individuals/workers are key actors within the economy. These actors operate in their respective space, place and scale, contributing to an overall understanding of the global economy. This overall understanding of the global economy is critical. Thus, the next section explores the key actors in the economy, particularly those within the production framework that drives economic growth, highlighting the evolving nature of geographies of production, supply chains and management as well as their disruptions and impacts.

The evolving geographies of production

As economic geographers are well aware, geographies of economic activities evolve over time (see Chapter 1 in this volume). There are three contrasting approaches to understanding the geography of production (Vanchan et al, 2018). One approach emphasizes the importance of local agglomerations, another highlights intra-firm mechanisms while the third approach underscores the global relationships, or global production network or global value chains. The importance of local agglomerations has been heralded by economic geographers in explaining industrial locations, local and regional economy since the work of Alfred Weber in the early 20th century. The agglomeration or clustering of industry develops when firms can gain external economies/savings from locating in the same place. This is evident in various sectors within the economy, such as the industrial design sector (Vanchan and MacPherson, 2008a, 2008b; MacPherson and Vanchan, 2010), optics and photonics industry (Clark, 2015), and furniture industry (Walcott, 2015). Geographically, industrial design companies are unevenly distributed across the country, reflecting an agglomeration economy and the nature of service specialization (MacPherson and Vanchan, 2010). Firms in these industries benefit from locating close to other firms and customers. In addition, the types of design services offered in any given metropolitan centre tend to mirror the structure of local production (that is, prominent or dominant sectors). Industrial design firms are more likely to locate close to their manufacturing clients. For example, automotive designers are located in Detroit, textile designers are in New York City and Los Angeles. On the other hand, the geography of production reflects the agglomeration economies in such that firms benefit from co-locating and available resources including but not limited to infrastructure, labour and capital.

Firms can gain efficiencies from both internal and external economies of scale. The evolution of firms has been a fascinating observation and topic of interest among economic geographers, including firms' roles in organizing economic activity. Corporate geography as an emerging subfield in 1970s and 1980s was a result of this (Watts, 1980; Taylor and Thrift, 1982) and firms continue to be a key institution for economic geographers (Clark et al, 2000; Sheppard and Barnes, 2000; Dicken, 2003; Barnes et al, 2004; Laulajainen and Stafford, 2005; Mackinnon and Cumbers, 2011; Coe et al, 2019). The complex nature of firms illustrates the sophisticated nature of their operations. It also underscores the intricate relationships among internal mechanisms in organizing their activities ranging from pre- to post-production and consumption. Alterations in internal mechanisms reflect the evolving geographies of production. My longitudinal empirical study on industrial design firms, for example, helps explain the geographies and key competitiveness of firms in this industry and their clients thus reflecting this approach in understanding the changing nature of geographies of production (MacPherson and Vanchan, 2010; Vanchan and Bryson, 2015).

Design plays an important role in corporate and national competitiveness. Design is related to culture and society as it is involved in incorporating place into product and product into place (Rusten and Bryson, 2010). Design not only concerns the shape and functionality of end products but is also implicated in the creation of sustainable or green products and in the development of inclusive products. Business performance was found to be associated with investment in human capital, technology upgrades and the provision of contract R&D services (Vanchan and MacPherson, 2008a). Evidence indicated that export-oriented design companies exhibit stronger business performance than their domestically focused counterparts, notably in terms of sales growth, employment creation, research spending and profitability. As firms seek to externalize their operations and optimize their production, their geography of production is altered. New geographies of production can then be explained by the circuit of capital theory involving internal and external expansion, obtaining new market access, avoiding sunk costs, and tapping cheaper labour and supplies. They can also be explained by the reorganization of division of labour within firms (see Stephen Hymer's (1960s) model) as well as the product cycle model by Raymond Vernon and colleagues. The latter emphasized the characteristics of products as a means in explaining relocation or internationalization process. John Dunning's eclectic paradigm outlines a range of motives related to accidents of history and the particular path dependencies of individual firms which explain why and when internationalization occurs.

As the internalization process occurs, the global relationships, or global production network (GPN) or global value chains (GVC), underscore another approach to understanding the geographies of production. Evidently, one of the major manufacturing transformations involves the continued restructuring of GVCs or GPNs. This process includes outsourcing, offshoring, reshoring and right-shoring. It also includes the application of new technologies, including artificial intelligence, robotics and autonomous systems (RAS). Manufacturing has transformed the relationship between work, worker and machine. This revolution has altered the existing geographies of manufacturing and, at the same time, transformed workplaces. Thus, the literature on commodity chains/networks needs to engage further with ongoing debates on evolutionary approaches to economic geography (Boschma and Martin, 2010) ensuring that change and dynamics are central to understanding the evolving geography of global production (see Chapter 14 in this volume). Recently, Coe and Yeung have recognized that the existing GPN/GVC frameworks under-theorized dynamics and overemphasized governance (Coe and Yeung, 2015; Yeung and Coe, 2015) while Ponte and Sturgeon have called for the development of a modular approach to theory building as they 'believe in multi-causality [and] view endless substitution of one partial theory with another as a self-limiting exercise' (2014: 196). As a result, Vanchan et al (2018) call for the need to develop a more 'operations'-focused account of global production beyond the original frameworks of GPN/GVC by Yeung and Coe (2015), by exploring the repatriation or reshoring of manufacturing to the US and UK. In this paper, we identified the drivers behind reshoring as the first stage towards developing a dynamic conceptual framework for understanding the global organization of production. The global production is the outcome of an accumulation of many incremental micro and macro decisions made by individuals, firms and governments. This accumulation includes the decisions that determine the subdivision of tasks and their geographies that lie above a production process. This not only reflects an ongoing evolution of a spatial division of labour, but also a balance between variable and fixed costs or between labour and machines and artificial intelligence. Firms, workers and governments are in a continual process of becoming. This is simultaneously social, political, cultural and economic, especially during time of crises. As such, this requires an understanding of the impacts and underscores the need for effective pandemic/crisis contingency plans to be developed (Bryson et al, 2021). In order to further understand the impacts, I now turn to the discussion of supply chains disruptions.

Global supply chain disruptions and management

During the global pandemic, growth in the global economy faltered. Policy choices became more difficult, with limited room to manoeuvre (IMF, 2021). All these uncertainties can be described as being part of a new epoch termed 'Jenga Capitalism', which represents a new form of risk society where globalization combined with technological convergence has led to new forms of non-calculable uncertainty and instability (Bryson, 2022). Interestingly, goods have become a focal point of the global supply chains crisis as shoppers have spent more on goods and less on services during the COVID-19 pandemic where inflation-adjusted spending on services was down 2 per cent compared to a 14.5 per cent increase on goods compared to pre-pandemic (Weissmann, 2021). The US imported more physical goods than ever before where imports were up 17 per cent in 2021 compared to those during the same time in 2019 (Oak, 2021). During COVID-19 the US economy experienced global supply chain disruptions, with media reports painting a grim picture of no deliverable toys, and shortages of needed goods ranging from foods to toilet paper. Industrial production was also impacted due to supply chain bottlenecks such as a lack of new cars amid the computer chip shortage (Tappe, 2021a). The world's delicate supply chains have been under extreme stress because of epic port congestion, lack of workers, particularly truck drivers, and computer chip shortages. Key measures have been outlined by President Biden to help the supply chain bottlenecks which include longer port hours, efforts to boost the number of truck drivers, and actions by those in the private sectors such as Walmart, FedEx and UPS to increase their overnight operations (Tappe, 2021b). Short-term remedies such as longer port hours or increases in overnight logistics operations (Tappe, 2021b) have not resolved these issues, with critics highlighting more systemic problems like crumbling infrastructure in the US (Klein, 2021). Global supply chains have been undergoing a paradigm shift from just-in-time delivery to resiliency, which requires technological improvements, industry investment and labour-union participation (Klein, 2021). The persistent chip shortages limited car production worldwide and stymied the production of medical devices and a vast range of electronic gadgets (Goodman, 2022).

The global economy has been facing many shocks alongside COVID, including those arising from conflict in Europe. Businesses that rely on rail transport from eastern China to western Europe through Russia have had to find new routes. These trains haul everything from laptops and smart phones to new cars and auto supplies (Navellier, 2022). As a result, these disruptions represent risks associated with globalization that requires reconceptualization of 'value' and 'risk' within the current GPNs framework as well as identification of key operational strategies in risk management and national security (Bryson and Vanchan, 2020). This called for reconceptualization of globalization and localization in the global production networks to avoid disruptions, manage risks and to increase national security which I termed 'glocalization' (Vanchan, 2021). Glocalization offers an alternative pathway to the configuration of supply chains and production management where firms balance risk versus reward and cost control with non-price-based forms of competitiveness. Glocalization can also be expanded and applied as a strategy for individuals and states. Since the heightened trade war between US and China in 2018, more American companies have decreased their dependence on the Asian market. In 2019, Abercrombie & Fitch, the American lifestyle retailer of casual wear, reduced their dependence on Chinese suppliers by more than 40 per cent (Stampler, 2019). In March 2021, Intel announced it would invest $20 billion into two new semiconductor plants in Arizona (Kessler, 2021). General Motors is reshoring its battery production to Michigan, with a new hub for lithium-based products. US Steel decided in 2022 to build its new $3 billion factory in Alabama or Arkansas rather than abroad, because of rapidly rising steel prices. Lockheed, General Electric and Thermo Fisher are reported to be considering reshoring activities (Kessler, 2021). An estimated 1.3 million jobs have been brought back to the US since 2010 because of reshoring activities (Reshoring Initiative, 2022). According to Reshoring Initiative, 1,800 US firms intended to reshore their whole business or at least parts of it in 2021, resulting in some 220,000 new jobs to be created in the US compared to only 6,000 new jobs over a decade ago (Kessler, 2021).

The US has been facing labour shortages, particularly in the manufacturing sector, for many years (Bryson et al, 2015; Vanchan and Bryson, 2015; Kessler, 2021). With the pandemic, the country has experienced what was called 'the great resignation' which dominated the headlines in 2021 where many people have quit their jobs (Kessler, 2021). As many as 4.5 million Americans quit their jobs in November 2021, based on data published in January 2022 (Zagorsky, 2022). These figures may seem alarming, but they only represent a piece of the puzzle as quitting rates were higher before the pandemic and the skilled labour shortage represents another problem for the US labour supply. In addition, the shortages and impacts are sector-dependent. Manufacturing workers in the steel, automotive and textiles industries were quitting their jobs at a monthly average rate of 2.3 per cent in November 2021 compared to 6.1 per cent in 1945, according to Zagorsky (2022). The highest quitting rate is among workers in the accommodation and food services followed by retail trade (Zagorsky, 2022). The discussion of turnover rates and worker demographics predate the pandemic, but the pandemic has brought this complex and evolving relationship to the forefront as we have experienced the labour shortages at a more personal level – for example, the shortages of frontline workers in transportation, education, food and retail businesses. Businesses have to find new ways to attract workers and retain them, as young people (16–24-year-olds) are more likely to switch and quit jobs than their older counterparts (Zagorsky, 2022). Giving workers a sense of purpose, letting them work in self-directed teams and providing better benefits are suggested to help minimize turnover (Zagorsky, 2022). Worker satisfaction involves many attributes, but promoting and maintaining them is key. Glocalization, within this context, heightens the need to balance economic value with values related to reliability, resilience and location. The final section of this chapter, therefore, concludes with a look at understanding the changing nature of the global economy, evolving geographies of production, supply chains disruptions and risk management.

Conclusion

Although deindustrialization processes in developed economies have reduced the contribution of manufacturing to those economies, manufacturing remains a transformative force in economic growth. It plays a key role in creating the evolving global economy. Thus, geographies of production require a comprehensive understanding of all actors involved at all scales and scopes. Economic geographers play a crucial role in developing this understanding. It is vital to highlight the transformations of production, and thus the evolving geographies of production, which require understanding change and dynamics and a conceptualization of production and GPN/GVC beyond the existing approaches. First, attention needs not just be given to governance of the production networks but to the very processes and tasks underlying each operation and decision-making process. This includes an appreciation of operational tasks and both the qualitative and quantitative drivers behind their geography. As Vanchan et al (2018) point out in their analysis of reshoring activities by the UK and US firms, reshoring is sector-dependent and is mainly driven by manufacturers' cost-management and quality strategies combined with the importance of manufacturing products close to market. This involves a total manufacturing cost analysis in which access to a set of tangible and intangible inputs are key drivers behind dynamics of GPN. Thus, understanding the evolving geography of global production is a complex task. Second, this latest pandemic and war in Europe revive the significant role of manufacturing in the global economy and underscore the vulnerability of the societies and economies around the world. It reinforces Bryson and Vanchan's (2020) argument for reconceptualization of 'value' and 'risk' within the current global production networks framework and responses in risk management and national security. A profit focus as a driver behind the configuration of value chains needs to be balanced with a concern for other values which include both monetary and non-monetary values. They also include balancing profits with environmental impacts. Firms, individuals, institutions and countries need to re-evaluate their priorities and reconfigure their operations and long-term goals. In sum, values need to be further analysed as 'value' for whom, what, when, where, why and how (Bryson and Vanchan, 2020).

From a risk reconceptualization perspective, the same can be said as firms try to balance their profit with risks. And the same goes for all other actors within the society and economy. Risks apply to all levels internal and external to the organizations, nations and individuals. Endogenous and exogenous risks need to be understood and expanded to also include risks such as microbial risks (Ali and Keil, 2006). Third, the pandemic and recent conflicts have also taught us to be aware and better prepared for times of crisis, including identifying vulnerabilities and managing risks. Any crisis response requires ongoing and rapid improvisation. This involves innovation and rapid actions at all levels from individual to state and development of policies to protect and promote individual, business and national capacity. Glocalization offers an alternative pathway and strategy in balancing risks and rewards for firms, individuals and states. It bolsters locality, reliability and resiliency amid connectivity. The ongoing global supply chain crisis not only elucidates the global production problems, but also the issues surrounding resources, consumption/utilities and management. It further demonstrates the need for reconfiguration and rebalancing of 'value' and 'risk' as well as the role of the state in response to crisis, and their performance assessment. Short-term and long-term approaches need to be considered when responding to an ongoing crisis. Only time will tell how well all these economic actors manage risks and how fast the global economic recovery will unfold, but we should be certain that these risks are not a single phenomenon and that a sound crisis management plan needs to be developed regardless. Thus, economic geographers, as mentioned throughout this chapter, have been well positioned to address these issues, but must develop a more comprehensive and timely approach to understanding the global crises, and the changing nature of production and the economy, as well as risk management and policy implementation. They must actively engage with decision and policy makers to effectively address those issues and prepare for the future.

References

Ali, S.H. and Keil, R. (2006) 'Global cities and the spread of infectious disease: the case of severe acute respiratory syndrome (SARS) in Toronto, Canada', *Urban Studies*, 43(3): 491–509.

Anderson, W.P. (2012) *Economic Geography*, New York: Routledge.

Barnes, T.J., Peck, J., Sheppard, E. and Tickell, A. (eds) (2004) *Reading Economic Geography*, Malden, MA: Blackwell.

Boschma, R. and Martin, R. (eds) (2010) *The Handbook of Evolutionary Economic Geography*, Cheltenham: Edward Elgar.

Bryson, J.R. (2022) 'Reading manufacturing firms: lost geographies of value/risk and the emergence of Jenga Capitalism', in J.R. Bryson, C. Billing, W. Graves and G. Yeung (eds) *A Research Agenda for Manufacturing Industries in the Global Economy*, Cheltenham: Edward Elgar, pp 211–44.

Bryson, J. and Vanchan, V. (2020) 'COVID-19 and alternative conceptualisations of value and risk in GPN research', *Tijdschrift voor Economische en Sociale Geografie*, 111(3): 530–42.

Bryson, J.R., Andres, L., Ersoy, A. and Reardon, L. (eds) (2021) *Living with Pandemics: Places, People and Policy*, Cheltenham: Edward Elgar.

Bryson, J.R., Clark, J. and Vanchan, V. (eds) (2015) *Handbook of Manufacturing Industries in the World Economy*, Cheltenham: Edward Elgar.

Clark, G.L., Feldman, M.P. and Gertler, M.S. (2000) *The Oxford Handbook of Economic Geography*, New York: Oxford University Press.

Clark, J. (2015) 'Hidden in plain sight: the North American optics and photonics industry', in J.R. Bryson, J. Clark and V. Vanchan (eds) *The Handbook of Manufacturing Industries in the World Economy*, Cheltenham: Edward Elgar, pp 245–66.

Coe, N.M. and Yeung, H.W.C. (2015) *Global Production Networks: Theorizing Economic Development in an Interconnected World*, Oxford: Oxford University Press.

Coe, N. M, Kelly, P.F. and Yeung, H.W.C. (2019) *Economic Geography: A Contemporary Introduction* (3rd edn), Hoboken, NJ: Wiley.

Dicken, P. (2003) '"Placing" firms: grounding the debate on the "global" corporation', in J. Peck and H.W.C. Yeung (eds) *Remaking the Global Economy*, Thousand Oaks, CA: Sage, pp 27–44.

Goodman, P.S. (2022) 'A normal supply chain? It's "unlikely" in 2022', New York Times, 1 February. Available from: https://www.nytimes.com/2022/02/01/business/supply-chain-disruption.html [Accessed 15 June 2023].

IMF (International Monetary Fund) (2021) *World Economic Outlook: Recovery During a Pandemic – Health Concerns, Supply Disruptions, and Price Pressures*, October, Washington, DC: IMF.

Kessler, S. (2021) 'Why US firms are reshoring their business', DW AKADEMIE, 12 August. Available from: https://www.dw.com/en/why-us-companies-are-reshoring-their-business/a-60054515 [Accessed 15 June 2023].

Klein, B.P. (2021) '24/7 ports won't fix America's supply-chain deficits', Barron's, 15 October. Available from: https://www.barrons.com/artic les/24-7-ports-wont-fix-americas-supply-chain-deficits-51634308297 [Accessed 15 October 2021].

Laulajainen, R. and Stafford, H.A. (2005) *Corporate Geography: Business Location Principles and Cases*, New York: Springer.

Mackinnon, D. and Cumbers, A. (2011) *An Introduction to Economic Geography: Globalization, Uneven Development and Place* (2nd edn), New York: Routledge.

MacPherson, A. and Vanchan, V. (2010) 'The outsourcing of industrial design by large US manufacturing companies: an exploratory study', *International Regional Science Review*, 33(1): 3–30.

Navellier, L. (2022) 'The global supply chain crisis is about to get worse: here's how you play it', Yahoo! Finance, 28 March. Available from: https://fina nce.yahoo.com/news/global-supply-chain-crisis-worse-132838808.html [Accessed 15 June 2023].

Oak, E. (2021) 'September shows slower import growth; holiday trends emerge', S&P Global Market Intelligence, 11 October. Available from: https://www.spglobal.com/marketintelligence/en/news-insights/ latest-news-headlines/september-shows-slower-import-growth-holiday-tre nds-emerge-66975050 [Accessed 15 October 2021].

Ponte, S. and Sturgeon, T. (2014) 'Explaining governance in global value chains: a modular theory-building effort', *Review of International Political Economy*, 21(1): 195–223.

Poon, J.P.H. (2005) 'Commentary: women in economic geography', *Environment and Planning A: Economy and Space*, 37(5): 765–8.

Reshoring Initiative (2022) 'Companies reshoring', Reshoring Initiative. Available from: https://reshorenow.org/companies-reshoring/ [Accessed 4 April 2022].

Rusten, G. and Bryson, J.R (eds) (2010) *Industrial Design, Competition, and Globalization*, Basingstoke: Palgrave Macmillan.

Sheppard, E. and Barnes, T.J. (eds) (2000) *A Companion to Economic Geography*, Malden, MA: Blackwell.

Stampler, L. (2019) Is Wall Street's Abercrombie and Fitch Love Affair over? *Fortune*. Available from: Abercrombie and Fitch [Accessed 19 January 2022].

Tappe, A. (2021a) 'Biden administration discusses moving to 24/7 operations at Los Angeles and Long Beach ports', CNN Business News, 13 October. Available from: https://edition.cnn.com/2021/10/13/economy/supply- chains-biden-ports/index.html [Accessed 13 October 2021].

Tappe, A. (2021b) 'Biden announced new measures today to help ease the supply chain crisis: here are key things to know', CNN Business News, 13 October. Available from: https://edition.cnn.com/business/live-news/sup ply-chain-issues-biden-10-13-21/index.html [Accessed 13 October 2021].

Taylor, M.J. and Thrift, N. (1982) *The Geography of Multinationals*, London: Croom Helm.

Vanchan, V. (2021) 'Global pandemic disruptions, reconfiguration and glocalization of production networks', in J.R. Bryson, L. Andres, A. Ersoy and L. Reardon (eds) *Living with Pandemics: Places, People and Policy*, Cheltenham: Edward Elgar, pp 195–201.

Vanchan, V. and Bryson, J.R. (2015) 'Design and manufacturing: the competitiveness of American, European and Chinese industrial design companies', in J.R. Bryson, J. Clark and V. Vanchan (eds) *Handbook of Manufacturing Industries in the World Economy*, Cheltenham: Edward Elgar, pp 147–62.

Vanchan, V. and MacPherson, A. (2008a) 'The competitive characteristics of US firms in the industrial design sector: empirical evidence from a national survey', *Competition and Change*, 12(3): 262–80.

Vanchan, V. and MacPherson, A. (2008b) 'The recent growth performance of U.S. firms in the industrial design sector: an exploratory study', *Industry and Innovation*, 15(1): 1–17.

Vanchan, V., Mulhall, R. and Bryson, J.R. (2018) 'Repatriation or reshoring of manufacturing to the U.S. and UK: dynamics and global production networks or from here to there and back again', *Growth and Change*, 49(1): 97–121.

Walcott, S. (2015) 'Finding a future for the U.S. furniture industry', in J.R. Bryson, J. Clark and V. Vanchan (eds) *Handbook of Manufacturing Industries in the World Economy*, Cheltenham: Edward Elgar, pp 206–16.

Weissmann, J. (2021) 'The absolute simplest explanation for America's supply chain woes', Slate, 15 October. Available from: https://slate.com/busin ess/2021/10/supply-chain-shortages-retail-united-states-explained.html [Accessed 15 October 2021].

World Bank Group (2022) *Global Economic Prospects, January 2022*, Washington, DC: World Bank.

Yeung, H.W.C. and Coe, N.M. (2015) 'Toward a dynamic theory of global production networks', *Economic Geography*, 9(1): 29–58.

Zagorsky, J.L. (2022) 'The conversation: are we really facing a resignation crisis?' World Economic Forum, 13 January. Available from: https://www. weforum.org/agenda/2022/01/great-resignation-crisis-quit-rates-perspect ive [Accessed 15 June 2023].

13

Entrepreneurship and Innovation: Who Is Forgotten?

Wenying Fu

Introduction

Innovation and entrepreneurship are the cornerstone of the modern economy, driving the creation of new economic opportunities. As a research area, it has gained traction among economic geographers as a spatially bounded phenomenon and regional event (see Chapters 9 and 16 in this volume). Processes of regional growth have shifted the attention from cost-based competitiveness to innovation-driven productivity (Feldman et al, 2012). The scholarly approach to understanding innovation has been also evolving from linear processes to ones that credit complexity and interactivity across a multiplicity of social actors and spatial scales (Cooke, 2001; Iammarino and McCann, 2015; Gong and Hassink, 2020). On the one hand, the highlight of Jacobian externalities on diversity, in terms of industry, population and cultures, shows the capacity of large metropolises to form new ideas and human capital spillovers (Neffke et al, 2011). Similarly, the massive positive externalities of R&D activities require economies of scale and spatial concentration to counteract the cost of technological spillover (Rodríguez-Pose, 2001). On the other hand, the innovation system approach attributes significance to innovation-supported institutions and regional innovation policy as the vital means through which competitiveness is attained (Cooke, 2001). Under such governance-based ontology as well as increasing attention to the role of nation state (Mayer et al, 2016; Fu and Lim, 2022), it could be postulated that the political economy of innovation favours cities with national and global influences and tends to marginalize the peripheral ones (see also Chapter 22 in this volume).

As a result, stylized facts and key evidence on regional innovation and entrepreneurship are heavily drawn upon a limited number of metropolitan centres, which celebrate the economies of externalities and knowledge spillovers underlying the non-linear processes of innovation. Since the late 2000s, scholars have been injecting incisive thinking into innovation studies by unravelling the unique ways innovation is nurtured, introduced and organized in peripheral regions (Doloreux and Dionne, 2008; Pugh, 2017; Fu and Lim, 2022). In the few innovation studies on peripheral regions, the definition of the periphery is manifold. Geographically speaking, the periphery includes regions and cities that have low population density and/ or are located beyond commuting distance of the primary metropolitan areas (Doloreux and Dionne, 2008). Tödtling and Trippl (2005) differentiate peripheral regions from old industrial regions and metropolitan regions their lack of industrial clusters and support organizations. From a relational economic geographical view, the periphery refers to regions that occupy a structurally weak position vis-à-vis the core regions in terms of value capture, corporate power and national positioning (compare Fu and Lim, 2022). The structurally disadvantaged periphery includes old industrial regions in the North, as well as resource peripheries and developing regions in the South. Economically and politically speaking, the peripheral could be also extended to certain social groups who are disadvantaged due to lack of access to regulatory protection and basic services such as education. As illuminatingly phrased by Iammarino et al (2019: 289), '[D]iversity of capable agents and territories is the most powerful tool for success in the open probability game of innovation and economic creativity' (see also Chapter 9 in this volume). Likewise, Pugh and Dubois (2021) propose an open-ended and integral view towards 'the peripheries' in economic geographical studies. For economic geographers, it is thus fundamental to understand *why* and *how* the boundary, in both spatial and social terms, of the periphery evolves and reconfigures within the contemporary innovation-driven capitalism.

Studies on learning economy approach (Asheim and Coenen, 2005), inspired by the contemporary turn of flexibly accumulated capitalism which takes knowledge as the crucial input, contend that small and medium-sized enterprises (SMEs) and their constituent networks are the vital organisms of knowledge production and innovation dissemination. These further attest to the vitality of numerous SME-based clusters in both developing and developed regions, participating actively in pushing forward the innovation boundaries of global capitalism. Regardless, evidence still suggests that large corporations play a key role as the lead firms and nodal network partners in the global production networks (Yeung and Coe, 2015), albeit they have to coordinate with strategic subcontractors and first-tier suppliers in improving, applying and disseminating the innovations. The inquiry on the key actors who are capable of leading technological innovation bears significant geographical implication. Does the dominance of large corporations over the SMEs indicate an obstinate value-dependence of the specialized clusters in the periphery? In a globalized context, is the development of the peripheral regions only tentative, meaning that they are subject to rounds of exploitation by the relentless expansion of highly mobile large capitalists? Indeed, the global cities thesis proposed by Sassen (1991) presciently captures the enlarging geographical divide between the city-regions with technological dominance, network power and market influence, and those without.

While acknowledging the rationale for research focusing on core regions and mainstream actors, this chapter critically examines the notion of spatial peripherality and social marginality in the process of innovation-driven capitalism. The fundamental contention is that innovation of the 'forgotten' – with its unique characters and organization for the 'creative destruction' process – deserves closer scrutiny for the sake of uneven geographical development and spatial injustice in the course of capitalist advancement. The chapter will focus on three 'forgotten' places and social groups that received insufficient attention in mainstream innovation studies, namely the peripheral regions, migrant entrepreneurs, and participants in the informal sector (see also Chapter 11 in this volume). It raises the question: whether and to which extent do these overlooked socio-spatial processes in the 'forgotten' corners shape the dynamics of contemporary innovation-driven capitalism?

Deciphering the innovation dynamics of the peripheral regions

To facilitate innovation processes, most peripheral regions face formidable barriers to development, ranging from limited market, inferior transport connection, low density of business networks and insufficient absorptive capacity, to a brain drain of talents and population ageing (Shearmur and Doloreux, 2016; Pugh, 2017; Iammarino et al, 2019).

The SMEs in peripheral regions, often specializing in traditional industries, differ fundamentally from their counterparts in large metropolitan areas of advanced economies which features high-growth start-up potential. Notably, SMEs in the core regions are deeply embedded into the entrepreneurial ecosystem dominated by lead firms, which is premised upon a sophisticated set of soft infrastructures including venture capital and legalized acquisition processes (see the case of Silicon Valley in Saxenian, 2002). The Silicon Valley model of entrepreneurship is indeed subject to increasing criticism. Over time, it is incapable of solving – or even is becoming part of the causes – for the most intractable issues in the contemporary economic landscape, namely the stagnant rate of income boost of 'the middle' and an escalating enlargement of social disparities even within their embedded regions (Florida and Mellander, 2016; Audretsch, 2021).

Au contraire, organization of SMEs in the peripheral regions are characterized by strong place-based relational assets and territorial embeddedness. One typical example is the *Mittelstand* in Germany, often family-owned SMEs located in rural or peripheral regions, featuring a high level of place-based social responsibility and commitment (Pahnke and Welter, 2019). Note that the local orientation does not necessarily point to lower rate of innovation, depending on how innovation is evaluated, as the *Mittelstand* in Germany are the hidden champions that enable the disruptive technological change in the production process rather than the visible innovative products in Silicon Valley (Pahnke and Welter, 2019).

There is also opposing evidence suggesting that peripheral regions, instead of being self-contained and locally bounded, benefit notably from exogenous knowledge and translocal connections. Studies found that firms in peripheral regions are more inclined to interact with distant partners than firms in the core regions (Lagendijk and Lorentzen, 2007; Grillitsch and Nilsson, 2015). Atta-Owusu (2019) points out the role of academics' collaboration activities as the major channel of knowledge transfer to peripheral regions. The notion of 'temporary cluster', developed by Maskell et al (2006), highlights the practices of firms in peripheral regions to access non-local knowledge via trade shows. In other words, the innovation dynamics in the peripheral regions depends crucially on its capacities to exploit extra-local networks (Trippl et al, 2018), and it has foregrounded the heterogenous place contexts of peripheral regions as an integrative part of global knowledge systems. Regardless of the positive views that innovation could still occur in these regions, connectivity in the periphery implies embedded power-relations in the spatial configurations of innovation. In the studies on 'temporary clusters', for instance, the knowledge access is mediated by the organizers as the market intermediaries, defining the scopes of exhibitors and visitors and facilitating/restraining certain types of knowledge learning (Rinallo and Golfetto, 2011).

Evidence further suggests that, if the peripheral regions already have a certain knowledge base, innovation potentials could be realized under a public institution-led approach (Doloreux and Dionne, 2008). Hence, the potential 'windows of opportunity' in the peripheral regions are strongly moderated through the political economy of both global capitalism and state structure. For example, Doloreux and Dione's (2008: 280) analysis on the small regional innovation system in La Pocatière, Canada, points out that institutional entrepreneurship is fundamental in enabling the momentum through 'conscious, deliberate and mobilizing' strategies. In this case, peripheral innovation systems go beyond the conventional notion of the firm network, but rather hinge upon the cross-scalar institutional network through which the agency of regional-based actors is enabled (Dawley et al, 2015). Meanwhile, agency is also constituted and constrained by the larger-scale structure and geographical forces. Fu and Lim (2022), through their study on a peripheral city's coupling process to global production networks (GPNs) in China, contends that the regional actors' ability to engage in strategic coupling for local industrial upgrading are constituted by the national structure in the Chinese context. Of particular significance in this case is the relatively passive role of the local government in the peripheral city in the initial coupling process, which reflects the constraining effects of a highly unequal and spatially selective approach to economic development across China. In parallel with the state structural constraints are the state structural opportunities upon which regional actors strategically act to foster an open-ended process of GPN coupling.

Interestingly in the studies of innovation dynamics of the periphery, state apparatus stands out as the key promoter for innovation. This spans from the territorially systemic approach to public-led efforts in organizing innovation in the Global North, to the pronounced state interventions in the Southern nations for technological catching-up through the anchorage of flagship transnational firms by pecuniarily subsidizing or institutionally benefiting foreign investment (Murphy, 2019). Recent studies on the role of the state have questioned the viability of neoliberal critique in the Southern context because the state has been growing its capacity in controlling capital to determine the ways of organizing the economy – one that could conflict, overlap or coalesce with the profit maximization rationale in neoliberal governance (Parnell and Robinson, 2012). Following this, the spatial outcome of state involvement is mixed. On the one hand, the state support proves to be pivotal for capacity building and absorption of knowledge in the peripheries across many Southern nations (Habiyaremye et al, 2020). The state institutions and national strategies, on the other hand, sometimes even create new forms of spatial inequality by framing and maintaining discernible institutional 'borders' between places within state space (Berndt, 2013). While it reflects how the opportunities of the periphery to catch up are constitutive of the state structures, it raises the question as to what extent and in what manner state intervention is justified and effective in terms of reducing the spatial imbalance in innovation dynamics.

Innovation and entrepreneurship on the move

The enlargement of urban–rural divide and rising spatial inequality, both in the Global North and the Global South, has created a massive flow of rural–urban/interregional migration seeking economic opportunities and social mobility in metropolitan core regions (Meng, 2011; Fu, 2020). Indeed, migration is another channel, vis-à-vis the spatial redistribution of income, through which socio-economic inequality may be reduced. However, the geographical migration to more economically developed regions per se does not automatically guarantee asset accumulation by the poor; rather, it is imperative to inquire whether the migrants have been granted equal opportunities and resources to participate in the innovation–driven capitalist production, including high value-added occupations or opportunity-driven entrepreneurial activities, in the metropolitan cores.

Migrants are often related to the push side of entrepreneurial motives, partly owing to their inferior social position in the host country or region. It is hence postulated by previous studies that migrants have a proclivity towards self-employment, as they are excluded or given limited access to the host labour market. Bonacich's (1973) theory of middleman minorities is the most influential theory in the study of self-employment among immigrant minorities. She explains the persistence of small trade and commerce businesses through ethnic ties, family labour and resistance to integrate. It is implied that social deprivation and marginality serves as a decisive factor in their employment choice and pushes them towards starting their own, often small and narrowly oriented, businesses. Exclusive social engagement within their own ethnic community also creates considerable levels of social capital, following which trust has been firmly established to lubricate transactions of 'ethnic business'.

Alongside a long-standing body of literature on migrant entrepreneurs that focuses on their reliance on ethnicity-based social networks (see Wang 2012 for synthetic and critical review), economic geographers have been paying increasing attention to the migrants' openness to value-enhancing experiences and opportunity-driven entrepreneurship (Martynovich, 2017; Fu, 2020). Saxenian's (2002) seminal study on the Asian engineers in Silicon Valley has challenged the ethnicity-bounded assumption by revealing the economic contributions of Asian immigrants as both entrepreneurs and trade facilitators. Indeed, migrants are increasingly viewed as the source of regional economic revitalization and social restructuring (Assudani, 2009). In an ever-globalizing era, knowledge and network about the outside world help the immigrant entrepreneurs to grasp niche market opportunities. There are numerous examples of immigrant businesses that reach far beyond ethnic communities, such as Japanese immigrants developing the Brazilian coffee and cotton industries (Makabe, 1981), Chinese immigrants contributing to the industrialization of South-East Asian economies (Hamilton, 1996), and Taiwanese- and Indian-run businesses constituting over a quarter of high-growth firms in Silicon Valley (Saxenian, 2002). Personal success stories like the Swatch founder, a Lebanese immigrant in Switzerland, and one of Korea's biggest conglomerates, Lotte Corporation, started up by a Korean immigrant in Japan, well illustrate the entrepreneurialism of migrants.

The push side of migrant entrepreneurship, namely inadequate assimilation into and embeddedness within the host region, and its pull side, namely the openness to adventurous experiences, are two sides of the same coin. The social hierarchies and background of economic agents, as suggested by the notion of enclosed immigrant businesses, means that the specific set of regional advantages is asymmetric within a geography-bounded economic system, access to which embodies a social filtering process for migrant entrepreneurs. The finding by Fu (2020), that opportunity-driven entrepreneurship among migrants is driven by extra-local connectedness to greater market areas – compared to the endogenous exploitation of a localized firm network by local entrepreneurs – further implies a disconnection between endogenous and exogenous entrepreneurial and innovative resources. As such, it engenders a dual structure of innovation and entrepreneurial opportunities not only between places but also within place, creating a form of otherness that prevails in everyday economic practices. Furthermore, the fact that many migrants seek self-employed opportunities in the urban informal sector as a long-term livelihood strategy (Meng, 2011) exacerbates the layered structures of opportunities within megacities (see also Chapter 23 in this volume). The next section will turn to this essential point.

Entrepreneurship embodied through informal sector

In the Global South, with insufficient public finances and inferior formal governance structures (Nzeadibe and Anyadike, 2010), informality is a prevailing feature in many industrial sectors as well as the social service sector. The informal sector is defined by Portes and Böröcz (1988: 17) as 'all productive and distributive income earning activities which take place outside the scope of public regulation on the macrosocietal level'. Essentially, informality creates spaces for the 'others' that are discounted or discriminated against by the formal institutions, including but not limited to the migrants, to seek livelihood and growth opportunities.

Understanding the causes and outcomes of uneven innovation-driven capitalism demands a deep investigation into the informal sectors. Central to this research agenda is the negation of a dualist lens that separates and marginalizes the informal sector from the formal economy (see Bacchetta et al, 2009). Instead, this chapter argues that activities in informal sector embodies opportunity-driven entrepreneurship, and meanwhile constitutes reproduction of structural inequality orchestrated by the formal sectors. First, the informal sector has notable implications for development in terms of encouraging knowledge accumulation as well as nurturing innovative economic and social practices (Muchie et al, 2016). Indeed, activities in the informal sector often embody opportunity-driven entrepreneurship and innovation potentials in broader terms. More importantly, the informal sector is resilient because it is able to mutate and transform to accommodate formality if they see opportunities in it (see Keane and Zhao, 2012 for analysis of the *shanzhai* (imitation or counterfit) mobile producers in Guangdong, China).

While the entrepreneurship side of informality reflects the agency of the grassroots actors, it is meanwhile constituted by the encompassing processes of capitalism (Phillips, 2011; Yusuff, 2011). This structuralist perspective regards informality as a form of labour utilization that the global capitalist elites *consciously* establish to exploit the deficient institutions and lax labour regulation primarily in the developing countries. Specifically, Phillips (2011: 380) argues that 'informality is created and exploited within GPNs in a top-down manner – that is, by capital, firms, employers and states'. This suggests that the formal sector is trying to manoeuvre the features – low cost and flexibility – in informality to reinforce its powerful positions. Take e-waste sector as an example, Corwin (2020) points out that the narratives to conflate environmental pollution with informal labour is constructed to secure corporate e-waste markets. A typical case in e-waste is the regulatory measure of 'extended producer responsibility' (EPR), which proves to be problematic depending on the manner of its implementation (Kojima et al, 2009). Often, these EPR projects are highly subsidized by the state, severely skewing the level playing field between large corporates in the formal sector and small business operators in the informal one. In China, for instance, the government subsidized 90 per cent of the fund for EPR and it is expected that the fund will grow into deficit of $33 billion from 2012 to 2030 (Gu et al, 2017). Therefore, it could be expected that the formal industrial sector – for example, the large recycling enterprises – will still have to negotiate and exploit the flexible informal sector when the subsidy programme wanes. In essence, the strong profit orientation of global corporates acts as the 'pull' factor, while the state, with its excessive regulation and distributive *injustice*, acts as the 'push' factor that underlines the flourishing informal sector in the Global South.

Understanding the informal sector from a non-dualist perspective helps advance innovation studies in two aspects. First, the institutional turn in economic geography conceptualizes 'institutional thickness' as the cornerstone in securing external economies for dynamic innovations (Amin and Thrift, 1994), which foregrounds the rationale of systemic innovation supported by the establishment of formal organizations and regulations. However, it is under-theorized within the context of the Global South whereby formal institutional set-up is far from mature and stable, and a great deal of interaction and learning occur in the informal setting facilitated by social norms, values, cultures and ethnicity (Fu et al, 2013). In the Western school of regional innovation studies, informal institutions are situated as lubricants to facilitate the network functioning of the 'thick' formal organizations (see the notion of localized learning and proximity revisited by Malmberg and Maskell, 2006), while the tensions, interdependence and transition between formal and informal institutions are overlooked in the exploitation of new market and technological opportunities. As argued earlier, the grassroots forces challenge existing formal institutions as well as the business models of established corporates (for example, the *shanzhai* mobile producers). Therefore, the informal sector is worthy of further investigation as to how politico-economic processes working at multiple scales underpin the state's manipulative in/exclusion of the marginalized groups into the economy, and concomitantly how the changing boundaries between these two interfaces influences the regional innovation dynamics in a dialectical manner.

Second, the significance of the informal sector in regional innovation, not least within emerging and developing economies, deserves closer investigation with regard to the ways through which it is integrated with global capitalism. On one hand, the conscious exploitation of sectors and actors operating within the fuzzy boundaries of formality and informality provide sufficient surplus value to sustain the costly R&D functions in the developed economies. On the other hand, the informal sector also creates creative solutions and competitive dynamics that feed into the relentless round of capitalist accumulation.

Conclusion

Innovation and entrepreneurship constitute the indispensable ingredients in contemporary capitalism, yet a large proportion occurs within the bulk 'iceberg' of economy hidden under the water. In essence, it is the numerous small and medium-sized business operating in the peripheral regions, in the immigrant entrepreneurial communities, and in the Southern informal sector that sustain *and* confront the mainstream innovation, which is advocated by Schumpeter (1942) as the large corporate monopoly that the society has to pay for innovation. For the three peripheral groups under discussion in this chapter, the desires to link up with the outside world, both in geographical and societal terms, exist in parallel with strong commitment to their own localities and communities characterized by the everyday struggle of selection and resistance to mainstream capitalist practices (Gibson-Graham, 2008; see also Chapter 4 in this volume). This could come in the form of dependence/interdependence as well as reciprocity/tension, which is subject to technological cycles, domestic policy narratives and geopolitical complexities. Hence, the investigation of the innovation dynamics within the *peripheral capitalism* transcend the neoliberal leitmotif, and comes down to a deeper issue of contested political economy and the power struggle of everyday practices.

Inherent paradox within the peripheral capitalism is epitomized by high levels of fluctuation and precarity, but meanwhile manifesting agility and flexibility that are pressured by external markets and the institutional environment. However, the resilience of the peripherals should not be treated as a desired outcome, as the state and corporate regulatory forces from the top down will probably actively (re)produce and exploit this agility and precarity. In this sense, economic geographers should be alert to capturing the potential livelihood and developmental outcomes that accompany the 'heroic' exploitation of institutional and market opportunities by the peripheral regions and actors existing as the 'forgotten' corners from the mainstream capitalist economy.

References

Amin, A. and Thrift, N. (1994) 'Living in the global', in A. Amin and N. Thrift (eds) *Globalization, Institutions, and Regional Development in Europe*, Oxford: Oxford University Press, pp 1–19.

Asheim, B.T. and Coenen, L. (2005) 'Knowledge bases and regional innovation systems: comparing Nordic clusters', *Research Policy*, 34(8): 1173–90.

Assudani, R.H. (2009) 'Ethnic entrepreneurship: the distinct role of ties', *Journal of Small Business and Entrepreneurship*, 22(2): 197–205.

Atta-Owusu, K. (2019) 'Oasis in the desert? Bridging academics' collaboration activities as a conduit for global knowledge flows to peripheral regions', *Regional Studies, Regional Science*, 6(1): 265–80.

Audretsch, D.B. (2021) 'Have we oversold the Silicon Valley model of entrepreneurship?', *Small Business Economics*, 56(2): 849–56.

Bacchetta, M., Ernst, E. and Bustamante, J.P. (2009) *Globalization and Informal Jobs in Developing Countries*, Geneva: International Labour Organization and World Trade Organization.

Berndt, C. (2013) 'Assembling market b/orders: violence, dispossession, and economic development in Ciudad Juárez, Mexico', *Environment and Planning A: Economy and Space*, 45(11): 2646–62.

Bonacich, E. (1973) 'A theory of middleman minorities', *American Sociological Review*, 38(5): 583–94.

Cooke, P. (2001) 'Regional innovation systems, clusters, and the knowledge economy', *Industrial and Corporate Change*, 10(4): 945–74.

Corwin, J. (2020) 'Between toxics and gold: devaluing informal labor in the global urban mine', *Capitalism Nature Socialism*, 31(4): 106–23.

Dawley, S., MacKinnon, D., Cumbers, A. and Pike, A. (2015) 'Policy activism and regional path creation: the promotion of offshore wind in North East England and Scotland', *Cambridge Journal Regions, Economy and Society*, 8(2): 257–72.

Doloreux, D. and Dionne, S. (2008) 'Is regional innovation system development possible in peripheral regions? Some evidence from the case of La Pocatière, Canada', *Entrepreneurship and Regional Development*, 20(3): 259–83.

Feldman, M.P., Link, A.N. and Siegel, D.S. (2012) *The Economics of Science and Technology: An Overview of Initiatives to Foster Innovation, Entrepreneurship, and Economic Growth*, New York: Springer.

Florida, R. and Mellander, C. (2016) 'The geography of inequality: difference and determinants of wage and income inequality across US metros', *Regional Studies*, 50(1): 79–92.

Fu, W. (2020) 'Spatial mobility and opportunity-driven entrepreneurship: the evidence from China labor-force dynamics survey', *Journal of Technology Transfer*, 45(5): 1324–42.

Fu, W. and Lim, K.F. (2022) 'The constitutive role of state structures in strategic coupling: on the formation and evolution of Sino–German production networks in Jieyang, China', *Economic Geography*, 98(1): 25–48.

Fu, W., Revilla Diez J. and Schiller, D. (2013) 'Interactive learning, informal networks and innovation: evidence from electronics firm survey in the Pearl River Delta, China', *Research Policy*, 42(3): 635–46.

Gibson-Graham, J.K. (2008) 'Diverse economies: performative practices for "other worlds"', *Progress in Human Geography*, 32(5): 613–32.

Gong, H. and Hassink, R. (2020) 'Context sensitivity and economic-geographic (re)theorising', *Cambridge Journal of Regions, Economy and Society*, 13(3): 475–90.

Grillitsch, M. and Nilsson, M. (2015) 'Innovation in peripheral regions: do collaborations compensate for a lack of local knowledge spillovers?', *Annals of Regional Science*, 54(1): 299–321.

Gu, Y., Wu, Y., Xu, M., Wang, H. and Zuo, T. (2017) 'To realize better extended producer responsibility: redesign of WEEE fund mode in China', *Journal of Cleaner Production*, 164: 347–56.

Habiyaremye, A., Kruss, G. and Booyens, I. (2020) 'Innovation for inclusive rural transformation: the role of the state', *Innovation and Development*, 10(2): 155–68.

Hamilton, G.G. (1996) 'The organizational foundations of western and Chinese commerce: a historical and comparative analysis', in G.G. Hamilton (ed) *Asian Business Networks*, Berlin: de Gruyter, pp 43–57.

Iammarino, S. and McCann, P. (2015) 'Multinational enterprises innovation networks and the role of cities', in D. Archibugi and A. Filippetti (eds) *The Handbook of Global Science, Technology, and Innovation*, Chichester: Wiley, pp 290–312.

Iammarino, S., Rodríguez-Pose, A. and Storper, M. (2019) 'Regional inequality in Europe: evidence, theory and policy implications', *Journal of Economic Geography*, 19(2): 273–98.

Keane, M. and Zhao, E.J. (2012) 'Renegades on the frontier of innovation: the *Shanzai* grassroots communities of Shenzhen in China's creative economy', *Eurasian Geography and Economics*, 53(2): 216–30.

Kojima, M., Yoshida, A. and Sasaki, S. (2009) 'Difficulties in applying extended producer responsibility policies in developing countries: case studies in e-waste recycling in China and Thailand', *Journal of Material Cycles and Waste Management*, 11(3): 263–9.

Lagendijk, A. and Lorentzen, A. (2007) 'Proximity, knowledge and innovation in peripheral regions: on the intersection between geographical and organizational proximity', *European Planning Studies*, 15(4): 457–66.

Makabe, T. (1981) 'The theory of the split labor market: a comparison of the Japanese experience in Brazil and Canada', *Social Forces*, 59(3): 786–809.

Malmberg, A. and Maskell, P. (2006) 'Localised learning revisited', *Growth and Change*, 37(1): 1–18.

Martynovich, M. (2017) 'The role of local embeddedness and non-local knowledge in entrepreneurial activity', *Small Business Economics*, 49(4): 741–62.

Maskell, P., Bathelt, H. and Malmberg, A. (2006) 'Building global knowledge pipelines: the role of temporary clusters', *European Planning Studies*, 14(8): 997–1013.

Mayer, H., Sager, F., Kaufmann, D. and Warland, M. (2016) 'Capital city dynamics: linking regional innovation systems, locational policies and policy regimes', *Cities*, 51: 11–20.

Meng, X. (2011) 'The informal sector and rural–urban migration: a Chinese case study', *Asian Economic Journal*, 15(1): 71–89.

Muchie, M., Bhaduri, S., Baskaran, A. and Sheikh, F.A. (eds) (2016) *Informal Sector Innovation: Insights from the Global South*, Abingdon: Routledge.

Murphy, J.T. (2019) 'Global production network dis/articulations in Zanzibar: practices and conjunctures of exclusionary development in the tourism industry', *Journal of Economic Geography*, 19(4): 943–71.

Neffke, F., Henning, M. and Boschma, R. (2011) 'How do regions diversify over time? Industry relatedness and the development of new growth paths in regions', *Economic Geography*, 87(3): 237–65.

Nzeadibe, T.C. and Anyadike, R.N.C. (2010) 'Solid waste governance innovations: an appraisal of recent developments in the informal sector niche in urban Nigeria', *Geography Compass*, 4(9): 1284–96.

Pahnke, A. and Welter, F. (2019) 'The German Mittelstand: antithesis to Silicon Valley entrepreneurship?', *Small Business Economics*, 52(2): 345–58.

Parnell, S. and Robinson, J. (2012) '(Re)theorizing cities from the Global South: looking beyond neoliberalism', *Urban Geography*, 33(4): 593–617.

Phillips, N. (2011) 'Informality, global production networks and the dynamics of "adverse incorporation"', *Global Networks*, 11(3): 380–97.

Portes, A. and Böröcz, J. (1988) 'The informal sector under capitalism and state socialism: a preliminary comparison', *Social Justice*, 15(3/4): 17–28.

Pugh, R. (2017) 'Universities and economic development in lagging regions: "triple helix" policy in Wales', *Regional Studies*, 51(7): 982–93.

Pugh, R. and Dubois, A. (2021) 'Peripheries within economic geography: four "problems" and the road ahead of us', *Journal of Rural Studies*, 87: 267–75.

Rinallo, D. and Golfetto, F. (2011) 'Exploring the knowledge strategies of temporary cluster organizers: a longitudinal study of the EU fabric industry trade shows (1986–2006)', *Economic Geography*, 87(4): 453–76.

Rodríguez-Pose, A. (2001) 'Is R&D investment in lagging areas of Europe worthwhile? Theory and empirical evidence', *Papers in Regional Science*, 80(3): 275–95.

Sassen, S. (1991) *The Global City: New York, London, Tokyo*, Princeton, NJ: Princeton University Press.

Saxenian, A. (2002) 'Silicon Valley's new immigrant high-growth entrepreneurs', *Economic Development Quarterly*, 16(1): 20–31.

Schumpeter, J. (1942) *Capitalism, Socialism and Democracy*, New York: Harper.

Shearmur, R. and Doloreux, D. (2016) 'How open innovation processes vary between urban and remote environments: slow innovators, market-sourced information and frequency of interaction', *Entrepreneurship and Regional Development*, 28(5/6): 337–57.

Tödtling, F. and Trippl, M. (2005) 'One size fits all? Towards a differentiated regional innovation policy approach', *Research Policy*, 34(8): 1203–19.

Trippl, M., Grillitsch, M. and Isaksen, A. (2018) 'Exogenous sources of regional industrial change: attraction and absorption of non-local knowledge for new path development', *Progress in Human Geography*, 42(5): 687–705.

Wang, Q. (2012) 'Ethnic entrepreneurship studies in geography: a review', *Geography Compass*, 6(4): 227–40.

Yeung, H.W.C. and Coe, N.M. (2015) 'Toward a dynamic theory of global production networks', *Economic Geography*, 91(1): 29–58.

Yusuff, O.S. (2011) 'A theoretical analysis of the concept of informal economy and informality in developing countries', *European Journal of Social Sciences*, 20(4): 624–36.

14

Consumption: Advancing Postcolonial Perspectives from the Global South

Luiza Sarayed-Din and Alex Hughes

Introduction

Studies of spaces of consumption have long been positioned at the intersection of economic and cultural geography, embracing the interplay between industry and commerce and the lifeworlds through which goods and services are purchased, used and experienced. Since the 1990s we have witnessed the development of multidisciplinary and critical consumption studies through a period of neoliberalization when the global economy has been significantly market led (see Chapter 12 in this volume). Geographical studies of consumption have been a part of this field, exploring the spaces through which goods and services are marketed, purchased and incorporated into daily life, as well as addressing the practices and spaces of disposal and discard (Crewe, 2011; Mansvelt, 2014; Meah and Jackson, 2017). Economic geographers have played a role in mapping and conceptualizing the commodity chains linking consumers with local, regional and global systems of production, as well as understanding landscapes of retail and household economies (Mansvelt, 2014; Hall, 2015; Lane and Mansvelt, 2020).

Spaces of consumption in the Global North have tended until recently to be centre stage in geographies of consumption, and Western concepts and practices have dominated analysis (Crang and Hughes, 2015). This chapter seeks to unsettle dominant narratives of consumption driven by Western framings. We suggest that perspectives of postcolonial economy can help to foreground more inclusive and diverse geographies of consumption and theorization from Global South settings. To demonstrate this, we take food as our focus and examine changing discourses of food consumption in Brazil. We concentrate on food justice discourses emerging during the 12 years of left-wing government from 2003. With 24.7 per cent of the population living in poverty (IBGE, 2020) and 10.3 million people affected by hunger and malnutrition (IBGE, 2020), Brazil is usually portrayed in terms of its long history of hunger when discussing food consumption. However, the intention here is to use a postcolonial lens to broaden the analysis of domestic food consumption in Brazil, revealing its plural contingencies and histories.

Plural perspectives on geographies of consumption

Social science research has developed critical perspectives on consumption as material culture (Miller, 1998; Gregson and Crewe, 2003), with food featuring prominently (Mansvelt, 2014; Jackson, 2015). In terms of research into consumer practices, Evans (2019) has followed the work of sociologist Alan Warde in defining the key 'moments' of consumption as acquisition, appropriation and appreciation, adding devaluation, divestment and disposal to capture waste, re-use and recycling (see also Holmes and Ehgartner, 2020). Regarding discourses shaping these moments and practices, influences of the state, business and civil society – incorporating issues of safety, quality, sustainability, health and lifestyle – are addressed in the literature (Liu et al, 2019).

Geographical research has focused on the spaces through which food, as an essential material resource with cultural significance, is traded, purchased and embedded in everyday life. Critical engagement with the implications of globalizing food supply chains and retail foreign direct investment for consumers and consumption has been an important part of this research, considering 'threats' to traditional market formats (Coe and Wrigley, 2007), implications for food access through the creation of food deserts (Del Casino, 2015; Peyton et al, 2015), changing food cultures (Cook et al, 2008), and implications for health including food safety scares (Gong and Jackson, 2012; Jackson, 2015) and food insecurity (Del Casino, 2015; Battersby and Crush, 2016). Western framings of health, regulation and the commercial labelling of food products can often frame analysis (Guthman, 2013; Colls and Evans, 2014).

A complementary field of geographical research concerns the ethics and politics of consumption, focusing on the social and environmental consequences of consumers' purchasing choices. The 'responsibilization' of consumers has been argued to arise from a neoliberal context where politics are often practised through the market (Bryant and Goodman, 2004; Barnett et al, 2011; Evans et al, 2017). Examples of explicit forms of ethical consumption are afforded by markets for fair trade foods and beverages, organic produce and locally produced goods (Guthman, 2002; Slocum, 2007; Clarke et al, 2008; Barnett et al, 2011). However, Agyeman and McEntee (2014), discussing a wider food justice movement, are critical of such ethical initiatives and solutions to food access problems that are essentially routed through the market. Rather, they argue for a food justice movement more deeply interrogating 'the insidious causes [of food injustice], which are rooted in the commodification of food and deregulation of the marketplace' (Agyeman and McEntee, 2014: 217). This demands not only a critique of consumption's part in the circuits of capital and the practice of 'consumer choice' bound up in neoliberalization, but also a conceptualization of food and consumption beyond Western models of capitalism and neoliberalization.

Over time critical geographical research on food consumption has broadened to consider consumption discourses and practices in a diverse range of settings. See, for example, research on urban China (Liu et al, 2019; Chen and Liu, 2022), studies of ethical food consumption in Brazil and Chile (Ariztia et al, 2016) and engagement with ordinary ethical consumption in South Africa (McEwan et al, 2015). Some of this literature has pointed out that ethical consumption beyond the Global North can be less about a care for distant others in global supply chains shaped by colonial pasts, and rather more about 'ordinary consumption with ethical effects' (Gregson and Ferdous, 2015: 244; Ariztia et al, 2016).

We draw inspiration from economic geography engaging postcolonial critique to unsettle perspectives of food consumption dominated by insights from the Global North and Western frames of reference. Pollard et al (2009, 2011) propose a fruitful dialogue between economic geography and postcolonial perspectives, understanding the 'postcolonial' as 'a political, anti-colonial sensibility and a suite of theoretical approaches that seek to disrupt and contest hegemonic Western ways of knowing, writing and seeing the world' (Pollard et al, 2011: 1–2). They identify three helpful dimensions of a postcolonial economic geography. First, they call for theorization of the economic 'as plural, contested, and above all situated' (Pollard et al, 2011: 3). Second, they argue for a cultural economy perspective acknowledging the intertwining of lifeworlds and resource production and distribution. And third, they call for knowledge production avoiding universalizing economic knowledges. For geographies of consumption, this means acknowledging the ways in which landscapes and practices of consumption have so often been read through Western conceptual framings, including production network and value chain theories (Gereffi et al, 2005; Coe, 2021) and notions of neoliberal responsibility (Barnett et al, 2011). It means researching and theorizing consumption from places in the Global South as well as North and engaging with the histories of consumption in those places (see Wilson, 2013).

Domestic food consumption in Brazil

Brazil is a country with continental dimensions and a large variety of food traditions linked to its different regions and histories. Brazil is also the result of different encounters and confrontations. Its food traditions are marked by Indigenous cultures, a long Portuguese colonial past based on African slaves, and impacts of Italian, German, Japanese and other immigration in the 19th and 20th centuries. However, and conscious of the reductionism of any grouping process, certain common features and traditions related to food are possible to identify as a contemporary Brazilian way of eating. The national Household Budget Survey (Pesquisa de Orçamentos Familiares) conducted between May 2008 and May 2009 by the Brazilian Institute of Geography and Statistics (IBGE; Instituto Brasileiro de Geografia e Estatística) identified that 69.5 per cent of what a typical Brazilian consumer eats is natural or minimally processed food (IBGE, 2011). With a sample of 30,000 Brazilians covering all regions of the country, the Household Budget Survey has indicated that almost a quarter of the population's energy intake derives from a combination of rice and beans, followed by meats, cassava, fruits, fish and vegetables. They have also revealed that more than 40 million Brazilians have most of their diet (85 per cent) based on natural or minimally processed food.

However, the same survey indicated that 21.5 per cent of Brazilian energy intake is provided by ultra-processed food and 9 per cent by processed food. Based on these data, Brazilian scientists from the Centre for Epidemiological Research in Nutrition and Health (NUPENS) of the University of São Paulo highlighted the impact of ultra-processed food consumption on both certain diseases and the environment (IBGE, 2020). They also argued that particular types of food processing have implications for modes of production and environmental impact. Oliveira and Amparo-Santos (2018: 213) argue that the manufacture of ultra-processed food requires 'intensive animal production systems and extensive monoculture to supply inputs such as soyabeans and corn …, producing, in general, degradation and environmental pollution, reduction of biodiversity and jeopardizing water reserves, energy and other natural resources'.

This context of domestic food consumption in Brazil thus reveals certain supply chain challenges in the country. Focusing on food production and making use of data from the First Agricultural Census of 2006, the government argued that 75 per cent of what Brazilians eat is produced by family farming in the country. Based on the everyday food of Brazilians, already described, the importance of family farming is therefore evident, since it is responsible for the production of 69.6 per cent of beans, 83.2 per cent of cassava (*mandioca*) and 33.1 per cent of the rice consumed in the country (IBGE, 2009). Conversely, representing 24.3 per cent of GDP (CEPEA, 2021) and making

Brazil a leading country in agricultural commodities export, agribusiness is the agricultural model receiving greatest investment (financially and politically) in Brazil. Based on monoculture, intense use of mechanization, irrigation and industrial inputs, and driven by the international market, agribusiness receives 75 per cent of the total government agricultural incentives. Moreover, while 25 per cent of the agricultural area of Brazil is occupied by 84.4 per cent of the agricultural establishments dedicated to family farming, the other 75 per cent of the land is dominated by only 15.6 per cent of non-family/employer farming businesses (IBGE, 2009).

This blend of value chains characterized by local smallholder and 'big capital' agribusiness, with a continuing emphasis on the importance of the smallholder, is important for understanding the food systems shaping Brazilian domestic food consumption. Drawing on Pollard et al's (2011) call for a cultural economy perspective acknowledging the intertwining of lifeworlds and resource production and distribution, the description of such complex food systems is important for understanding the structural inequalities and cultures of consumption expressed in different areas of the country. This includes the agricultural model most financially supported, which in the case of Brazilian agribusiness represents the old oligarchies historically owning the land (*latifundia*) and holding power since colonial times.

We shed light next on the influential food consumption discourses emerging from the specific sociopolitical and economic context in Brazil, which connect to the values of these different agricultural models (agribusiness and family farming). We focus specifically on the processes through which two editions of the influential *Dietary Guidelines for the Brazilian Population* (DGBP) were developed. Exploring the values of both editions of the DGBP as an emblematic case, the next section briefly presents the *policies* and *models* that have shaped food production, and consequently consumption, in Brazil in the last 20 years.

Dietary Guidelines for the Brazilian Population

The DGBP is a federal government document for the promotion of healthy and adequate food, first published in 2006 and later revised in 2014. The two editions reflect the contingencies and influences of different discourses of food consumption: the first edition is based on a hegemonic nutritional epidemiological discourse and the second focused on the sociocultural aspects of eating (Oliveira and Amparo-Santos, 2018).

The first edition of the DGBP was published in 2006 as a deliverable of the first term of the left-wing President Lula. Elected to the presidential chair for the first time in 2003, the Working Party incorporated representatives of social movements and academia within the government, who occupied both ministerial positions and seats on various participatory councils. Responsible for driving the discussion of food as a development axis of the government, the National Council for Food and Nutritional Security (CONSEA) was reactivated in 2003. Initially organized with representatives of key social movements fighting against hunger in 1993, it was dismantled one year later and reactivated at the beginning of Lula's presidency, incorporating representatives of different sectors of society and government. From its creation in 2003 until 2019, when it was officially dissolved as one of the first actions of the far-right elected President Jair Bolsonaro, CONSEA became the leading participatory body of food security and food sovereignty policy in Brazil. The co-crafted discourse in which such policy emerged defends food and food sovereignty as a basic human right and, significantly, it has family farming as one of its key pillars. This can be observed in the revision of the Programme of Food Acquisition (PAA) in 2003 offering flexibility in the bidding process of food acquisition, giving priority to products from family agriculture. Following the same path, in 2009 the National School Feeding Programme (PNAE) stipulated that 30 per cent of school meals in all public schools of Brazil should be purchased from family farms. In addition to increasing the productivity and income of family agriculture and food quality for the population, this programme was a key driver for Brazil leaving the United Nations World Hunger Map in 2014 for the first time. The development of those policies and other programmes tackling social inequality issues and hunger in the country during the first two terms of the left-wing party (2003–06 and 2007–10) are important for understanding the mix of political and economic variables from which the first and second editions of the DGBP emerged.

The first edition of the DGBP was released at the beginning of the aforementioned construction of the political, legal and technical/scientific apparatus concerning food and nutritional security in the country. It was issued in the same year as the publication of the Organic Law for Food and Nutritional Security (LOSAN), which in addition to formally registering the concept of family farming, offered the basic legal framework for the development of the National Policy for Food and Nutritional Security. In contrast to the second edition, which was developed after ten years of discussion and with a more consolidated legal and political apparatus on food security and sovereignty, the first edition featured graphics and scientific and technical terms embedded in a hegemonic nutritional epidemiological discourse (Oliveira and Amparo-Santos, 2018). For example, on the first page of the guide, the document is immediately classified as a 'norms and technical manual'. Drawing on Ratner and Riis's (2014) reflections on the domain of scientific/nutritional/epidemiological discourses, Oliveira and Amparo-Santos (2018: 212) highlight that the first DGBP 'disregards the daily life complexity of human beings in order to encourage individuals to follow the guidelines'. Moreover, the Western framings of health and nutrition informing the DGBP's first edition are evident.

In 2008 and 2009, during the second term of President Lula, the Household Budget Survey was applied with a broad sample and covering all regions of Brazil. The results represented the importance of family agriculture in numbers for the first time. From the analyses of the Household Budget Survey data, the Centre for Epidemiological Research in Nutrition and Health (NUPENS) of the University of São Paulo developed the NOVA classification (Monteiro et al, 2010), which rather than classifying food according to its nutritional components, identified three categories of food based on its processing level: food, food ingredients and food products. Subsequently, in 2011 the DGBP began a long and participatory process of revision, deeply conscious of the realities of Brazilian everyday life. Ensuring that the sociocultural realities of everyday life of different parts of Brazil were represented, a two-year collective round of discussions took place in the 26 states and federal districts of the country to revise and translate the DGBP. Having the 4th Conference on Food and Nutritional Security of 2011 (involving some 2,000 participants) as a starting point of the revision process and led by CONSEA, the working groups of each state held regular meetings, the outcomes of which were translated into the principles and guidelines of the second edition, incorporating Brazilian sociocultural aspects of eating and conscious of the impact of ultra-processed food on both human health and the environment. This process demonstrates how the policies and guidelines were intentionally shaped by cultural geographies of food (Liu et al, 2019; Wilson, 2013), and the ways in which connections were made between the food system and Brazilian lifeworlds shaping food consumption.

Rather than tables, graphs and academic language prescribing quantities and food types, the second edition of the DGBP explores the multidimensional nature of food, including its cultural as well material aspects, and was published in 2014. Emphasis of the second edition was therefore very much upon engendering healthy eating practices through Warde's (2014) second moment of consumption – appreciation. As described in the quotations that follow, the second DGBP endeavoured both to represent the diversity of the Brazilian population as well as a variety of food combinations, recipes and culinary cultures strongly rooted in the different regions of the country. In the case of the basic everyday dish composed of rice and beans, the second DGBP incorporates a variety of preparations of such ingredients depending on the region in Brazil, stimulating the consumption of *in natura* and minimally processed food, advocating against ultra-processed food, and embedded in a food sovereignty discourse:

> One attempt was made to represent in the [meal] examples both genders, all age groups (as of the age of 10), all classes of income, urban and rural settings, and the five big regions of the country. … The meals illustrated here are of course not in any sense 'set menus' or rigid

recommendations. Variations among the combinations presented are crucial [and] also allow for regional and personal preferences. (Brasil, Ministério da Saúde, 2014: 55–6)

The combination of rice and beans is present in almost all the selected majority of Brazilians who opt for natural or minimally processed foods and indeed, most of the Brazilian population in general. (Brasil, Ministério da Saúde, 2014: 59)

'[H]owever, there are many other preparations made with beans that are appreciated by Brazilians, such as tutu à mineira, black-eyed peas, feijoada (bean and meat stew), bean soup, acarajé, among many others … Rice is the main cereal in Brazil. It is most commonly served with beans, but, [is] an extremely versatile food (Brasil, Ministério da Saúde, 2014: 68–9)

Another interesting feature of the second edition is the purposeful usage of images, including photographs, depicting regional, cultural, gendered, class-based and racial identities of Brazil. This can be observed in photographs of a family cooking together, in which the man is cooking and the woman and child are preparing the food together in a happy and harmonious moment, emphasizing the role of cooking skills as part of healthy eating. Another example is the depiction of friends eating together (Figures 14.1 and 14.2),

Figure 14.1: Eating a typical Brazilian meal together

Source: Brasil, Ministério da Saúde (2014: 94, 95)

Figure 14.2: Picnic with friends: eating together

Source: Brasil, Ministério da Saúde (2014: 101)

where fruits from different regions of Brazil, as well as people of different races and genders, are positioned together. Overall, the second DGBP provides tips for eating better, valuing food culture, and links are made between consumption and local fresh or minimally processed food production. Reflecting ethical food consumption beyond Global North assumptions of caring for distant others (Gregson and Ferdous, 2015), the second DGBP focuses on 'ordinary consumption practices related to issues of health and well-being, responsibility, and care for resources at the everyday household scale' (Ariztia et al, 2016: 898).

It is important to mention that Lula went to power with a fragile agreement of different power players in Brazil, from industry to social movements and agribusiness. Such agreement was embodied in the coexistence of the two contrasting agricultural models: family farming and agribusiness. While the Food and Nutritional Security Policy was developed through a multistakeholder process and a co-crafted discourse of food sovereignty and family farming echoed in the second edition of the DGBP, agribusiness enjoyed significant public subsidies and was supported by a highly organized and politically influential, rural caucus (known as *bancada ruralista*). A critical historical review of this context therefore reveals a Brazilian 'third way', in which family farming as a pillar of food sovereignty coexisted with agribusiness in a leading food exporting country. Sencébé et al (2020), however, reflect on the coexistence of these two agricultural models as uneasy and fraught with inequalities. Concurring with Sencébé et al (2020) and reflecting on the two editions of DGBP published against the backdrop of the rising consumption of processed foods, we argue that domestic food consumption in Brazil is influenced by myriad, sometimes opposing, discourses. While an increase in consumption of ultra-processed foods associated with food industry power and an agribusiness model receiving significant public subsidies is acknowledged, most Brazilians continue to eat fresh and minimally processed food produced mainly by family farms.

An influential discourse on changing approaches to healthy eating practices therefore emerged through Brazil's left-wing government from 2003. This discourse, enshrined in the two editions of the DGBP, is considerate of the impacts of the food industry on health, nutrition and basic human rights. The second edition illustrates values of food consumption beyond the travelling values and models of the Global North and rather emphasizes Brazilian cultural values in all their regional sociocultural diversity and, crucially, their connections to a food system based on family farming.

Conclusion

We have identified geographical research on consumption discourse and practice beyond the Global North, aiming to resist theorization of consumption driven by western framings. We have taken inspiration from perspectives of postcolonial economy to argue for situating consumption in particular histories and geographies, to embrace the ways in which practices of consumption are at once economic and culturally embedded, and to understand consumption through perspectives beyond Western views and models (see also Chapters 11 and 27 in this volume).

Focusing on the case of the DGBP, we have illustrated attempts to encourage healthy food consumption in Brazil through state initiatives shaped by policy makers and activists working in a multistakeholder dialogue with a left-wing government at that time. The guidelines engender consumption of natural and minimally processed foods against the backdrop of the rising consumption of processed foods. A model of agriculture based on the family farm, coexisting but contrasting with 'big capital' agribusiness in Brazil, underpins the guidelines.

Throughout the guide, especially in its second edition, Indigenous culinary values are promoted, acknowledging Brazil's regional diversity. The focus here is upon appreciating fresh food and incorporating it into everyday life through regional and national cuisine. Notably, regarding the economic and environmental implications of food consumption, the guide is less about mobilizing consumer support for family farming through a neoliberal mechanism of sustainable food consumption routed through the market and consumer choice (Barnett et al, 2011). Rather, it works in support of smallholder agriculture by encouraging consumers to appreciate natural or minimally processed foods through regional culinary culture and inclusive food preparation practices in the home. As such, the guidelines are powerful examples of locally and regionally situated policy and practice, understood through framings alternative to universalizing economic knowledges. They were shaped by state-led institutions and values that challenge both the commodification of food associated with powerful agribusiness and market-led pathways to healthy food consumption popular in many high-income countries (for example, expensive organic produce and brands associated with healthy food products). This resonates with Agyeman and McEntee's (2014) perspectives on the food justice movement. Engagement with the dietary guidelines, their underpinning values, and their emergence through particular political and cultural histories of Brazil, illustrates the kinds of plural geographies of consumption to be written beyond the Global North. Economic geographers committed to telling these plural stories have much to offer this important project.

Funding
ESRC award ES/R005303/1.

References

Agyeman, J. and McEntee, J. (2014) 'Moving the field of food justice forward through the lens of urban political ecology', *Geography Compass*, 8(3): 211–20.

Ariztia, T., Kleine, D., Bartholo, R., Brightwell, G., Agloni, N. and Afonso, R. (2016) 'Beyond the "deficit discourse": mapping ethical consumption discourses in Chile and Brazil', *Environment and Planning A: Economy and Space*, 48(5): 891–909.

Barnett, C., Cloke, P., Clarke, N. and Malpass, A. (2011) *Globalizing Responsibility: The Political Rationalities of Ethical Consumption*, Chichester: Wiley-Blackwell.

Battersby, J. and Crush, J. (2016) 'The making of urban food deserts', in J. Crush and J. Battersby (eds) *Rapid Urbanisation, Urban Food Deserts and Food Security in Africa*, Cham: Springer, pp 1–18.

Brasil, Ministério da Saúde (2014) *Guia alimentar da população brasileira* (2nd edn), Brasília: Secretaria de Atenção a Saúde, Departamento de Atenção Básica.

Bryant, R.L. and Goodman, M.K. (2004) 'Consuming narratives: the political ecology of "alternative consumption"', *Transactions of the Institute of British Geographers*, 29(3): 344–66.

Center for Advanced Studies on Applied Economics (CEPEA) (2021) GDP figures. Available at: https://www.cepea.esalq.usp.br/en/brazilian-agrib usiness-gdp.aspx [Accessed 15 January 2022].

Chen, J. and Liu, C. (2022) 'Takeaway food consumption and its geographies of responsibility in urban Guangzhou', *Food, Culture & Society*, 25(3): 354–70.

Clarke, N., Cloke, P., Barnett, C. and Malpass, A. (2008) 'Spaces and ethics of organic food', *Journal of Rural Studies*, 24(3): 219–30.

Coe, N.M. (2021) *Advanced Introduction to Global Production Networks*, Cheltenham: Edward Elgar.

Coe, N.M. and Wrigley, N. (2007) 'Host economy impacts of transnational retail: the research agenda', *Journal of Economic Geography*, 7(4): 341–71.

Colls, R. and Evans, B. (2014) 'Making space for fat bodies? A critical account of "the obesogenic environment"', *Progress in Human Geography*, 38(6): 733–53.

Cook et al, I. (2008) 'Geographies of food: mixing', *Progress in Human Geography*, 32(6): 821–33.

Crang, M. and Hughes, A. (2015) 'Globalizing ethical consumption: editorial', *Geoforum*, 67: 131–4.

Crewe, L. (2011) 'Life itemised: lists, loss, unexpected significance, and the enduring geographies of discard', *Environment and Planning D: Society and Space*, 29(1): 27–46.

Del Casino, V.J. Jr (2015) 'Social geographies I: food', *Progress in Human Geography*, 39(6): 800–8.

Evans, D. (2019) 'What is consumption, where has it been going, and does it still matter?', *Sociological Review*, 67(3): 499–517.

Evans, D., Welch, D. and Swaffield, J. (2017) 'Constructing and mobilizing "the consumer": responsibility, consumption and the politics of sustainability', *Environment and Planning A: Economy and Space*, 49(6): 1396–412.

Gereffi, G., Humphrey, J. and Sturgeon, T. (2005) 'The governance of global value chains', *Review of International Political Economy*, 12(1): 78–104.

Gong, Q. and Jackson, P. (2012) 'Consuming Anxiety?', *Food, Culture & Society*, 15(4): 557–78.

Gregson, N. and Crewe, L. (2003) *Second-Hand Cultures*, Oxford: Berg.

Gregson, N. and Ferdous, R. (2015) 'Making space for ethical consumption in the South', *Geoforum*, 67: 244–55.

Guthman, J. (2002) 'Commodified meanings, meaningful commodities: rethinking production–consumption links through the organic system of provision', *Sociologia Ruralis*, 42(4): 295–311.

Guthman, J. (2013) 'Too much food and too little sidewalk? Problematizing the obesogenic environment thesis', *Environment and Planning A: Space and Economy*, 45(1): 142–58.

Hall, S.M. (2015) 'Everyday ethics of consumption in the austere city', *Geography Compass*, 9(3): 140–51.

Holmes, H. and Ehgartner, U. (2020) 'Lost property and the materiality of absence', *Cultural Sociology*, 15(2): 252–70.

IBGE (Instituto Brasileiro de Geografia e Estatística) (2009) *Censo Agropecuário 2006, Agricultura Familiar, Primeiros Resultados: Brasil, Grandes Regiões e Unidades da Federação*, Rio de Janeiro: IBGE.

IBGE (Instituto Brasileiro de Geografia e Estatística) (2011) 'Pesquisa de Orçamentos Familiares 2008–2009: análise do consumo alimentar no Brasil', Rio de Janeiro: IBGE. Available from: https://www.ibge.gov.br/estatisticas/sociais/populacao/9050-pesquisa-de-orcamentos-familiares.html?edicao=9051&t=destaques [Accessed 20 July 2021].

IBGE (Instituto Brasileiro de Geografia e Estatística) (2020) *Pesquisa nacional de saúde 2019: Informações sobre domicílios, acesso e utilização dos serviços de saúde – Brasil, grandes regiões e unidades da federação*, Rio de Janeiro: IBGE.

Jackson, P. (2015) *Anxious Appetites: Food and Consumer Culture*, London: IBGBloomsbury.

Lane, R. and Mansvelt, J (2020) 'New consumption geographies: introduction to the special section', *Geographical Research*, 58(3): 207–13.

Liu, C., Valentine, G., Vanderbeck, R.M., McQuaid, K. and Diprose, K. (2019) 'Placing "sustainability" in context: narratives of sustainable consumption in Nanjing, China', *Social and & Cultural Geography*, 20 (9): 1307–1324.

Mansvelt, J. (2014) 'Consumption–reproduction', in P. Cloke, P. Crang and M. Goodwin (eds) *Introducing Human Geographies* (3rd edn), Abingdon: Routledge, pp 378–90.

McEwan, C., Hughes, A. and Bek, D. (2015) 'Theorising middle class consumption from the Global South: a study of everyday ethics in South Africa's Western Cape', *Geoforum*, 67: 233–43.

Meah, A. and Jackson, P. (2017) 'Convenience as care: culinary antinomies in practice', *Environment and Planning A: Economy and Space*, 49(9): 2065–81.

Miller, D. (1998) 'Why some things matter', in D. Miller (ed) *Material Cultures: Why Some Things Matter*, London: UCL Press, pp 3–21.

Monteiro, C.A., Levy, R.B., Claro, R.M., Castro, I.R.R. de and Cannon, G. (2010) 'A new classification of foods based on the extent and purpose of their processing', *Cadernos de Saúde Pública*, 26(11): 2039–49.

Oliveira, M.S.S. and Amparo-Santos, L. (2018) 'Food-based dietary guidelines: a comparative analysis between the Dietary Guidelines for the Brazilian Population 2006 and 2014', *Public Health Nutrition*, 21(1): 210–17.

Peyton, S., Moseley, W. and Battersby, J. (2015) 'Implications of supermarket expansion on urban food security in Cape Town, South Africa', *African Geographical Review*, 34(1): 36–54.

Pollard, J.S., McEwan, C. and Hughes, A. (2011) 'Introduction: postcolonial economies', in J. Pollard, C. McEwan and A. Hughes (eds) *Postcolonial Economies*, London: Zed Books, pp 1–20.

Pollard, J.S., McEwan, C., Laurie, N. and Stenning, A. (2009) 'Economic geography under postcolonial scrutiny', *Transactions of the Institute of British Geographers*, 34(2): 137–42.

Ratner, R.K. and Riis, J. (2014) 'Communicating science-based recommendations with memorable and actionable guidelines', *PNAS*, 111(S4): 13634–41.

Sencébé, Y., Pinton, F. and Cazella, A.A. (2020) 'On the unequal coexistence of agrifood systems in Brazil', *Review of Agricultural, Food and Environmental Studies*, 101(2/3): 191–212.

Slocum, R. (2007) 'Whiteness, space and alternative food practice', *Geoforum*, 38(3): 520–33.

Warde, A. (2014) 'After taste: culture, consumption and theories of practice', *Journal of Consumer Culture*, 14(3): 279–303.

Wilson, M. (2013) *Everyday Moral Economies: Food, Politics and Scale in Cuba*, Chichester: Wiley-Blackwell.

15

Governance: Climate Change and Land Use in the Anthropocene

Janelle Knox-Hayes

Introduction

Climate change governance is a crucial issue for contemporary economic geographers as climate change is disrupting the fundamental conditions of human life. Its impacts are also profoundly unequal. Climate change exacerbates existing inequities by placing further burdens on communities that are already vulnerable. While some individuals and communities will have the resources to adapt to or avoid the worst impacts of climate change, others will find their homes becoming uninhabitable, their livelihoods vanishing, and their health and security threatened (Oppenheimer and Antilla-Hughes, 2016). Sea level rise alone will create up to 1 billion climate refugees by 2100 (Hauer et al, 2020). While such inequities are routinely noted, scholars and policy makers have largely failed to grasp the magnitude of their impact or to craft commensurate responses.

For economic geographers the nature of the problem poses questions of how communities, industries and infrastructure will be reconfigured to respond to the worst impacts (see Chapters 27 and 29 in this volume). Solutions that aim to increase resilience often focus on technological fixes and economic metrics rather than on the social and ecological complexities of the problem and the ways in which solutions require holistic approaches. For problems, such as climate change and environmental degradation, siloization of the problem suggests that it can be addressed through the privatization of rights to the environment (Bumpus and Liverman, 2008), and the free exchange of these rights on a market system (Knox-Hayes, 2013). The problem is reduced to a series of pricing metrics – the allocation of rights to emit greenhouse gases – and the enablement of the exchange of these credits.

In contrast, an economic geography approach suggests the consideration of the interconnected dynamics between resource and social systems.

These issues are apparent within the main critiques within economic geography which question how commensuration and privatization influence the establishment of more equitable climate responses. Governance regimes operating under neoliberalism reduce the social norms and ideals of democracy, such as contestation and deliberation to a series of economic measurements and assessments of profitability. In this regard a range of values – as well as the processes under which such values might be considered, weighted and distributed in the allocation of governance – are reduced to exchange value and weighted only according to perceived profitability. Privatization diminishes the influence of a range of social considerations.

When public institutions are privatized the decisions of these institutions – how best to respond to heat waves, to reduce coastal vulnerability or to secure the supply of clean water and adequate food and energy resources – are reduced to a series of profit metrics. Consideration of the social value of clean water, let alone whether or not water is a human right is discounted through considerations of individuals' ability to pay (Bakker, 2010). Simultaneously neoliberalism compartmentalizes the function of industries into silos. Water is treated as independent from land use, the production of energy, forestry or even agriculture.

Ultimately, the issues that surround the transformation of social governance through neoliberalism revolve around the reduction of social values to a particular form of economic value – exchange value. Price is a singular metric that discounts not only social attributes of valuation, why and for what purpose clean water has value, but also the material nature of value – namely, what is required to produce clean water. Water becomes not a component of a system but a seemingly distinct and isolatable commodity. Effective governance requires a better assessment of the values inherent in commodities as well as a consideration of their interconnections.

Economic geography in environmental governance and land-use planning

Economic geographers have long been interested in understanding the relationships between economic activities, environmental governance and social outcomes (Barnes and Sheppard, 2019). They study how economic systems interact with the natural environment and how environmental policies are shaped by economic interests and power relations (Palsson et al., 2013). Economic geographers also examine how environmental governance is influenced by global economic processes, such as trade, investment and finance (Bridge et al, 2013).

There is growing recognition of the need to address climate change and environmental challenges more broadly. Economic geographers have thus increasingly focused on the study of climate governance, exploring questions such as the role of markets, policy instruments and governance structures in addressing climate change (Johnson, 2015). They also examine the social and environmental implications of climate policies, particularly for marginalized communities and vulnerable populations (Knuth, 2022).

While economic geography shares common themes with political ecology and political economy, there are also some important differences. Political ecology tends to focus on the ways in which environmental problems are rooted in social relations and power structures (Robbins, 2012), while political economy focuses on the relationship between economic systems and political power (Hudson, 2016). Economic geography, on the other hand, combines insights from both fields to examine the interactions between economic activities, environmental governance and social outcomes (Peet and Hartwick, 2015).

Female economic geographers have made important contributions to the study of environmental governance and climate change. Leigh Johnson, for example, has examined the role of corporations in shaping climate policy (Johnson, 2015), while Sarah Knuth has explored the impacts of carbon markets on rural communities (Knuth, 2022). Kelly Kay has focused on the gendered dimensions of environmental governance (Kay, 2018), while Tanya Matthan has examined the intersection of climate change and food systems (Matthan, 2022). Jamie Shinn has studied the political economy of renewable energy transitions (Shinn, 2016), and Carlson and Caretta have explored the role of grassroots movements in shaping environmental governance (Carlson and Caretta, 2021).

Overall, economic geographers are uniquely positioned to contribute to an understanding of the complex relationships between economic activities, environmental governance and social outcomes. Female economic geographers, in particular, have broadened perspectives of socio-economic systems and address the complex and pressing environmental challenges facing the world.

Economic geographers have highlighted the ways in which land use and adaptation planning is often built around the seemingly innocuous concept that the economic value of land should be maximized, especially as land becomes more scarce (see Chapters 8 and 22 in this volume). The highest economic use is not only rarely to the highest public benefit, but often also confers direct and untold social and environmental cost. For one thing, the logic that unused land is wasted is a logic that has been used across the world to dispossess Indigenous peoples of their lands (Wolfe, 2006; Domínguez and Luoma, 2020). For another, and interrelatedly, climate change is not a singular problem of greenhouse gas emissions, but rather symptomatic of deeper mismatches between natural and human resource cycles. By virtually every measure, the Earth's biosphere is in decline as a consequence of unrelenting development. Underpinning this is the idea that biosphere can be compartmentalized into sectors (Steffen et al, 2015). In laying the groundwork for governance in a civic rationale, the well-meaning principle of maximizing land product has laid the groundwork for untold destruction, a consequence increasingly felt by those facing the worse impacts of climate change.

For most Indigenous cultures land is relational, not a thing to be controlled, but an entity that sits in relation (a mother, a sister, a brother) to the community that inhabits it (Wolfe, 2006). The world view of many Indigenous peoples also includes the principle of connectivity – that everything in the universe is linked. The spirit world is connected to the mortal world, the sea is connected to the land, and the sky is connected to the ground. Connectivity explains the linkages people have to their communities, their traditional territories and the ecosystem on those lands. In this way land is also inseparable from the complex ecosystem it generates. The use of land exists in reciprocity: it provides the resources a community needs, but only if they carefully steward and renew it in their practices. How would industries function if they were not industries (energy, water, forestry, real estate, agriculture and so on) but rather manifestations of the health and functional use of the ecosystems embedded in land? The idea is challenging in the context of modern capitalism, but less difficult in the context of the radical socio-economic, cultural and environmental transformations that attenuate climate change, and its severe impacts.

The temporal and systemic challenge of climate change

Neoliberalism frames climate change as a phenomenon that can be addressed from a siloed approach: market mechanisms to stimulate energy transition. Greenhouse gases (primarily carbon dioxide (CO_2), but also others such as methane and hydrofluorocarbons) are emitted by industrial activity. The increasing concentration of greenhouse gases, over time, leads to a net increase in temperature at the Earth's surface. The core components of the problem then are industrial and economic processes that emit greenhouse gases, shifting atmospheric chemistry as greenhouse gas concentrations increase, and rising global temperatures. As the average global temperature increases, a host of climatic changes occur: glaciers melt, sea levels rise and weather patterns change.

The solution is also seemingly simple and discrete; prevent greenhouse gases from being emitted into the atmosphere to avoid altering atmospheric chemistry and the ensuing climactic effects. However, as the repeated failure of global climate negotiations suggests, the apparently simple solution presents substantial complexity. The key to managing carbon emissions is to internalize them in economic transactions. Internalizing the cost of carbon emissions requires both a political solution, the creation of regulation to mandate the reduction CO_2 emissions, and an economic solution, the construction of a priced carbon externality and an economic infrastructure that can exchange and transmit the value of the priced carbon externality. The challenge is that nearly all the energy infrastructure underpinning the modern political economy emits carbon dioxide.

The apparent simplicity of both the problem and solution is belied by the obvious difficulties states and societies have in addressing climate change. For one thing, climate change is a spatial and temporal macro problem, operating at a global scale and over a long-term horizon. Because climate is structural and systemic, people do not experience the climate so much as they experience weather, which is local and changes hourly or daily and thus apparently belies claims of general trends. The mismatch in temporal and spatial scale creates a problem of felt impact. Over decades and at a global scale temperature will rise and climate patterns will shift, but the weather at a local level is variable and relatively unpredictable. The apparent disconnect between abstract claims about the climate and the concrete experience of weather can help drive scepticism as to whether or not climate change exists and is anthropogenic.

The neoliberal approach to climate change similarly suggests that the problem arises out of the failure to price externalities. For example, the burning of fossil fuels results in the emission of CO_2 and other greenhouse gases which are not accounted for in the price of energy unless a carbon-pricing scheme is put in place. Treating climate change as a matter of externality pricing is symbolic of ecological modernization – the idea that markets can integrate environmental and social equity into economic instruments through the recalibration of exchange value. Ecological modernization takes a sociopolitical problem, removes it from the realm of political discourse, and recasts it in economic, technical language (Knox-Hayes and Hayes, 2014; Ioris, 2015). Accordingly, the market mechanism-based economic framing of climate change situates the solutions to the problem of climate change as technocratic matters that require only the proper implementation of economic theory.

Towards an economic geography of climate valuation

The application of economic values for the assessment and management of a full range of social and environmental problems is problematic on two counts. First, the economic values of neoliberalism are miscalibrated to the social and environmental realties they are designed to represent.

In particular, neoliberal economics treats all value as though it were absent of spatial and temporal dimensions. In fact, questions of how and where value actually exists are central to the provision of social welfare. A more considered appraisal of the interface of economic theory and the environment suggests that the core assumptions upon which market-based governance is built lack a full conceptualization and integration of value. While in conventional calculations of price and quantity only exchange value is theorized, the operation of the natural environment – water purification, carbon sinks – draws attention to the importance of use value and the significance of time.

Take, for example, the question of ensuring energy security. From an exchange value perspective, the solution focuses on managing the price of fossil fuels. Accounting for use value, however, brings in considerations of utility and consequently a focus on renewability and limitations on energy use to increase efficiency. However, use and exchange only go so far to address the modern failure to adequately conceptualize value. Notably, both use and exchange value deal with the *present* possibilities of a good or service. Reconsidering this temporal fixation draws attention to the distinction between potential and realized value, which in turn highlights the interplay objective and subjective conceptions of value. Realized value is value that exists in the present. Potential value has yet to be created, and thus has the possibility to exist in the future. Because the future is undetermined, potential value is subjective and only arises through the fulfilment of particular conditions. Since future value is not situated in an objective reality, it is not truly commensurate with value that has already come to exist.

By failing to recognize these spatial and temporal distinctions, the systems and instruments of economic valuation miss a critical aspect of resource governance – where, when, and how value exists across space and time. The spatial and temporal distinctions of value can be illustrated through a typology (Figure 15.1). Clarifying the relationship of space and time to these forms of value illuminates the missing link of use in time in economic valuation and market-based governance for problems like climate change. The matrix in Figure 15.1 represents a typology of value that accounts for spatial and temporal dynamics. The vertical axis divides space into socio-economic and socio-environmental relations. The horizontal axis divides time into present (realized economy) and future (potential economy). Four distinct types of value are identified: use, exchange, derived (for example, derivatives like wheat options) and external (externalities, or value unaccounted by present use and exchange). Consider a common commodity like a bushel of wheat. Use value is the value acquired from using or consuming the bushel. Exchange value is the value of exchanging the wheat for something else, usually money. Derived value is the value

Figure 15.1: Typology of the spatial and temporal dynamics of value

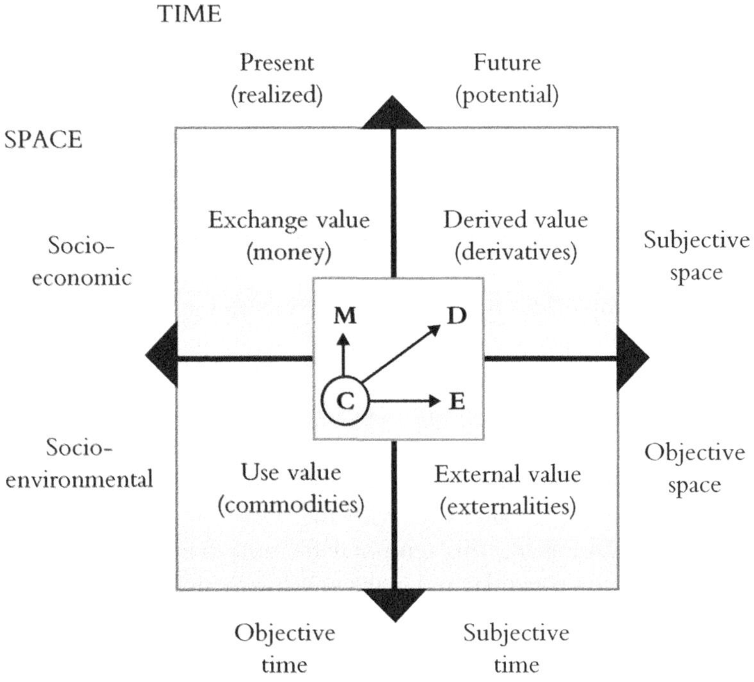

derived from the exchange of the commodity in the future: a contract to sell a bushel of wheat at a certain price at a future time. External value is the value external to the production of the commodity; for example, the loss of value from depleted soil or polluted water.

The typology makes some important distinctions with respect to the value of resources. The valuation of resources develops from use value. The ultimate objective of any resource is use, whether now or in the future. Value is objectively embodied in physicality and realized through the use of the commodity. Although use value is ultimate objective of a commodity, the only metric to account the value of the resource is exchange value. Value is measured relative to price. For this reason, carbon pricing is used to try to solve climate change. The challenge is that the solutions actually require a direct transformation of use (shifting energy resources) and price does not guarantee a particular use. In order to effectively manage problems like climate change, the spatial and temporal dimensions of value must be considered

Finally, in reducing social values into economic exchange value, a range of social and environmental attributes are stripped out (how people want to live, where and why). We must recognize what consumption does to the planet and we must change course not just because it is profitable, but because we understand what we value as society as well as how to realize these values (Sayer, 2015). A sustainable economy would not compress these values so that their only form of recognition might be the profitability of their exchange, but it should instead give them space for expression, consideration and realization. Such a realization empowers forms of governance that operate beyond neoliberal privatization and marketization.

Value proposition: towards the integration of systems around use

Climate change requires thus attention to two critical dynamics: (1) managing the balance of time between socio-economic and environmental systems, and (2) understanding the flows of hydrocarbon cycles and their interrelationship with ecosystems. The solution generated by neoliberal economies to solve climate change, carbon pricing, is designed to generate exchange value for the absence of negative externalities (greenhouse gas emissions) and a market signal to stimulate the deployment of renewable energy. Numerous renewable energy technologies already exist: photovoltaic, wind, hydroelectric, geothermal and so on. Within each field there has been development and experimentation of technologies to respond to social and environmental resistance. For example, wind energy has been moved offshore, developed into a floating technology, and integrated with different storage solutions. 'DeepWind' projects, which can be sited as far as 50 km offshore, have the potential to operate at greater capacity because of the stronger winds offshore; however, they experience greater variability of wind speed and as a consequence higher transmission need (Waite and Modi, 2019). The distance from shore helps to minimize sight impact concerns, as well as impacts on fisheries and other wildlife located closer to shore. Some researchers have suggested more systematic approaches that integrate wind with hydroelectric seasonal storage, and even floating photovoltaic panels can help to generate stable transmission rates and to reduce transmission lines (Farfan and Breyer, 2018). However, full integration of energy systems is not common.

Climate change cannot be isolated as a singular phenomenon, but must rather be understood and addressed from the standpoint of systemic impacts across time. This idea is also found within the concept of planetary boundaries (Steffen et al, 2015). The Earth has at least nine planetary boundaries at risk from resource depletion and overproduction including: loss of genetic diversity, loss of functional diversity, land–system change, freshwater depletion, phosphorus and nitrogen soil depletion, ocean acidification, atmospheric aerosol loading, stratospheric ozone depletion and climate change from the atmospheric greenhouse gas effect. Addressing each of these ecological dynamics and imbalances in chemical cycles is critical to generating

Figure 15.2: A new value proposition: the integration of chemical and nutrient cycles through cyclical industries

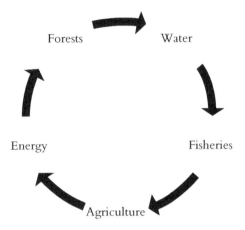

a more holistic and sustainable approach to climate change. Working across this system dynamics also represents the possibility of generating use and external value across developed and developing places and sustained in time.

Coming back to the idea that climate change is situated within the temporal bounds of cycling chemical systems, the solution might be to better integrate the productivity of human systems with these natural cycles. Rather than address climate change in a silo, as a by-product of fossil-fuel-based energy, it could instead be considered within a system of planetary boundaries. As a consequence, land-based industries, such as forestry, water provision, energy, agriculture, fisheries and even real estate might be integrated into comprehensive systems (Figure 15.2).

The idea that land is a commodity leads to siloed production: real estate, agriculture, energy, water and ecosystem services are all different uses. Industries frequently experience challenges in their competing use of land. Rather than see each industry as a distinct land-use decision, with a single economic commodity, it is, rather, important to understand these industries as interconnected systems. The idea that land is relational leads to the generation of more productive systems. Healthy, biodiverse forests are necessary to filter water (Broadmeadow and Nisbet, 2004). Fresh water is a necessary ingredient for agriculture and aquaculture (Beveridge and Brummett, 2015). Healthy forests are also essential to the sustenance of pollinators for agricultural crops. A range of forestry, agricultural and aquaculture by-products can be used to generate hydro and biochar to enhance soil productivity, and to capture carbon dioxide (Zhang et al, 2019). Finally, from a chemical standpoint various agricultural and hydrological cycles can be used to create green fuels such as green hydrogen and green methanol (Li and Tsang, 2018). These fuels could be critical to building a clean energy transition until conventional renewable resources such as wind and solar, with new technologies for storage, can operate at the scale of the present economy.

The integration of industries would lead to a more holistic approach to managing critical social and ecological systems. Across each of the domains, this kind of approach would generate co-benefits, better entrain the temporality and relationality of different systems, and generate cyclical economies. This approach is critical to managing the sustained use of resources across time and the generation of intergenerational social and ecological value.

Conclusion

Climate change is the greatest challenge of our time. It asks us to fundamentally reconsider our economies and the physical, social and environmental infrastructures that underpin them. Climate change also presents an opportunity to transform our social and economic systems to benefit all members of society and to better integrate social and ecological outcomes. Resilience strategies must address not just critical physical infrastructure but also the socio-economic and cultural interdependencies of human and natural systems. This is the only way to truly bring human and natural systems into a more sustainable relationship.

The construction of financial markets to serve as systems of governance challenges environmental processes, which are embedded in physical materiality (Daly, 1992; O'Neill, 2007). While the productivity of economic (the rate of good and service production for example) and social systems (the rate and scale of communication for example) can be accelerated through the operation of digital networks, environmental systems cannot withstand the pressures to accelerate their rate of productivity in line with financialization. Overconsumption of these systems will lead to collapse. Markets to conserve forests can trade the exchange value of the trees around the globe instantaneously, but the trees still require decades, if not centuries, to reproduce themselves. Their use value, if not their intrinsic value, is deeply embedded in space and time. In divorcing the spatial and temporal scale of use value from exchange value, financial markets are unlikely to address the very real and material demands our society places on the natural environment. Furthermore, the isolation of land uses into distinct commodities leads to a missed opportunity to generate more cyclical and productive socio-economic systems.

To be made more effective, economic systems must be made to account for spatial and temporal scale. From the standpoint of finance, there are a number of ways in which this could be envisioned, including having instruments that have geographic limits on the extent to which they can be traded, forcing accountability and linkage between the revenue of projects and the credits to which they belong. Additionally, there could be temporal restrictions placed on the exchange of environmental instruments such that their rate of turnover is slowed to better represent the underlying physical processes of the natural environment valued by the instruments. It might even be possible to imagine a system through which property rights could be transformed such that instruments of environmental finance could have fixed use but flexible exchange parameters. In such an instance, the instruments would allow for the generation of exchange value, but guarantee a specific type and quality of use value to the natural environment.

From an industry perspective, the integration of energy, water, forestry, agriculture and aquaculture into holistic industries could better entrain both temporal and chemical nutrient cycles to produce cyclical and sustainable economies (see also Chapter 29 in this volume). To accommodate the function of environmental systems, the economies must seek to entrain the spatial and temporal scale of production and reproduction between the socio-economic, and socio-environmental worlds. Finally, from a social standpoint, addressing climate change requires the realization and enactment of a range of values beyond economic profitability. The best way to challenge neoliberalism is to empower these alternative discourses and practices of values.

Climate change is a multifaceted problem, which signals the dangers of current economic activities and of the increasing disconnect between socio-economic and environmental productivity (Newell and Paterson, 2010). Environmental finance is almost certainly capable of generating exchange value, but to be meaningful it must make real the promise of an economy capable of countering the ecological waste and destruction of an economic system that is designed only to extract and never to return value. Sustainable governance requires policies and institutions that spread wealth over a time horizon that is almost always long term. The effects of these policies ensures that the types of value generated from conventional industries are balanced across use, exchange, external and derived formats. Critically, such a balance ensures wealth is not rapidly exhausted by a few private entities, but rather preserved for public benefit for generations to come. For economic geographers, the nature of the climate change problem raises a challenge of integrating socio-economic and ecological systems, bridging industries, and seeking equitable long-term solutions that engage a range of stakeholders.

Acknowledgements

I acknowledge and thank Geoforum for permission to reproduce parts of my paper Knox-Hayes, J. (2013) 'The spatial and temporal dynamics of value in financialization: analysis of the infrastructure of carbon markets', *Geoforum*, 50: 117–28.

References

Bakker, K. (2010) *Privatizing Water: Governance Failure and the World's Urban Water Crisis*, Ithaca, NY: Cornell University Press.

Barnes, T.J. and Sheppard, E. (eds) (2019) *Spatial Histories of Radical Geography: North America and Beyond*, John Wiley & Sons.

Beveridge, M.C.M. and Brummett, R.E. (2015) 'Aquaculture and the environment', in J.F. Craig (ed) *Freshwater Fisheries Ecology*, Chichester: Wiley-Blackwell, pp 794–803.

Bridge, G., Bouzarovski, S., Bradshaw, M. and Eyre, N. (2013) 'Geographies of energy transition: space, place and the low-carbon economy', *Energy Policy*, 53: 331–40.

Broadmeadow, S. and Nisbet, T.R. (2004) 'The effects of riparian forest management on the freshwater environment: a literature review of best management practice', *Hydrology and Earth System Sciences*, 8(3): 286–305.

Bumpus, A.G. and Liverman, D.M. (2008) 'Accumulation by decarbonization and the governance of carbon offsets', *Economic Geography*, 84(3): 127–55.

Carlson, E.B. and Caretta, M.A. (2021) 'Legitimizing situated knowledge in rural communities through storytelling around gas pipelines and environmental risk', *Technical Communication*, 68(4): 40-55. Available from: https://www.ingentaconnect.com/content/stc/tc/2021/00000068/00000004/art00004

Daly, H.E. (1992) 'Allocation, distribution, and scale: towards an economics that is efficient, just, and sustainable', *Ecological Economics*, 6(3): 185-93.

Domínguez, L. and Luoma, C. (2020) 'Decolonising conservation policy: how colonial land and conservation ideologies persist and perpetuate indigenous injustices at the expense of the environment', *Land*, 9(3): 65–86.

Farfan, J. and Breyer, C. (2018) 'Combining floating solar photovoltaic power plants and hydropower reservoirs: a virtual battery of great global potential', *Energy Procedia*, 155: 403–11.

Hauer, M.E., Evans, J.M. and Mishra, D.R. (2020) 'Millions projected to be at risk from sea-level rise in the continental United States', *Nature Climate Change*, 10(5): 443–50.

Hudson, R. (2016) *Approaches to Economic Geography: Towards a Geographical Political Economy*, London: Routledge.

Ioris, A.A.R. (2015) 'Cracking the nut of agribusiness and global food insecurity: in search of a critical agenda of research', *Geoforum*, 63: 1–4.

Johnson, L. (2015) Catastrophic fixes: Cyclical devaluation and accumulation through climate change impacts. *Environment and Planning A*, 47(12): 2503-21.

Kay, K. (2018) 'A hostile takeover of nature? Placing value in conservation finance', *Antipode*, 50(1): 164–83.

Knox-Hayes, J. (2013) 'The spatial and temporal dynamics of value in financialization: analysis of the infrastructure of carbon markets', *Geoforum*, 50: 117–28.

Knox-Hayes, J. and Hayes, J. (2014) 'Technocratic norms, political culture and climate change governance', *Geografiska Annaler Series B: Human Geography*, 96(3): 261–76.

Knuth, S. (2022) 'New political ecologies of renewable energy', *Environment and Planning E: Nature and Space*, 5(3): 997–1013.

Li, M.M.J. and Tsang, S.C.E. (2018) 'Bimetallic catalysts for green methanol production via CO_2 and renewable hydrogen: a mini-review and prospects', *Catalysis Science & Technology*, 8(14): 3450–64.

Matthan, T. (2022) 'Speculative crops: Gambling on the onion in rural India', *Geoforum*, 130: 115–22.

Newell, P. and Paterson, M. (2010) *Climate Capitalism: Global Warming and the Transformation of the Global Economy*, Cambridge: Cambridge University Press.

O'Neill, J. (2007) *Markets, Deliberation and Environmental Value*, Abingdon: Routledge.

Oppenheimer, M. and Anttila-Hughes, J. K. (2016) 'The science of climate change', *The Future of Children*, 26(1): 11–30.

Palsson, G., Szerszynski, B., Sörlin, S., Marks, J., Avril, B., Crumley, C., ... and Weehuizen, R. (2013) 'Reconceptualizing the 'Anthropos' in the Anthropocene: Integrating the social sciences and humanities in global environmental change research', *Environmental Science & Policy*, 28: 3–13.

Peet, R. and Hartwick, E. (2015) *Theories of Development: Contentions, Arguments, Alternatives*, New York: Guilford.

Robbins, P. (2012) *Political Ecology: A Critical Introduction* (2nd edn), Chichester: Wiley.

Shinn, J.E. (2016) 'Adaptive environmental governance of changing social-ecological systems: Empirical insights from the Okavango Delta, Botswana', *Global Environmental Change*, 40: 50–59.

Steffen, W., Richardson, K., Rockström, J., Cornell, S.E., Fetzer, I., Bennett, E.M., Biggs, R., Carpenter, S.R., de Vries, W., de Wit, C.A., Folke, C., Gerten, D., Heinke, J., Mace, G.M., Persson, L.M., Ramanathan, V., Reyers, B. and Sörlin, S. (2015) 'Planetary boundaries: guiding human development on a changing planet', *Science*, 347(6223). Available from: https://doi.org/10.1126/science.1259855 [Accessed 15 June 2023].

Waite, M. and Modi, V. (2019) 'Impact of deep wind power penetration on variability at load centers', *Applied Energy*, 235: 1048–60.

Wolfe, P. (2006) 'Settler colonialism and the elimination of the native', *Journal of Genocide Research*, 8(4): 387–409.

Zhang, Z., Zhu, Z., Shen, B. and Liu, L. (2019) 'Insights into biochar and hydrochar production and applications: a review', *Energy*, 171: 581–98.

16

Creativity: An Evolving Critical Debate

Suntje Schmidt

Introduction

Creativity in economic geography has primarily been addressed from two perspectives: one that takes a sectoral approach by investigating spatial dynamics in cultural and creative industries, and a second that is interested in creativity as a practice – either on an individual or a collective level. The first perspective was developed against the background of indicating how regional development stems from creative processes. Creativity here is expressed by economic activities in cultural and creative organizations and occupations with working routines and organizational forms of work that differ from other industrial sectors. Creative work hence is project-based and working contracts are often temporal. Therefore, careers in creative sectors develop less within but across organizations and projects, which is why workers in creative sectors develop boundaryless and subjective careers (Khapova et al, 2007). The second perspective conceptualizes (creative) work as practices 'necessary for the material and immaterial reproduction of society' (Kruker et al, 2002: 248). This perspective seeks to carve out the multiple spatial dynamics of practices and routines of creating novel and useful outlets. Against this background, such discourses are rather embedded in knowledge economy and knowledge society discourses addressing spatial dynamics and spatial dimensions of generating novelty in form of new knowledge (see also Chapter 13 in this volume).

Both perspectives, however, suggest that creativity in the form of creative work in creative sectors or as creative practices seldom crystalizes within a single organization or location, but instead combines several on- and offline places and likewise creates new places and spaces. Recent discourses point towards particular places that are embedded in multilocal creative practices, such as homes (Reuschke et al, 2021), hacker spaces (Toupin, 2014), creative hubs (Virani and Gill, 2019) or Open Creative Labs (Schmidt, 2019). In fact, if creativity-driven work and practices unfold across organizations and projects, some scholars argue that such places may take over governing functions in creative work (Doussard et al, 2018) and thus become central elements in the context of creativity and space. Many of these spaces such as coworking, maker, hacker or collaborative workspaces postulate openness, underlining their accessibility to all kinds of users, and thus seem to naturally suggest differences to be integrated in the conceptualization of creative work (Reimer, 2016; Crewe and Wang, 2018; Morgan, 2020; McLean, 2021). However, very seldom this has been critically tackled by scholars.

Against this background the aim of this sections is threefold. First, despite the heterogeneity and plurality of topics, themes and perspectives in economic geography this chapter seeks to elaborate and appreciate the major strands of exchange within the discipline, focusing especially on creative work and creative processes. This section hence aims to depicture some of the main contributions of economic geography scholars to better understand the transformation processes in (primarily Western) contemporary economies driven by knowledge- and creativity-driven work. Second, the chapter then continues to particularly illuminate how critical perspectives in economic geography have helped us to better address, for example, new dimensions of inclusion or exclusion and new forms of vulnerabilities of certain groups within labour markets due to the transformation processes and the shifting attention of academic research. Finally, the chapter concludes by tentatively addressing potential consequences for future critical work in economic geography.

Creativity

Creativity can be regarded as the capacity to generate valuable novelty (Amabile, 1996) – or, as Malecki (2013: 79) pointed out as the 'art of creating the new'. At a very basic level, creative capacity, the ability to generate new ideas and imaginations are thus 'expressions for the inherited and learned characteristics attached to the individual' (Törnqvist, 2004: 228). However, despite this seemingly individual capacity, creative processes do not take place in isolation, but are inherently collaborative processes (Richardson, 2016) as new ideas are generated through the interaction with one's surrounding environment (Törnqvist, 2004: 228) and by interacting with other individuals or organizations.

From an economic geography point of view these perspectives opened a number of discourses, of which a comprehensive overview would exceed the scope of this section. Most prominently are, for example, discourses on the creative class, creative cities and regions, creative milieus or places of creativity such as Open Creative Labs/Hubs or other forms of collaborative work places: studios, laboratories, universities. Acknowledging creativity as the capacity to generate new, valuable knowledge, creativity has therefore been also interpreted as the key resource for economic actors to successfully take part in a global competition (Leslie and Rantisi, 2012). Therefore, research streams on creativity in economic geography are sometimes embedded in a larger set of discourses on spatial dynamics in knowledge economies and societies. While this shift promised new 'no-collar' workplaces accompanied with values such as autonomy, self-expression and flexibility, to some it also devalued seemingly non-creative jobs, most often characterized as less flexible, dependent on decisions of hierarchies, low-skilled and low-paid that are often occupied by women, ethnic minorities, younger or elderly employees (Leslie and Rantisi, 2012), even though at the same time the demand for exactly this type of work increases (Moretti, 2012). Already, critical perspectives on creativity-driven economies in economic geography are increasingly addressing the vulnerability and precariousness of creative work due to a widening income gap between core and peripheral creative workers, changing professional identities as well as a reinforcing unequal participation in creative labour markets along, for example, gender lines and of different ethnic groups (Christopherson, 2008; McDowell and Christopherson, 2009; McDowell, 2011). Against this backdrop I now highlight some of the critical voices in economic geography that open up further research avenues for the discipline.

Richard Florida's work (Florida, 2002) certainly marked a cornerstone that ignited numerous studies investigating the creative potential of cities and regions, but also invited somewhat critical perspectives especially on creative processes and – most prominently – on creative cities' policies and creative work (for example, Bontje and Musterd, 2009). But, discourses on the (however defined) creative class did create a sensitivity for work outside standardized organizational and spatial forms as well as add a complementary perspective on questions of creative and knowledge-generating processes by asking who is doing creative knowledge work, how and where.

Creative processes and work can be understood as collaborative, interactive practices (Malecki, 2013) that often require diverse forms of either physical and or technologically mediated forms of co-presence (Gertler, 1995), for example for the simultaneous productions and consumption of creativity (in concerts, for instance) or for the interactive work for generating novelty (in form of cooperation between creative service providers and customers or among peers to co-create a new software, for instance). The need for cooperation and interaction in knowledge-generating and creative processes also underlines the importance of networks the governance form for coordinating and organizing creative processes (Grabher, 2004a; Amin and

Roberts, 2008) or in form of social networks that support dealing with creative labour market–related uncertainties (Ibert and Schmidt, 2014).

Research in economic geography also addresses new organizational forms of work in creative work environments, most prominently in terms of temporary organizations such as projects and events and – in consequence – flexibility in terms of when, how and where creative work is organized. Creative processes are thereby often characterized by temporary organizational structures that are set up to reach predefined objectives without clear hierarchical structures within and across non-temporary organizations (Janowicz-Panjaitan et al, 2009). Grabher (2004b) points out that temporary organizations such as projects may be regarded as temporary settings for learning and knowledge flows. Projects thus provide a temporary organizational form for creative processes at the intersections of permanent organizations, communities and networks (Grabher and Ibert, 2011). Other temporary forms of organizing creative processes are events such as fairs, festivals, conferences and other forms of temporary clusters, but also temporal event-like settings such as hackathons (Gibson and Bathelt, 2014; Power and Jansson, 2008). Studies in economic geography have demonstrated how such events contribute to creating a 'buzz' that supports informal and formal knowledge flows, networking within and across industries, or serendipitous encounters (Storper and Venables, 2004). Additionally, temporality is also strategically organized as an instrument in creative processes for reaching particular interim results, for instance in form of hackathons or rapid prototyping session.

In consequence, these characteristics of creative processes and creative work radically change working practices, requirements and expectations from creative workers. Under the umbrella of the term 'flexibility', scholars addressed a variety of spatial dynamics in creative processes and of creative work. For instance, temporary forms of organizing creativity are closely linked to temporary forms of income-related work, which is why creatives built up careers across projects and across organizations rather than within a few enterprises (Comunian and Jacobi, 2015). Additionally, repeatedly shifting work arrangements frequently promote or require spatial mobility across organizations, but also across regions and cities (Zhang and Dai, 2021). Furthermore, creative industries are characterized by high shares of non-standardized forms of institutionalized work and freelance work (Vinodrai, 2013). The latter is frequently interpreted as a form of work that offers freedom, self-fulfilment and individual control, but also as a precarious and uncertain form of income. In consequence, acknowledging that creative work encompasses flexible working structures and often lacks fixed organizational forms, creatives also flexibly seek workplaces according their needs, combining, for instance diverse places of work such as home, coworking spaces, workshops studios, cafés, or trains (Schmidt, 2019).

Creative work / creative economy: some critical debates

Economic geography scholars have developed quite a comprehensive body of research streams debating creativity. Around some of the major foci outlined earlier, such as networking, collaboration and interaction, modes of organizing creativity and new forms of work as well as sectoral differentiations, critical debates contributed to better understanding the ambivalence, ambiguities, vulnerabilities and new lines of inclusion or exclusion of taking part in creative processes. Though these critical voices become increasingly numerous and diverse, they are still selective in terms of their research objectives and their systematic integration in creativity research. The following subsections seek to introduce some of these pioneering voices before discussing some further research conceptual and empirical implications for economic geography.

Networking

In the context of creative work and creative processes, networks can be considered a resource (in the form of social capital for dealing with uncertainties or for building up ties within a particular creative field) or a governance mechanism that steers and coordinates creative processes. Networking as a practice to build up and activate resources requires intensive labour, often unpaid and in informal work environments that mingle private and working time. Critical perspectives not only underline the blurring boundary between work and leisure in this regard, but also point towards new lines of in/exclusion based on when and where networks are formed.

Angela McRobbie (2002), for instance, investigated the characteristics of work and employment in the UK economy and illustrated that clubs become places where networks are established and fostered. Furthermore, she illustrates how informal networking in clubs eventually also provides the base for further creative work. This, however, creates strong critical impacts on who can participate in creative work practices, and in what way, especially when considering age and domestic (therefore gendered) responsibilities. Women, she argues, face a dual struggle as new ways of working challenge established boundaries for those who carry out domestic work, for example care work for family members, and who therefore have only limited resource to actively engage with the night-time economy, where networking often shapes work-related ties. At the same time, the night-time economy establishes boundaries with regard to age (for example, being accessible and attractive to the 'middle youth') (McRobbie, 2002: 526) that eventually extends to a long-hours working culture in creative occupations.

Networking as a social practice may also affect who dominates leading positions within (creative) industries. For the example of design as one of the central sectors in creative economies, Suzanne Reimer (2016) demonstrates that design occupations are quite male dominated, which may be explained by dominant networking practices, both with other members of the industry and with clients. Tying in with McRobbie's findings, Reimer (2016) finds that design industries are characterized by a normalization of long and often unpredictable hours of working and socializing with clients that extends to third places such as restaurants, bars or clubs. Her investigation uncovers that gender thus contributes to unequal possibilities of participating in networking practices, which leads to likewise unbalanced career advancements, with fewer women in senior positions within the design industries.

Crewe and Wang also find gender and age inequalities in the advertising industry that result from 'social, structural and institutional factors rather than individual choice, lack of "talent" or the absence of mentors or appropriate role models' (Crewe and Wang, 2018: 671). Crewe and Wang interpret networks not only as social capital, but as important governance mechanisms for creating and sharing tacit knowledge. Networks are thus a necessary social infrastructure for circulating knowledge, information and business secrets in addition to functioning as labour-market mediators (Crewe and Wang, 2018: 677).

Non-standardized forms of work and temporary organizing

Creative industries exhibit a comparatively high share of part-time, temporal work contracts, a high share of freelance work and other forms of self-employment leading to uncertain, sometimes precarious working conditions. Critical perspectives in economic geography are therefore concerned with precarious working conditions with regard to temporal aspects, pay gaps and chances to participate in creative labour markets.

Tying in with the previous discussion, social practices as a resource-building networking strategy clearly differ along gender lines, but also with regard to social background. Virani and Gill (2019: 136) demonstrate that this applies not only to education and training, but also for entering creative industries, as it seems a prerequisite to work for free or for a low income especially in the early phases of creative careers – a practice that, for example, social groups with working-class backgrounds or individuals who take over care responsibilities struggle to do, and which excludes many from participating in creative working environments early on. Such inequalities then manifest further as even though the participation of women in creative occupations has increased, inequalities in terms of income significantly manifested as well (Inglada-Pérez et al, 2021).

Creative work is organized by temporary organizations, such as projects or events, requiring an increasing flexibility in terms of how and when work is conducted. Cockayne (2021) argues that the term 'flexibility', however, disguises labour-market deregulations affecting already vulnerable social groups as work is being pushed into private lives conceptually, rhetorically and materially. Others argue that, affiliations with companies being lacking, freelance work, especially in creative occupations, often remains hidden or invisible (Merkel, 2015).

Identity constructions

Linda McDowell's work stresses the relevance of gender relations and identity constructions in the knowledge-based service economy building a foundation for many further critical contributions in economic geography (see, for example, Chapter 6 in this volume). McDowell (2011, 2015) focuses on male and female social relations in and at work, accentuating gender, skin colour, age, bodily appearance and language as elements in labour markets. Building on McDowell's work, studies in creative work contexts added further critical insights into identity construction. Reimer (2016: 1039), for instance, demonstrates how design is imbued by a social construction of masculinity, because design seems to be strongly linked to craft. Craft skills thus are constructed as masculine, encompassing physical skills, manual labour with materials, and intuitive artistic and aesthetic performances on the job. This may also extend sexualized masculinity constructions in some creative fields as Warren's (2016) findings underline 'blokey masculinity' in surf board industries (Warren, 2016: 50). Thus, within the creative field of craft, boundaries are constructed not only along gender lines, but also with regard to sexual orientation and sexism (Gill, 2014; Reimer, 2016).

For the example of musical performers Ibert and Schmidt (2014) illustrate how musical performers create multiple identities in order to circumvent being stereotyped in their labour markets. Musical performers are trained in acting, dancing and singing. This training enables them to not only compete for positions in musical shows, but also in the fields of, for example, theatre performance, filming and other stage-related roles. However, from the perspective of producers and directors their training is perceived as too diverse, lacking in-depth skills in specialized performing arts. Therefore, musical performers tend to create different CVs, depending on what kinds of roles they compete for.

Organizing without organization

A central question in geography naturally is the question of the spatiality of creative industries. However, it seems that the site of the employers in creative fields is less central for creatives, because they lack a fixed contract with the employer or their work requires a high degree of mobility, for example, to visit clients or the locations of projects. Against this background new collaborative workplaces such as coworking spaces, makerspaces or start-up accelerators partially take over organizing functions for community building (Waters-Lynch and Potts, 2017) and creative working practices (Friederici, 2016) – functions formerly in the hands of formal employers and organizations.

Even though collaborative workspaces are still a comparatively new research object in economic geography (Schmidt, 2019), some critical investigations have already uncovered boundaries of inclusion and exclusion in creative practices that make use of these spaces, for example based on gender, age or association with particular creative communities. Morgan (2020: 156), for example, points out that 'communities are often not open and egalitarian; instead, their membership is curated in ways that may serve to exclude people from certain social backgrounds'. Likewise, Johns and Hall (2020) found with the example of a FabLab in Manchester that, despite its vision of involvement and connection, users were marginalised or even rejected by other users of the space. Hence, communities associated with collaborative workspaces clearly influence who may be attracted to a particular space – or who is excluded. The exclusion stems not only from the habits, postulated community values or identity constructions of users of collaborative spaces, but are also carefully curated (Merkel, 2015; Virani and Gill, 2019). Within this context, curation is a practice closely associated with the founder or manager of a space who seeks to build up the 'right' community, which includes '"intense segmentation and hierarchy" along race and gender lines' as Virani and Gill (2019: 132) observed in creative hubs.

While curation is creating gender- and age-based boundaries, so do practices of appropriating spaces (Bingel, 2019), for example in the form of far-reaching and expensive behaviour in the physical-material sense of making use of a space, but also in the form of openly exhibiting artistic scenes, subcultures or political positions. For instance, Bingel (2019) observed boundary constructions between free artists and freelance and self-employed workers in culture and creative industries. Against this background, it is not surprising that collaborative workspaces sometimes develop towards a particular profile, such as coworking spaces for bloggers and free journalists or spaces for micro-enterprises or explicitly inviting a particular group of users (for example, women or members of the LBTGQIA+ community) while also explicitly excluding others (male members, for instance) (Toupin, 2014).

Open Creative Labs are collaborative workspaces that actively promote their openness to all kinds of users (Schmidt, 2019), in particular those labs registered as associations – which is why one could have expected less obvious and strict lines of exclusion. However, we (author and colleagues) observed quite clear lines of exclusion. For instance, some labs set up procedures of taking on board new members, for example the existing membership decides who may take part in the lab, which eventually promotes homogeneity in terms of shared values, interests and community fit. In addition, even though the share of female members is indeed a sensitive topic and some lab communities seek to support a gender balance, we also observed instances where female members felt the need to create their own subgroup for a few meetings, because they wanted to create a secure space allowing women to escape from a male-dominated communication culture.

Conclusion

Scholars from economic geographies have already contributed critical conceptual and empirical perspectives in the context of creative work and processes. Across the discourses I have discussed here, inequalities, forms of inclusion and exclusion, and unequal opportunities to participate in creative work are primarily disclosed on the basis of gender constructions and age. The role of social, cultural or ethical identities in creative processes and work are hardly addressed, though. An outstanding contribution offered by critical perspectives in economic geography relates to discourses on identity constructions. Contributions here not only stem from cases within creative industries, but also extend to creative work, for example in service industries. These contributions clearly carve out how gender is performed and constructed by individuals and how these gender constructions also impact what work identities are cautiously developed by women in particular (see also Chapters 6, 11, 18 and 25 in this volume). Again, the main contribution of critical approaches in identity constructions in creative work environments are discussed from gendered perspectives, lacking systematic investigations along dimensions such as age, cultural, religious, ethical or social belonging.

Despite these briefly addressed valuable contributions, critical economic geography still needs to be pushed further. This includes considering what critical economic geography actually can contribute. Barnes and Christophers suggest that critical thinking is critical 'in its very nature' (2018: 114), meaning that it asks researchers to question what we take for granted and to reconceptualize existing approaches when necessary. Reflecting on the discourses already discussed, inequalities are primarily addressed along gender dimensions; few studies address age or cultural backgrounds too. The concept of intersectionality (Crenshaw, 1990) might contribute to critical economic geographical thinking as it may be applied to understanding the interaction of multiple identities and experiences of exclusion and subordination (Davis, 2008: 67) and thereby seek to focus not on one, but on multiple dimensions of inequality. Understanding the social and spatial underpinnings of creative work thus considers practices of performing occupations that are framed by collective construction processes of social positions (Dean, 2005). A further field for critical economic geography in the context of creativity relates to the dominating focus of income-related creative work. Less attention, for example, is paid to the spatiality of cultural, artistic work, creative activism or creative work outside the university-educated, middle-class professions from a critical perspective (McLean, 2021). Thus, critical perspective may bring a greater range of creative practices to the focus of analysis seeking to understand collective agency and power relations within creative processes (Reid-Musson et al, 2020).

References

Amabile, T.M. (1996) *Creativity in Context*, Boulder, CO: Westview Press.

Amin, A. and Roberts, J. (2008) *Community, Economic Creativity, and Organization*, Oxford: Oxford University Press.

Barnes, T.J. and Christophers, B. (2018) *Economic Geography: A Critical Introduction*, Hoboken, NJ: Wiley.

Bingel, K. (2019) *Dritte Orte kreativ-urbaner Milieus: Eine gendersensible Betrachtung am Beispiel Braunschweig*, Bielefeld: transcript.

Bontje, M. and Musterd, S. (2009) 'Creative industries, creative class and competitiveness: expert opinions critically appraised', *Geoforum*, 40(5): 843–52.

Christopherson, S. (2008) 'Beyond the self-expressive creative worker: an industry perspective on entertainment media', *Theory, Culture & Society*, 25(7/8): 73–95.

Cockayne, D. (2021) 'The feminist economic geographies of working from home and "digital by default" in Canada before, during, and after COVID-19', *Canadian Geographer/Le Géographe canadien*, 65(4): 499–511.

Comunian, R. and Jacobi, S. (2015) 'Resilience, creative careers and creative spaces: bridging vulnerable artists' livelihoods and adaptive urban change', in H. Pinto (ed) *Resilient Territories: Innovation and Creativity for New Modes of Regional Development*, Newcastle upon Tyne: Cambridge Scholars, pp 151–66.

Crenshaw, K. (1990) 'Mapping the margins: intersectionality, identity politics, and violence against women of color', *Stanford Law Review*, 43(6): 1241–99.

Crewe, L. and Wang, A. (2018) 'Gender inequalities in the City of London advertising industry', *Environment and Planning A: Economy and Space*, 50(3): 671–88.

Davis, K. (2008) 'Intersectionality as buzzword: a sociology of science perspective on what makes a feminist theory successful', *Feminist Theory*, 9(1): 67–85.

Dean, D. (2005) 'Recruiting a self: women performers and aesthetic labour', *Work, Employment & Society*, 19(4): 761–74.

Doussard, M., Schrock, G., Wolf-Powers, L., Eisenburger, M. and Marotta, S. (2018) 'Manufacturing without the firm: challenges for the maker movement in three US cities', *Environment and Planning A: Economy and Space*, 50(3): 651–70.

Florida, R. (2002) *The Rise of the Creative Class, and How It's Transforming Work, Leisure, Community and Everyday Life*, New York: Basic Books.

Friederici, N. (2016) *Innovation Hubs in Africa: Assemblers of Technology Entrepreneurs*, DPhil thesis, University of Oxford.

Gertler, M.S. (1995) '"Being there": proximity, organization, and culture in the development and adoption of advanced manufacturing technologies', *Economic Geography*, 71(1): 1–26.

Gibson, R. and Bathelt, H. (2014) 'Field configuration or field reproduction? The dynamics of global trade fair cycles', *Zeitschrift für Wirtschaftsgeographie*, 58(4): 216–31.

Gill, R. (2014) 'Academics, cultural workers and critical labour studies', *Journal of Cultural Economy*, 7(1): 12–30.

Grabher, G. (2004a) 'Learning in projects, remembering in networks? Communality, sociality, and connectivity in project ecologies', *European Urban and Regional Studies*, 11(2): 103–23.

Grabher, G. (2004b) 'Temporary architectures of learning: knowledge governance in project ecologies', *Organization Science*, 25(9): 1491–514.

Grabher, G. and Ibert, O. (2011) 'Project ecologies: a contextual view on temporary organizations', in P.W.G. Morris, J.K. Pinto and J. Söderlund (eds) *The Oxford Handbook of Project Management*, Oxford: Oxford University Press, pp 175–98.

Ibert, O. and Schmidt, S. (2014) 'Once you are in you might need to get out: adaptation and adaptability in volatile labor markets – the case of musical actors', *Social Sciences*, 3(1): 1–23.

Inglada-Pérez, L., Coto-Millán, P., Casares, P. and Inglada, V. (2021) 'Profile of creative women: a comprehensive quantitative approach for Spain', *European Planning Studies*, 29(10): 1798–818.

Janowicz-Panjaitan, M., Cambré, B. and Kenis, P. (2009) 'Introduction: temporary organizations – a challenge and opportunity for our thinking about organizations', in P. Kenis, M. Janowicz-Panjaitan and B. Cambré (eds) *Temporary Organizations: Prevalence, Logic and Effectiveness*, Cheltenham: Edward Elgar, pp 1–12.

Johns, J. and Hall, S.M. (2020) ' "I have so little time … I got shit I need to do": critical perspectives on making and sharing in Manchester's FabLab', *Environment and Planning A: Economy and Space*, 52(7): 1292–312.

Khapova, S.N., Arthur, M.B. and Wilderom, C.P. (2007) 'The subjective career in the knowledge economy', in H. Gunz and M. Peiperl (eds) *Handbook of Career Studies*, Thousand Oaks, CA: Sage, pp 114–30.

215

Kruker, V.M., Schier, M. and von Streit, A. (2002) 'Geography and gendered labour markets', *GeoJournal*, 56(4): 243–51.

Leslie, D. and Rantisi, N.M. (2012) 'The rise of a new knowledge/creative economy: prospects and challenges for economic development, class inequality, and work', in T.J. Barnes, J. Peck and E. Sheppard (eds) *The Wiley-Blackwell Companion to Economic Geography*, Chichester: Blackwell, pp 458–71.

Malecki, E.J. (2013) 'Creativity: who, how, where?', in P. Meusburger, J. Glückler and M. el Meskioui (eds) *Knowledge and the Economy*, Heidelberg: Springer, pp 79–93.

McDowell, L. (2011) 'Doing gender, performing work', in A. Leyshon, R. Lee, L. McDowell and P. Sunley (eds) *The SAGE Handbook of Economic Geography*, London: Sage, pp 338–50.

McDowell, L. (2015) 'Roepke Lecture in Economic Geography – The Lives of Others: body work, the production of difference, and labor geographies', *Economic Geography*, 91(1): 1–23.

McDowell, L. and Christopherson, S. (2009) 'Transforming work: new forms of employment and their regulation', *Cambridge Journal of Regions, Economy and Society*, 2(3): 335–42.

McLean, H. (2021) 'Spaces for feminist commoning? Creative social enterprise's enclosures and possibilities', *Antipode*, 53(1): 242–59.

McRobbie, A. (2002) 'Clubs to companies: notes on the decline of political culture in speeded up creative worlds', *Cultural Studies*, 16(4): 516–31.

Merkel, J. (2015) 'Coworking in the city', *Ephemera: Theory & Politics in Organizations*, 15(1): 121–39.

Moretti, E. (2012) *The New Geography of Jobs*, Boston, MA: Houghton Mifflin Harcourt.

Morgan, G. (2020) '"Meaning and soul": co-working, creative career and independent co-work spaces', in S. Taylor and S. Luckman (eds) *Pathways into Creative Working Lives*, Cham: Springer, pp 139–58.

Power, D. and Jansson, J. (2008) 'Cyclical clusters in global circuits: overlapping spaces in furniture trade fairs', *Economic Geography*, 84(4): 423–48.

Rantisi, N.M. (2014) 'Gendering fashion, fashioning fur: on the (re)production of a gendered labor market within a craft industry in transition', *Environment and Planning D: Society and Space*, 32(2): 223–39.

Reid-Musson, E., Cockayne, D., Frederiksen, L. and Worth, N. (2020) 'Feminist economic geography and the future of work', *Environment and Planning A: Economy and Space*, 52(7): 1457–68.

Reimer, S. (2016) ' "It's just a very male industry": gender and work in UK design agencies', *Gender, Place & Culture*, 23(7): 1033–46.

Reuschke, D., Clifton, N. and Fisher, M. (2021) 'Coworking in homes: mitigating the tensions of the freelance economy', *Geoforum*, 119: 122–32.

Richardson, L. (2016) 'Sharing knowledge: performing co-production in collaborative artistic work', *Environment and Planning A: Economy and Space*, 48(11): 2256–71.

Schmidt, S. (2019) 'In the making: Open Creative Labs as an emerging topic in economic geography?', *Geography Compass*, 13(9): art e12463. Available from: https://doi.org/10.1111/gec3.12463 [Accessed 16 June 2023].

Storper, M. and Venables, A.J. (2004) 'Buzz: face-to-face contact and the urban economy', *Journal of Economic Geography*, 4(4): 351–70.

Törnqvist, G. (2004) 'Creativity in time and space', *Geografiska Annaler Series B: Human Geography*, 86(4): 227–43.

Toupin, S. (2014) 'Feminist hackerspaces: the synthesis of feminist and hacker cultures', *Journal of Peer Production*, 5. Available from: http://pee rproduction.net/issues/issue-5-shared-machine-shops/peer-reviewed-artic les/feminist-hackerspaces-the-synthesis-of-feminist-and-hacker-cultures/ ?format=pdf [Accessed 16 June 2023].

Vinodrai, T. (2013) 'Design in a downturn? Creative work, labour market dynamics and institutions in comparative perspective', *Cambridge Journal of Regions, Economy and Society*, 6(1): 159–76.

Virani, T.E. and Gill, R. (2019) 'Hip hub? Class, race and gender in creative hubs', in R. Gill, A.C. Pratt and T.E. Virani (eds) *Creative Hubs in Question: Place, Space and Work in the Creative Economy*, Cham: Palgrave Macmillan, pp 131–54.

Warren, A. (2016) 'Crafting masculinities: gender, culture and emotion at work in the surfboard industry', *Gender, Place & Culture*, 23(1): 36–54.

Waters-Lynch, J. and Potts, J. (2017) 'The social economy of coworking spaces: a focal point model of coordination', *Review of Social Economy*, 75(4): 417–33.

Zhang, X. and Dai, J. (2021) 'Cultural and creative production in the era of globalization: exploring the trans-border mobility of Chinese media and entertainment celebrities', *Geoforum*, 120: 198–207.

17

Industrial Landscapes: From the Geographies of Production to Everyday Life

Chantel Carr and Natasha Larkin

Introduction

Transitioning contemporary industrial landscapes towards a lower-carbon future is a challenging proposition. Workforces in carbon-intensive sectors and regions are vulnerable as energy transitions accelerate rapidly. Globally, the concept of *just transitions* is gaining traction among policy makers, academics and organizations such as the International Labour Organization (ILO) and the UN Environment Programme (UNEP). The meaning and scope of a just transition is now formalized in the ILO's *Guidelines for a Just Transition* (2015) and was adopted in the preamble to the Paris Climate Agreement. A focus on just transitions recognizes that the effects of climate change mitigation will be felt unevenly across societies, and that governments have a responsibility to ensure people adversely affected by decarbonizing economies are supported (ILO, 2015). Geography is an important factor in this debate (Tonts, 2010; Fleming and Measham, 2015), since the economic and social cost of failing to adequately plan for such transitions will be borne unevenly.

In Australia, the current outlook for well-planned and socially just transitions away from carbon-intensive energy generation and industrial production is not positive. As the world's largest net exporter of coal wrestles with the move to a post-carbon economy, a national debate that pits concern for the environment against industrial and resource sector jobs is becoming increasingly intractable. Studies of industrial transformation show successive governments have shown limited capacity to anticipate and plan for change (Rainnie et al, 2004; Beer, 2018;

Weller, 2019). Empirical work on industrial transitions in Australia has predominantly taken a political-economic lens, contributing valuable insights into the negative effects of reactive, top-down and disjointed policy making on regional workers and communities (Sheldon et al, 2018; Snell, 2018; Weller, 2019). In a compelling account of the failure of a multilevel approach to engage with very material fears of 'poverty, disempowerment and disenfranchisement' in a thermal coal region, Weller (2019: 313) argues for a much deeper engagement with place and people, particularly in regional communities dependent on a single industry. Recently, Edwards et al (2022) have advocated for an approach to transition that looks beyond workers in specific industries to the broader community, since decarbonizing heavy industrial and resource-based regions will affect not only the whole supply chain, but adjacent service industries. The implication is that the scale and pace of decarbonizing industrial regions will resonate far beyond those whose paid work is directly affected. This raises questions of what analytical tools are needed to understand the effects of these changes, and how to support those communities most affected. As industrial transformation continues to radically reshape everyday lives, it is crucial that economic geographers remain attuned to the ways capital interests make decisions that resonate unevenly across sites and scales, including the household and community (Hall, 2016).

In this chapter, we set out the parameters of a research agenda informed by labour process and feminist economic geography, that seeks to refocus attention on industrial landscapes at a time of intense change. This focus is timely – indeed urgent – in a context where industrial and resource sector capital is becoming increasingly sensitive to global imperatives around carbon reduction. We begin with an overview of geographical work on industrial landscapes. Here the contributions of feminist economic geographers and those who have written about embodied labour process continue to inspire and inform our own empirical analyses, prompting a more holistic approach to work, skill, households, and everyday life (see also Chapters 2, 11, 20 and 24 in this volume). We then turn to examples from recent projects led by the authors in the steel and coal sectors to illustrate two overlooked aspects of industrial landscapes in contemporary economic geography: invisible labour and workers beyond the workplace. We conclude by calling for a broader emphasis on the lived experiences and myriad social relations of workers, households and communities in future analyses of industrial transitions. With an era of fossil-fuel profligacy coming to an end, such work is urgently needed to support those communities on the front line of a new wave of structural change that is already transforming industrial landscapes.

Legacies and limitations: industrial landscapes and economic geography

Industrial landscapes have provided the empirical basis for the development of many key concepts in economic geography throughout the 20th century, enriching analyses of capital-class relations, markets, regions, value and gender among others.[1] While it is impossible to do justice to the breadth of this work in a short chapter, in this section we explore two conceptual threads that might inform a renewed interest in industrial landscapes, at a time of profound change. We proceed by tracing out the dominant legacy of political–economic analysis of industrial landscapes. This work has made substantial progress in understanding the collective experiences and concerns of industrial workers. We suggest, however, that an emphasis on the social relations of production has served to obscure other types of social and material relations in the industrial landscape (Swanton, 2013; Carr, 2017). Guided by the contributions of both industrial sociologists and feminist economic geographers, we identify two key directions economic geographers might pursue in analyses of industrial landscapes on the cusp of further structural transformation: an attentiveness to everyday embodied labour processes and material engagements; and a focus on how workers are embedded in social relations beyond the paid workplace.

Geographical interest in industrial landscapes first began to gather pace after the Second World War, a 'golden' period described by Marxian economists and sociologists as monopoly capitalism (Burawoy, 1979). Industrial enterprises held a dominant role in world markets, and the rapid expansion of production beyond urban centres provided a fruitful empirical source for the largely apolitical spatial-locational analytical methods that characterized industrial geography at the time (Scott, 2000). Beyond being instrumentalized as an input into the production process, workers were generally excluded from early geographical analyses of industrial landscapes (Castree, 2007; Coe and Jordhus-Lier, 2011). The point worth emphasizing here is that economic geography's long-standing interest in industrial landscapes emerged – and arguably remains – at the intersection of firms, markets, space and place.

An alternative, and perhaps better starting point for understanding the lived experiences of workers under monopoly capitalism is Braverman's (1974) *Labor and Monopoly Capital*. Preceded by many years on the tools as a craft metal worker, Braverman's concern was with the degradation of skill, as management sought to break work down into smaller, discrete tasks. He argued that this Taylorist tactic stifled dissent under monopoly capitalism, by reducing workers to interchangeable units of production. Together, with Burawoy's (1979) *Manufacturing Consent*, Braverman's work consolidated a resurgent interest in Marxian labour process in industrial sociology, that flourished well into the 1980s (Thompson, 1983; Smith, 2015). Labour process takes as its departure point the body at work. It requires that close attention be paid to how value is created through the relationship between worker and the work at hand (Marx [1867] 1976: 284). Yet curiously, labour process (and the body more generally) has been under-theorized in industrial economic geography. Even within the subfield of labour geography, where industrial landscapes provided a productive avenue (and a receptive, union-oriented workforce) for much of the early work on worker agency, an emphasis on organized labour has served to obscure labour process (Herod, 1997; Castree, 2007; Coe and Jordhus-Lier, 2011). Relatively little has been written in economic geography, for example, about the socio-material relations industrial workers engage in as they go about their everyday work, or how tasks and labour processes vary for workers, or how technology impacts on differentiated skills (Swanton, 2013; Carr, 2017; Warren, 2019). Yet we would argue that such knowledge is vital in understanding the capacity of industrial regions to meet the challenges ahead. As industrial regions, and societies more broadly, grapple with the issue of decarbonization, uneven geographies of skill and the capacities of workers to adapt to new labour processes will inevitably become key issues for achieving socially just transitions.

If the industrial landscapes of the Global North in the 1950s and 1960s were characterized by periods of transformational growth, the 1970s saw the emergence of instability and crisis (for contemporary discussion of crises see Chapters 12 and 21 in this volume). Bigger structural forces came into play: by shifting to regions with lower labour costs, global capital was already rewriting the space-economy when the global energy crisis began in 1973. The repercussions continued into the next decade, with unemployment and inflation remaining high in industrial economies (Scott, 2000). Neoclassical location theory was an inadequate analytical tool for understanding the structural injustices set in train by deindustrialization. Marxian political economy emerged in response, bringing new critical questions to industrial landscapes and processes of capital accumulation in the 1970s (Harvey, 1973; Walker and Storper, 1981; Bluestone and Harrison, 1982; Massey, 1984). Job losses and class conflict provided the empirical focus for understanding how regional industrial decline intersected with power and capital (Massey and Meegan, 1982). During this period, those working within a framework of geographical political economy took important steps in identifying labour as a social process (Peck, 2018); however, a focus on resistance in the paid workplace meant other aspects of working and community life were commonly overlooked (Taksa, 2000; Ettlinger, 2002). This lacuna in many ways continues to shape what is understood to be industrial geographies today.

Where the metanarratives of class struggle and capital–labour relations served to obscure other kinds of social relations in industrial regions in the 1970s and 1980s, the work of Doreen Massey is, of course, an important exception. *Spatial Divisions of Labour* (1984) was a remarkable, deep engagement with the ways capital intersected with social change in the deindustrializing landscapes of the UK. Massey demonstrated the profound value of examining how these landscapes are shaped simultaneously by social and cultural histories, capital interests, the physical environment, material affordances and political context (see Chapter 1 in this volume). She also emphasized the need to understand how different scales were interconnected within and beyond the industrial region, from the household through to the global. This relational scalar framing is critical to understanding how everyday lived realities in industrial landscapes are shaped by broader structural forces, as much as they are produced within the home and community. Massey's work remains vital to understanding contemporary industrial landscapes, because it provides the conceptual foundations for exploring how working lives are shaped both within the workplace, and at a range of scales beyond it.

Since the 1980s, feminist economic geographers have continued to build on Massey's work, closely examining how paid and unpaid work are deeply entwined in spaces dominated by global capital (Mackenzie and Rose, 1983; McDowell and Massey, 1984; Hanson and Pratt, 1988; McDowell, 1991, 2003, 2004, 2008; Pratt and Hanson, 1991; Gibson, 1992; Gibson-Graham, 1993, 1996, 2006; England and Lawson, 2005). This body of work has expanded the possibilities for understanding industrial landscapes by foregrounding other sites and scales of analysis, including the household (Gibson, 1992; Gibson-Graham, 2006; Bamberry, 2016) and community (Cameron and Gibson, 2005). Households, for example, have their own internally complex politics and practices, informed by unique configurations of gender, age, class, financial obligations and familial structures, which provide crucial context for navigating labour-market change (Cravey, 1997; Oberhauser, 1995). Households make sense both to the people who live in them, and to policy makers: as social units, as sites through which it is logical to understand financial and employment risk, and as a scale through which to understand and anticipate economic restructuring (compare Head et al, 2013). Workers and households are not easily separable, yet contemporary analyses of how workers negotiate transforming industrial landscapes often tend to isolate workers from this social context (Bamberry, 2016; Beer et al, 2019; Warren, 2019; Strauss, 2020). As the decarbonization of industrial landscapes gathers pace, it is important to examine not only how households are shaped by industrial change, but also how the configuration of the household shapes workers' capacities to navigate industrial change. That is, socially just transitions in industrial landscapes must account for how changes in working lives are planned for, experienced and rationalized in spaces enrolled in – but not reducible to – capitalist relations.

In this section we have traced out an abbreviated history of the economic geographies of industrial landscapes. We have focused on some of the legacies and limitations of this work, and identified two key directions economic geographers might pursue considering mounting imperatives to decarbonize production. The first draws on the work of industrial sociologists, suggesting that a return to labour process is needed to understand the everyday, embodied work practices and material engagements of industrial workers. Navigating decarbonizing industrial landscapes will require a much deeper understanding of the skills, knowledges and tasks that constitute contemporary industrial work, and how these might be adapted (or not) to meet the needs of emergent industries and new modes of production. Second, we build on the work of feminist economic geographers to suggest a renewed focus on social relations beyond the paid workplace. This broader view is essential to understanding the broader impacts of change on households and communities, recognizing that industrial transformation resonates far beyond the enterprise. In what follows, we turn to examples from our own empirical work in Australia's steel and metallurgical coal sectors, exploring two overlooked aspects of industrial landscapes where these conceptual tools have led to new insights.

From the geographies of production to everyday life

In this section, we draw on examples from two projects, both located in the Illawarra region of New South Wales where the steel and coal sectors remain operational today. The first project is current as at the time of writing, and involves working with coal miners and their families, to understand their plans and aspirations for the future, in the context of growing concern around the resources sector. The second project draws from Carr's PhD work (see also Carr, 2017), which explored the lives of repair and maintenance workers at Australia's largest steelworks. Inspired by Massey (1984) and McDowell (1992, 2003) together these projects represent a decade of research with industrial workers *in place* – that is, within the community in which we ourselves live and work (see Hall, 2017). The examples speak to the opportunities for deeper understandings of industrial landscapes to emerge through close attentiveness to labour process, and social relations beyond the workplace.

Invisible labour

Feminist economic geographers have consistently drawn attention to the invisible labour that sustains social infrastructures (Pratt, 1999; England and

Dyck, 2012; McDowell, 2015; Strauss, 2015; Cox, 2018). More recently, the infrastructural 'turn' in geography has highlighted the invisible labour that goes into repairing and maintaining physical infrastructures, itself a form of care (Mattern, 2018; Millington, 2019; De Coss-Corzo, 2021). It is perhaps unsurprising then, that invisible labour is also a feature of the industrial landscape. From 2012 to 2016, I (Carr) undertook an ethnography of repair and maintenance workers at the Port Kembla steelworks. Looking beyond 'the steelworker' as a cohesive working identity, I focused on the labour processes, material engagements and cognitive skills of this work. Maintenance and repair workers undertake work that keeps production processes rolling. They are highly attuned to the potential for disruption and breakdown. Yet to senior management always searching for cost savings, these workers – and their vast practical knowledges accumulated over time – were all but invisible. I began to explore this absence further, observing that not only were repair and maintenance workers overlooked in the workplace, they had rarely been explicitly discussed within scholarly accounts of industrial production.[2] Drawn to the task of remediating this oversight, feminist labour geography provided the conceptual tools for exploring the invisibility of repair and maintenance work within industrial landscapes.

The labour process literature provided a framework for more closely examining how this work proceeded, and how vulnerable workers were to restructuring. Many aspects of Braverman's (1974) deskilling thesis resonate with the experiences of industrial workers today (Warren, 2019). Yet a close examination of the labour process of repair crews revealed that this work was difficult to routinize, and so it had continued to elude Taylorist-style management techniques (see also Blum, 2000). At Port Kembla, small, multi-trade teams work on rotating shifts, responding to breakdowns. Located close by a production control room, their work proceeds in fits and starts, depending on how the mill is running. Repair crew workers are often required to exercise creativity and deploy tacit knowledges in the moment, sometimes under extraordinary pressure (Carr, 2017). Without these workers production would cease, a subtle yet significant form of agency intimately bound up with particular bodies and identities.

Together, these insights point to an imperative to account for many kinds of skills and capacities among industrial workers, some of which had been consistently overlooked in both scholarly and management contexts throughout the 20th century. In discussions of industrial transformation, there is currently very little emphasis on the role skills play in achieving socially just outcomes. Yet within an industrial landscape such as the Port Kembla steelworks, a multitude of shop floors, labour categories, production processes, material transformations, worker subjectivities (class, age, gender, ethnicity, ability) and social relations to contend with, the effects of industrial change will always be uneven, to say the least. Developing a much more detailed knowledge of worker skills and capacities is critical to supporting those workers as industrial regions begin to navigate the upheaval of decarbonization. With an analytic sensitivity to context and the specificities of place and time, economic geographers are well positioned to make insightful contributions that can guide future transition processes.

Workers beyond the workplace

The second example where feminist perspectives bring new insights to industrial landscapes is through a consideration of the lives of workers beyond the workplace. Here we focus on one aspect: identity. While work is an important element of identity, our interviews with coal workers and their families continue to reveal the complex ways work identities intersect with and challenge other aspects of life. The excerpt is from an interview with Justin, a coal miner who has worked in the industry for 13 years:

> 'I classify myself as an environmentalist. We all want to leave this planet better off than we found it. You know I campaigned against housing developments … I've bloody been arrested. I've chained myself up to cars and that, to try and stop bulldozers getting in, so you know, it was a big debate in my head to get into it to start with. You are ripping a layer of the ground out, but in the end, you have to provide for your family.'

Justin was the first person we interviewed for this project. Among other things, his comments reveal the importance of place and time in determining what economic opportunities are available to workers, and how these opportunities are taken up (Massey, 1984). Hearing a coal worker describe themselves as an environmentalist and talk about their activism was certainly unexpected (though we have now heard similar sentiments expressed by other participants). Mining is an increasingly challenging topic in Australian public life due to growing awareness of its environmental impacts, and these insights are at odds with pervasive media and political narratives that are often intended to divide. This tension is evident where several participants have since described their discomfort in responding to the inevitable 'So what do you do?' in social situations.

Yet Justin's comments remind us that we should be wary of using work as a proxy for particular environmental or political perspectives. This much more nuanced entanglement of environmental and occupational identities cautions us to avoid moralizing responses to complex issues. If we had interviewed Justin only about his paid work, we would have missed these insights. Here McDowell's (2003, 2004, 2008) work has been particularly instructive. It has taught us the value of seeing workers as 'whole selves' – asking about their daily lives beyond the workplace, observing how they interact with their environments, how they use their bodies and skills in other spaces, how they are placed within families and communities, and how they envision their futures. This broader analytical frame offers a way of understanding what motivates and engages people whose voices are rarely heard in conversations about the future of industrial landscapes – their interests and fears, their relationships to place, and their politics. It is critical that such perspectives are heard and amplified by economic geographers, in ways that can inform dialogue around industrial transitions.

Conclusion

In a world so fractured, it is both a privilege and a responsibility to talk to people about the work they do, and the role it plays in their identity and their everyday life. We have found work to be a window into how people experience the world, but it is only a starting point for a broader discussion that inevitably ends up speaking to the qualities and complexities of people's lives: the decisions they make (to have children, to migrate), the relationships they value, and their politics, which are inevitably more complex than we expect. We are motivated by Castree's (2007: 859–60) sentiments that our responsibilities lie with understanding:

> the geographies of employment and labour struggle not in themselves but as windows onto the *wider* question of how people live and seek to live. Such analyses are, admittedly, hard-won. They demand of researchers extraordinarily close attention to the social and geographical tapestry (I use the metaphor advisedly) of workers' lives so they are represented as what they really are: lives of people who are far more than just 'workers'.

Australia's industrial landscapes contribute to the world's carbon intensity, and are under increasing pressure as global capital interests begin to reconsider their investment profiles. In this chapter, we have set out an agenda for future geographical research, that places workers, households and communities at the centre of planning for future industrial transformation. We suggest two key directions that provide the conceptual tools necessary to support those living and working in industrial landscapes. First, a return to labour process, where a tightly scaled focus on tasks, skills and practices is needed to understand the capacities of workers to navigate decarbonizing industrial landscapes. Second, the work of feminist economic geographers provides a basis for focusing on social and material relations beyond the workplace. This broader analytical frame recognizes that industrial transformation resonates far beyond the enterprise.

Notes

1   An unwieldy string of references would serve as a distraction here. A very truncated and selective list might include contributions by Bluestone and Harrison (1982), Massey (1984), McDowell and Massey (1984), Hudson and Sadler (1989), Florida and Kenny (1992), Gibson (1992), Modell (1998), Sadler and Thompson (2001), McDowell (2003), Sadler (2004) and Hudson (2005), among many others.

2   Though the corpus of Roger Penn and Elaine Scattergood is an important exception (Penn and Scattergood, 1985).

References

Bamberry. L. (2016) 'Restructuring women's work; labour market and household gender regimes in the Greater Latrobe Valley, Australia', *Gender, Place & Culture*, 23(8): 1135–49.

Beer, A. (2018) 'The closure of the Australian car manufacturing industry: redundancy, policy and community impacts', *Australian Geographer*, 49(3): 419–38.

Beer, A., Ayres, S., Clower, T., Faller, F., Sancino, A. and Sotarauta, M. (2019) 'Place leadership and regional economic development: a framework for cross-regional analysis', *Regional Studies*, 53(2): 171–82.

Bluestone, B. and Harrison, B. (1982) *The Deindustrialization of America: Plant Closings, Community Abandonment, and the Dismantling of Basic Industry*, New York: Basic Books.

Blum, J.A. (2000) 'Degradation without deskilling: twenty-five years in the San Francisco shipyards', in M. Burawoy, J.A. Blum, S. George, Z. Gille and T. Gowan, L. Haney, M. Klawiter, S.H. Lopez, S. Ó Riain, and M. Thayer *Global Ethnography: Forces, Connections and Imaginations in a Postmodern World*, Oakland: University of California Press, pp 106–36.

Braverman, H. (1974) *Labor and Monopoly Capital: The Degradation of Work in the Twentieth Century*, New York: Monthly Review Press.

Burawoy, M (1979) *Manufacturing Consent: Changes in the Labor Process Under Monopoly Capitalism*, Chicago: University of Chicago Press.

Cameron, J. and Gibson, K. (2005) 'Alternative pathways to community and economic development: the Latrobe Valley community partnering project', *Geographical Research*, 43(3): 274–85.

Carr, C. (2017) 'Maintenance and repair beyond the perimeter of the plant: linking industrial labour and the home', *Transactions of the Institute of British Geographers*, 42(4): 642–54.

Castree, N. (2007) 'Labour geography: a work in progress', *International Journal of Urban and Regional Research*, 31(4): 853–62.

Coe, N.M. and Jordhus-Lier, D.C. (2011) 'Constrained agency? Re-evaluating the geographies of labour', *Progress in Human Geography*, 35(2): 211–33.

Cravey, A.J. (1997) 'The politics of reproduction: households in the Mexican industrial transition', *Economic Geography*, 73(2): 166–86.

Cox, R. (2018) 'Gender, work, non-work and the invisible migrant: au pairs in contemporary Britain', *Palgrave Communications*, 4: art 4. Available from: https://doi.org/10.1057/s41599-018-0174-9 [Accessed 16 June 2023].

De Coss-Corzo, A. (2021) 'Patchwork: repair labor and the logic of infrastructure adaptation in Mexico City', *Environment and Planning D: Society and Space*, 39(2): 237–53.

Edwards, G., Hamner, C., Park, S., MacNeil, R., Bojovic, M., Kucic-Riker, J., Musil, D. and Viney, G. (2022) Towards a Just Transition for Coal in Australia?, April. Sydney: Sydney Environment Institute. Available from: https://www.sydney.edu.au/content/dam/corporate/documents/sydney-environment-institute/publications/reports/just_transition_from_coal_in_aus_summary_report.pdf [Accessed 16 June 2023].

England, K. and Dyck, I. (2012) 'Migrant workers in home care: routes, responsibilities, and respect', *Annals of the Association of American Geographers*, 102(5): 1076–83.

England, K. and Lawson, V. (2005) 'Feminist analyses of work: rethinking the boundaries, gendering, and spatiality of work', in L. Nelson and J. Seager (eds) *A Companion to Feminist Geography*, Malden, MA: Wiley-Blackwell, pp 77–92.

Ettlinger, N. (2002) 'The difference that difference makes in the mobilization of workers', *International Journal of Urban and Regional Research*, 26(4): 834–43.

Fleming, D.A. and Measham, T.G. (2015) 'Income inequality across Australian regions during the mining boom 2001–2011', *Australian Geographer*, 46(2): 203–16.

Florida, R. and Kenny, M. (1992) 'Restructuring in place: Japanese investment, production, organisation, and the geography of steel', *Economic Geography*, 68(2): 146–73.

Gibson, K. (1992) 'Hewers of cake and drawers of tea: women, industrial restructuring and class processes on the coalfields of central Queensland', *Rethinking Marxism*, 5(4): 29–56.

Gibson-Graham, J.K. (1993) 'Waiting for the revolution, or how to smash capitalism while working at home in your spare time', *Rethinking Marxism*, 6(2): 10–24.

Gibson-Graham, J.K. (1996) *The End of Capitalism (As We Knew It): A Feminist Critique of Political Economy*, Oxford: Blackwell.

Gibson-Graham, J.K. (2006) *A Postcapitalist Politics*, Minneapolis: University of Minnesota Press.

Hall, S.M. (2016) 'Everyday family experiences of the financial crisis: getting by in the recent economic recession', *Economic Geography*, 16(2): 305–30.

Hall, S.M. (2017) 'Personal, relational and intimate geographies of austerity: ethical and empirical considerations', *Area*, 49(3): 303–10.

Hanson, S. and Pratt, G. (1988) 'Spatial dimensions of the gender division of labor in a local labor market', *Urban Geography*, 9(2): 108–202.

Harvey, D. (1973) *Social Justice and the City*, London: Edward Arnold.

Head, L., Farbotko, C., Gibson, C., Gill, N. and Waitt, G. (2013) 'Zones of friction, zones of traction: the connected households in climate change and sustainability policy', *Australian Journal of Environmental Management*, 20(4): 351–62.

Herod, A. (1997) 'From a geography of labor to a labor geography: labor's spatial fix and the geography of capitalism', *Antipode*, 29(1): 1–31.

Hudson, R. (2005) 'Rethinking change in old industrial regions: reflecting on the experiences of North East England', *Environment and Planning A: Economy and Space*, 37(4): 581–96.

Hudson, R. and Sadler, D. (1989) *The International Steel Industry: Restructuring, State Policies and Localities*, London: Routledge.

ILO (International Labour Organization) (2015) *Guidelines for a Just Transition: Towards Environmentally Sustainable Economies and Societies for All*, Geneva: ILO.

Mackenzie, S. and Rose, D. (1983) 'Industrial change, the domestic economy and home life', in J. Anderson, S. Duncan and R. Hudson (eds) *Redundant Spaces in Cities and Regions? Studies in Industrial Decline and Social Change*, London: Academic Press, pp 155–200.

Marx, K. ([1867] 1976) *Capital Volume I*, B. Fowkes (trans), London: Penguin.

Massey, D. (1984) *Spatial Divisions of Labour: Social Structures and the Geography of Production*, Basingstoke: Macmillan.

Massey, D. and Meegan, R. (1982) *Anatomy of Job Loss: The How, Why and Where of Employment Decline*, London: Methuen.

Mattern, S. (2018) 'Maintenance and care', Places Journal, November. Available at: https://doi.org/10.22269/181120 [Accessed 21 March 2019].

McDowell, L. (1991) 'Life without father and Ford: the new gender order of post-Fordism', *Transactions of the Institute of British Geographers*, 16(4): 400–19.

McDowell, L. (1992) 'Doing gender: feminism, feminists and research methods in human geography', *Transactions of the Institute of British Geographers*, 17(4): 399–416.

McDowell, L. (2003) *Redundant Masculinities? Employment Change and White Working Class Youth*, Malden, MA: Wiley-Blackwell.

McDowell, L. (2004) 'Masculinity, identity and labour market change: some reflections on the implications of thinking relationally about difference and the politics of inclusion', *Geografiska Annaler Series B: Human Geography*, 86(1): 45–56.

McDowell, L. (2008) 'Thinking through class and gender in the context of working class studies', *Antipode*, 40(1): 20–4.

McDowell, L. (2015) 'Roepke Lecture in Economic Geography – The Lives of Others: body work, the production of difference, and labor geographies', *Economic Geography*, 91(1): 1–23.

McDowell, L. and Massey, D. (1984) 'A woman's place?', in D. Massey and J. Allen (eds) *Geography Matters! A Reader*, Cambridge: Cambridge University Press, pp 128–47.

Millington, N. (2019) 'Critical spatial practices of repair', Society + Space, 26 August. Available from: https://www.societyandspace.org/articles/criti cal-spatial-practices-of-repair [Accessed 19 January 2021].

Modell, J. (1998) *A Town Without Steel: Envisioning Homestead*, Pittsburgh, PA: University of Pittsburgh Press.

Oberhauser, A. (1995) 'Towards a gendered regional geography: women and work in rural Appalachia', *Growth and Change*, 26(2): 217–44.

Peck, J. (2018) 'Pluralizing labour geography', in G. Clark, M. Feldman, M. Gerler and D. Wójcik (eds) *The New Oxford Handbook of Economic Geography*, Oxford: Oxford University Press, pp 465–84.

Penn, R. and Scattergood, E. (1985) 'Deskilling or enskilling? An empirical investigation of recent theories of the labour process', *British Journal of Sociology*, 36(4): 611–30.

Pratt, G. (1999) 'From registered nurse to registered nanny: discursive geographies of Filipina domestic workers in Vancouver, B.C.', *Economic Geography*, 75(3): 215–36.

Pratt, G. and Hanson, S. (1991) 'On the links between home and work: family-household strategies in a buoyant labour market', *International Journal of Urban and Regional Research*, 15(1): 55–74.

Rainnie, A., D'Urbano, T., Barrett, R., Paulet, R. and Grobbelaar, M. (2004) 'Industrial relations in the Latrobe Valley: myths and realities', *Labour and Industry*, 15(2): 25–46.

Sadler, D. (2004) 'Cluster evolution, the transformation of old industrial regions and the steel industry supply chain in North East England', *Regional Studies*, 38(1): 55–66.

Sadler, D. and Thompson, J. (2001) 'In search of regional industrial culture: the role of labour organisations in old industrial regions', *Antipode*, 33(4): 661–86.

Scott, A. (2000) 'Economic geography: the great half-century', *Cambridge Journal of Economics*, 24(4): 483–504.

Sheldon, P., Junankar, R. and Pontello, A. (2018) The Ruhr or Appalachia? Deciding the Future of Australia's Coal Power Workers and Communities – *IRRC Report for CFMMEU Mining and Energy*, Sydney: Industrial Relations Research Centre and University of New South Wales.

Smith, C. (2015) 'Continuity and change in labor process analysis: forty years after *Labor and Monopoly Capital*', *Labor Studies Journal*, 40(3): 222–42.

Snell, D. (2018) '"Just transition?" Conceptual challenges meet stark reality in a "transitioning" coal region in Australia', *Globalizations*, 15(4): 550–64.

Strauss, K. (2015) 'Social reproduction and migrant domestic labour in Canada and the UK: towards a multi-dimensional concept of subordination', in L. Waite, G. Craig, H. Lewis and K. Skrivankova (eds) *Vulnerability, Exploitation and Migrants: Insecure Work in a Globalised Economy*, London: Palgrave Macmillan, pp 59–71.

Strauss, K. (2020) 'Labour geographies III: precarity, racial capitalism and infrastructure', *Progress in Human Geography*, 44(6): 1212–24.

Swanton, D. (2013) 'The steel plant as assemblage', *Geoforum*, 44: 282–91.

Taksa, L. (2000) 'Like a bicycle, forever teetering between individualism and collectivism: considering community in relation to labour history', *Labour History*, 78: 7–32.

Thompson, P. (1983) *The Nature of Work: An Introduction to Debates on the Labor Process*, Basingstoke: Macmillan.

Tonts, M. (2010) 'Labour market dynamics in resource dependent regions: an examination of the Western Australian goldfields', *Geographical Research*, 48(2): 148–65.

Van Doorn, N. (2017) 'Platform labor: on the gendered and racialized exploitation of low-income service work in the "on-demand" economy', *Information Communication & Society*, 20(6): 898–914.

Walker, R. and Storper, M. (1981) 'Capital and industrial location', *Progress in Human Geography*, 5(4): 473–509.

Warren, A. (2019) 'Labour geographies of workplace restructuring: an intra-labour analysis', *Antipode*, 51(2): 681–706.

Weller, S.A. (2019) 'Just transition? Strategic framing and the challenges facing coal dependent communities', *Environment & Planning C: Politics and Space*, 37(2): 298–316.

18

Labour: Reckoning with Inequality through 'Divisions of Labour'

Nancy Worth

Introduction

This chapter examines the economic geographies of labour and highlights how geographers are reckoning with inequality within labour (see also Strauss's excellent series of reports for *Progress in Human Geography*: Strauss, 2018a, 2018b, 2019; see also Chapter 24 in this volume). There are a myriad number of ways to approach this diverse topic: Herod (2018: 5) calls labour a 'resource unlike any other' because it is both *object* (labour is bought and sold on the market like a commodity) and *subject* (workers are agential and embodied). In this contribution I use the labour-as-subject lens, considering how workers can actively intervene in the means of production, considering forms of agency and workers' relationship to structural power. Scaling up from attention on labour, my approach here is also guided by research in the diverse economies framework (Gibson-Graham, 2008), which examines economic difference, considering work beyond wage labour, and challenging us to think beyond the imperatives of capitalism (see Chapter 4 in this volume).

To centre inequality, I use 'divisions of labour' as an organizing strategy for the main section of this chapter. Labour can be divided in many ways to show different power structures, relationships and spatiality. Although not my focus here, perhaps the most famous is Marx's (via Adam Smith) 'technical division of labour', where workers specialize in different parts of the production process, allowing workers to build up their skills and increase efficiency – consider the many jobs involved in a car assembly line. Instead, I use various spatial and social divisions of labour, understanding why different places and people do different forms of labour (see 'social division of labour' in Marx, [1867] 1992). Divisions of labour reveal power and inequality – for example, within the gendered division of labour, women do the majority of unpaid work, are more likely to be in informal or low-wage work and are more likely to be in work that is insecure and hazardous. Moreover, following Dutta (2016), across the chapter I highlight research that listens to workers, prioritizing their narratives within wider descriptions of economic change. The chapter proceeds with two main sections – the first examines five different divisions of wage labour, while the second moves beyond wage labour, gesturing towards the many forms of work beyond formal employment.

Divisions of wage labour

Within each of the following divisions of labour I begin with a brief definition; I then highlight examples from the literature that centre the lives of workers and I feature an important concept that geographers are developing: social division of labour (*precarity*), spatial division of labour (*restructuring*), migrant labour (*unfreedom*), gendered labour (*care*) and digital labour (*entrepreneurial affect*).

Social division of labour

One of the first things many of us learn as students of economic geography is that the economy is divided into different sectors – primary (agriculture, extractive industries), secondary (manufacturing), tertiary (service industries) and quaternary (knowledge work). Economic geographers are interested in how these sectors have expanded and contracted over time, from the Industrial Revolution and the rise of manufacturing to the growth of service (and now knowledge) economies. Each of these sectors involves a group of workers, which gives us the social division of labour, or workers doing different types of jobs. This matters as different kinds of work have different demands on workers. For example, in manufacturing, working on the assembly line involves showing up for work at the right time and completing your task. With service work, especially work focused on interactions with customers, a whole range of embodied and aesthetic labour comes into play as part of or alongside the job (McDowell, 2009, 2012). While we might begin with seeing labour as solely an economic concern, McDowell's research demonstrates how work is bound up with questions of identity and power. For example, hotels have been a productive workplace to examine the nuances of service work; according to Jordhus-Lier and Underthun (2015) hotel labour is simultaneously embedded in national labour markets, hierarchical workplaces, the practices of working bodies and workers' agency to contest the conditions of their labour. Digging into this complexity is a highlight of this kind of case study research that examines the specific dynamics and actors within a workplace (see also Dyer et al, 2008 on care work in a hospital).

Most workers in the Global North now work in the service and knowledge economy. A key issue is the insecurity of these jobs, especially when compared to the perceived stability of much manufacturing work before the 1970s. In contrast to the 'standard employment relationship' (a full-time, permanent job with benefits, often with standard hours), low-wage service work is increasingly precarious. This involves work that is often contract, part-time, unpredictable and with few benefits – these are some of the empirical measures of *precarity*, which in a subjective sense 'conjures life worlds that are inflected with uncertainty and instability' (Waite, 2009: 416). My own work on precarity sets out how this insecurity about work invades other aspects of our lives – we can 'feel precarious' (Worth, 2016). As this low-wage, insecure service class expands, so too does higher-paid, more secure knowledge work – this polarization was forcefully exposed (again) during the COVID-19 pandemic, where precarious service workers faced either unemployment or risky 'essential' work while most knowledge workers quickly shifted to the security of working from home (Worth and Karaagac, 2020).

Spatial division of labour

The spatial division of labour is one of economic geography's key contributions; it examines the changing dynamics of where labour happens, especially in relation to capital. Massey's (1984) *Spatial Divisions of Labour* examines this process at a regional level in the UK. She considers how the uneven development of capitalism is created through narratives of regional 'dominance and dependence' (see Chapter 1 in this volume). Powerful centres (like London) were at the top of the hierarchy, where headquarters were located, and decisions and profits were made. In the North of England, branch plant manufacturing (and blue-collar jobs) depended on decisions from the south. Since the 1970s and 1980s, economic geographers have traced periods of *restructuring*, where firms reorganize their operations to maximize profits. The changing spatial division of labour is one form of restructuring, with the most prominent feature being the outsourcing of manufacturing work from the Global North to the Global South, and the proportional rise of service work in the Global North, as mentioned earlier. Outsourcing occurs as firms aim to take advantage of lower labour costs, or more permissive regulatory regimes. This global shift in labour is also called the new international division of labour (Fröbel et al, 1980).

Economic geographers have traced the consequences of manufacturing labour moving into new spaces. Wright' s (1999: 1615) work on maquiladoras (duty-free factories in Mexico owned by foreign firms) is instructive: 'capitalism is, in the first instance, a local phenomenon. The ideas behind it may have a global dimension, but the working out of capitalism occurs when individuals are identified to represent varying kinds of capitalist subjects'. For Wright's ethnography of the maquila, the nature of men's work versus women's work and the status of American managers over Mexican workers come into broad relief. Werner builds on this foundational work, examining garment factories operating in a trade zone on the Dominican Republic–Haiti border. Werner interrogates labouring bodies through the 'coloniality of power'. This analytic is the 'terrain … linking hierarchical, colonial forms of social difference to capital accumulation, a process that not only reproduces (with difference) race, gender, and nation, but one that also renews capital accumulation' (Werner, 2011: 1591). Her analysis offers more nuance than the shift of manufacturing labour from North to South – many more subtle divisions are at play. Beyond manufacturing, Kleibert (2015) details services offshoring, where international firms locate key services (like call centres) in large urban centres like Manila – creating 'islands of globalization' that mimic aspects of cities in the Global North. Her work examines how the economic logic of the spatial division of labour (finding lower labour costs) has powerful impacts on the territory and workers where capital touches down.

Migrant division of labour

Beyond economic sectors and geographical spaces, we can also consider divisions about labour based on workers themselves. The migrant division of labour highlights workers with different immigration statuses, which leads to differential treatment in the labour market (including access to work, worker protection and welfare) (Wills, 2017). Much work in economic geography has traced the differences among migrants, from 'elite migrants' working in global financial services who have the power to crisscross borders fluidly, to temporary foreign workers who are often in highly restricted precarious work. Understanding the relative agency of migrant workers is critical; a useful concept here is *unfreedom*, defined as a 'continuum of exploitation' (Strauss, 2012: 137), 'between freedom (to commodify one's labour) and unfreedom (the various forms of compulsion that require one to do so under varying conditions)' (Strauss, 2012: 140). Many economic migrants face restrictions as part of their visa status – limiting them to a particular industry or even a single employer. When economic security (and perhaps the potential for future settlement is at stake) it can be very difficult for migrants to contest their working conditions (see Pratt, 2012; and the testimonial play that examines Canada's temporary foreign worker programme from the perspective of Filipino live-in caregivers Pratt et al, 2020).

May et al (2007) use the migrant division of labour to understand occupational polarization in London, where low-wage work is increasingly performed by migrants. Beyond issues of pay, they also highlight the 'deskilling' of migrants, who often are working in positions that do not require their academic or professional qualifications. Rather than positioning migrants on the 'fringes' of the labour market, the authors emphasize their centrality. May et al (2007: 161) emphasize that 'the economy is a political construction'; the role of the state, in the UK and elsewhere, deserves more focus within the migrant division of labour – creating the entry conditions for migrant workers and often limiting access to welfare and other social supports.

Gendered division of labour

The gendered division of labour refers to both the stereotypical expectations of masculine work and feminine work, as well as the resulting occupational segregation we see in many parts of the labour market (both horizontal, where men and women do different kinds of jobs, and vertical, where men are more likely to hold senior roles). Feminized work often involves aspects of nurturing and *care*, building on and contributing to sexist norms about women's 'natural' abilities. This segregation is directly tied to assumptions about value: occupations dominated by men tend to be higher paid than those dominated by others. Geographers have traced the social and economic consequences of this division of labour; in Quintal-Marineau's (2017) case study of Kangiqtugaapik, Nunavut, the community experienced the shift to wage labour (rather than a land-based economy) over one generation. Inuit women's experiences of wage labour often extended their traditional caring roles. Quintal-Marineau traces Inuit girls' socialization into domestic labour and the needs of the family into their preparation for wage work – 'Mothers would comment on their son being too shy to look for a job and their daughter being resourceful and being mature enough to deal with wage employment responsibilities' (2017: 343). This connects to the social division of labour and the rise of 'feminized' service work, work that often involves the emotional labour of deference and care (see also Chapters 11, 20, 21, 23, 24 and 27 in this volume).

While to some extent operating within a binary, the most revealing aspects of this division of labour involve norms of masculinity and femininity rather than a binary framing of gender. However, research on the gendered division of labour for the most part has been cisnormative. Moreover, experiences of labour and the workplace are often not centred in trans geographies; Todd (2021) (although see Rush-Morgan, 2023) calls 'for further geographical research to turn to the minutiae of trans people's everyday lives in their full diversity and complexity, and continue to move beyond representations of trans lived experience as marginal and solely traumatic'. More trans geographies of work and the workplace would be a productive addition to the gendered division of labour and economic geography more broadly.

Digital division of labour

The digital division of labour operates like a technical and spatial division of labour; technically, digital work, especially in the form of crowdsourcing websites like Amazon's Mechanical Turk, can involve discrete (often repetitive) tasks, like the assembly line in manufacturing where workers specialize in a different skill (see Chapter 30 in this volume). Spatially, it refers to work that happens (or is arranged through) digital spaces, rather than offline. At an intimate scale, in the lives of workers, 'technologies extend and intensify work, rendering the boundaries of the workplace emergent' (Richardson, 2018: 244). For example, many people engage with the digital labour of email, more frequently and beyond typical work hours. Within the intensive work ethic of tech sector start-up firms, Cockayne (2016: 462) identifies an *entrepreneurial affect*, or a connection to work that blurs work/ life boundaries: 'the seductive character of entrepreneurialism is located in the affective and economic sense of satisfaction in one's work, which is also satisfaction in one's self'. As a result, for some it is not a sacrifice to work long hours in risky ventures – it was a marker of their commitment.

At the global scale, geographers have examined digital outsourcing, through the rise of digital work in Africa. Anwar and Graham (2020) argue that this work can contribute to significant insecurities for workers – while there is some perception of autonomy and entrepreneurship as workers can choose their tasks, workers often work long hours for low wages, with little chance of advancement. Within platform labour, where tasks are advertised on apps and workers are crowdsourced, people can end up competing against each other, depressing pay per task. Moreover, regulation (including greater worker security) of this new form of work is challenging, especially in economies that are highly informal, as work is not tied to physical place and can easily move elsewhere.

Moving beyond wage labour

As wage labour is only one form of work in the economy, it is vital to consider a more inclusive framing of labour (Gibson-Graham, 2008; Monteith et al, 2021). Looking at the diversity of labour seen in Figure 18.1, a version of the Diverse Economies Iceberg based on my freelancing research, this chapter so far has stayed above the waterline, prioritizing wage labour. To some extent this represents where research on labour has historically happened in economic geography – based on narrow definitions of 'the economic'.

Figure 18.1: Economic iceberg of freelancers

Paid freelance work

Looking for work

Volunteering

Building work networks

Caring   Working for free

Chasing invoices

Cooking

Bartering   Maintenance

Cleaning

Training

But building on the influential work of Gibson–Graham and other feminist geographers the terrain of labour within economic geography is getting more expansive.

Beyond the selections that follow, geographers also examine indentured and enslaved labour through the lens of racial capitalism (Kothari, 2013; Fraser, 2018; Hawthorne, 2019). For Bledsoe et al (2022: 288), 'the afterlives of settler colonialism and chattel slavery inform the realities of present-day capitalism', a key point of reckoning before thinking through what alternatives to capitalism could look like. Using examples from Detroit and Washington, DC, Bledsoe et al (2022) consider how cooperative enterprises geared to food security for the local community contest capitalist dispossession through self-reliance and labour for the commons. Geographers are also examining the diverse (un)paid work that happens within social reproduction (see Chapter 24 in this volume) among many other forms of labour. In this section, I consider self-employment (and the concept of *organizing*), and informal labour (considering *agency*).

Self-employment (working for yourself rather than for an employer) is a growing employment relationship in many countries in the Global North, from gig workers in the platform economy who are often categorized as 'independent contractors', to freelancers in knowledge work who move from project to project. This employment relationship means workers are not employees and are often left out of state employment protections and employer benefits (like pensions and health care). This reduced responsibility for firms can incentivize misclassification, where firms seek to categorize workers as self-employed rather than as their employees. Self-employment is often valorized for its flexibility – but for many, especially those working for low pay, it can be lonely and insecure. Economic geographers have examined the spatiality of freelancers and the workplaces they seek out or build for themselves, especially co-working spaces and innovation labs (Avdikos and Kalogeresis, 2017). These collaborative workplaces create opportunities for innovation and networking, while also functioning as a supportive space for this often-insecure form of work. In my own research on freelancing, I focus on the interrelationship of paid and unpaid work (see Figure 18.1), where often only a small portion of work 'counts' – especially when rates are preset. I am also interested in the role of freelancing in the labour market; self-employment offers another way of thinking about what counts as 'work', and who is responsible for regulating and protecting these 'new' ways of working (Worth and Karaagac, 2022).

Another focus of geographers is the potential for the self-employed to improve their pay and job security. Similar to the just-in time nature of assembly-line work, Wells et al (2020) argue that platforms like Uber create 'just-in-place labour' where workers are sent to specific places to pick up passengers. While this labour arrangement creates a fragmented workforce with limited agency, the authors consider how this work arrangement also impacts *organizing* – the potential for workers to build solidarity and challenge their working conditions through collective action. The authors detail a form of temporary solidarity that emerged at an airport, where drivers were grouped into a pick-up area. This 'emplacement' by Uber provided a rare opportunity to strategize with other drivers – physical space became a key component to begin to organize independent contractors. Organizing among self-employed workers remains challenging, as the work itself often keeps people apart.

Informal labour, productive work that is not taxed or regulated by government, involves 2 billion workers across the world, predominantly in the Global South (ILO, 2018). Surprisingly, informal labour often receives only brief attention from economic geographers; more often, urban and development geographers attend to the diversity of informal labour. Livelihood studies has been a productive lens for development geographers, considering all the strategies people employ to survive, including labour that moves between formality and informality. Returning to the social division of labour, most informal labour occurs in the primary sector (agriculture), involving self-provisioning – growing food to survive. Yet informal labour occurs in all sectors of the economy. Urban geographers researching cities in the Global South often connect informal labour with the informal economy more broadly (including housing and infrastructure). In Thieme's (2018) research with informal waste workers in Nairobi, she digs into the 'hustle' of informal work, examining the urgency, engagement and uncertainty of everyday economic survival.

Within the concept of 'hustle' is an understanding of *agency*, or a worker's ability to make choices about their labour. For informal workers, especially in relation to other more powerful actors including the state and police, agency is often nuanced and contingent. Muñoz (2016: 339) employs agency in her work with Latino/a street vendors in Los Angeles; vendors are 'often in precarious, vulnerable situations, [yet] are able to reconfigure economic spaces and create viable economic strategies making informal labour a choice within fluid and temporal complex restrictive systems'. Some street vendors chose this work as it gave them more flexibility (in their hours, bringing kids to work) than they could find within formal wage work, but it also regularly put them in contact with police who threatened them with fines. Here, agency was not (only) about building collective rights for vendors, it also involved a negotiation with limited options. Importantly, Muñoz challenges simplifications of informal work, seeing this labour as an integral part of a wider economic system that is uneven and exclusionary. Research on informal labour is often published outside the subdiscipline of economic geography, yet informal labour (and all its included economic activities) are an integral part of economic life in the Global South. Contemporary economic geographies would benefit from understanding the full nature and interrelations of economic activity (including informal labour and unpaid work); in the short term this means engaging with the existing scholarship on labour within development and urban geography and beyond. In the longer term this involves expanding what contemporary economies geographies understands as 'the economic'.

Conclusion

To conclude I briefly reflect on considering labour in economy geography through the lens of inequality. Economic geographers have most often thought about inequality in terms of social class, including through the social division of labour where different jobs led to different amounts of power and status in society (who is a worker and who owns the means of production). In this chapter I've highlighted other ways of thinking about inequality, including race, gender, gender identity, citizenship status, employment relation and geographic location – who and where we live as workers matters. This borrows a labour geography approach of centring the worker, but also expands our focus beyond formal wage labour and social class. This expansive understanding of labour opens up contemporary economic geography to both the detail of a worker's lived experience as well as a grounding in the diversity of economic relations within and beyond capitalism. The subdiscipline of economic geography is always in the making, yet as Rosenman et al (2020: 515) powerfully demonstrate the dominant 'core' of economic geography has not meaningfully engaged with long-standing concerns of feminist economic geographers: 'economic geographical research on women, categories of social difference, and non-traditional and informal employment relationships are still largely framed as outside stalwart disciplinary traditions'. Moreover, in their analysis of economic geography publications, 'there appears to be a gap between recognizing female scholars as top contributors to the field of economic geography and systematically and substantively publishing the research of women and other non-male identified scholars in top economic geography journals' (Rosenman et al, 2020: 525). As a result, it's important to recognize that vital research on labour is often published outside of economic geography journals.

Finally, when thinking about the role of labour in the economy more broadly, it's important to consider the rise of anti-work and post-work thinking within discourses about the future of work (Reid-Musson et al, 2020). Geographers have been inspired by Weeks's (2011) *The Problem with Work*, which digs into the politics of work, rather than seeing it as a given in society. Weeks argues that the primacy of wage labour stops us from thinking about other ways of organizing economic life. Yet in times of crisis, the seemingly impossible becomes possible: when many people lost jobs or were furloughed at the height of the COVID-19 pandemic, many countries in the Global North provided emergency funding directly to citizens, galvanizing debates about universal basic income policies and the need for a more equitable economic system. Going forward, to deeply examine labour, economic geographers need to be attentive to what is new: work organized through digital platforms, the rise of automation, knowledge work that is increasingly disconnected from physical place, but also all the ways that inequalities within labour under capitalism endure. As technology creates change in the lives of workers, exploitation may take new forms, but the pressure to extract value from workers remains. Understanding labour means reckoning with the agency and subjectivity of workers in all parts of the economy – across divisions of wage labour and beyond the limits of wage labour itself.

References

Anwar, M.A. and Graham, M. (2020) 'Digital labour at economic margins: African workers and the global information economy', *Review of African Political Economy*, 47(163): 95–105.

Avdikos, V. and Kalogeresis, A. (2017) 'Socio-economic profile and working conditions of freelancers in co-working spaces and work collectives: evidence from the design sector in Greece', *Area*, 49(1): 35–42.

Bledsoe, A., McCreary, T. and Wright, W. (2022) 'Theorizing diverse economies in the context of racial capitalism', *Geoforum*, 132: 281–90.

Cockayne, D.G. (2016) 'Entrepreneurial affect: attachment to work practice in San Francisco's digital media sector', *Environment and Planning D: Society and Space*, 34(3): 456–73.

Dutta, M. (2016) 'Place of life stories in labour geography: why does it matter?', *Geoforum*, 77: 1–4.

Dyer, S., McDowell, L. and Batnitzky, A. (2008) 'Emotional labour/body work: the caring labours of migrants in the UK's National Health Service', *Geoforum*, 39(6): 2030–8.

Fraser, N. (2018) 'Roepke Lecture in Economic Geography – From Exploitation to Expropriation: historic geographies of racialized capitalism', *Economic Geography*, 94(1): 1–17.

Fröbel, F., Heinrichs, J. and Kreye, O. (1980) *The New International Division of Labour*, Cambridge: Cambridge University Press.

Gibson-Graham, J.K. (2008) 'Diverse economies: performative practices for "other worlds"', *Progress in Human Geography*, 32(5): 613–32.

Hawthorne, C. (2019) 'Black matters are spatial matters: Black geographies for the twenty-first century', *Geography Compass*, 13(11): art e12468. Available from: https://doi.org/10.1111/gec3.12468 [Accessed 19 June 2023].

Herod, A. (2018) *Labor*, Cambridge: Polity Press.

ILO (International Labour Organization) (2018) *Women and Men in the Informal Economy: A Statistical Picture* (3rd edn), Geneva: ILO.

Jordhus-Lier, D. and Underthun, A. (eds) (2015) *A Hospitable World? Organising Work and Workers in Hotels and Tourist Resorts*, Abingdon: Routledge.

Kleibert, J.M. (2015) 'Islands of globalisation: offshore services and the changing spatial divisions of labour', *Environment and Planning A: Economy and Space*, 47(4): 884–902.

Kothari, U. (2013) 'Geographies and histories of unfreedom: indentured labourers and contract workers in Mauritius', *Journal of Development Studies*, 49(8): 1042–57.

Marx, K. ([1867] 1992) *Capital Volume I*, B. Fowkes (trans), London: Penguin.

Massey, D. (1984) *Spatial Divisions of Labour: Social Structures and the Geography of Production*, Basingstoke: Macmillan.

May, J., Wills, J., Datta, K., Evans, Y., Herbert, J. and McIlwaine, C. (2007) 'Keeping London working: global cities, the British state and London's new migrant division of labour', *Transactions of the Institute of British Geographers*, 32(2): 151–67.

McDowell, L. (2009) *Working Bodies: Interactive Service Employment and Workplace Identities*, Chichester: Wiley-Blackwell.

McDowell, L. (2012) 'Post-crisis, post-Ford and post-gender? Youth identities in an era of austerity', *Journal of Youth Studies*, 15(5): 573–90.

Monteith, W., Vicol, D.O. and Williams, P. (eds) (2021) *Beyond the Wage: Ordinary Work in Diverse Economies*, Bristol: Policy Press.

Muñoz, L. (2016) 'Agency, choice and restrictions in producing Latina/o street-vending landscapes in Los Angeles', *Area*, 48(3): 339–45.

Pratt, G. (2012) *Families Apart: Migrant Mothers and the Conflicts of Labor and Love*, Minneapolis: University of Minnesota Press.

Pratt, G., Zell, S., Johnston, C. and Venzon, H. (2020) 'Performing Nanay in Winnipeg: Filipino labour migration to Canada (creative intervention)', *Studies in Social Justice*, 2020(14/1): 55–66.

Quintal-Marineau, M. (2017) 'The new work regime in Nunavut: a gender perspective', *Canadian Geographer/Le Géographe canadien*, 61(3): 334–45.

Reid-Musson, E., Cockayne, D., Frederiksen, L. and Worth, N. (2020) 'Feminist economic geography and the future of work', *Environment and Planning A: Economy and Space*, 52(7): 1457–68.

Richardson, L. (2018) 'Feminist geographies of digital work', *Progress in Human Geography*, 42(2): 244–63.

Rosenman, E., Loomis, J. and Kay, K. (2020) 'Diversity, representation, and the limits of engaged pluralism in (economic) geography', *Progress in Human Geography*, 44(3): 510–33.

Rush-Morgan, R. (2023) 'Geographies of queer economies', *Geography Compass*, 17(8): e12719.

Strauss, K. (2012) 'Coerced, forced and unfree labour: geographies of exploitation in contemporary labour markets', *Geography Compass*, 6(3): 137–48.

Strauss, K. (2018a) 'Labour geography 1: towards a geography of precarity?', *Progress in Human Geography*, 42(4): 622–30.

Strauss, K. (2018b) 'Labour geography II: being, knowledge and agency', *Progress in Human Geography*, 44(1): 150–9.

Strauss, K. (2019) 'Labour geography III: precarity, racial capitalisms and infrastructure', *Progress in Human Geography*, 44(6): 1212–24.

Thieme, T.A. (2018) 'The hustle economy: informality, uncertainty and the geographies of getting by', *Progress in Human Geography*, 42(4): 529–48.

Todd, J.D. (2021) 'Exploring trans people's lives in Britain, trans studies, geography and beyond: a review of research progress', *Geography Compass*, 15(4): art e12556. Available from: https://doi.org/10.1111/gec3.12556 [Accessed 19 June 2023].

Waite, L. (2009) 'A place and space for a critical geography of precarity?', *Geography Compass*, 3(1): 412–33.

Weeks, K. (2011) *The Problem with Work: Feminism, Marxism, Antiwork Politics, and Postwork Imaginaries*, Durham, NC: Duke University Press.

Wells, K.J., Attoh, K. and Cullen, D. (2020) '"Just-in-Place" labor: driver organizing in the Uber workplace', *Environment and Planning A: Economy and Space*, 54(2): 315–31.

Werner, M. (2011) 'Coloniality and the contours of global production in the Dominican Republic and Haiti', *Antipode*, 43(5): 1573–97.

Wills, J. (2017) 'Migrant division of labor', in D. Richardson, N. Castree, M.F. Goodchild, A. Kobayashi, W. Liu, and R.A. Marston (eds) *International Encyclopedia of Geography: People, the Earth, Environment and Technology*, Oxford: Wiley. Available from: https://onlinelibrary.wiley.com/doi/full/10.1002/9781118786352.wbieg0173 [Accessed 19 June 2023].

Worth, N. (2016) 'Feeling precarious: millennial women and work', *Environment and Planning D: Society and Space*, 34(4): 601–16.

Worth, N. and Karaagac, E.A. (2020) *Working from Home? New Work Arrangements (for some) in the Context of COVID-19, Region of Waterloo White Paper*. Waterloo, ON: University of Waterloo. Available from: https://uwaterloo.ca/environment/sites/ca.environment/files/uploads/files/economywork_3_working_from_home_worth_karaagan.pdf [Accessed 19 June 2023].

Worth, N. and Karaagac, E.A. (2022) 'Accounting for absences and ambiguities in the freelancing labour relation', *Tijdschrift voor Economische en Sociale Geografie*, 113(1): 96–108.

Wright, M.W. (1999) 'The politics of relocation: gender, nationality, and value in a Mexican maquiladora', *Environment and Planning A: Economy and Space*, 31(9): 1601–17.

19

Economic Development: Political Ecologies of Race

Sharlene Mollett

Introduction

Since the early 2010s, feminist economic geography, largely underpinned by feminist political economy (FPE), has emerged to lead renewed feminist geographic scholarly interest in questions of difference. As Werner et al (2017: 1) note, 'FPE is an approach that understands social difference – including but not limited to gender – to be integral to the functioning of political economic systems and knowledge production processes'. Central to feminist critiques of the 'masculinist' tone of economic geography writ large are appeals for 'emancipatory change' and a 'retaining of steely materialism'. While the broader field of feminist geography has long been committed to the role difference plays in geographic knowledge production, renewed attention to difference in the broader subfield of economic geography seems deeply influenced by the emergent subfields of Indigenous and Black geographies. In addition to bringing about important scholarly interrogations of Indigeneity and Blackness, this raises the importance of complicating spatial processes underpinned by capitalist logics and single axis analyses. With this push, there is currently a growing plethora of work that draws on conceptual frames open to multiple logics of power, namely racial capitalism and a reinvigorated adoption of intersectionality. While the latter has long been operationalized by a small group of feminist geographers largely since the 1990s, intersectionality's almost ubiquitous invocation in critical literature appears to have found firm footing in the subfield of feminist geography more broadly and feminist political ecology in particular.

Racial capitalism too is intersectional. Racial capitalism refers to '[t]he development, organization, and expansion of capitalist society pursued essentially racial directions, so too did social ideology. As a material force ... racialism would inevitably permeate the social structures emergent from capitalism' (Robinson in Melamed, 2015: 77). Which, as Melamed (2015) offers, means that certainly across geographic subfields race and capitalism are tightly woven, and with a concomitant acknowledgement that '[c]apitalism is racial capitalism' (Melamed, 2015: 77). How the term is operationalized, in many cases, seemingly suffers a similar challenge to that of intersectionality, namely an emptying out of race (see Mollett and Faria, 2018). With a frequent tendency to begin geographic understandings of economic change through a reliance on Harvey's 'accumulation by dispossession' as an ongoing process that is structurally required for capitalist production – the consequence of such a narrow focus on the economy means that too often racial and cultural difference are explained, as Fields and Raymond write, 'an unfortunate by-product of overaccumulation, the final stages in a system prone to ever-deepening divides' (Fields and Raymond, 2021: 1629). Even worse, as the case often with intersectionality, race disappears altogether.

This chapter serves as a meaningful reminder that race, whether as part of intersectionality or racial capitalism among others, is not a secondary hierarchal category. Rather, attention to race and racialization, 'allows us to see how racial and cultural differences have instead been deployed to reconcile a conception of the universal (as encapsulated by the notion of humanity) with a notion of the particular (of difference as marked in bodies and spaces)' (Chakravarty and Ferreira da Silva, 2012: 370). Thus, in this chapter, I employ the concept 'postcolonial intersectionality' to attend to multiple kinds of power in the spatial processes of tourism development shaping access to land and livelihoods for Afro-Panamanian women on Panama's Caribbean coast. Through the work of decolonial scholars Anibal Quijano and Maria Lugones, I link contemporary pejorative representations of Afro-descendants, often held by state, elite and other hegemonic groups, to the past. In so doing, I demonstrate through postcolonial intersectional analysis, how gender, race and sexuality, as mutually constituted forms of power, shape space. I centre the intersectional logics of power in Bocas as a former United Fruit Company (UFC) plantation turned tourism enclave, to examine the way Afro-Panamanian women in Old Bank, Bastimentos Island acquiesce to, and quietly contest, an array of dispossessions unfolding in the name of tourism development. These struggles inform feminist political ecologies of place through the embodied meanings of intersectionality, Afro-descendant peoples' struggles for space, and the intersectional logics of power that make visible the need for feminist political ecologists to attend to racial power. This chapter reflects upon the multiple ways Afro-Panamanian women lead a multiscaled, material and symbolic process of place making, one that prioritizes life in spite of, and via struggles over, carnal, gendered and racialized dispossession.

Economic geography, feminist political economy and postcolonial intersectionality

Attention to difference in the subfield of feminist economic geography is part of a collective goal to produce more complete understandings of the spatial–human–environmental dynamics of power operating through the Global South. Building on the early work of feminist political ecologists, FPE pays particular attention to the role that gendered power relations play in shaping access to, control of and distribution of land and natural resources (Rocheleau et al, 1996). More recently, 'new feminist political ecologies' call for a deeper engagement with other kinds of difference beyond gender (and class), building upon a small cluster of scholars already committed to this agenda (Gururani, 2002; Asher, 2009; Mollett, 2010; Radcliffe and Pequeño, 2010); in an effort to establish FPE as a 'feminist and justice oriented project' (Harris, 2015: xxii). These dialogues are occurring alongside, and through interaction with feminist and development economic geographies.

I enthusiastically share in the optimism of FPE's feminist and justice-oriented ambitions. Yet while traces of this move grow, and despite the plethora of intersectionality talk, somehow race and racialized processes (as factors of gendered meanings) receive scant attention in FPE *even while* embracing 'intersectionality' (Buechler and Hanson, 2015; Harcourt and Nelson, 2015). This 'indifference' to racial difference is curious given that Black feminist thinkers, then and now, argue that '[intersectionality's] production was not located outside the field of race and gender power but was an active and direct engagement with issues and dynamics that embodied such power' (Cho et al, 2013: 789; see also Collins, 1991; Lugones, 2007). For Black feminists and radical women of colour, intersectionality makes visible forms of power and oppression that are *invisible* within single axis analyses (hooks, 1984; Collins, 1991; Cho et al, 2013; Mollett and Faria, 2013; Moraga and Anzaldúa, 2015).

Thus,

> postcolonial intersectionality acknowledges the way patriarchy and racialized processes are consistently bound in a postcolonial genealogy that embeds race and gender ideologies within nation building and international development processes. This concept reflects the way people are always marked by difference whether or not they fit nicely in colonial racial categorizations, as cultural difference is also racialized. (Mollett and Faria, 2013: 120)

Hence, postcolonial intersectionality helps us understand the development landscape for Afro-Panamanian women and offers a fuller picture of their multiple and simultaneous struggles over livelihoods, access to natural resources and the right to be recognized as *human*. These are also key areas of research and debate within economic geography (see Chapters 11, 14, 20, 21, 23, 27 and 29 in this volume).

Coloniality of power, racialized gender and postcolonial intersectionality

Focusing in on a particular geographical context, a 'coloniality of power' approach helps explain anti-Black racism in Latin America. Through the work of Peruvian sociologist and decolonial scholar Anibal Quijano, a 'coloniality of power' outlines how cultural and racial presuppositions, designed by the 'Conquest' of 1492, produce the racialized geographies that inform regimes of exploitation and accompanying struggles of contemporary capitalist accumulation (Quijano and Ennis, 2000). Indeed, colonial and postcolonial power in Latin America comprises both modernity and coloniality, where racial subjugation and superiority are materialized through the entangled processes of land appropriation, religious hegemony, and the forced labour of Indigenous and Black bodies (Quijano and Ennis, 2000; Mollett, 2016). Building from Quijano, Argentine feminist and philosopher Maria Lugones argues that while colonialism introduced contemporary racial thinking, it 'did not impose pre-colonial European gender arrangements on the colonized' (2007: 186). Rather 'a new gender system' produced distinct formations for 'colonized males and females' different from Euro-American colonizers. For Lugones (2007: 187) historicizing gender is salient to avoid 'centering [an analysis of patriarchy ...] that rests on male supremacy without any clear understanding of the mechanisms by which heterosexuality, capitalism, and racial classification are impossible to understand apart from each other'. The spatiality of a 'coloniality of power' produced gender meanings along 'racial' lines. For Lugones:

> only white bourgeois women have consistently counted as women so described by the West. Females excluded from that description were not just their subordinates. They were also understood to be animals in a sense that went further than the identification of white women with nature, infants and small animals. They were understood as animals in the deep sense, 'without gender', sexually marked as female, but without the characteristics of femininity. (Lugones, 2007: 202–3)

Thus gender, rather the 'idea' of gender, became an instrument of power of a colonial civilizing masculinized project. Lugones's insistence that Latin

American society is imbued with heterosexist biases, a particularly animalized version for Afro-descendant (and Indigenous) women, offers salient insight to how ADW (Afro-descendant women) activists must continue to fight for recognition as human beings; that Black people are human is not a given. The experiences of ADW and their communities are instructive for developing more critical engagements with intersectionality, understanding the formations of racialized genders and sexualized racializations that I contend economic geography and 'new feminist political ecologies' must take on.

'Persistent misrecognition' as *less-than-human* (Gilroy, 2015)

In Latin America, Afro-descendant populations comprise 200 million (30 per cent) of the region's roughly 500 million people. While life experiences vary throughout the region, Afro-descendants disproportionately fall among the poor. In fact, more than 50 per cent of Afro-descendants live in poverty, a rate that intensifies in rural areas (World Bank, 2008; IDB, 2011). Despite the fact that most Latin American countries are signatories to a variety of international conventions that make racial discrimination illegal, anti-Black racism means Afro-descendants are persistently excluded from basic education, secure employment, adequate housing, healthcare, access to water and food, and are commonly harassed, criminalized, beaten, killed and imprisoned by police, explained in the words of a Garifuna activist, 'simply for being' (IPS, 2010; personal communication, 2016). For ADW there is a growing rise in sexual violence operationalized by alarming incidences of domestic slavery, sex trafficking and femicide (OAS/IAHR, 2011).

ADW's struggles for rights are imbued with the struggle to be recognized as *human*, to disrupt a history that presupposes their inhumanity in the present. As such, many ADW activists argue that recognition of their humanity must 'precede the restructuring of a democratic State *that incorporates from its very foundation a perspective on citizenship and participation which questions formal models of equality which [in its current form] cannot adequately incorporate a diverse plural array of identities*' (Lassén, 2010: 9, my emphasis). The legitimacy of these concerns among ADW activists is confirmed by a report published by the Rapporteurship on the Rights of People of African Descent, sponsored in part by the Inter-American Court of Human Rights. The report asserts that racism and the denial of racism are both salient in everyday lexicon in Latin America. For instance, the very term 'negro' (meaning Black) is considered derogatory and yet it is widely used in news media and in state and public discourse. In fact, anti-Black stereotypes are pervasive. Afro-descendants are frequently accused of smelling like animals, particularly monkeys, and are called such in the streets and newspapers through such terms as *macaco* (monkey) and *besta* (animal) in Brazil. The discursive denigration of Blackness is never far from the physical and material violence against Black bodies and their environments. Said differently, the dehumanizing narratives that target Afro-descendants are never just words, but render legitimate multiple kinds of material and violent embodied dispossessions.

Afro-Panamanian women and tourism development in Panama

The province and archipelago of Bocas del Toro, located on the Atlantic Coast of Panama represents 'a landscape both haunted and developed by old and new hierarchies of humanness' (McKittrick, 2006: xviii). Afro-Panamanian and Ngäbe Indigenous peoples have a long history in Bocas. Afro-Panamanian residents link their presence on the coast to periods of both forced and unforced labour migration, from slavery in the 17th century to plantation work with the UFC throughout the 20th century. While recognized as the 'original' inhabitants of the Bocas coast, Ngäbe presence in the archipelago was interrupted by Miskito raids and attacks that displaced Ngäbe communities (formerly referred to as Guaymí) inland. According to Bourgois (1989), the Ngäbe were forced to evacuate the region in the 17th and 18th centuries, which left the lands open to colonists, private fruit farmers and eventually the UFC. Thus, it is notable that the current popularity of Bocas as a tourist destination builds upon a regional history that links Indigenous and Black land displacement and slavery and coerced labour in the 17th and 18th centuries to export agriculture, wage labour and cocoa farming until the late 20th century.

At the time of writing (2023), Bocas's population numbers roughly 18,000 people who live across nine islands. The population is multicultural and in addition to Afro-Panamanians and Ngäbe peoples, includes Guna peoples, mestizos, predominately White foreigners from Europe and North America, and a growing Chinese merchant population. Panamanian nation building, like elsewhere in the region, did not simply focus on economic development but employed regional cultural narratives of *mestizaje* in the making of the nation (Guerrón-Montero, 2006). *Mestizaje* called for racial mixing between European elites and Indigenous and Black populations as part of a broader nationalist project of civilization. At the heart of *mestizaje* was the process of *blanqueamiento* (whitening) and the idealization of White bodies, Euro-American cultural practices, and the denigration of Black and Indigenous peoples and their cultural practices (Vasconcelos, [1925] 1997; Guerrón-Montero, 2006). But by the early 1900s, US control of both Canal operations and the UFC management spatialized Jim Crow racial policies in both Panama City and on the coast. In Bocas, White supremacy and racial purity aligned with the idealizations of Whiteness embedded in ideals of *blanqueamiento*, despite the growing celebration of Panama as a *mestizo* (mixed race) nation (Milazzo, 2013). These overlapping logics remain close to the surface in present-day Bocas, and unfold in curious ways as Afro-Antillean women negotiate their complex and subjugated emplacement punctuated by multiple oppressions.

Empirical insights from Afro-Antillean women

In this section, I illustrate through ethnographic testimonies the ways in which this postcolonial plantocracy turned tourism enclave shapes Afro-Antillean women's collective claims to livelihood, land security and the right to be recognized as *human*.

Lorraine

Despite growing discontent over foreign ownership and land investment in the name of tourism development, many Afro-Panamanian women desire jobs in tourism. While the tone regarding domestic work is consistently grim, some Afro-Panamanian women in Old Bank tend to see domestic service as a step towards more attractive prospects 'in the future'. At 25, Lorraine is unmarried, lives with her grandparents and works as a housekeeper at one of the medium-sized hotels in Bocas Town, Colon Island. She maintains that "in high school our teachers told us to study because hotels want 'educated' people as employees" (Lorraine, personal communication, 2012). With a high school diploma, Lorraine resides in the Archipelago "to help [her] grandparents".

Lorraine tells me about her job: "I work as a maid for a Panamanian family from the city. They run a 12-room hotel. It's me, and two Indian girls, they are Ngäbe you know Ngäbes?" (Lorraine, personal communication, 2012). She explains that the wife is the boss but it is the husband who supervises. She seems proud of her job particularly since she started working right after high school. However, she does not like her boss, because "her husband is a dog and she lets him be that way". She continues:

> 'The husband is always around and he watches us girls. He is always trying to start something – you know? (She whispers) he wants to have sex with us. One day he told me to meet him in room 6. I said no, because I already knew what he did with the Indian girls in there.' (Lorraine, personal communication, 2012)

However, when she refused, Lorraine's boss (the wife) suspended her for a week. She recounts that after returning to work that "[she] was told [by the husband] to clean up the dog shit and clean out the chicken coop (located about 100 metres behind the hotel) … [she] also had to clean bloodstained sheets at the pila, even though the washing machines are inside". Lorraine maintains that "the husband kept calling me a 'bad girl' and that 'only good girls work inside'". Despite this experience, Lorraine maintains that she would never quit her job, and cogently states that she needs to work, besides "most maid jobs are the same, your boss either ignores you or treats you like a slave".

Lorraine's exploitation is truly disturbing. At the same time, the spatiality of her punishment has meaning in Bocas. Being forced to work outside without 'modern' technology to do the work hygienically (gloves, masks, washing machine) aligns with a history of racial and ethnic labour hierarchies in Bocas. Under the UFC regime the worst kinds of jobs went to those at the bottom of socio-racial hierarchies (Bourgois, 1989). While Afro-Antilleans were subject to deplorable working conditions then, this changed in the 1950s because of significant shifts in UFC administration that led to Afro-Antillean social mobility. As a result, in the 1950s Ngäbe workers were heavily recruited and sometimes 'stolen' from their communities, to work as harvesters. Harvesting is repeatedly cited as the worst job on the plantation (Bourgois, 1989). Lorraine's punishment, however inverted from the past, reflects previous UFC labour practices in a number of ways. Due to a lack of proper sanitation at one UFC operation, Ngäbe men were forced to harvest bananas in the same fields in which plantation employees defecated. Ngäbe workers were also ordered to spray pesticides but were denied available technologies that would have protected them from the poison (safety goggles and masks/ gloves). Once they inevitably fell sick, they were sent back to their villages up river with very little, if any, compensation (Bourgois, 1989). According to the memories of Old Bank residents whose parents (and grandparents) spent their lives working for UFC in Bocas, in the minds and narratives of UFC managers those who worked outside were not just unskilled, but uncivilized, "more animal" (Mollett fieldnotes, 2011; Stephens personal communication, 2011). Similarly, Lorraine was placed outside, even though she worked inside a hotel, as outside work, in the lingering logics of the UFC plantation is, in borrowing phrase from McKittrick (2013: 6), 'incongruent with humanness'.

Michael

There is a bar in Bocas, I will call Paradise. While sitting at my table with backpackers from England, we could not avoid hearing a man named Michael, giving some 'advice' to male backpackers looking to 'hook up' with a 'black girl'. While we clearly missed the beginning part of the conversation, in a loud voice Michael blurts out:

'[N]o, no, no, you've got it all wrong. Easy guys, you can get a darky anytime … *Wari wari* girls are wild, you will get more than you want …

trust me. I know, when I first got here I got with a few *wari wari* girls and almost died of a heart attack, they clawed me good … But after a few months of that … as a man, you learn that that's not normal, you have to get sensible, you need a lady.'

With a full audience, Michael explains that what these newcomers really want is an "Indian girl". He says: "they are 'good' girls, ladies, quiet and always happy. If you are going to stay a long time, that's what you need … They don't understand much English [everyone laughs], but they aren't looking for trouble either, they just want someone to take care of them" (Micheal, in fieldnotes, 2012).

A couple of days later, I randomly found Michael near the Bocas Town pier with a group of what I later confirmed were tourists interested in 'buying property in Bocas'. In this monologue, Michael explains that in his former life, he was a wealthy stockbroker from Tennessee who had done well until the 2008 financial crisis when he fled the US. After a few years in Bocas he now 'owns' a piece of land on the island of La Luna. Michael insists that it is 'easy' to purchase property in Bocas and in fact, he speculates that 'the government [Panamanian] wants foreigners to bring back the coastal economy that was here when United Fruit Company was booming' (Mollett fieldnotes, 2012). After detailing some property buying 'tricks', he insists that "all that is needed is to purchase rights of possession from a local" because people "are so poor they will sell it for nothing" [group laughter]. According to Michael, he previously purchased his land after he and a local young Ngäbe woman, named Lela, "became lovers" and he was looking to "settle down" [again, lots of laughter]. But, according to island rumours, Michael did not pay for the land (Mollett fieldnotes, 2012). Rather, he holds de facto rights to the plot of land where he has a house and runs a 'bed and breakfast' business. Apparently, Lela's father allows Michael to use the land 'in exchange' for 'taking care' of Lela and her younger sister. Lela cooks for guests and she and her sister do the daily housekeeping.

Towards 'plantation logics': intersectional logics of power in Bocas

The UFC plantation is long gone but a 'plantation logic' remains (McKittrick, 2013: 3). These traces of past land uses and social relations contextualize how residential tourism development informs our expectations of specific development imaginaries and practices. Indeed, one of the conditions tied to foreign-owned land concessions for tourism development requires that the developer (foreigner/urban elite) hire 'unskilled labor' (Mollett fieldnotes, 2012). This condition lines up with government assurances that tourism will boost employment and reduce poverty (World Bank, 2008). While mainstream development may consider this 'trickle-down theory' at work, on the ground it is difficult to ignore how the act of locking labour to those who control land, as part of residential tourism development, resembles overlapping racial projects of plantation agriculture and settler colonialism. Plantations are bound to a wider global political economy that becomes empowered by the '"persistent underdevelopment" and "persistent poverty" of black life' (Beckford, 1972 in McKittrick, 2013: 3). A 'coloniality of power' gels in 'the interlocking workings of modernity and blackness [coloniality] which culminate in long-standing, uneven racial geographies' that travel through time in '[a] racialized economy that linger[s] long after [the abolition of slavery and nation-building movements] in the Americas' (McKittrick, 2013: 3).

That Lorraine works as a domestic worker is not remarkable, as Black and Indigenous women commonly comprise a disproportionate role in domestic service (Wade, 2013). The intimate spatialities of hotel work and cleaning homes do not simply offer opportunities for abuse but, as Wade theorizes, 'domestic service is a site where various historically specific dimensions of race, gender, class and age *together* produce a particular and intense form of sexualization' (Wade, 2013: 189, my emphasis). Domestic work, like plantation agriculture, illuminates and discloses how dehumanizing Afro-descendants maintains currency from the past, used to inform geographic formations in the present (McKittrick, 2013).

Plantation logics are not the only racial project in Bocas. Locking 'unskilled labor' to tourism developers and foreign land control is settler colonialism, as settler colonialism is in part a 'land centered' project with an aim to 'eliminate' Indigenous societies (Wolfe, 2006: 393). But this elimination is not simply about the 'disappearance' of Indigenous bodies, but the disavowal of land rights to all those considered inferior to White people and against whose cultures Euro-American cultural practices are deemed superior: this includes Afro-Panamanian women. Proximity to Whiteness for Ngäbe peoples (Michael and Lela) characterizes settler colonialism where Whites have a 'possessive investment' in 'nativeness' in the ways in which the power of Whiteness is articulated in the way 'native peoples disappear into whiteness so that white people in turn become the worthy inheritors of all that is indigenous' (Smith, 2012: 74). Hence, it makes little difference whether Michael bought the land from Lela's father or was gifted the property; it was his relationship to Lela that set the context and legitimated the land exchange. As Riviera Cusicanqui writes 'Western notions of development, and patron client politics impose a patriarchal political culture in which [Indigenous women] figure solely as symbolic elements of transaction within dominant (male) strategies of power' (Cusicanqui, 2010: 43). Cusicanqui's insight also makes clear that not only does Lela rely on Michael for her well-being and employment, but Michael too, relies on Lela (and her family) to fulfil his plans to '*settle* down' in Bocas. Together, women in both groups serve as the '(gendered) racial other whose degradation confirmed [foreigners and elite] identities as white … entitled to the land and the full benefits of citizenship' (Razack, 2002: 126). Hence, slavery, canal building, UFC plantation agriculture, and settler colonialism qua residential tourism development, are inseparable, linked by the logics of White supremacy, patriarchy and racialized modernities.

Conclusion

In closing, feminist political ecologists largely emerge from disciplines (anthropology and geography) with cogent colonial and imperialist tendencies that we have not fully overcome. One of the ways these tendencies continue to manifest is through the constant reduction of racial and cultural difference and concomitant power to economic logics. With new enthusiasm to incorporate multiple and intersectional ways of knowing the future of economic geography promises to reflect the 'realities' of the world including international development, particular for those classified as subaltern. Moreover, charting the dispossessive logics of a variety of geographic processes, like tourism development and or land titling, within frameworks that punctate race enables a way of seeing how race is salient and co-constitutive of the requisite proliferation of capitalist systems of which geographers have long been concerned.

Acknowledgements

I am grateful to the residents of the Bocas del Toro Archipelago for participating in my ongoing research in Panama. This is an adaptation of my paper, Mollett, S. (2017) 'Irreconcilable differences? A postcolonial intersectional reading of gender, development and Human Rights in Latin America, *Gender, Place & Culture*, 24(1): 1–17. All personal names and some place names are pseudonyms. Any mistakes or oversights are my responsibility.

References
Asher, K. (2009) *Black and Green: Afro-Colombians, Development, and Nature in the Pacific Lowlands*, Durham, NC: Duke University Press.
Beckford, G.L. (1972) *Persistent Poverty: Underdevelopment in Plantation Economies of the Third World*, Kingston: University of West Indies Press and Oxford: Oxford University Press.
Bourgois, P.I. (1989) *Ethnicity at Work: Divided Labor on a Central American Banana Plantation*, Baltimore, MD: Johns Hopkins University Press.
Buechler, S. and Hanson, A.M. (eds) (2015) *A Political Ecology of Women, Water and Global Environmental Change*, Abingdon: Routledge.

Chakravartty, P. and Da Silva, D.F. (2012) 'Accumulation, dispossession, and debt: the racial logic of global capitalism – an introduction', *American Quarterly*, 64(3): 361–85.

Cho, S., Crenshaw, K.W. and McCall, L. (2013) 'Toward a field of intersectionality studies: theory, applications and praxis', *Signs*, 38(4): 785–810.

Collins, P.H. (1991) *Black Feminist Thought: Knowledge, Consciousness and the Politics of Empowerment*, New York: Routledge.

Cusicanqui, S.R. (2010) 'The notion of "rights" and the paradoxes of postcolonial modernity: Indigenous peoples and women in Bolivia', M. Geidel (trans), *Qui Parle*, 18(2): 29–53.

Fields, D. and Raymond, E.L. (2021) 'Racialized geographies of housing financialization', *Progress in Human Geography*, 45(6): 1625–45.

Gilroy, P. (2015) 'Antipode RGS-IBG Lecture "Offshore Humanism"', [film] Antipode Online, 10 December. Available from: https://antipodefoundation.org/2015/12/10/paul-gilroy-offshore-humanism [Accessed 19 June 2023].

Guerrón-Montero, C. (2006) 'Racial democracy and nationalism in Panama', *Ethnology*, 45(3): 209–28.

Gururani, S. (2002) 'Forests of pleasure and pain: gendered practices of labor and livelihood in the forests of the Kumaon Himalayas, India', *Gender, Place & Culture*, 9(3): 229–43.

Harcourt, W. and Nelson I.L. (eds) (2015) *Practising Feminist Political Ecologies. Beyond the 'Green Economy'*, London: Zed Books.

Harris, L.M. (2015) 'A quarter century of knowledge and change: pushing feminism, politics, and ecology in new directions with feminist political ecology', in S. Buechler and A.M. Hanson (eds) *A Political Ecology of Women, Water and Global Environmental Change*, Abingdon: Routledge, pp xix–xxiii.

Hooks, B. (1984) *Feminist Theory: From Center to Margin*, Cambridge, MA: South End Press.

IDB (Inter-American Development Bank) (2011) 'IDB and People of African Descent in Latin America', IDB, 16 November. Available from: http://www.iadb.org/en/news/webstories/2011-11-16/idb-and-the-year-for-people-of-african-descent,9672.html [Accessed 19 June 2023].

IPS (Inter Press Service) (2010) 'Central America: Identity of Black People Recognized, but Needs Neglected', IPS, 8 October. Available from: https://www.ipsnews.net/2010/10/central-america-identity-of-black-people-recognised-but-needs-neglected/ [Accessed 19 June 2023].

Lassén, I.A.R. (2010) *Afrodescendant Women: Our Gaze Fixed on the Intersections of Race- and Gender-based Organizing*, concept document, July, Brasília: Network of Afro-Latin American, Afro-Caribbean and Diaspora Women. Available from: https://www.researchgate.net/publication/282971625_Afrodescendant_women_our_gaze_fixed_on_the_intersections_of_race-_and_gender-based_organizing [Accessed 19 June 2023].

Lugones, M. (2007) 'Heterosexualism and the colonial/modern gender system', *Hypatia*, 22(1): 186–209.

McKittrick, K. (2006) *Demonic Grounds: Black Women and the Cartographies of Struggle*, Minneapolis: University of Minnesota Press.

McKittrick, K. (2013) 'Plantation futures', *Small Axe*, 17(3): 1–15.

Melamed, J. (2015) 'Racial capitalism', *Critical Ethnic Studies*, 1(1): 76–85.

Milazzo, M. (2013) 'White supremacy, White knowledge and anti-West Indian discourse in Panama: Olmedo Alfaro's *El peligro antillano en la América Central*', *The Global South*, 6(2): 65–86.

Mollett, S. (2010) 'Está listo (are you ready)? Gender, race and land registration in the Río Plátano Biosphere Reserve', *Gender, Place & Culture*, 17(3): 357–75.

Mollett, S. (2016) 'The power to plunder: rethinking land grabbing in Latin America', *Antipode*, 48(2): 412–32.

Mollett, S. and Faria, C. (2013) 'Messing with gender in feminist political ecology', *Geoforum*, 45: 116–25.

Mollett, S. and Faria, C. (2018) 'The spatialities of intersectional thinking: fashioning feminist geographic futures', *Gender, Place & Culture*, 25(4): 565–77.

Moraga, C. and Anzaldúa, G. (eds) (2015) *This Bridge Called My Back: Writings by Radical Women of Color* (4th edn), Albany, NY: SUNY Press.

OAS/IAHR (Organization of American States/Inter-American Court for Human Rights) (2011) *The Situation of People of African Descent in the Americas*, OEA/Ser.L/V/II, Doc. 62, 5 December. Available from: https://www.oas.org/en/iachr/afro-descendants/docs/pdf/afros_2011_eng.pdf [Accessed 19 June 2023].

Quijano, A. and Ennis, M. (2000) 'Coloniality of Power, Eurocentrism, and Latin America', *Nepantla: Views from South*, 1(3): 533–80.

Radcliffe, S. and Pequeño, A. (2010) 'Ethnicity, development and gender: Tsáchila Indigenous women in Ecuador', *Development and Change*, 41(6): 983–1016.

Razack, S.H. (2002) 'Gendered racial violence and spatialized justice: the murder of Pamela George', in S.H. Razack (ed) *Race, Space and the Law: Unmapping a White Settler Society*, Toronto: Between the Lines, pp 121–56.

Rocheleau, D., Thomas-Slayter, B. and Wangari, E. (1996) *Feminist Political Ecology: Global Issues and Local Experience*, London: Routledge.

Smith, A. (2012) 'Indigeneity, settler colonialism, White supremacy', in D.M. HoSang, O. LaBennett, and L. Pulido (eds) *Racial Formation in the Twenty-First Century*, Berkeley: University of California Press, pp 66–90.

Vasconcelos, J. ([1925] 1997) *The Cosmic Race: A Bilingual Edition*, D.T. Jaén (trans), Baltimore, MD: Johns Hopkins University Press.

Wade, P. (2013) 'Articulations of eroticism and race: domestic service in Latin America', *Feminist Theory*, 14(2): 187–202.

Werner, M., Strauss, K., Parker, B., Orzeck, R., Derickson, K. and Bonds, A. (2017) 'Feminist political economy in geography: why now, what is different, and what for?', *Geoforum*, 79: 1–4.

Wolfe, P. (2006) 'Settler colonialism and the elimination of the native', *Journal of Genocide Research*, 8(4): 387–409.

World Bank (2008) *PA Sustainable Tourism: Project Information Document*, World Bank Report No. AB3759, Washington, DC: World Bank. Available from: http://documents.worldbank.org/curated/en/330481468146415 665/Panama-Sustainable-Tourism-Project [Accessed 19 June 2023].

20

Poverty and Inequality: Austerity, Welfare Reforms and Insecurity

Amy Greer Murphy

Introduction

This chapter explores how austerity-driven poverty and inequality in the Global North impact women and mothers, and the engagement with the topic in some of the contemporary economic geography literature. The link is made between these policies, the values underlying them and the impact they have on poorer communities, as well as the connection to invisible care work and how it increases exposure to the risk of poverty. The chapter draws on research into mothers' experiences of deprivation and inequality to illustrate how gendered care work and caring is more than incidental to 'the economic', how it facilitates and precedes it. This is particularly relevant in the context of the paradox of recent prolonged austerity measures, which have reframed choice and depleted opportunities, reconfigured community capacities and diminished agency. The peripheralization of care work in the field of economic geography echoes its invisibility – in understanding economy and of society in the field it is seen as incidental and not preceding (see also Chapter 27 in this volume).

The invisibility of socially reproductive labour is one of the core issues at the heart of the gendered inequalities women experience in contemporary UK society, one that drives higher rates of poverty and experiences of deprivation among women. This experience is consistently demonstrated by university research and by the government's own data (DWP, 2019). As feminist geographers in the recent past have indicated, there is an ongoing need to include formal and informal care work in discussions of work, the economy and value, so often notable in its absence (Strauss and Meehan, 2015; Teeple Hopkins, 2015; Horton, 2022; see also Chapters 6 and 24 in this volume). This need is more urgent than ever, as we see diminishing redistribution and rising geographic inequality. The field of economic geography can benefit from more complex understanding of what constitutes 'the economic'. By attending to the impacts of deprivation, poverty and inequality, economic geography can incorporate more completely a fuller range of types of work, the role of social reproduction, and account for how care work plays a central role in sustaining the life of communities, families and individual workers.

In the first section of this chapter, I discuss a range of economic geography literature on poverty and inequality, focusing on Western states with liberal economic and social policies. I demonstrate that these countries, with advanced 'neoliberal' economies and complex state architecture (Davies, 2016) engage in a set of practices that perpetuate and exacerbate inequality, and concentrate high levels of wealth for an ever-decreasing group of people (Davies, 2018). In the next section I outline the impacts on poverty and inequality of austerity policies in the UK in particular, focusing specifically on the years 2010–18. These policies, I argue, have generated and widened gendered, economic, social and spatial inequality, especially so in the context of invisible care work. In the next section I discuss the consequences for respondents of austerity policies and the invisibility of their care work. I then discuss the austerity policies and cuts in relation to impacts on their wider communities. In concluding, I advocate for more fully articulating the connectedness of unpaid and paid care work, social reproduction and wage-work within economic geography to more fully understand the rising precarity and insecurity experienced by many in the UK.

Poverty and inequality in the field of economic geography

Economic geography literature examining poverty and inequality provides nuanced and diverse insights into the causes and consequences of poverty, such as income inequality, income distribution, and regional and localized factors. Literature from the US, for example, has examined the role of deindustrialization, urbanization and social welfare provision across the country to demonstrate that inequality and poverty is experienced in geographically, racially and socio-economically uneven ways. Massey et al (2003) charted the declining geographical and demographic spread of wealth and economic prosperity in the US, indicating that the spaces poorer and more affluent people inhabit are increasingly disparate, charting this decline from the 1950s to the early 2000s (see Chapter 1 in this volume). More contemporary work, such as that from Schrecker (2016) and Hacker and Pierson (2010) has examined the health consequences and public policy underpinning of income and wealth inequality, work that has challenged the dominant economic narratives of public and economic policy in the US.

Some literature has examined the role of health equity in tackling social injustices, the root cause of poverty and inequality, in the specific context of the neoliberal state (Musolino et al, 2020). Literature from Canada has illustrated the consequences of weak employment protections in increasingly precaritized labour markets. McIntyre et al (2014) demonstrated rising food insecurity among Canadian households where the adults were in paid employment, clearly illustrating that work is not a sufficient protection from food scarcity, particularly for BAME communities. Peck's (2001) important work has examined the emergence of the 'workfare' state, and how the turn to 'responsible citizenship' through labour–market engagement has generated risks and forced families and workers into precarious work and removed the welfare safety net. Some use quantitative data to examine localized and regional phenomena (Beatty and Fothergill, 2014, 2018), others through the lens of affect and the psychosocial (Stenning, 2020) or lived experience (Jupp, 2017b), and others still through examining the experiences of childhood and youth in the context of economic and social precarity (Horton et al, 2021).

Many continue the tradition of examining poverty in an urban context, as in the case of Lee et al's (2016) work on wage inequality in UK cities. Crossley (2017), for example, examined the politics of representation in places that are stigmatized as 'poor', what is said about living with poverty and how this forms narratives and shapes biases, which have considerable social and policy implications.

Others, such as Robinson (2019) have examined inequality through phenomena such as energy poverty, with its distinct gendered and spatial dimensions, within households. Jupp's (2017b) and Stenning's (2020) work has also, from different angles, examined practices within the household, their gendered dimensions and what contributions these can make to our understanding of poverty and inequality. In Stenning's work, the juxtaposition between coping and thriving for respondents lays bare the harms austerity policies create within households and families and for individuals.

What this literature demonstrates is that through a variety of methods, perspectives and vocabularies, there is a coherent academic body of work showing that poverty and inequality are heavily influenced through public policies, and the impact for communities, families and individuals who live with the consequences of such policy making. The literature focusing on households and youth in particular demonstrates how so much of the experiences of poverty and inequality are shouldered by women, children and young people, obscured within the black box of private family relationships and spaces.

Poverty, inequality and austerity in the UK

Austerity policies in the UK have had a great impact on inequality, child poverty, household poverty and gender relations. This chapter examines such phenomena between 2010 and 2018 (the years the empirical work in question was concerned with). What was initially proposed as a measure to address the budget deficit following the global financial crisis of 2008 under Prime Minister David Cameron, became a complex series of cuts and changes to the benefit system (Konzelmann, 2014) which has reshaped the relationship between citizens and social security, healthcare, housing and other public services. The Conservative government drew on the long-standing 'scrounger versus striver' narrative, to make these cuts acceptable to the general public, as well as wielding the concept of public sector (and specifically welfare) overspend and a 'culture' of welfare dependence, and linked this to the conflation of national and household budgets to simplify the argument (Bishop, 2016; Painter, 2017).

Poverty in the UK is increasing, as many groups have highlighted (JRF, 2020). The widening inequality is in many ways a continuation of the neoliberal logic of welfare cuts and privatization in place since the 1970s (Blyth, 2013). It cannot be separated from historical processes of class stratification in UK society (Pattinson and Warren, 2018). It has a negative impact on many already disadvantaged communities and its legacy contributes to the increase in pre-existing spatial and health inequalities (Pearce, 2013) as well as gender inequalities (Bennett, 2015; Greer Murphy, 2017).

Poverty is gendered, classed and racialized in intersecting and complex ways (Hall et al, 2017). Women are subject to an 'invisible inequality' whereby economic, political and social factors intersect to amplify the aspects of women's lives that reinforce gender-based inequality and which are subsumed under beliefs rooted in stereotyping and traditional gender roles. Some of the mechanisms through which women have attained a reasonable standard of living – through social security payments or public sector employment, have been gradually withdrawn, generating risks for many women. The roll-out of Universal Credit, and the government's response to the COVID-19 lockdowns have also had well-documented gendered dimensions (Women's Budget Group, 2021).

As communities and families manage during the COVID-19 pandemic and beyond, there is a continuing strain on families. The pandemic has widened inequalities, and will have long-lasting effects on health, well-being and economic resilience in poorer communities, particularly in the North-East (Bambra et al, 2020) and for women (Women's Budget Group et al, 2020). The dynamics of gender inequality's economic, social and cultural roots have been examined extensively both within human geography and its subdisciplines, and across the social sciences

(Bhattacharyya, 2015; Holloway and Pimlott-Wilson, 2016). This chapter represents a vital contribution to that.

Empirical research: poverty, inequality and making invisible care visible

In this section I present empirical findings relating to experiences of life on a low income, the depletion of community resources, experiences of poverty and the invisibility of caring work respondents were carrying out. I use quotations from respondents to illustrate points relating to unpaid care, work, 'being a mam' and the impact of cuts on families and communities. These findings highlight the important role women play within families and communities as caregivers. They draw attention to the complexities austerity measures bring to those occupying caring roles, and reinforce how central care work is to maintaining the formal economy and of sustaining culture and society.

Community and the cuts

The research showed how austerity policies increased inequality and experiences of poverty. This was evident through how the community resources were being depleted, as well as the pressure respondents felt from actors associated with the state. Many respondents lived in areas with multiple and complex issues of deprivation. One respondent had been told to remove the name of her estate from job applications, to only use the postcode as the estate had a bad reputation. This is an example of how certain places are rendered tainted or blemished – 'territorial stigma' (Wacquant et al, 2014).

Respondents discussed how the cuts impacted their imagined futures – a future with more playgrounds, open community centres and activities for young people, which jarred with their expected futures, ones in which welfare reform intensified, mould in the wall didn't get treated, health got worse and no jobs came. Respondents described being unable to move away from material circumstances that were less than fortuitous or which were stopping them, their partners or their children from getting on. A common reference point was the lack of work, and what this meant for 'getting on'. As Anne stated:

> 'There's not much chance of getting on in Stockton, cos there's not much jobs. ... It's alright to say "we'll send you to college, get you an apprenticeship", that keeps you ticking over and over, so they're off the books. And then at the end of the course there's no job for them. There's just nothing there. There's no hope for young people.

I've got a grandson, 16 today. He's going in the army in September.'
(Anne, Wave II)

As Shildrick et al (2012: 163) found in their research, 'living and growing up
in neighbourhoods of multiple and concentrated deprivation meant that the
interviewees faced wider disadvantage beyond their difficulties in accessing
decent, lasting employment', and these experiences were no different for
my respondents.

Women and mothers – being 'just a mam'

Many of the mothers I interviewed were involved in volunteering and took
courses at the local children's centres which had been rebranded from Sure
Start Children's Centres. Sure Start had been an important poverty-reduction
initiative during the Blair Labour government of the late 1990s, but the
local centres were now privatized. Respondents were very clear that their
volunteering was very important to them, but they had no desire to move
this towards paid work. They were busy taking care of young families, and
getting a job at a nursery or children's centre would have disrupted their
caring duties. They were happy to have what little benefits were available to
their families, and were happy to get by on reduced incomes during their
children's younger years.

> 'I haven't thought 'bout it as a career. In the Star centre we do voluntary.
> So I'm looking on doing that next year when me daughter goes to
> the nursery properly and I was hoping since she was going to the
> nursery I wouldn't have to look after her and can help out with the
> volunteering.' (Trish, Wave I)

Most felt that austerity cuts were making it more difficult to manage their
money and time, and that this was causing them stress and worry. One
respondent stated:

> 'They've reduced the age at which mothers have to go out and find
> work. And they want to be a mam, and they want to stay at home
> and be a role model to their children in that way. But they can't
> cos now they're forced to look for a job. The cuts in tax credits,
> the benefit cap, all of these things, financially have an impact
> on women. And the lack of services in the local area to support
> women.' (Jill, Wave I)

Informal care work and the work of social reproduction within the home
and community was highly valued by respondents. But respondents felt

their work was devalued, through welfare conditionality and the push by the state for women to enter paid work (Fletcher et al, 2016). Women were and are increasingly expected to earn a wage, but the care that needs to take place remains inadequately commodified (Allen and Taylor, 2012; Lewis and West, 2016). It is segregated into low-paid, precarious sectors, or carried out by women after their paid jobs end. Where paid work was available, it was often in sectors like social care that was poorly paid and at difficult hours for parents of younger children, as in many regions in the UK (Holloway and Pimlott-Wilson, 2016). Respondents found themselves in a difficult position – expected by their partners, the Department for Work and Pensions, others in society, to go out to work as well as juggling care and domestic work, while the only jobs available for women, as one respondent put it, were "low paid jobs, that's all there is. You can walk into a job, and it's social caring, cleaning houses, in nursing homes" (Anne, Wave II).

Ongoing narratives within mainstream tabloid media and from Conservative politicians claim that those not actively engaged in work or seeking paid work are lazy, work-shy, unproductive and do not contribute to society (Skeggs, 2005; Tyler, 2013). This runs contrary to the lived experience and testimonies of my respondents. Much of the work available to respondents was located in sectors of the economy considered 'low skilled' and thus low paid. At the same time, this work, when undertaken informally, was devalued or invisible. Mixed messaging and punitive sanctions make it difficult for respondents to make choices in their best interests. Ultimately, social and economic policies disenfranchised those carrying out care work, paid and unpaid (Fraser, 1989). For respondents, occupying the role of mother and primary caregiver was incredibly important. Caregiving required their constant attention and took a great deal of time throughout the day and night. Respondents placed great significance on their work, and knew how important it was to their families and communities.

Respondents reflected with nuance on the complexities, disadvantages and contradictions in their lives. Concerns around household finances and debt, managing food budgets, affording phone credit, and good opportunities for their kids, hopes for and pride in the area they came from and love for their families dominated our conversations. Their everyday care work, characterized in feminist social theory as 'social reproduction' is the work that produces and maintains social bonds (Fraser, 2013). These acts shaped the everyday lives of respondents, embedded in their expectations and their life courses. But they were aware of how this work was not valued by the government, staff at the job centre or the housing officers they encountered. Their value for themselves lay somewhere else entirely.

Discussion: poverty and insecurity – reframing care and value

The findings set out in the previous section illustrate important points about how poverty and insecurity impact communities and families, the connection between austerity and gender, and how focusing on the experiences of mothers illustrates how central care is to healthy communities and individuals. It highlighted that what happens at macro, micro and meso-levels can influence how likely people are to experience poverty or inequality or what supports they have to buffer or insulate themselves. The closure of community amenities such as community centres, libraries and children's centres hit the most vulnerable hardest. The lack of quality paid work led to experiences of unemployment, underemployment or precarious employment. Sustained welfare reform and conditionality meant that mothers who wanted to be the main carer for their families risked being on the receiving end of benefit sanctions and welfare conditionality.

Women like the respondents in my research wanted to be there for their children and families, and were willing to forgo income in order to do so. The state, by invoking welfare conditionality and labour-market activation without accounting for the quality of work available or caring duties, forced respondents to make decisions that were not in their best interests. The work they carried out – years of caring for small children, meticulously calculating budgets, shopping for elderly neighbours, long nights spent up with ailing parents – was not giving the level of respect it deserves by the government, society or the media. These factors combine to produce invisible inequalities for women, and illustrate how state and society do not value care work.

How 'work' is articulated, characterized and conceptualized within economic geography does not always contribute to the valuing of care work. Since the 1970s, great strides have been made in the field of economic geography to see economic activity as more than financialized, macroeconomic, formal-labour-market–oriented and productive in the field of economic geography in the UK (Pollard, 2013; McDowell, 2016; see also Chapter 6 in this volume). Respondents had to make difficult choices with real-world economic and social implications – to choose work of low pay and low status, or to do most of the informal care in their families, subject to welfare conditionality and sanctions from the government. Their experiences were part of the 'invisible inequality' of many women's experiences (Greer Murphy, 2019). They wanted to do care work that paid them nothing and that many others did not even see as work. This is an issue so rarely addressed in mainstream economic geography – the peripheralization of the diverse forms of value creation, specifically the contribution of unpaid care work which sustains families, workers and communities.

Conclusion

This chapter explored the topics of poverty and inequality in the economic geography literature, as it relates to the practices of liberal states. It then moved on to discuss austerity policies in particular, as a facet of neoliberal state regimes in the 2010s. It discussed the implications of austerity for women living with poverty, disadvantage and inequality, by referencing the extensive amount of unpaid care work they carried out. It demonstrated how austerity measures and cuts impacted their roles and practices as mothers, and damaged the communities they live in. At the centre of this has been the reality of their invisible care work. Geographers within mainstream economic geography should consider both the experiences of those living with poverty and the significance of unpaid care work, to more fully theorize concepts of value, the future of work, social security and wages and distribution within households.

This chapter has articulated that the ever-growing precarity and economic, social and lived insecurity experienced by many as a consequence of austerity policies has been ongoing for over a decade. I re-emphasize the need, as Reid-Musson et al (2020: 1464) call for 'broadening the scope of what counts as work', focusing on the consequences of periods of upheaval such as public health emergencies and economic crises (Brewer and Patrick, 2021), as well as to engage in enduring and sustained critique of the detrimental impact of austerity policies. I advocate for understanding the significance of social reproduction in its diverse forms to fully interrogate questions of economic and sociocultural change in the UK. This should not be the domain of heterodox economic geographers but fully acknowledged in the mainstream.

Acknowledgements

The author would like to thank Thrive Teesside for their contribution to the research, and in particular to one much-missed member, Kath, who has since passed away.

References

Allen, K. and Taylor, Y. (2012) 'Placing parenting, locating unrest: failed femininities, troubled mothers and riotous subjects', *Studies in the Maternal*, 4(2). Available from: https://doi.org/10.16995/sim.39 [Accessed 19 June 2023].

Bambra, C., Munford, L., Alexandros, A., Barr, B., Brown, H., Davies, H., Konstantinos, D., Mason, K., Pickett, K., Taylor, C., Taylor-Robinson, D. and Wickham, S. (2020) *COVID-19 and the Northern Powerhouse: Tackling Inequalities for UK Health and Productivity*, Newcastle upon Tyne: Northern Health Science Alliance.

Beatty, C. and Fothergill, S. (2014) 'The local and regional impact of the UK's welfare reforms', *Cambridge Journal of Regions, Economy and Society*, 7(1): 63–79.

Beatty, C. and Fothergill, S. (2018) 'Welfare reform in the UK 2010–16: expectations, outcomes, and local impacts', *Social Policy & Administration*, 52(5): 950–68.

Bennett, F. (2015) 'The impact of austerity on women', in L. Foster, A.C. Brunton, C. Deeming and T. Haux (eds) *In Defence of Welfare 2*, London: Social Policy Association, pp 59–61. Available from: http://www.social-policy.org.uk/wordpress/wp-content/uploads/2015/04/IDOW-Complete-text-4-online_secured-compressed.pdf [Accessed 19 June 2023].

Bhattacharyya, G. (2015) *Crisis, Austerity, and Everyday Life: Living in a Time of Diminishing Expectations*, Basingstoke: Palgrave Macmillan.

Bishop, M. (2016) 'What if the national economy is like a household budget?', Sheffield Political Economy Research Institute, 19 September. Available from: https://web.archive.org/web/20210524112931/http://speri.dept.shef.ac.uk/2016/09/19/what-if-the-national-economy-is-like-a-household-budget/ [Accessed 19 June 2023].

Blyth, M. (2013) *Austerity: The History of a Dangerous Idea*, Oxford: Oxford University Press.

Brewer, M and Patrick, R. (2021) *Pandemic Pressures: Why Families on a Low Income Are Spending More During COVID-19*, Resolution Foundation Briefing Note. Available from: https://www.resolutionfoundation.org/publications/pandemic-pressures/ [Accessed 19 June 2023].

Crossley, S. (2017) *In Their Place: The Imagined Geographies of Poverty*, London: Pluto Press.

Davies, W. (2018) 'The neoliberal state: power against "politics"', in D. Cahill, M. Cooper, M. Konings and D. Primrose (eds) *The Sage Handbook of Neoliberalism*, London: Sage, pp 273–83.

DWP (Department for Work and Pensions) (2019) 'National statistics: households below average income, 1994/95 to 2017/18', GOV.UK, 28 March. Available from: https://www.gov.uk/government/statistics/households-below-average-income-199495-to-201718 [Accessed 19 June 2023].

Fletcher, D.R., Flint, J., Batty, E. and McNeill, J. (2016) 'Gamers or victims of the system? Welfare reform, cynical manipulation and vulnerability', *Journal of Poverty and Social Justice*, 24(2) 171–85.

Fraser, N. (1989) *Unruly Practices: Power, Discourse, and Gender in Contemporary Social Theory*, Minneapolis: University of Minnesota.

Fraser, N. (2013) *Fortunes of Feminism: From State-Managed Capitalism to Neoliberal Crisis*, London: Verso.

Greer Murphy, A. (2017) 'Austerity in the United Kingdom: the intersections of spatial and gendered inequalities', *Area*, 49(1): 122–4.

Greer Murphy, A. (2019) 'Mothers in austerity', in C. Bambra (ed) *Health in Hard Times: Austerity and Health Inequalities*, Bristol: Policy Press, pp 201–32.

Hacker, J.S. and Pierson, P. (2010) 'Winner-take-all politics: public policy, political organisation, and the precipitous rise of top incomes in the United States', *Politics & Society*, 38(2): 152–204.

Hall, S.M., McIntosh, K., Neitzert, E., Pottinger, L., Sandhu, K., Stephenson, M.A., Reed, H. and Taylor, L. (2017) *Intersecting Inequalities: The Impact of Austerity on Black and Minority Ethnic Women in the UK*. Available from: https://barrowcadbury.org.uk/wp-content/uploads/2017/10/Intersect ing-Inequalities-October-2017-Full-Report.pdf [Accessed 19 June 2023].

Holloway, S.L. and Pimlott-Wilson, H. (2016) 'New economy, neoliberal state and professionalised parenting: mothers' labour market engagement and state support for social reproduction in class-differentiated Britain', *Transactions of the Institute of British Geographers*, 41(4): 376–88.

Horton, A. (2022) 'Financialisation and non-disposable women: real estate, debt and labour in UK care homes', *Environment and Planning A: Economy and Space*, 54(1): 144–59.

Horton, J., Pimlott-Wilson, H. and Hall, S.M. (eds) (2021) *Growing Up and Getting By: International Perspectives on Childhood and Youth in Hard Times*, Bristol: Policy Press.

JRF (Joseph Rowntree Foundation) (2020) *UK Poverty Report, 2019–2020*, York: JRF. Available from: https://www.jrf.org.uk/report/uk-poverty-2019-20 [Accessed 19 June 2023].

Jupp, E. (2017b) 'Home space, gender and activism: the visible and the invisible in austere times', *Critical Social Policy*, 37(3): 348–66.

Konzelmann, S. (2014) 'The political economics of austerity', *Cambridge Journal of Economics*, 38(4): 701–41.

Lee, N., Sissons, P. and Jones, K. (2016) 'The geography of wage inequality in British cities', *Regional Studies*, 50(10): 1714–27.

Lewis J. and West, A. (2016) 'Early childhood education and care in England under austerity: continuity or change in political ideas, policy goals, availability, affordability and quality in a childcare market?', *Journal of Social Policy*, 46(2): 331–48.

Massey, D.S., Fischer, M.J., Dickens, W.T. and Levy, F. (2003) 'The geography of inequality in the United States, 1950–2000 [with comments]', *Brookings-Wharton Papers on Urban Affairs*. Available from: https://www.jstor.org/sta ble/25067394 [Accessed 19 June 2023].

McDowell, L. (2016) 'Reflections on feminist economic geography: talking to ourselves?', *Environment and Planning A: Economy and Space*, 48(10): 2093–9.

McIntyre, L., Bartoo, A.C. and Emery, J.C. (2014) 'When working is not enough: food insecurity in the Canadian labour force', *Public Health Nutrition*, 17(1): 49–57.

Musolino, C., Baum, F., Freeman, T., Labonté, R., Bodini, C. and Sanders, D. (2020) 'Global health activists' lessons on building social movements for health for all', *International Journal for Equity in Health*, 19: art 116. Available from: https://doi.org/10.1186/s12939-020-01232-1 [Accessed 19 June 2023].

Painter, J. (2017) 'Why we need to talk about money', *Soundings*, 66: 34–9.

Pattison, J. and Warren, T. (2018) 'Class disparities and social inequalities', in P. Dunleavy, A. Park and R. Taylor (eds) *The UK's Changing Democracy: The 2018 Democratic Audit*, London: LSE Press. Available from: https://press.lse.ac.uk/site/chapters/e/10.31389/book1.ag/ [Accessed 19 June 2023].

Pearce, J. (2013) 'Commentary', *Environment and Planning A: Economy and Space*, 45(9): 2030–45.

Peck, J. (2001) *Workfare States*, New York: Guilford Press.

Pollard, J.S. (2013) 'Gendering capital: financial crisis, financialization and (an agenda for) economic geography', *Progress in Human Geography*, 37(3): 403–23.

Robinson, C. (2019) 'Energy poverty and gender in England: a spatial perspective', *Geoforum*, 104: 222–33.

Reid-Musson, E, Cockayne, D, Frederiksen, L. and Worth, N. (2020) 'Feminist economic geography and the future of work', *Environment and Planning A: Economy and Space*, 57(7): 1457–68.

Schrecker, T. (2016) 'Neoliberalism and health: the linkages and the dangers', *Sociology Compass*, 10(10): 952–71.

Shildrick, T, MacDonald, R. Furlong, A. Roden, J. and Crow , R. (2012) 'Are "cultures of worklessness" passed down the generations?', Joseph Rowntree Foundation, December 2012, https://research.tees.ac.uk/ws/portalfiles/portal/6445722/Publisher_s_PDF.pdf

Skeggs, B. (2005) *Class, Self, Culture*, London: Routledge.

Stenning, A. (2020) 'Feeling the squeeze: towards a psychosocial geography of austerity in low-to-middle income families', *Geoforum*, 110: 200–10.

Strauss, K. and Meehan, K. (2015) 'Introduction: new frontiers in life's work', in K. Meehan and K. Strauss (eds) *Precarious Worlds: Contested Geographies of Social Reproduction*, Athens: University of Georgia Press, pp 1–22.

Teeple Hopkins, C. (2015) 'Feminist geographies of social reproduction and race', *Women's Studies International Forum*, 48: 135–40.

Tyler, I. (2013) *Revolting Subjects: Social Abjection and Resistance in Neoliberal Britain*, London: Zed Books.

Wacquant, L., Slater, T. and Pereira, V.B. (2014) 'Territorial stigmatisation in action', *Environment and Planning A: Economy and Space*, 46(6): 1270–80.

Watts, B., Fitzpatrick, S., Bramley, G. and Watkins, D. (2014) *Welfare Sanctions and Conditionality in the UK*, September, York: Joseph Rowntree Foundation.

Women's Budget Group, The Fawcett Society, London School of Economics and Queen Mary's University London (2020) 'Parenting and Covid-19: research evidence', August. London: Women's Budget Group. Available from: https://wbg.org.uk/wp-content/uploads/2020/08/Coronavirus-the-impact-on-parents-20.08.2020.pdf [Accessed 19 June 2023].

PART III

Charting Future Research Agendas for Economic Geographies

21

Housing Struggles: Dwelling in Crisis Economies

Mara Ferreri

Introduction

Contemporary economic geographies have been profoundly marked by two recent global crises. The first, the 2008 global[1] financial crisis, was first and foremost a crisis of financialization of everyday life, and notably of mortgage debt, which triggered a still ongoing crisis (at the time of writing) of housing affordability and security worldwide, exacerbated by the implementation of austerity measures and neoliberal logics (Rolnik, 2013). The second is the still ongoing (again, at the time of writing) crisis that developed in response to the economic impacts of the COVID-19 global pandemic (see also Chapter 12 in this volume). This one, too, has placed housing and home at the centre, through containments policies and support measures that revolved around home confinement and home-working.

In both cases, policy responses revealed a profound gap between the normative imaginaries of home/work underpinning governments' approaches, and the economic and dwelling realities of the majority of the world's population, across both Global North and South (Saleem and Anwar, 2020; Vilenica et al, 2020). At the same time, the experience of vulnerable dwellers showed a further retrenchment of processes of residential precarization, through less visible but fundamentally transformative processes of digital control and extraction.

In this chapter, I reflect on the centrality of dwelling to recurring crises for understanding economic geographies of urban living, with a specific focus on less visible practices in global cities. The chapter begins with a reflection on the invisibilization of everyday reproductive activities that informed the pandemic discourse of the economy 'grinding to a halt', and its roots in the persistent binarism between economies within and outside the home (see also Chapter 27 in this volume). Challenging normative imaginaries of home, I draw on two ethnographic vignettes to argue for a renewed focus on dwelling as a way of addressing emerging areas of economic geographies, frontiers of extractivism, and their intersection with forms of resistance and self-organization.

Dwelling in the shadow of the economy 'grinding to a halt'

In March 2020, while many governments began introducing varying degrees of restrictions to everyday productive activities to contain the unknown effects of the COVID-19 pandemic, photographs of deserted cityscapes became viral representations of global economic activities 'grinding to a halt' (The Economist, 2020). Post-apocalyptic urban imaginaries of cities devoid of human life, first in Wuhan, China, then in Lombardy, Italy, then across many larger and smaller cities, were reproduced and disseminated through a digital media frenzy. Such headlines and images revealed the full poverty of culturally hegemonic understandings of what constitutes 'the economy' and the vision dominated political debates across the following months. All measures of containment and control of the spread of the virus were discursively measured against the needs of *the economy*. This line of argument is much influenced by an understanding of crisis that implies a rupture in the normal order of things, 'a scission of the dominant order which rips into existing society, its values and hierarchies, taking hold of old experiences and transforming them, almost beyond recognition' (Heslop and Ormerod, 2020: 149). The dominant order was clearly associated with the singularly univocal designation of *some* economic activities as a totality; as an aside, such a pandemic economic synecdoche can be seen as proof that moments of crisis are as much an opportunity for alternatives as they are a chance to reinforce orthodox economic narratives.

The compliance with which such a reductivist view was accepted and reproduced by analysts and public commentators offers an excellent example of the dominance of classical understandings of economic processes and their spatial articulations. In this vision, the (singular) economy is made of monetized, formal and visible productive activities that take place in the world 'outside' the home; anything that belongs to domestic and informal spaces and practices, and any agents involved with those activities, are, to a smaller or greater extent, erased as uncounted and uncountable. The invisibilization of domestic, reproductive activities from such a vision has been central to the critique of 'gender blind' economics developed by early feminist approaches to economic geographies. Androcentric economic frameworks and indicators persist, despite a long and diverse lineage of feminist economic scholarship across both Global North and South (Gibson-Graham, 2008; Carrasco and Corral, 2017).

However, as the pandemic extended geographically and temporally, this monolithic vision began to shift. Many began arguing that the pandemic, rather than producing a rupture in so-called economic normality, had helped making visible longer-term social and economic issues that classical economic frameworks had brushed under the carpet. Rather than the singular economy coming to a halt, the argument went, the pandemic revealed the interconnected plural and multiple economic and social infrastructures that make cities tick. In the continuities and the disruptions caused by lockdowns, in the interruption of globalized fluxes and in infrastructural fail (Graham, 2010), cities can be comprehended and understood anew.

Critical voices, particularly from radical feminist and postcolonial approaches, have pushed back against this. In contrast, they argued that the crises triggered by COVID-19 were an extension of existing and overlapping crises of healthcare, housing, labour insecurity, everyday bordering and other intersecting gendered and racialized forms of economic oppression. As feminist political economists remind us, capitalism is reproduced through logics and practices that marshal difference into categories of value (Werner et al, 2017), and that larger swathes of urban populations are constantly devalued and rendered disposable. Large proportions of urban inhabitants globally were and continue to be 'in crisis', inhabiting precarious geographies of insecure livelihood, particularly in terms of places and practices of *dwelling* (Lancione and Simone, 2020). I am here referring not just to the inadequacy or outright impossibility of the so-called 'new normal' of widespread home-working and home-schooling in overcrowded or unsafe homes – as if housing/home were not or had never been spaces of work (Cox, 2013). Rather, I point to the chasm between the normative imaginaries of home underpinning governments' containment measures that revolved around home confinement and home-working policies, on the one hand, and the economic and dwelling realities of many, on the other (Saleem and Anwar, 2020). COVID-19 was an emergency within a crisis landscape still governed by fantastical normative visions of what both contemporary home and work, and, by extension, of what is and isn't counted as economics (see Chapters 4, 6 and 24 in this volume).

In this chapter, I maintain that housing and home, as commodities but also as labour and processes, need to take once again centre stage in economic geography. Not as bounded entities (the household) and as sites of exploitative labour and economic relations (as in the first wave of feminist approaches to economic geographies) but rather, in line with a wider critique of the global/local binary, in the profound interconnection of scales and dynamics that inform economies and politics of dwelling (Gibson-Graham, 2002). Given the centrality of housing and home to global economic processes,

I argue that a more plural reading of dwelling, focusing on the position of precarious inhabitants, can shed light on neglected and emerging areas of economic geographies, and how they intersect with forms of resistance and rearticulation. In what follows I explore these intersections through situated reflections from my own research in two global cities.

Home, informal urban livelihoods and self-organized care

A warm early summer in 2020, three women and a teenage girl sit around a public fountain as they wait for their pitchers to be filled with water to bring home. The women are chatting, one of them holding onto a supermarket trolley filled with metal and other valuable scraps gleaned from refuse bins. The teenage girl looks bored as she scrolls messages on the screen of her mobile phone. Women at a fountain are almost a pictorial genre on its own right, representing gendered reproductive labour, a canon in ancient Western and non-Western visual art. Waste pickers are also a common enough subject of global urbanization: in Brazil they are called *catadores* (Millar, 2014), in Spain *chatarreros* (Climent and Porras Bulla, 2018). The women belong to a mostly uncountable number of those whose livelihood depends on the unlawful occupation of land and property, at a time when squatting has become one of the markers of contemporary responses to the crisis of affordability and a common form of direct action for housing (Ferreri, 2020; Martinez, 2020).

A week later, a few hundred metres away, a block of flats is violently evicted (Figure 21.1). It had been occupied on 8 March 2020, by a group of women activists under the slogan 'Let's make feminist homes'[2] (Betevé, 2020). Women had taken centre stage in the struggle for the right to decent homes in a handful of women-only collective squats across the city, such as this one. Local neighbourhood housing and feminist organizing, as well as social media networks, chiefly Twitter and Instagram, were key to the mobilization, which extended and intersected with global calls for action in what organizers have called a Feminist Strike – part of the global movement to reclaim power and the visibility of women's paid and unpaid work. The ten women-only households included migrants and single-adult households with dependents. Their occupation responded to unliveable conditions of overcrowding, speculation and discrimination they faced in the private rented sector, but it was also a political act that denounced the lack of welfare provision and public housing for unemployed and low-income households. Politicizing home was not simply about obtaining physical shelter, but importantly also about reshaping a set of social relations around home and care. The slogans, during the marches and the anti-eviction protests in multiple cities across the globe (Cavallero et al, 2021), drew attention to

Figure 21.1: Women's belongings piled in a public square after the eviction of a feminist squat, Barcelona, 25 June 2020

Source: Author's photo

relations of care that emerge and are self-organized autonomously from a neglectful welfare system: 'The state does not take care of me, my (women) friends take care of me' (in Spanish: 'El estado no me cuida, me cuidan mis amigas').[3]

Care and interdependence have been key themes in feminist critique of mainstream understanding of economic systems, and have been taken up more recently in response to the intersecting crises triggered by the global financial crisis of 2008 (Carrasco and Corral, 2017). The web of interrelations and labours that make possible life and its sustenance are key to this critique. As explained by the *Care Manifesto*, the devaluing of activities that are considered 'reproductive' and not productive still dominates political imaginaries, while social reproduction was and continues to be a 'constitutive outside' in urban scholarship (Peake et al, 2021). In this context, human and non-human life interdependence is still culturally and politically framed in terms of pathologies, deficiencies and lack of autonomy (The Care Collective, 2020). In their proposal for a radical reformulation of care as a guiding principle in self-organization, they bring the focus to kinship beyond the family, highlighting the 'care deficit' of normative households, as well as opening up new horizons for more caring social and spatial practices. In recent critical geographical scholarship too, practices of home-making and home-unmaking are inseparably interwoven with the politics of social reproduction (Muñoz, 2018; Baxter and Brickell, 2014), in a renewed reckoning with life-sustaining relations and economies of care.

The short-lived feminist squat mentioned earlier is a small example of the intersection of struggle for home with broader struggles for transformative social and economic relations within and beyond households. In the short period between occupation and eviction, the women squatters were actively involved in local solidarity food banks and in self-organized activities around online schooling for children. The focus on solidarity economies through self-organized 'making kin' thus expanded beyond housing and home, to intersect and establish autonomous practices to address exclusion and oppression, and work towards greater social and urban justice (Grazioli, 2017). Pre-pandemic forms of self-organizing have been the bedrock of geographies of solidarity and mutual aid, which have found a recent renewed resurgence (Spade, 2020; Springer, 2020). Pandemic solidarity practices emerged and have been central to sustaining life already affected by the most precarious infrastructures of livelihood – which appear informal only when seen from the detached standpoint of state regulations – at a time of ostensible suspension of all but the most 'necessary' economic activities.

A focus on people as infrastructure that sustains urban life (Simone, 2004) extends here to incorporate organized and coordinated attempts to address the differential disposability of certain bodies in the city, before and during the pandemic emergency. Difference and the scale of migratory fluxes are key to the reconfiguration of the 'home–city nexus' (Blunt and Sheringham, 2019), as well as to its politicization. In a growing body of geographical and interdisciplinary literature, for example, practices of refugee solidarity have been shown to intersect with geographies of housing struggles, as squats becomes sites of resistance and collectivization of care through the enactment of transversal equality (Kapsali, 2020), often against the threat of criminalization (Dadusc and Mudu, 2022). As much as migratory flows should be incorporated into any account of contemporary economic geographies, so should be the forms of resistance and autonomous reinvention of relations of support and care, in a wider politicization of practices of interdependency across the formal–informal economic and housing continuum.

Platform economies, mediation and home

A wet early autumn day in 2020. The floor in the entrance of the block of flats is littered with parcels (Figure 21.2). Small and large, the Amazon logo is repeated on many, alongside fast fashion, food boxes and other e-commerce providers and intermediaries. Around lunch and dinner time, day after day, the intercom is buzzing with deliveries. Rain or shine, the drivers cross the main door: they are usually young, often migrants, carrying on their bodies the corporate insignia of gig economy companies. On any given day, in the

Figure 21.2: Parcels in the entrance lobby of an apartment block, London, 1 November 2020

Source: Author's photo

eerie vacant streets they huddle at the corners of busy intersections, shoulders bent, staring at their mobile phones, awaiting jobs, reviews, evaluations, ready to spring into action on their bicycles or motorcycles. This could be any block of flats in any relatively privileged global city where e-commerce became the backbone of life sustenance for those who by necessity or choice worked from home during local or national lockdowns or other restrictions.

Platform economies have been a feature of global urban living since the early 2010s (Caprotti and Liu, 2020; Leszczynski, 2020; Sadowski, 2020b), but the pandemic triggered a deepening and retrenching of households' reliance on deliveries for more or less essentials goods, in an unprecedented expansion (Brydges et al, 2021). The home-working reality of some urban dwellers was predicated upon the expansion of fully digitalized warehousing and just-in-time delivery infrastructures which are replacing traditional retailing, leading to predictable if unprecedented levels of profit maximization (Weise, 2021). This pod living of 24-hour digital connectivity, presented as self-contained and autonomous, and affectively perceived as the most isolated and individualistic urban everyday, was only possible through highly coordinated economic networks and the digital and material processes that support them. A vast, complex, more-than-human assemblage stretched out and through the cocoon of the hyperindividualized experience of home-working, self-isolation and e-commerce.

While the pandemic emergency acted as a brief societal reminder of collective interdependency, talking about interdependency without qualifiers risks neglecting the differential relations that allowed privileged practices of lockdown home/work, which are underpinned by deeply exploitative labour dynamics and vastly unjust distribution of resources. Maintaining the spatial, social and cultural shift of working 'from home' has required vast geographical networks of production and distribution: the crowdworkers that make it possible (Scholz, 2016); the spaces (warehousing) expanding and engulfing more and more suburban and urban landscapes; the social and environmental impact of packaging, of transportation, of maintaining just-in-time logics (Malin and Chandler, 2017). Unable or unwilling to engage in life-sustaining practices, home-workers are not only multiplying practices of online consumption and production through digital connectivity but are also becoming ever more reliant and enmeshed in platform economy life.

In this enmeshing are to be found new frontiers of extractivism shaping economic geographies in what has been called a new iteration of 'rentier capitalism' (Sadowski, 2020a). In platformed economic landscapes, critical questions include not only the economic activities that are digitally mediated, but also the role of data as a valuable commodity and mode of control. Corporate digital platform companies increasingly act as repository and guardians of vast amount of information and govern the access of that information to clients and secondary users, and this is becoming central to the management of use through tenancies. In industry reports, the minute management of tenants' data is presented as enhanced customer service and as a response to the ways in which 'the on-demand economy is reshaping tenant expectations' (Deloitte Insights, 2020: 9), leading the real estate industry to focus on what they call '*end user* or the *day-to-day consumer* of that space: a retail shopper; a resident living in a multifamily property; an employee working in an office space; or a manufacturer using a warehouse'

(Deloitte Insights, 2020: 9, emphasis added). These shifts are taking place through wider, global, property and housing geographies of PropTech, or Platform Real Estate (Shaw, 2020; Fields and Rogers, 2021).

The language of *use* marks the new subject positions of dwelling mediated by digital platforms. The renaming of commercial and residential tenants as 'end users' shifts the emphasis on uses of spaces, but also of the platforms that mediate such use, and that generate data through that mediation. Tenants as 'end users', bound by opaque 'contractual' agreements, draw up new territories that exist in parallel to sanctioned definitions, rights and contractual obligations based on tenure, exacerbating discriminatory dynamics against minorities (Allen, 2019). When prospective tenants become 'end users' of the platforms which mediate their access to dwelling spaces, there are powerful if invisible forces to extract, shape and control. Digital platform companies' 'increasing power over and insight into the lives of tenants, and in which surveillance and monitoring regimes are extended to make access to shelter and housing contingent on factors well beyond the payment of monthly rents' (McElroy et al, 2020).

The extension of surveillance and monitoring regimes has significant implications for housing, for urban economies and for political struggles, as seen in the recent wave of mass global mobilizations against waves of eviction and eviction threats. The advancement of capillary data collection through digital platforms has become an even more visible instrument of control and discipline '[a]s anxious landlords contend with tenant rent strikes, eviction moratoriums, and remote property management' (McElroy et al, 2020), with worrying implications in terms of present and future exclusion and victimization of poorer urban residents. In April 2020, for example, the tenant management Canadian company Naborly wrote to its clients – property owners and managers – asking them to report tenants who had missed payments due to the economic impact of the pandemic, hinting to the creation of a 'tenants blacklist' (Hauen, 2020). Real-time dataveillance (surveillance by data) combined with the increasing adoption of geolocational media and the precarious position of tenants, appears to be ushering in new modalities of social control in digitally networked cities (Iveson and Maalsen, 2019).

Interdependence, a key concept to think relationally about practices of and through dwelling, is becoming captured by digital mediation, driving data extraction, surveillance and the possibility of exclusion, especially for tenants, towards a 'digital informalisation' of housing (Ferreri and Sanyal, 2022). The mediation of everyday life by digital platforms, mostly in the hands of the corporate sector, is a powerful shaper of present and future housing; the place of home becomes fundamental as a site of struggle against racial profiling and 'automated gentrification', and its roots in carcerality and racial capitalism (McElroy and Vergerio, 2022). The creep of digital platform economies into increasingly greater aspects of dwelling globally, and its intersection with practices and forms of resistance through dwelling in crisis, is a clear issue that research into economic geographies will need to address.

Conclusion

Throughout the last two global crises, geographers attuned to the experiences of those precariously housed have been painfully aware of how normative understandings of housing and home underpin both scholarship and political debates. Reinforced by mainstream definitions of 'the economy' as external to places of dwelling, this vision is reproduced in an ongoing neglect of housing and home as fundamental to both production and social reproduction. Thinking about housing from the margins, from the 'constitutive outside' of social reproduction, requires bringing a renewed attention to questions of care and interdependency, and to the relevance of housing struggles for understanding contemporary economic geographies.

In this chapter I have drawn on two contrasting ethnographic vignettes to explore two contemporary sets of issues concerning societal responses to intersecting crises. The first concerned the intersection between struggles for dwelling through self-organization at the urban margins. The second, at apparently the other end of the spectrum, explored the role of digital platforms in mediating urban livelihood and introducing new forms of management and dataveillance, with implications for self-organization and resistance. If in one case a politics of interdependency is invoked as key to rethinking economies of care, in the other interdependency is exposed as increasingly mediated by extractivist digital platforms. While the two vignettes may appear at the polar opposites of the housing question, both coexist in contemporary cities and may, in practice, overlap. Digital mediation of dwelling is not radically separate from the formal–informal economic continuum discussed earlier; rather, it presents yet another way in which multiple crises – and market-based responses to them – continue to affect the most vulnerable and precarious urban dwellers.

Key terms of care, interdependence and self-organization, but also platform-mediated management and extraction, I argue, are redrawing the boundaries of contemporary and future housing struggles. In an effort to sketch out more plural future directions of geographical research, the intersection between housing struggles and economic processes should be made both theoretically and empirically. At the intersection of extended crises and recurrent emergencies, research into housing practices and policies is become more and more necessary (Rogers and Power, 2020). But such plural geographies of dwelling praxis are not contained by policy definitions, the measurable units of households or the metrics of the real estate sector. Placing housing and home at the centre of contemporary economic geographies means to address dwelling in all its facets, across a formal–informal continuum, to engage with processes of extraction, control and dispossession, but also forms of resistance and reconfiguration.

At the start of the COVID-19 pandemic, writer and poet Anne Boyer sensed the possibility of a societal opening. She wrote, 'We now have to live as daily evidence that we believe there is value in the lives of the cancer patient, the elderly person, the disabled one, the ones in unthinkable living conditions, crowded and at risk' (Boyer, quoted in Lewis, 2020). Her call was to recognize, acknowledge and value life at its most vulnerable, and the spaces where it takes place, in those unthinkable living conditions. Taking this call to arms into the realm of geographical scholarship, we need to bring a renewed attention to dwelling as a plural praxis, different and multifaceted, and a challenge to the normative blind spots that relegate life-support practices to the margins of what is understood as housing. It requires being mindful of the centrality of the 'marshalling of difference into categories of value' in what feminist economic scholarship has defined as the 'capital–life conflict' (Pérez Orozco, 2014), and placing intersectional axes of difference at the core of our understanding.

Notes

[1] I call it global, mindful that clearly not all places and territories were equally vulnerable to processes of financialization or were affected at the same scale.
[2] Catalan: Fem llars feministes.
[3] See also Women's Strike 2021, https://womenstrike.org.uk/2021/03/07/womens-strike-2021/ [Accessed 28 June 2023].

References

Allen, J.A. (2019) 'The color of algorithms: an analysis and proposed research agenda for deterring algorithmic redlining', *Fordham Urban Law Journal*, 46(2): art 1. Available from: https://ir.lawnet.fordham.edu/ulj/vol46/iss2/1/ [Accessed 27 June 2023].

Baxter, R. and Brickell, K. (2014) 'For home un making', *Home Cultures*, 11(2): 133–43.

Betevé (2020) 'Desallotjat un edifici de la Bordeta conegut com Ca la Cristina', Betevé, 25 June. Available from: https://beteve.cat/societat/desallotjament-edifici-ca-la-cristina-mossos-esquadra/ [Accessed 27 June 2023].

Blunt, A. and Sheringham, O. (2019) 'Home-city geographies: urban dwelling and mobility', *Progress in Human Geography*, 43(5): 815–34.

Brydges, T., Heinze, L., Retamal, M. and Henninger, C.E. (2021) 'Platforms and the pandemic: a case study of fashion rental platforms during COVID-19', *Geographical Journal*, 187(1): 57–63.

Caprotti, F. and Liu, D. (2020) 'Emerging platform urbanism in China: reconfigurations of data, citizenship and materialities', *Technological Forecasting and Social Change*, 151: art 119690. Available from: https://doi.org/10.1016/j.techfore.2019.06.016 [Accessed 27 June 2023].

Carrasco, C. and Corral, C.D. (2017) *Economía feminista: Desafíos, propuestas y alianzas*, Barcelona: Entrepueblos.

Cavallero, L., Presta, F., Gago, V., Vilenica, A. and Muñoz, S. (2021) 'Housing struggles and domestic territories in Argentina during the pandemic', *Radical Housing Journal*, 3(1): 53–9.

Climent, V. and Porras Bulla, J. (2018) 'An analysis of informal work: the case of SubSaharan scrap metal waste pickers in the city of Barcelona', *Intangible Capital*, 14(4): 536–68.

Cox, R. (2013) 'House/work: home as a space of work and consumption', *Geography Compass*, 7(12): 821–31.

Dadusc, D. and Mudu, P. (2022) 'Care without control: the humanitarian industrial complex and the criminalisation of solidarity', *Geopolitics*, 27(4): 1205–30.

Deloitte Insights (2020) Report, Availbale from: https://www2.deloitte.com/content/dam/Deloitte/de/Documents/real-estate/Commercial-real-estate-outlook.pdf

Ferreri, M. (2020) 'Contesting displacement through radical emplacement and occupations in austerity Europe', in P. Adey, J.C. Bowstead, K. Brickell, V. Desai, M. Dolton, A. Pinkerton and A. Siddiqi (eds) *The Handbook of Displacement*, Cham: Palgrave Macmillan, pp 739–52.

Ferreri, M. and Sanyal, R. (2022) 'Digital informalisation: rental housing, platforms, and the management of risk', *Housing Studies*, 37(6): 1035–53.

Fields, D. and Rogers, D. (2021) 'Towards a critical housing studies research agenda on platform real estate', *Housing, Theory and Society*, 38(1): 72–94.

Gibson-Graham, J.K. (2002) 'Beyond global vs. local: economic politics outside the binary frame', in A. Herod and M.W. Wright (eds) *Geographies of Power: Placing Scale*, Oxford: Blackwell, pp 25–60.

Gibson-Graham, J.K. (2008) 'Diverse economies: performative practices for "other worlds"', *Progress in Human Geography*, 32(5): 613–32.

Graham, S. (ed) (2010) *Disrupted Cities: When Infrastructure Fails*, New York: Routledge.

Grazioli, M. (2017) 'From citizens to *citadins*? Rethinking right to the city inside housing squats in Rome, Italy', *Citizenship Studies*, 21(4): 393–408.

Hauen, J. (2020) '"Unconscionable": landlord service Naborly draws criticism for creating "blacklist" of tenants who missed April 1 rent', QP Briefing, 6 April. Available from: https://www.qpbriefing.com/archives/unconscionable-landlord-service-naborly-draws-criticism-for-creating-blacklist-of-tenants-who-missed-april-1-rent [Accessed 28 June 2023].

Heslop, J. and Ormerod, E. (2020) 'The politics of crisis: deconstructing the dominant narratives of the housing crisis', *Antipode*, 52(1): 145–63.

Iveson, K. and Maalsen, S. (2019) 'Social control in the networked city: datafied dividuals, disciplined individuals and powers of assembly', *Environment and Planning D: Society and Space*, 37(2): 331–49.

Kapsali, M. (2020) 'Political infrastructures of care', *Radical Housing Journal*, 2(2): 13–34.

Lancione, M. and Simone, A.M. (2020) 'Bio-austerity and solidarity in the COVID-19 space of emergency: episode one', EPD: Society and Space, 19 March. Available from: https://www.societyandspace.org/articles/bio-austerity-and-solidarity-in-the-covid-19-space-of-emergency [Accessed 28 June 2023].

Leszczynski, A. (2020) 'Glitchy vignettes of platform urbanism', *Environment and Planning D: Society and Space*, 38(2): 189–208.

Lewis, S. (2020) 'The coronavirus crisis shows it's time to abolish the family', OpenDemocracy, 24 March. Available from: https://www.opendemocr acy.net/en/oureconomy/coronavirus-crisis-shows-its-time-abolish-fam ily/ [Accessed 28 June 2023].

Malin, B.J. and Chandler, C. (2017) 'Free to work anxiously: splintering precarity among drivers for Uber and Lyft', *Communication, Culture & Critique*, 10(2): 382–400.

Martinez, M.A. (2020) *Squatters in the Capitalist City: Housing, Justice, and Urban Politics*, New York: Routledge.

McElroy, E. and Vergerio, M. (2022) 'Automating gentrification: landlord technologies and housing justice organizing in New York City homes', *Environment and Planning D: Society and Space*, 40(4): 607–26.

McElroy, E., Whittaker, M. and Fried, G. (2020) 'COVID-19 crisis capitalism comes to real estate', Boston Review, 7 May. Available from: https://www. bostonreview.net/articles/erin-mcelroy-meredith-whittaker-genevieve-fried-covid-19-and-tech/ [Accessed 28 June 2023].

Millar, K.M. (2014) 'The precarious present: wageless labor and disrupted life in Rio de Janeiro, Brazil', *Cultural Anthropology*, 29(1): 32–53.

Peake, L., Koleth, E., Tanyildiz, G.S. and Reddy, R.N. (eds) (2021) *A Feminist Urban Theory for Our Time: Rethinking Social Reproduction and the Urban*. John Wiley & Sons.

Pérez-Muñoz, C. (2018) 'Participation income and the provision of socially valuable activities', *The Political Quarterly*, 89(2): 268–72.

Pérez Orozco, A. (2014) *Subversión feminista de la economía: Aportes para un debate sobre el conflicto capital-vida*, Madrid: Traficantes de Sueños.

Rogers, D. and Power, E. (2020) 'Housing policy and the COVID-19 pandemic: the importance of housing research during this health emergency', *International Journal of Housing Policy*, 20(2): 177–83.

Rolnik, R. (2013) 'Late neoliberalism: the financialization of homeownership and housing rights', *International Journal of Urban and Regional Research*, 37(3): 1058–66.

Sadowski, J. (2020a) 'The internet of landlords: digital platforms and new mechanisms of rentier capitalism', *Antipode*, 52(2): 562–80.

Sadowski, J. (2020b) 'Cyberspace and cityscapes: on the emergence of platform urbanism', *Urban Geography*, 41(3): 448–52.

Saleem, A. and Anwar, N.H. (2020) 'Urban life in the COVID-19 space of emergency: field notes from Karachi', *Identities Journal*, 16 April. Available from: http://www.identitiesjournal.com/4/post/2020/04/urban-life-in-the-covid-19-space-of-emergency-field-notes-from-karachi.html [Accessed 28 June 2023].

Scholz, T. (2016) *Uberworked and Underpaid: How Workers Are Disrupting the Digital Economy*, Cambridge: Polity Press.

Shaw, J. (2020) 'Platform Real Estate: theory and practice of new urban real estate markets', *Urban Geography*, 41(8): 1037–64.

Simone, A.M. (2004) 'People as infrastructure: intersecting fragments in Johannesburg', *Public Culture*, 16(3): 407–29.

Spade, D. (2020) 'Solidarity not charity: mutual aid for mobilization and survival', *Social Text*, 38(1): 131–51.

Springer, S. (2020) 'Caring geographies: the COVID-19 interregnum and a return to mutual aid', *Dialogues in Human Geography*, 10(2): 112–15.

The Care Collective (2020) *Care Manifesto: The Politics of Interdependence*, London: Verso Books.

The Economist (2020) 'Much of global commerce has ground to a halt', The Economist, 21 March. Available from: https://www.economist.com/business/2020/03/21/much-of-global-commerce-has-ground-to-a-halt [Accessed 28 June 2023].

Vilenica, A., McElroy, E., Ferreri, M., Fernández, M., García-Lamarca, M. and Lancione, M. (2020) 'Covid-19 and housing struggles: the (re)makings of austerity, disaster capitalism, and the no return to normal', *Radical Housing Journal*, 2(1): 9–28.

Weise, K. (2021) 'Amazon's profit soars 220 percent as pandemic drives shopping online', New York Times, 29 April. Available from: https://www.nytimes.com/2021/04/29/technology/amazons-profits-triple.html [Accessed 28 June 2023].

Werner, M., Strauss, K., Parker, B., Orzeck, R., Derickson, K. and Bonds, A. (2017) 'Feminist political economy in geography: why now, what is different, and what for?', *Geoforum*, 79: 1–4.

22

Urban Economies: Learning from Post-Socialist Contexts

Elena Trubina

Introduction

The study of urban economies is a key example of the challenge of 'provincializing' economic geography: that is, expanding disciplinary conceptual and empirical foci towards the non-Western parts of the world. City-specific case-study research remains pivotal for understanding the multi-scalar dynamic of contemporary capitalist development (Robinson, 2016). While many cities continue growing, others shrink (Haase et al, 2014) and these multifaceted processes are linked to both the advantages and disadvantages stemming from the international economic integration, at least for some world regions and subnational regions. These uneven trends have substantial impact on governments' responses to globalization and economic shocks which include protectionism, resource nationalism and the backlash against globalization (see Chapter 12 in this volume).

Post-socialist cities[1] provide a fertile ground for comparatively and relationally examining a periodic reshaping of urban alliances in order to cope with difficulties in financing the development of cities. They are also a significant context upon which to reflect on the expansion of state and transnational institutions and the promotion of market logic across all spheres of life. Economic geographers' interest in global economic integration has prompted scholars to advance relational and comparative analysis of cities, revealing radically interlocked and differently scaled links and networks among different practices and policies in the cities of the Global Easts (Robinson, 2016; Gentile, 2018). While cities in general comprise part of the expanding 'geographies of contemporary economic geography' (Cockayne et al, 2018: 1514), the focus has been Western-centric, rather than developing a global perspective, and thus there remain cities and urban economies that typically remained marginal to the production of urban knowledge (Galuszka, 2022) and to traditional economic geography (Smith and Stenning, 2006). Post-socialist cities are a prime example. These cities' economic practices combined the informal post-socialist economy (Morris and Polese, 2014), regional variegations of capitalism with a recent socialist past and the repercussions of the global financial crisis of 2008–09 as well as the 2014 Russian financial crisis (Yakovlev, 2021).

Following John Agnew's argument that economic geography's 'fuller focus on politics is very much in the interest of making the field more realistic in accounting for the very economic phenomena that remain its focus of description and analysis' (2012: 569), with this chapter I argue that attention to various ways in which politics and economy become intertwined is needed to demonstrate the ways in which economic geography has been influenced by methodologies that problematize purportedly neutral accounts of economy (Ndlovu and Makoni, 2014; Reid-Musson et al, 2020). These accounts were widely employed to depict the transition of the formerly socialist countries to a market economy. Peck's (2012: 169) diagnosis ('readings of both the state and alternative economies are distorted by the analytical habit of staring into the bright light of the market') can be applied to many studies of transitional economies. These include the analysis of high technology entrepreneurial firms in Russia (Ahlstrom and Bruton, 2010), the study of the effects of measurable market reforms on reallocation and the creation of productive jobs in Eastern Europe (Brown and Earle, 2008), and development, lifecycles and outcomes of Slovakian enterprises along ownership, financing and governance dimensions (Wilson et al, 2016) and many others.

To develop this argument, I first outline key features of urban economies beyond the West, focused in particular on post-socialist and Central and Eastern Europe countries. I then move on to describe in detail the role that urban development plays in political governance, at city, national and international scales. I then home in on the issue of uneven urban economies, using the example of mega-events. I close with reflections for economic geographies, and argue that a place-based understanding beyond Western contexts is crucial for pluralizing urban economic geographies (see also Chapters 13, 14, 19, 23 and 27 in this volume).

Urban economies beyond the West

Foundational research on post-socialist economies in urban studies and economic geography was conducted on the consequences for cities of the economic turmoil of the 1990s (Stanilov, 2007) and on the predominant trajectories of urban development. While some scholars claimed that the urbanization in Central and Eastern Europe (CEE) can be interpreted as a hybrid one – combining quick adaptation to the capitalist economy and path-dependency (Taubenböck et al, 2019) – others argued that Western modernity – the free-market global economy coupled with liberal democracy – is the future at which almost all post-socialist countries are destined to arrive (Sýkora and Bouzarovski, 2012). The nexus between governance transitions, neoliberalization of 'transition' economies and the whole range of economic, political and social forces both endogenous and exogenous was considered by Bohle and Greskovits (2012) and Drahokoupil and Myant (2015). As, for instance, Drahokoupil and Myant (2015) demonstrated, in the course of the economic liberalization which the formerly socialist countries and states underwent beginning from the 1990s, the new EU member states governments followed the increasingly neoliberal recommendations of the EU. This resulted in a growing casualization of labour and in undermined collective bargaining mechanisms.

Shevchenko (2009), Marcińczak and Sagan (2011) and Temelová et al (2016) all write of the cost borne by urban citizens of the formerly communist countries of Eastern Europe and Central Asia, as a result of the emergence of the new trajectories of economic growth. They show how the collapse of the centrally planned economic systems produced new vulnerabilities of both citizens and cities of the former Eastern Bloc: those of citizens most notably were in relation to employment and income distribution while those of cities were in relation to political and economic autonomy. These resulted in the growth of illiberal entrenchment, conservatism and nationalism (Neumann et al, 2014; Hajnal et al, 2021). Instability in the region has continued. For instance, the annexation of Crimea by Russia and the escalation of military conflict in Eastern Ukraine in 2014 have resulted in policies of sanctions and other restrictions imposed by the Western governments on Russia (as a response to the breach of international law). These events coincided with the growth of popularity of the populist authoritarian regimes in Belarus and Hungary (Hajnal and Rosta, 2019) and were followed by the ongoing (at the time of writing, summer 2022) Russian–Ukrainian war. The economic repercussions of these processes, already enormous, will be experienced for decades. While some cities in Ukraine were completely destroyed, the urban population of the aggressor country – Russia – increasingly deals with the consequences of the unprecedented economic blockade organized by the Western governments and of the ongoing state capture by the Russian elites.

In the CEE countries, China and Russia, the hybrids of neo-authoritarianism (where a powerful state oversees the market) and neoliberalism emerged (Duckett, 2020; Stubbs and Lendvai-Bainton, 2020). While the term 'neoliberalism' hardly needs explanation, the term 'neo-authoritarianism' is often used to grasp both the Chinese form of authoritarianism (Xiao,

2019) and the current tendencies in Eastern Europe and Russia. Used interchangeably with 'illiberal democracy' and 'authoritarianism' (Pech and Scheppele, 2017: 4), it captures several traits of the current political configurations in the region. These include various 'hybrids' of liberal democracy and neoliberalism, conservative and nationalist policies and references to the past varieties of the far-right governments, including the fascist ones (Tacik, 2019: 33). Apart from Poland and Hungary, the term is used to analyse the Russian (Yildirim, 2018) and Belarussian (Usov, 2008) politics.

These coercive varieties of neoliberal governance not only have a significant impact on the institutional, operational and ideological dimensions of urban development in the region, but also testify to the uniformity of a neoliberal global system of governance (Rustin and Massey, 2015). This system advances market-led economic and social restructuring which subjugates economic and social policy to the private sector's priorities. Central governments then increasingly employ finance to exert their power on localities (Ashton et al, 2016) but also use finance to extend state power (Gotham, 2016).

Urban development and political governance

On the scale of urban development, this often amounts to the multiplying of projects, processes and ways of governance that are non-transparent and closed to public scrutiny (Bruff, 2014). Urban megaprojects often become the popular ways to realize neoliberal agendas with help of central state interventions which include the creation of new regulatory agencies, as Grubbauer and Čamprag (2019) show in their analysis of the Belgrade Waterfront project. The strong links between urban development and political governance forms and policies are examined by Büdenbender and Golubchikov (2018). They demonstrated numerous connections among real estate globalization and diverse geopolitical interests and considerations. These connections are materialized through both external impact on domestic real estate markets and state-led megaprojects, in which the power of the central state plays a role of an external force which largely distorts local planning priorities.

The importance for authorities of proposing ambitious designs with questionable feasibility was considered in the case of two proposed (yet unrealized) island megaprojects in the city of Baku, Azerbaijan (see Harris-Brandts and Gogishvili, 2018). The grand projects become more and more questionable by virtue of their enormous cost, associated displacement of urban citizens and businesses, and environmental consequences, yet the lure of spectacular architecture remains significant. Neoliberalism therefore prioritizes urban entrepreneurialism (Lauermann, 2018) which, in turn, promotes the competition among countries and places for investors and tourists. Such competitiveness-based ideologies inform an econometric analysis including the one conducted on CEE countries (Rusu and Roman, 2018) in search for competitive advantage that these countries and cities may have. Urban projects are, after all, also national projects.

The external neoliberal forces undergirding the post-Soviet transition include the all-European economic policies and decisions promoted by the EU. These severely impacted the geographical distribution of economic activity across Europe when the expansion of the EU took place. Extensive deindustrialization of the post-socialist economies included the rapid privatization of state-owned enterprises which have led to a growing dependence on foreign direct investment as a source of infrastructure improvement and technological modernization. The role of the World Bank and the International Monetary Fund (IMF) in shaping national social policies as part of the neoliberal reforms is persuasively criticized by Kopiński and Wróblewski (2021). Austerity packages imposed between 2008 and mid-2012 particularly negatively impacted on household income. However, many governments welcomed the financial help provided by these international financial organizations (Aidukaite, 2014). Bohle and Greskovits (2012) argue that the Baltic post-Soviet states especially eagerly promoted the neoliberal restructuring. This was seen as part of the return to Europe and the nation-building processes post-1991 (Bohle and Greskovits, 2012). The 'neoliberal model of development' which was employed by these states included 'the nation state–based coupling of regulation and accumulation' (Neilson, 2020: 87). The active use of this developmental model had to do with the electoral interests of the governments and political leaders who wanted to increase their influence by radically distancing themselves from the social and Soviet legacy. The actors of the neoliberal transition in Eastern Europe skilfully used the spectre of 'zombie socialism' – an ideological tool used to self-responsibilize the population and indoctrinate it into neoliberal dogmas (Chelcea and Druță, 2016: 522). Such zombie socialism has been used in political discourse to justify the excesses of market fundamentalism and the absence of social justice and social housing within urban economies.

Eglitis and Lāce (2009) sceptically evaluate the outcomes of the neoliberal restructuring path which many Baltic states pursued and posit that poverty alleviation was never on national governments' agendas. In Latvia, Lithuania and Estonia, both the urban and rural population had to face the consequences of the economic restructuring, including deindustrialization, the dissolution of collective farms, the massive disappearance of jobs, reduction of work places, increase of poverty and joblessness from the 1990s through to the 2010s, and so on. The specificity of the post-socialist circumstances includes the increased influence of the supranational actors and a lack of concern nationally for the marginalized parts of the population. This can be seen in the consequences of the global economic crisis in Latvia (Plakans, 2009). Lativa's GDP decreased 26 per cent between 2008 and 2010. Having received in 2008 a €7.5 billion rescue grant from the EU, Latvia also appealed to the IMF for financial aid (Lannin, 2009). The conditions of the lenders were the introduction of austerity measures that included pension and salaries cuts (Penfold, 2009). This has been just one of the many episodes when the negligence towards social policy marked the interactions of the transnational (the EU) and national political players. Among the determinants of urban economic performance, the network of interdependencies between the external economic actors (the EU), the national governments and the local municipalities (often acting only as recipients of various 'help') prevents urban economies from transforming themselves into operating more efficiently.

Urban economies are also embedded into the complex processes of centralization (and over-centralization), on the one hand, and peripheralization on the other. The towns and cities which didn't make it into the league of thriving capitals are often deemed 'left behind'. The intensity of peripheralization in Eastern Europe prompted the inclusion into the Territorial Agenda 2020 of the EU the statement that it is important 'to avoid polarization between capitals, metropolitan areas and medium-sized towns on the national scale' (Kühn, 2015: 367). When describing the consequences of peripheralization in the neighbouring Estonia, Pfoser (2018) argues that the inhabitants of provinces are depicted as lacking agency since the analysis is, as a rule, based on the macroeconomic processes which make places and their inhabitants peripheral (see Sgibnev and Ismailbekova, 2015 for a similar analysis of the processes in Central Asia). This has been exacerbated by the predominant spatial stereotypes and perceptions. Pfoser posits that 'In comparison to these macro-approaches, there is relatively little work on how people living in peripheral areas experience and actively deal with the negative consequences of economic and political restructuring in their everyday lives' and that focusing on the narratives of peripheralization helps to challenge 'the success story' of the economic and political restructuring in Eastern Europe (Pfoser, 2018: 391, 402). Pfoser importantly draws attention to the ways in which populations at the margins are negatively depicted by the media which, also informed by the hegemonic imaginary of the need to take initiative in order to get one's share of resources, are busy 'blaming the victim' for its failures and calls for 'a differentiated analysis of peripheral communities that takes into account the diversity of strategies that actors employ to inhabit, negotiate, contest and reproduce peripheralities' as well as the need to embed them in a wider political and economic analysis (2018: 402).

Uneven urban economies: the example of mega-events

If in Western Europe the policy responses to the consequences of the economic crises (Higgins and Larner, 2017) generated widespread opposition and resistance, and grassroots activism contested austerity governance, in the CEE countries, China, Belarus, Kazakhstan and Russia the waves of anti-government rallies were severely suppressed (Gabowitsch, 2017; Wynnyckyj, 2019). The global economic crisis has been 'sold' to the local populace as an external threat. The governments, corporate actors and property developers of the large cities in many CEE countries continue to seek economic growth while exacerbating uneven development stemming from accumulation by dispossession. As Trubina (2015) and Brenner (2018) demonstrate, the neoliberal rhetoric, which includes such buzzwords as 'global cities', 'smart cities', 'creative cities', 'sustainable cities' and the like, operates as a legitimizing tool for the local elites. Post-socialist urban development thus becomes a variety of 'classic' capitalist development. The growth machines in the post-socialist cities have adopted neoliberal policies and advance global, market-led urban development by, in part, hosting mega-events (Müller and Pickles, 2015), and using the cities for demonstrating geopolitical ambitions (Koch, 2013).

While it is well-known that such mega-events inevitably become a burden for the local economies while the global financial crisis continues, authorities and other stakeholders go on investing, symbolically and economically, in new events and ambitious projects. The examples are the 2012 UEFA European Football Championship in Poland and Ukraine, the 2012 Eurovision Song Contest in Baku, the 2012 APEC Summit in Vladivostok, the 2013 Universiade in Kazan, the 2014 Winter Olympic Games in Sochi, the 2018 FIFA World Cup in Russia. Economic geographers are well placed to examine a reduced public sector's role in determining and purveying the urban development, such as in these examples of urban mega-events. This includes elucidating the complex dynamics of the impact of neoliberal globalization on cities with a need to shift to a more sustainable economies in the 21st century. As Schulz and Bailey (2014: 277) posit, 'predominant conceptual approaches to emerging modes of economic orientation continue to examine economic transitions somewhat unreflexively within the context of traditional growth paradigms'. As such, there is a need for greater attentiveness to the consequences of decades-long promotion of growth-based ideologies and policies, including the ones in the less-studied regions of post-Soviet countries.

The cities of the Global East (which includes a variety of post-Soviet, CEE and Baltic countries) are facing many challenges caused by both the embedded structural inequalities and the realities of global recession and climate change. Economic geographers respond to these challenges by reconsidering traditional approaches in a search for productive alternatives. The following two examples illustrate this tendency. Rather than adopting country- and city-based logics of investigation (typical for area studies), Pavlínek (2020) places urban production in Eastern European cities in the larger context of the European motor industry. Western and Eastern Europe are relationally depicted in his account as the centre and integrated periphery: driven by cost-cutting interests, car companies relocate production to Czechia and Slovakia to get greater profit opportunities. The dependence on foreign firms and large international suppliers prevented domestic firms and locations in Eastern Europe from benefiting from the massive job creation in the region by foreign firms between 2005 and 2016. Elaborating on the concept of territoriality in the context of global value chain theory, Thomsen (2016) demonstrates the importance of geography and institutional context for the sourcing strategies and practices and supply-chain entry barriers examined in the three countries and five urban centres (Astana and Almaty in Kazakhstan, Bishkek in the Kyrgyz Republic, and Dushanbe and Khujand in Tajikistan) and concludes that, because of transportation constraints, Central Asian suppliers are less successful in the Russian market than their Russian competitors. The uneven urban growth and varying density of the transportation networks comprise part of enormous path-dependency of the cities of Eastern Europe, Russia and Central Asia.

It is thus pivotal to reflect on the reasons why growth-based ideologies and policies retain popularity in post-Soviet countries, and express themselves in a tiresome seeking of new iconic projects and mega-events. Yet in the realization of the mega-event, the city's existence becomes subsumed to the mega-event's needs. The fixed deadline for a mega-event becomes the only certainty amid the sea of uncertainties. The urgency of measures to be undertaken is part of the enormous scope of demands made by the organizations like FIFA and the IOC. Exempted from accountability, these organizations and their local counterparts produce a climate of exceptionality and engineer radical urban transformations. While the official invocation of mega-events attempts to highlight them as beneficial for the local communities and positive for society overall, they remain inextricably intertwined with wider global processes and interests of the players who are, as a rule, located quite far from the sites of the events. Contemporary cities often have too little autonomy when it comes to fostering 'their own development models, address[ing] urban inequalities or develop[ing] low carbon and sustainable modes of living' (Bulkeley et al, 2018: 703). Bidding for and organizing mega-events further increases the dependence of cities on 'external forces'.

Conclusion

Economic geographers are well placed to advance a rapidly evolving conversation about the ways in which the neoliberal agenda has been promoted internationally resulting in implementation of remarkably similar models of growth. These include deregulation, privatization and country- and place-promotion via mega-events' organizing. They are also advancing the discussion of how global processes reverberate in cities around the world, including those of the Global East. They undoubtedly benefited from the opportunities that emerged 'in the post-Soviet era' while also proved incapable of coping with widening inequalities. As such, a place-based understanding beyond Western contexts is crucial for pluralizing urban economic geographies

Note
[1] I use 'post-socialist cities' and 'the cities of Global East' synonymously to emphasize the new attempts to categorize the set of cities in countries that emerged in the place of the former Soviet Union and the Eastern bloc as well as to problematize the specific teleology inherent in the notion of post-socialist cities.

References
Agnew, J. (2012) 'Putting politics into economic geography', in T.J. Barnes, J. Peck and E. Sheppard (eds) *Wiley-Blackwell Companion to Economic Geography*, Chichester: Blackwell, pp 567–80.

Ahlstrom, D. and Bruton, G.D. (2010) 'Rapid institutional shifts and the co-evolution of entrepreneurial firms in transition economies', *Entrepreneurship Theory and Practice*, 34(3): 531–54.

Aidukaite, J. (2014) 'Transformation of the welfare state in Lithuania: towards globalization and Europeanization', *Communist and Post-Communist Studies*, 47(1): 59–69.

Ashton, P., Doussard, M. and Weber, R. (2016). 'Reconstituting the state: City powers and exposures in Chicago's infrastructure leases', *Urban Studies*, 53(7): 1384–400.

Bohle, D. and Greskovits, B. (2012) *Capitalist Diversity on Europe's Periphery*, Ithaca, NY: Cornell University Press.

Brenner, N. (2018) 'Debating planetary urbanization: for an engaged pluralism', *Environment and Planning D: Society and Space*, 36(3): 570–90.

Brown, J.D. and Earle, J.S. (2008) 'Creating productive jobs in East European transition economies: a synthesis of firm-level studies', *National Institute Economic Review*, 204(1): 108–25.

Bruff, I. (2014). 'The rise of authoritarian neoliberalism', *Rethinking Marxism*, 26(1): 113–29.

Büdenbender, M. and Golubchikov, O. (2018) 'The geopolitics of real estate: assembling soft power via property markets', in *The Globalisation of Real Estate*, Routledge, pp 75–96.

Bulkeley, H., Luque-Ayala, A., McFarlane, C. and MacLeod, G. (2018) 'Enhancing urban autonomy: towards a new political project for cities', *Urban Studies*, 55(4): 702–19.

Chelcea, L. and Druță, O. (2016) 'Zombie socialism and the rise of neoliberalism in post-socialist Central and Eastern Europe', *Eurasian Geography and Economics*, 57(4/5): 521–44.

Cockayne, D., Horton, A., Kay, K., Loomis, J. and Rosenman, E. (2018) 'On economic geography's "movers" to business and management schools: a response from outside "the project"', *Environment and Planning A: Economy and Space*, 50(7): 1510–18.

Drahokoupil, J. and Myant, M. (2015) 'Putting comparative capitalism research in its place: varieties of capitalism in transition economies', in M. Ebenau, I. Bruff and C. May (eds) *New Directions in Comparative Capitalisms Research: Critical and Global Perspectives*, Basingstoke: Palgrave Macmillan, pp 155–71.

Duckett, J. (2020) 'Neoliberalism, authoritarian politics and social policy in China', *Development and Change*, 51(2): 523–39.

Eglitis, D. and Lāce, T. (2009) 'Stratification and the poverty of progress in post-communist Latvian capitalism', *Acta Sociologica*, 52(4): 329–49.

Gabowitsch, M. (2017) *Protest in Putin's Russia*, Cambridge: Polity Press.

Galuszka, J. (2022) 'Transcending path dependencies: why the study of post-socialist cities needs to capitalise on the discussion on urbanisation in the South (and vice versa)', *Urban Studies*, 59(12): 2411–30.

Gentile, M. (2018) 'Three metals and the "post-socialist city": reclaiming the peripheries of urban knowledge', *International Journal of Urban and Regional Research*, 42(6): 1140–51.

Gotham, K.F. (2016). 'Re-anchoring capital in disaster-devastated spaces: financialisation and the Gulf Opportunity (GO) Zone programme', *Urban Studies*, 53(7): 1362–83.

Grubbauer, M. and Čamprag, N. (2019) 'Urban megaprojects, nation-state politics and regulatory capitalism in Central and Eastern Europe: the Belgrade Waterfront project', *Urban Studies*, 56(4): 649–71.

Haase, A., Rink, D., Grossmann, K., Bernt, M. and Mykhnenko, V. (2014) 'Conceptualizing urban shrinkage', *Environment and Planning A: Economy and Space*, 46(7): 1519–34.

Hajnal, G. and Rosta, M. (2019) 'A new doctrine in the making? Doctrinal foundations of sub-national governance reforms in Hungary (2010–2014)', *Administration and Society*, 51(3): 404–30.

Hajnal, G., Jeziorska, I. and Kovács, E.M. (2021) 'Understanding drivers of illiberal entrenchment at critical junctures: institutional responses to COVID-19 in Hungary and Poland', *International Review of Administrative Sciences*, 87(3): 612–30.

Harris-Brandts, S. and Gogishvili, D. (2018) 'Architectural rumors: unrealized megaprojects in Baku, Azerbaijan and their politico-economic uses', *Eurasian Geography and Economics*, 59(1): 73–97.

Higgins, V. and Larner, W. (eds) (2017) *Assembling Neoliberalism: Expertise, Practices, Subjects*, New York: Palgrave Macmillan.

Koch, N. (2013) 'Why not a world city? Astana, Ankara, and geopolitical scripts in urban networks', *Urban Geography*, 34(1): 109–30.

Kopiński, D. and Wróblewski, M. (2021) 'Reimagining the World Bank: Global public goods in an age of crisis', *World Affairs*, 184(2): 151–75.

Kühn, M. (2015) 'Peripheralization: theoretical concepts explaining socio-spatial inequalities', *European Planning Studies*, 23(2): 367–78.

Lannin, P. (2009) 'IMF Would Back Latvian Devaluation', Reuters (26 March), www.reuters.com.

Lauermann, J. (2018) 'Municipal statecraft: revisiting the geographies of the entrepreneurial city', *Progress in Human Geography*, 42(2): 205–24.

Morris, J. and Polese, A. (eds) (2014) *The Informal Post-Socialist Economy: Embedded Practices and Livelihoods*, Abingdon: Routledge.

Marcińczak, S. and Sagan, I. (2011) 'The socio-spatial restructuring of Łódź, Poland', *Urban Studies*, 48(9): 1789–809.

Müller, M. and Pickles, J. (2015) 'Global games, local rules: mega-events in the post-socialist world', *European Urban and Regional Studies*, 22(2): 121–7.

Ndlovu, M. and Makoni, E.N. (2014) 'The globality of the local? A decolonial perspective on local economic development in South Africa', *Local Economy*, 29(4/5): 503–18.

Neilson, D. (2020) 'Bringing in the "neoliberal model of development"', *Capital and Class*, 44(1): 85–108.

Neumann, L., Berki, E. and Edelényi, M. (2014) 'Austerity and politically motivated changes: wage bargaining in Hungarian municipal services', *Transfer: European Review of Labour and Research*, 20(3): 431–44.

Pavlínek, P. (2020) 'Restructuring and internationalization of the European automotive industry', *Journal of Economic Geography*, 20(2): 509–41.

Pech, L. and Scheppele, K.L. (2017) 'Illiberalism within: rule of law backsliding in the EU', *Cambridge Yearbook of European Legal Studies*, 19: 3–47.

Peck, J. (2012) 'On the waterfront', *Dialogues in Human Geography*, 2(2): 165–70.

Penfold, C. (2009) 'Latvia cuts pensions, salaries to avoid bankruptcy', Deutsche Welle, 16 June. Available from: https://web.archive.org/web/20210525014225/https://www.dw.com/en/latvia-cuts-pensions-salaries-to-avoid-bankruptcy/a-4320882 [Accessed 28 June 2023].

Pfoser, A. (2018) 'Narratives of peripheralisation: place, agency and generational cohorts in post-industrial Estonia', *European Urban and Regional Studies*, 25(4): 391–404.

Plakans, A. (2009) 'Latvia: normality and disappointment', *East European Politics and Society*, 23(4): 518–25.

Reid-Musson, E., Cockayne, D., Frederiksen, L. and Worth, N. (2020) 'Feminist economic geography and the future of work', *Environment and Planning A: Economy and Space, 52*(7): 1457–68.

Robinson, J. (2016) 'Starting from anywhere, making connections: globalizing urban theory', *Eurasian Geography and Economics*, 57(4/5): 643–57.

Rustin, M. and Massey, D. (2015) 'Rethinking the neoliberal world order', *Soundings*, 58: 110–29.

Rusu, V.D. and Roman, A. (2018) 'An empirical analysis of factors affecting competitiveness of CEE countries 2017', *Economic Research/Ekonomska istraživanja*, 31(1): 2044–59.

Schulz, C. and Bailey, I. (2014) 'The green economy and post-growth regimes: opportunities and challenges for economic geography', *Geografiska Annaler Series B: Human Geography*, 96(3): 277–91.

Sgibnev, W. and Ismailbekova, A. (2015) 'As long as the capital is far away: multi-scalar peripheralization in Central Asia', in T. Lang, S. Henn, W. Sgibnev and K. Ehrlich (eds) *Understanding Geographies of Polarization and Peripheralization: Perspectives from Central and Eastern Europe and Beyond*, Basingstoke: Palgrave Macmillan, pp 80–97.

Shevchenko, O. (2009) *Crisis and the Everyday in Postsocialist Moscow*, Bloomington: Indiana University Press.

Smith, A. and Stenning, A. (2006) 'Beyond household economies: articulations and spaces of economic practice in postsocialism', *Progress in Human Geography*, 30(2): 190–213.

Stanilov, K. (2007) 'Political reform, economic development, and regional growth in post-socialist Europe', in K. Stanilov (ed) *The Post-Socialist City: Urban Form and Space Transformations in Central and Eastern Europe After Socialism*, Dordrecht: Springer, pp 21–34.

Stubbs, P. and Lendvai-Bainton, N. (2020) 'Authoritarian neoliberalism, radical conservatism and social policy within the European Union: Croatia, Hungary and Poland', *Development and Change*, 51(2): 540–60.

Sýkora, L. and Bouzarovski, S. (2012) 'Multiple transformations: conceptualising the post-communist urban transition', *Urban Studies*, 49(1): 43–60.

Tacik, P. (2019) 'A new popular front, or, on the role of critical jurisprudence under neo-authoritarianism in Central-Eastern Europe', *Acta Universitatis Lodziensis*, 89: 31–44.

Taubenböck, H., Gerten, C., Rusche, K., Siedentop, S. and Wurm, M. (2019) 'Patterns of Eastern European urbanisation in the mirror of Western trends: convergent, unique or hybrid?', *Environment and Planning B: Urban Analytics and City Science*, 46(7): 1206–25.

Temelová, J., Novák, J., Kährik, A. and Tammaru, T. (2016) 'Neighbourhood trajectories in the inner cities of Prague and Tallinn: what affects the speed of social and demographic change?', *Geografiska Annaler: Series B, Human Geography*, 98(4): 349–66.

Thomsen, L. (2016) 'Exporting to Russia? Entry barriers for food suppliers in a territory in transition', *Journal of Economic Geography*, 16(4): 831–47.

Trubina, E. (2015) 'Manipulating neoliberal rhetoric: clientelism in the run-up to international summits in Russia', *European Urban and Regional Studies*, 22(2): 128–42.

Usov, P. (2008) 'The neo-authoritarian regime in the Republic of Belarus', *Lithuanian Foreign Policy Review*, 21: 86–110.

Wilson, N., Ochotnický, P. and Káčer, M. (2016) 'Creation and destruction in transition economies: the SME sector in Slovakia', *International Small Business Journal*, 34(5): 579–600.

Wynnyckyj, M. (2019) *Ukraine's Maidan, Russia's War: A Chronicle and Analysis of the Revolution of Dignity*, Stuttgart: Ibidem.

Xiao, G.Q. (2019) 'China's four decades of reforms: a view from neo-authoritarianism', *Man and the Economy*, 6(1): art 20190003. Available from: https://doi.org/10.1515/me-2019-0003 [Accessed 28 June 2023].

Yakovlev, A. (2021) 'Composition of the ruling elite, incentives for productive usage of rents, and prospects for Russia's limited access order', *Post-Soviet Affairs*, 37(5): 417–34.

Yildirim, E. (2018) 'The political economy of the transformation of the Russian state from 1990s to 2000s: towards a neo-authoritarian regulative state model', *Fiscaoeconomia*, 2(1): 103–40.

23

Migration and Cross-Border Trading

Charlotte Wrigley-Asante and Mariama Zaami

Introduction

Since the 1990s, studies in migration have received significant attention in development studies in general and geographical studies in particular, with a focus on labour migration and its implications for development (see for instance Momsen, 1999; McDowell, 2018). Among human geographers and economic geographers in particular, the emphasis has been on the physical movement of persons from one place to another – either within one's country (internal migration) or outside one's country (international migration) – with a focus on the factors that influence people to migrate, and the effects on the lives of the migrants. Thus, the push and pull theories have traditionally been the focus of most geographical studies on migration (see Hanson and Pratt, 1988; de Haan, 1999; Castles et al, 2014) in understanding both the reasons that people move and the situation at the sending and destination areas (de Haas, 2011; Massey, 1990).

Following this, substantial bodies of work have been developed by feminist economic geographers in both the Global North and Global South to show how migrant women have been recruited and absorbed into the migration systems resulting in the feminization of global social reproduction and care work (Momsen, 1999; Silvey, 2007; McDowell, 2018; see also Chapters 2, 4 and 8 in this volume). While these major themes have been researched in both the Global North and Global South, there still remains limited focus on the linkages between gender, migration and cross-border trading and that is what this chapter seeks to highlight. It discusses scholarly work done within the African continent on women's experiences in informal cross-border trading and their opportunities, challenges and vulnerabilities, while highlighting grey research areas within this theme that economic geographers need to focus on.

We begin by discussing the migration research work conducted by feminist economic geographers broadly, followed by work done specifically within the African region along two major themes: migration and household poverty; and migration as a livelihood strategy for women using the case of women in informal cross-border trading, using Ghana as an example. The concluding section summarizes the key research areas that economic geographers have been involved in both globally and specifically in Africa while outlining new research agendas for economic geography.

Migration and economic geography

While, traditionally, migration research has been masculinized in nature, there has been an increasing knowledge of feminist approaches in studying migration and this stems from the fact that gender influences the process of migration (Momsen, 1999; Attanapola, 2004; Awumbila and Ardayfio-Schandorf, 2008). Feminists have argued that sociocultural factors do influence decision making in the migration process, as prevailing gender norms shape migrants' decisions, including economic and cultural, as well as individual and family, status (see Momsen,1999; Silvey, 2007). In all of these, economic geographical research has focused on how the migration process itself shapes the lives of female migrants, whether in rural or urban settings, in both the Global North and Global South (Momsen, 1999; McDowell, 2018; Awumbila et al, 2019) with scholarly research focusing on female migrants either as industrial or domestic workers. For instance, Silvey (2012) highlights, among others, the centrality and necessity of social reproduction and care work by female migrants; the significance of migrants' bodies and households as key sites for understanding how labour markets and national economies are produced and reproduced through gendered and racialized social practices. Similarly, McDowell (2018) explains how the spread of the capitalist relations of production in Britain exploited women industrial workers and those who moved to work on rural farms. But that transformed gender relations between men and women at the household level (see Chapters 6, 18 and 21 in this volume).

In the Global South, feminist geographers have looked at the challenges that female migrants face in terms of legal issues, immigration laws and contractual agreements in the context of domestic workers (see Momsen, 1999; Awumbila et al, 2019). Others have also explored female migrants' participation in the labour market either as domestic or industrial workers and linkages to issues of (dis)empowerment (see Attanapola, 2004; Wrigley-Asante, 2014); as well as poverty and vulnerability especially among young female migrants (see Awumbila and Ardayfio-Schandorf,

2008; Teye et al, 2015). Thus, substantial bodies of work have been conducted to show how migrant women have been recruited and absorbed into the migration systems, reflecting the feminized nature of the migration process and the reproduction of care work (Momsen, 1999; Silvey, 2007; McDowell, 2018).

In more recent times, environmental push factors have contributed to geographical research in migration and climate change with a focus on how climate stress is affecting livelihoods and migration patterns (Arday-Cudjoe et al, 2012; United Nations, 2015; Wrigley-Asante et al, 2019; see also Chapter 27 in this volume). While there has been some research in this area generally, more has to be done on how climate stress impacts on the lives of particularly the left-behind in the household. This is one area in which critical research should be done especially in the context of Africa. Chant and McIlwaine (2016) have also examined the lives of female migrants in cities, their access to social services and their vulnerabilities. Again, while these issues have been looked at broadly within the Global South, it is important for economic geographers to consider context-specific research to highlight the spatial and gender differences in terms of migrants' access to social services such as water, health and housing. This will contribute greatly to economic geography.

In the next section, we will discuss the contribution of African feminist geographers to economic geography in terms of migration research. We will begin with the relationship between migration and household poverty. Then we will examine women in cross-border trading within the ECOWAS (Economic Community of West African States) subregion using studies conducted in Ghana while highlighting the remaining research gaps that economic geographers should explore further.

Migration and household poverty

Traditionally, economic geographical research in migration in Africa has focused on rural–urban migration since that has been the dominant form of migration. This is because the many decades of development and investment have been skewed in favour of the cities, making cities more attractive as a result of the availability of economic opportunities (Awumbila and Ardayfio-Schandorf, 2008; Agyei and Ofosu-Mensah Ababio, 2009).

Economic geographical scholars in Africa have analysed the migration behaviours of individuals and highlighted several reasons for migrating, which includes diversification of livelihoods; for family unification; political instabilities and conflicts; and environmental factors such as prolonged drought, and flooding (see Awumbila, 2018, Teye et al, 2018). For instance, Nabila (1986) and Benneh et al (1995) have shown how some male members of the family leave the rural areas for part of the year to look for paid work or to trade in far-off places such as the 'rich' cocoa and mineral belt zones, leaving behind women and children.

With increasing feminization of the migration process, Awumbila and Ardayfio-Schandorf (2008) began research on the socio-economic situation of female migrants in cities and how they fared. Their study focused on young females who had little or no education and moved independently from the rural areas to work as head porters (*kayayeis*)[1] in the cities. It provided a classic example of reasons for moving independently to cities and these were linked to poverty, lack of employment opportunities and the need to purchase requirements for preparation towards marriage (Awumbila and Ardayfio-Schandorf, 2008). In effect, household poverty and the desire to overcome it were considered major reasons in the migration process (Awumbila and Ardayfio-Schandorf, 2008). Their studies were in line with Chant's (1998) argument that while the decision to migrate is usually seen as an individual decision, migrating is not devoid of the household conditions that inform the process of migration.

Within African and Ghanaian societies in particular, which are predominantly patriarchal, gender as a social construct organizes the relations between males and females, shaping the reasons and processes of migration (Awumbila, 2015; Zaami, 2020). Traditionally, women do not have the same decision-making authority over access and ownership of assets as men and that decision to migrate is intrinsically linked to the household resources, gender roles and relations (de Haan, 1999; de Haan and Yaqub, 2010). Building on earlier studies, Awumbila (2015) and Zaami (2020) examined how gender roles and relations in the household shape the migration process. Their studies contributed to filling the knowledge gap within economic geography on household decisions concerning the migration process and the expectations from migrants. It highlights the fact that when migration becomes a household strategy, families could contribute to the migrants' journeys; thus, there is an expectation of the migrant returning remittances to the household to reduce poverty (Awumbila, 2018; Zaami, 2020).

While these studies have been done, there were other areas, such as the extent to which female migrants in cities become empowered through the migration process, that needed to be explored further. This became a research gap which Wrigley-Asante (2014) examined through her engagement with female migrants in the informal sector in cities and how their livelihoods supplement households' needs and income. Her study focused on the processes through which female migrants as economic actors had used migration as pathways to empowerment: through analyses of women's control over material and non-material resources, their choices in life and their ability to influence the direction of change, which in the long run is expected to lead to poverty reduction at the household level. Nevertheless, not much has been done within the households of migrants in ascertaining the actual impact of migration on the reduction of poverty levels. This is therefore an area which needs more research for economic geographers.

Women in cross-border trading within the ECOWAS

While traditionally women in West Africa have been involved in small-scale trade both within their countries and across borders (Robertson, 1976; Tsikata; 2009), women are increasingly trading across national frontiers, both within the ECOWAS subregion and transnational borders (Teye et al, 2015; Awumbila, 2017). Again, the neoliberal structural reforms and their associated economic trade liberalization policies in Africa, increasing urbanization, and globalization are all factors contributing to increased cross-border trading (Yusuff, 2014; Wrigley-Asante and Agyemang, 2019; Darkwah, 2021).

The Food and Agriculture Organization (FAO) reports that women constitute the largest share of informal cross-border traders, comprising more than half in Western and Central Africa and about 70 per cent in southern Africa (FAO, 2017). Also, cross-border traders in West Africa employ one or two persons and support an average of 3.2 children, in addition to 3.1 dependents who are not their children or spouses (UNIFEM, cited in Yusuff, 2014). This obviously is an important area that needs attention by economic geographers.

In Ghana, women in cross-border trading exist at all scales of operation; from carrying individual head loads at border towns to travelling by road within the ECOWAS, and by air to Europe, the US and newer trading areas, such as China and the United Arab Emirates. Women trade at different scales to acquire income to support themselves and their families in the face of increasing economic hardship (Wrigley-Asante, 2013a). There is some evidence to show that women in particular have been able to use global opportunities and have developed regional networks to enhance their living standards (Darkwah, 2007; Desai, 2009; Yusuff, 2014).

Scholarly work among cross-border traders has shown that women engage in such trade to improve their socio-economic status through the acquisition of income to support themselves and their families (Randriamaro, 2008: Wrigley-Asante, 2013b). Revenue from trade is a source of social safety as it provides basic needs such as health, education, nutrition and housing for their families, as well as improving women's resilience (United Nations Women, 2012). Engaging in cross-border trading activities opens up better opportunities for women to gain control over financial and material resources that improve their socio-economic status, including decision making at the household level and overall well-being (see for instance Wrigley-Asante, 2013b).

The cognitive evaluation of such women demonstrates a sense of satisfaction and contentment with their socio-economic status as some had investments such as savings in the bank, and assets such as land and houses (see Wrigley-Asante, 2013b). Deere (2010) notes that house ownership is a poverty-reducing strategy, especially for women, since it provides increased security. Assets could be empowering for women (Kabeer, 2010) as they constitute an important buffer during emergencies since they can be pawned or sold.

Despite the benefits of trading, women in informal cross-border trading along the ECOWAS face many challenges with 'harassment' by border officials being identified as a key challenge (Wrigley-Asante, 2013b). Other challenges identified included women's limited knowledge of rules and regulations authorizing various branches of government to request payments, and those that did seemed to know had only a vague idea of what the laws were with regard to import fees (Wrigley-Asante, 2013b). However, what is not clear and has not been extensively explored is women's knowledge of the tax system and how they perceive 'borders'. Indeed, borders are historically perceived and accepted as relatively porous due to social, cultural and economic ties transcending these political boundaries, such as the Ghana–Togo borders (Nugent, 2002). This is an area that economic geographers could explore further since many women traders considered these unlawful practices as a normal and regular part of the business (Wrigley-Asante, 2013a; Yusuff, 2014).

Establishing alliances with officials nevertheless served as a coping mechanism to sustain their business but these have been linked to accusations of the demand for sexual favours by some officials, which some often complied as a means of evading taxes (Wrigley-Asante, 2013b; Yusuff, 2014). This reiterates the need for economic geographers to conduct more research in this area to ascertain women's understanding of the tax system as against that of their male counterparts, the international trading protocols, and the gender differences on how they navigate or complied with the system. Again, particular attention needs to be paid to the social and institutional mechanisms that operate to exacerbate women's vulnerability as they migrate across borders to trade.

Another major insecurity that women in cross-border trading face is the fear of being attacked by armed robbers because of the relatively large amounts of physical cash women traders are known to carry (King, 2010; Wrigley-Asante, 2013a). With the increasing emergence of information and communication technologies (ICT) such as the mobile telephony system, trading off-the-road through cyberspace is increasingly becoming popular yet many women in informal cross-border trading are yet to utilize these systems (Wrigley-Asante and Agyemang, 2019). Economic geographers could explore the opportunities for cross-border traders by conducting more research in this area to ascertain ways in which women could take full advantage of ICT while examining the gender differences as well.

Within the ECOWAS subregion, there are numerous policy interventions; however, transport investments appear not to have fully enhanced the ease of freight movement associated with informal trade (Wrigley-Asante, 2013a; Wrigley-Asante and Agyemang, 2019). Studies have shown that there are issues with transportability as an inherent risk to trade since that leads to incessant violent robberies, pose safety and security concerns due to delays and poor transport networks (Dupuy, 2007; Wrigley-Asante, 2013a). This is an area where women in informal cross-border trading should be supported while educating them on, and sensitizing them to, the ECOWAS protocols guiding trading. Yet what has not been done, however, is the work on the types of transport and related systems that women would need along the West African trade corridors to improve security and safety issues. This again is a research and policy gap that could be explored by economic geographers.

The health implications for women in cross-border trading also warrants further attention. Studies have shown women's susceptibility to various diseases such as fatigue and stress resulting from the activities of border officials, gendarmes and concerns over left-behind children as they travel across national frontiers to trade, contributing greatly to psychosocial challenges (Wrigley-Asante, 2013a). But the relationship between women's productive and reproductive activities and how that impacts on their health and time poverty needs further research and may also be of interest to economic geographers.

Despite these challenges, women traders exhibit resilience as they travel across borders to sustain their livelihoods through their social networks (Wrigley-Asante, 2013a, 2018). The networks that cross-border traders depend on demonstrate women's sense of empathy, love and trust (Purkayastha and Subramanian, 2004; Wrigley-Asante, 2018). It is, however, important for economic geographers to explore further the types of social networks created beyond kinship ties and ascertain the level of reciprocity particularly in the context of globalization and transnational cross-border trading.

Conclusion

The chapter has outlined a substantial body of work within migration and economic geography in both the Global North and Global South. The initial focus of research was on labour migration issues and its implications for development, with a key focus on how migrant women were recruited and absorbed into the migration systems resulting in the feminization of global social reproduction and care work (Momsen, 1999; Silvey, 2007; McDowell, 2018). In the Global South, economic geographers involved in migration research have been interested in understanding the reasons why people move and the effects on the situation at the sending and destination areas (see Teye and Awumbila, 2015). While extensive work has been done, there are still gaps thus it is important for economic geographers to pay particular attention to, such as how the migration process impacts on the lives of the left-behind in the household especially in relation to climate stress and the actual impact of migration on the reduction of household poverty levels as well as migrants' access to social services such as water, health and housing while assessing the spatial and gender differences.

With increasing globalization and its associated increasing migration of females independently of males, economic geographers have examined migration as a pathway in addressing household poverty and engaging in and improving women's livelihoods (Wrigley-Asante; 2013a; Awumbila et al, 2014) but with very limited research on women in informal cross-border trading. Yet there are research gaps within the migration and cross-border trading discourse that warrant explanations by economic geographers.

Thus, another key research area that economic geographers need to explore is women's understanding of the tax system and the social and institutional mechanisms that contribute to exacerbating women's vulnerability as they migrate across borders to trade. Again, the use of ICT in trading and improving livelihoods of both male and females in cross-border trading could also be of research interest for geographers. The types of social networks used and the level of reciprocity, particularly in the context of globalization and transnational cross-border trading, the use of transport systems and how they are related to issues of safety and security along trade corridors are all new areas that require further and deeper research. Finally, it is important that the research targets the different categories of cross-border traders to ascertain the gender differences in terms of experiences and the differences within and between the different categories of women and men traders in different geographical spaces. This will hopefully provide a better understanding of the nexus between migration, gender and cross-border trade and enrich the contribution of feminist geographers to economic geography.

Note
[1] *Kayayei*: 'A name was given to female porters who carry the load on their heads for a negotiated fee' (Awumbila and Ardayfio-Schandorf, 2008: 171).

References

Agyei, J. and Ofosu-Mensah Ababio, E. (2009) 'Historical overview of internal migration in Ghana', in J.K. Anarfi and O.S. Kwankye (eds) *Independent Migration of Children in Ghana*, Legon, Ghana: Institute of Statistical Social and Economic Research, pp 9–42.

Arday-Codjoe, S.N., Atidoh, L.K and Burkett, V. (2012) 'Gender and occupational perspectives on adaption to climate extremes in the Afram Plains of Ghana', *Climatic Change*, 110(1/2): 431–54.

Attanapola, C.T. (2004) 'Changing gender roles and health impacts among female workers in export-processing industries in Sri Lanka', *Social Science & Medicine*, 58(11): 2301–12.

Awumbila, M. (2015) 'Women moving within borders: gender and internal migration dynamics in Ghana', *Ghana Journal of Geography*, 7(2): 132–45.

Awumbila, M. (2017) 'Drivers of migration and urbanization in Africa: key trends and issues', *International Migration*, 7(8): 1–9.

Awumbila, M. (2018) 'Dynamics of intra-regional migration in West Africa: implications for ECOWAS migration policy', in M. Awumbila, D. Badasu and J. Teye (eds) *Migration in a Globalizing World: Perspectives from Ghana*, Accra: Sub-Saharan Publishers, pp 9–30.

Awumbila, M. and Ardayfio-Schandorf, E. (2008) 'Gendered poverty, migration and livelihood strategies of female porters in Accra, Ghana', *Norsk Geografisk Tidsskrift/Norwegian Journal of Geography*, 62(3): 171–9.

Awumbila, M., Owusu, G. and Teye, J.K. (2014) *Can Rural–Urban Migration into Slums Reduce Poverty? Evidence from Ghana*, Working paper 13, Migrating out of Poverty, University of Sussex. Available from: https://opendocs.ids.ac.uk/opendocs/handle/20.500.12413/14825 [Accessed 28 June 2023].

Awumbila, M., Teye, J.K. and Yaro, J.A. (2017) 'Social networks, migration trajectories and livelihood strategies of migrant domestic and construction workers in Accra, Ghana', *Journal of Asian and African Studies*, 52(7): 982–96.

Awumbila, M., Deshingkar, P., Kandilige, L., Teye, J.K. and Setrana, M. (2019) 'Please, thank you and sorry: brokering migration and constructing identities for domestic work in Ghana', *Journal of Ethnic and Migration Studies*, 45(14): 2655–71.

Benneh, G., Kasanga, R.K and Amoyaw, D. (1995) *Women's Access to Agricultural Land in the Household: A Case Study of Three Selected Districts in Ghana*, FADEP Technical Series 8, Accra: Assemblies of God Literature Centre.

Castles, S., de Haas, H. and Miller, M.J. (2014) *The Age of Migration: International Population Movements in the Modern World* (5th edn), New York: Guilford Press.

Chant, S. (1998) 'Households, gender and rural–urban migration: reflections on linkages and considerations for policy', *Environment and Urbanization*, 10(1): 5–22.

Chant, S. and McIlwaine, C. (2016) *Cities, Slums and Gender in the Global South: Towards a Feminised Urban Future*, Abingdon: Routledge.

Darkwah, A. (2007) 'Work as duty and work as joy: understanding the role of work in the lives of Ghanaian female traders of global consumer items', in S. Harley (ed) *Women's Labor in the Global Economy: Speaking Multiple Voices*, New Brunswick, NJ: Rutgers University Press, pp 206–20.

Darkwah, A.K. (2021) 'African women and globalisation', in O. Yacob-Haliso and T. Falola (eds) *The Palgrave Handbook of African Women's Studies*, Section VIII, Cham: Palgrave Macmillan, pp 1805–20.

De Haan, A. (1999) 'Livelihoods and poverty: the role of migration–a critical review of the migration literature', *Journal of Development Studies*, 36(2): 1–47.

De Haan, A. and Yaqub, S. (2010) 'Migration and poverty: linkages, knowledge gaps and policy implications', in K. Hujo and N. Piper (eds) *South–South Migration*, Basingstoke: Palgrave Macmillan, pp 190–219.

De Haas, H. (2011) *The Determinants of International Migration: Conceptualising Policy, Origin and Destination Effects*, Working Paper 32, Oxford: International Migration Institute, University of Oxford.

Deere, C.D. (2010) 'Household wealth and women's poverty: conceptual and methodological issues in assessing gender inequality in asset ownership', in S. Chant (ed) *The International Handbook of Gender and Poverty: Concepts, Research, Policy*, Cheltenham: Edward Elgar, pp 347–52.

Desai, M. (2009) 'Women cross-border traders: rethinking global trade', *Development*, 52(3): 377–86.

Dupuy, R. (2007) *Sub-regional Approach to Advocacy for Women Cross-Border Traders: A Report Prepared for ActionAid Ghana*, Accra: ActionAid Ghana.

FAO (Food and Agriculture Organization) (2017) 'Harnessing rather than suppressing informal trade can give Africa a boost', FAO, 25 May. Available from: https://www.fao.org/news/story/en/item/888767/icode/ [Accessed 16 October 2021].

Hanson, S. and Pratt, G. (1988) 'Reconceptualizing the links between home and work in urban geography', *Economic Geography*, 64(4): 299–321.

Kabeer, N. (2010) 'Gender equality and women's empowerment: a critical analysis of the third Millennium Development Goal', *Gender and Development*, 13(1): 13–24.

King, R. (2010) 'Geography and diasporas', in M. Iorio and G. Sistu (eds) *Dove finisce il mare: scritti per Maria Luisa Gentileschi*, Cagliari: Sandhi, pp 195–212.

Massey, D.S. (1990) 'The social and economic origins of immigration', *Annals of the American Academy of Political and Social Science*, 510(1): 60–72.

McDowell, L. (2018) 'Moving stories: precarious work and multiple migrations', *Gender, Place & Culture*, 25(4): 471–88.

Momsen, J.H. (ed) (1999) *Gender, Migration and Domestic Service*, London: Routledge.

Nabila, J.S. (1986) 'Rural migration and its implications for rural development in Ghana', in C.K. Brown (ed) *Rural Development in Ghana*, Accra: Ghana Universities Press, pp 75–89.

Nugent, P. (2002) *Smugglers, Secessionists and Loyal Citizens on the Ghana–Togo Frontier: The Lie of the Borderlands Since 1914*, Oxford: James Currey.

Purkayastha, B. and Subramaniam, M. (2004) 'Introduction', in B. Purkayastha and M. Subramaniam (eds) *The Power of Women's Informal Networks: Lessons in Social Change from Asia and West Africa*, Lanham, MD: Lexington, pp 1–14.

Randriamaro, Z. (2008) *Trade, Poverty and Women's Economic Empowerment in Sub-Saharan Africa*, New York: UNDESA.

Robertson, C. (1976) 'Ga women and socioeconomic change in Accra, Ghana', in N.J. Hafkin and E.D. Bay (eds) *Women in Africa: Studies in Social and Economic Change*, Palo Alto, CA: Stanford University Press, pp 111–33.

Silvey, R. (2007) 'Mobilizing piety: gendered morality and Indonesian–Saudi transnational migration', *Mobilities*, 2(2): 219–29.

Silvey, R. (2012) 'Gender, difference, and contestation: economic geography through the lens of transnational migration', in T.J. Barnes, J. Peck and E. Sheppard (eds) *The Wiley-Blackwell Companion to Economic Geography*, Chichester: Blackwell, pp 420–30.

Teye, J.K., Anarfi, J.K., Kwasi, J., Sulemana, A., Anamzoya, A. and Adiku, G. (2018) 'Environmental change and migration in Africa', in M. Awumbila, D. Badasu and J. Teye (eds) *Migration in a Globalizing World: Perspectives from Ghana*, Accra: Sub-Saharan Publishers, pp 97–115.

Teye, J.K., Awumbila, M. and Benneh, Y. (2015) 'Intra-regional migration in the ECOWAS region: trends and emerging challenges', in A.B. Akoutou, R. Sohn, M. Vogl and D. Yeboah (eds) *Migration and Civil Society as Development Drivers: A Regional Perspective*, Bonn: WAI ZEI, pp 97–124.

Tsikata, D. (2009) 'Informalization, the informal economy and urban women's livelihoods in sub-Saharan Africa since the 1990s', in S. Razavi (ed) *The Gendered Impacts of Liberation: Towards 'Embedded' Liberalism?*, New York: Routledge, pp 131–62.

United Nations (2015) *Millennium Development Goals: Summary Report*, New York: United Nations.

United Nations Women (2012) 'Balancing the scales: groundbreaking legal cases that have changed women's lives', in *Progress of the World's Women 2011–2012: In Pursuit of Justice*, New York: United Nations, pp 16–21.

Wrigley-Asante, C. (2013a) 'Unraveling the health-related challenges of women in informal economy: accounts of women in cross border trading in Accra, Ghana', *GeoJournal*, 78(3): 525–37.

Wrigley-Asante, C. (2013b) 'Survival or escaping poverty: perspectives on poverty and well-being among Ghanaian women in cross-border trading', *Journal of Gender Studies*, 22(3): 320–34.

Wrigley-Asante, C. (2014) 'Accra turns lives around: female migrant traders and their empowerment experiences in Accra, Ghana', *Multidisciplinary Journal of Gender Studies*, 3(2): 341–67.

Wrigley-Asante, C. (2018) 'Women in ties: informal social networks among women in cross-border trading in Accra, Ghana', *Gender Issues*, 35(3): 202–19.

Wrigley-Asante, C. and Agyemang, E. (2019) 'Trading on-the-road and off-the-road: experiences of Ghanaian informal cross border traders', *Ghana Science Journal*, 16(1): 23–53.

Wrigley-Asante, C., Owusu, K., Egyir, I.S. and Owiyo, T.M. (2019) 'Gender dimensions of climate change adaptation practices: the experiences of smallholder crop farmers in the transition zone of Ghana', *African Geographical Review*, 38(2): 126–39.

Yusuff, S.O. (2014) 'Gender dimensions of informal cross border trade in West-African sub-region (ECOWAS) borders', *International Letters of Social and Humanistic Sciences*, 29: 19–33.

Zaami, M. (2020) 'Gendered strategies among northern migrants in Ghana: the role of social networks', *Ghana Journal of Geography*, 12(2): 1–24.

24

Care and Social Reproduction

Kendra Strauss

Introduction

I wrote the first draft of this chapter in the same that week the colonial (federal Canadian) government announced its first budget since the onset of the global coronavirus (COVID-19) pandemic in early 2020. Delivered by the first woman finance minister (and deputy prime minister), the budget was characterized by the government as 'very much a feminist plan' (Government of Canada, 2021). Two key foci were national investments in childcare and national standards for long-term care (institutional seniors' care), both dimensions of the 'crisis of care' intensified (though by no means instigated) by the pandemic (The Economist, 2021).

These key policy commitments appeared to reverse decades of state-led divestment, marketization and (re)privatization of services to support care and social reproduction, researched and theorized by feminist scholars, including feminist economic and labour geographers (see, for example, Bakker and Silvey, 2008; Molinari and Pratt, 2021; Schwiter et al, 2018a). They were precipitated by evidence in Canada and elsewhere that the economic impacts of the pandemic are gendered, and that both unemployment and the increased burden of unpaid labour have been disproportionately borne by feminized workers – impacts that will not have surprised feminist scholars of structural adjustment or the 2008 global financial crisis and austerity regimes in Europe. Pandemic-related unemployment and impacts on livelihoods are also racialized and classed, shaped by White supremacy, colonialism and imperialism (Krupar and Sadural, 2022; Neely and Lopez, 2022).

The current pandemic moment thus represents an intensification of trends that feminist economic geographers have long signalled (Nagar et al, 2002; McDowell, 2003; Mullings, 2005; Pollard, 2013), and has pulled back the curtain on the household as a domain of paid and unpaid work invisibilized or ignored in economic research (Ruwanpura, 2013; Pimlott-Wilson, 2015; Worth, 2018). The economic geographies of our present conjuncture are highly uneven, seemingly unprecedented, yet rooted in historical socio-spatial structures, processes and institutions of production and reproduction that shape the landscapes of racialized global capitalism today. They spur us to examine how feminists have long signposted an agenda for economic geography that understands economic development and crisis in relation to these socio-spatial relations and their exclusions, and seeks to ground economic geography's future in a more inclusive and politicized vision of the economy and understanding of who counts within it.

In what follows, I sharpen the focus on this moment of increased visibility of multiple crises of care to spotlight a broader crisis of social reproduction (Rao, 2021) that is also nothing new. I first examine the concept of social reproduction and the revival of analytical and research frameworks informed by social reproduction theory, as well as its stalled uptake in economic geography. I argue that attention to social reproduction deepens analyses of the relationship between uneven development and the socio-spatial construction of 'the economy'. I illustrate my arguments with a brief discussion of research on eldercare labour in Vancouver, BC and Shanghai, China,[1] and conclude by considering the role of feminist economic geography (as a knowledge project) and feminist economic geographers (as a community of praxis) in shaping the disciplinary future of economic geography.

Social reproduction theory from outside [the university] in

The origins of social reproduction theory are now relatively well documented in geography (for example, Mitchell et al, 2004; Meehan and Strauss, 2015; Winders and Smith, 2019; see also Chapters 1, 2 and 8 in this volume). Emerging from activist feminist engagements with Marx's theorization of the wage relation in capitalism (and lack of attention to domestic labour, in particular), the concepts of social production and social reproduction were central to a feminist articulations of struggles against both capitalism and patriarchy that sought to analytically centre women's work.

As the transnational coalition of *The Power of Women and the Subversion of Community* wrote: 'The specific social relation, which is capital, then, is the wage relation. And the wage relation can exist only when the ability to work becomes a saleable commodity. Marx calls this commodity *labour power* … *To describe its basic production and reproduction is to describe women's work*' (James, 2012: 51 emphasis in original; see also Dalla Costa and James, 1973). Mies (2014: 48) argued for this analysis of social production to include 'the general production of life, or subsistence production – mainly performed by the non-wage labour of women and other non-wage labourers such as slaves, contract workers and peasants in the colonies' in her exploration of the new international division of labour. In these arguments the goal was to put reproduction on equal footing with production, both theoretically and politically, and to decentre the wage. As Winders and Smith (2019: 872) argued, 'Faced with both committed Marxists' and mainstream economists' preoccupation with wages, labor productivity, returns to capital, and other normative measures of economic activity, feminists have long struggled not just to conceptualize but also to valorize social reproduction as entailing systemically fundamental forms of labor'.

However, despite the transnational and multiracial coalition building that undergirded movements like the Wages Against Housework (Federici, 2012), the location of women's oppression and exploitation in unpaid domestic labour in the male-breadwinner-headed household had the effect of eliding or downplaying differences among women. While James and others argued for a class–gender analysis, rejecting 'on the one hand class subordinated to feminism and on the other feminism subordinated to class' (James, 2012: 49), the 'triple jeopardy' (Davis, 1981) of women, race and class had already been theorized and analysed by Black intellectuals like Claudia Jones (Boyce Davies, 2007).[2] In her 1949 pamphlet, Jones cogently identified the ways that Black women 'had the responsibility of caring for the needs of the family, of militantly shielding it from the blows of Jim-Crow insults, of rearing children in an atmosphere of lynch terror, segregation, and police brutality, and of fighting for an education for the children'. They were also far more likely to engage in wage labour and to be the main breadwinners or heads of households than White women.

Moreover, Jones vigorously asserted the ways that the women's movement and radical (revolutionary) politics had to understand Black women's experiences at the intersection of class, race and gender as 'the vital link to this heightened political consciousness' (Jones, 1949). Far from suggesting that intersectional politics subordinate class or reinscribe rigid categories of identity, Jones's analysis situated intersectional experience as a locus of radical transformation of class and thus of capital as a social relation, without losing the historical and contemporary specificity of Black women's experience (both within the US and in transnational and diasporic contexts) (Boyce Davies, 2007). This is but one reason her writing rings so true today; she was also explicit about the ways that racial terror, police violence, White supremacy and discrimination in the labour market problematized universalizing claims about gender, the family, the household and the sexual division of labour (see also Chapter 23 in this volume). These insights cut to the heart of current and future research agendas that connect racial capitalism with both social reproduction and evolving economic geographies of accumulation and dispossession.

These various standpoints of critique from which social reproduction theory (SRT) emerged, and their relationship with liberation struggles, were transmuted by its institutionalization as feminist analysis slowly made inroads in the academic social sciences. From a politics of refusal – '[The movement] poses by its very existence and must pose with increasing articulation in action that *women refuse the myth of liberation through work*' (James, 2012: 59 emphasis added) – and demands (Weeks, 2011), SRT developed as a framework for feminist political economists to analyse structures, relations and struggles over production and reproduction. In this development, and the revival of interest in social reproduction among feminist academics since the 1990s, Mezzadri (2021: 1187) identified a split between 'understanding social reproduction as composed of circuits lying outside processes of value generation [and] early social reproduction analyses (ESRA), which instead theorized social reproduction as central to value'.

The concept of social reproduction was also broadened to encompass, on one hand, the institutional and material infrastructures of the welfare state that support the reproduction of both labour power and class relations, and on the other, the broader forms of unpaid work within and beyond the household that sustain communities. This broadening has had implications for the concept of social reproduction within and beyond SRT. Winders and Smith highlighted four imaginaries of social reproduction at work in geography and across other disciplines, which also represent conceptual schema and empirical social relations (2019: 873). Three of them (separate and unequal, overlapping duality of equals, and merged spheres in life's work and precarity) are defined in different ways by their relationship to productive labour, with the fourth instead centring relations of care involving migration and forms of global householding (Miraftab, 2011) that link the global and the intimate scales of the body and household without being defined in relation to production. Arguably, productive tensions between these imaginaries shape the ways that SRT is used to analyse contemporary capitalism in relation to current and future social, economic, political and ecological crises.

From social reproduction to care and back again: confronting the 'properly economic' in economic geography?

The evolution in approaches to social reproduction coincided with an increased interest in care and care work among feminist theorists (England and Dyck, 2012; Kofman, 2012; Boyer et al, 2017). Care offered both a broader and more heterodox starting point for describing and analysing the work of social and societal reproduction and maintenance, and a normative and ethical position from which to argue for its value (separate from the production of value). Theories of social reproduction and care were integral to feminist analyses of transnational migration (Pratt, 1999; Kofman and Raghuram, 2012); economic restructuring (McDowell, 2017); and the impacts of structural adjustment policies, welfare state retrenchment, and privatization (Katz, 2004; Mahon, 2006), which require attention to feminization and racialized, gendered and classed divisions of paid and unpaid labour that shape the contours of uneven development.

In economic geography, however, an interest in social reproduction among heterodox scholars of labour markets and production regimes (Peck, 1996; Kelly, 2009) in the 1990s waned somewhat a decade later. In the process of this shift, reproductive and domestic labour, the household and the production of social difference were left to feminist geographers (Werner et al, 2017) as 'mainstream' economic geography debated the benefits and challenges of heterodoxy (Barnes and Sheppard, 2010; compare Rosenman et al, 2019) while remaining wedded to a largely unchanged geographical imagination of the economy. The concept of social reproduction gained popularity in the social sciences, especially after the 2007–08 financial crisis, but while the number of papers on the topic of social reproduction in geography journals (317 between 1900 and 2021) was second only to those in sociology journals (373 in the same period), few of those were published in the main economic geography journals: two in *Economic Geography* (by Diane Perrons and Jamie Peck) and one in *Journal of Economic Geography* (by Al James and Bhaskar Vira).[3]

These are rough metrics, but they suggest that while an increasing number of geographers are using the social reproduction in their analyses, this research (including when published by economic and labour geographers) falls outside of the 'core' of economic geography. As Rosenman et al (2019: 515) write:

> Despite feminist economic geographers' success at identifying the fundamental relationships between such processes as economic production and social reproduction … economic geographical research on women, categories of social difference, and non-traditional and informal employment relationships are still largely framed as outside stalwart disciplinary traditions like industrial restructuring. This is despite more than 25 years of feminist economic geographers' rigorous evidence showing how dominant approaches to economic restructuring explain the transition of only a narrow portion of the economy in a small number of places.

Theorizing crisis through care: politics, social reproduction and future agendas for economic geography

The COVID-19 pandemic is merely the latest crisis to highlight just how insufficient theories of crisis and restructuring are when they focus only on 'a narrow portion of the economy in a small number of places' (Rosenman et al, 2019: 515) (see also Chapter 12 in this volume). If crisis is inherent to globalized capitalism, these crisis tendencies manifest in material and interrelated, if distinct, ways in the domains of social reproduction and production. The COVID-19 pandemic has simply pulled back the curtain on capitalism's 'hidden abodes' (Fraser, 2014). In other words, the processes that have been the focus of much research in economic geography (the ongoing socio-spatial restructuring of global production, financialization, technological change and digitalization, and the rise and fall of regions in the context of new spatial divisions of labour) have been accompanied by equally significant and interrelated changes in socio-spatial configurations of social production and reproduction.

In geographies of production regimes, research by feminist and labour geographers has undoubtedly shifted firm-centric approaches, yet there is still a tendency in economic geography that even if labour is acknowledged to be more than an input or factor of production, research stops at the factory gates (or their digital equivalent) (Bair, 2015). Sectors that employ huge numbers of workers, like retail, and health and social care, receive scant attention from economic geographers, as do informal labour and livelihoods. Geographies of finance and financialization (Christopherson et al, 2013) have developed themes of financial inclusion and exclusion and the financialization of everyday life, analyses of financial centres and practices beyond 'the West' (Hanieh, 2020; Lai and Pan, 2021; see also Chapter 26 in this volume), and are rapidly incorporating analyses of shifting technologies (Grindsted, 2016; Wójcik, 2021) and domains like climate finance and new debt regimes (Knox-Hayes, 2013; Potts, 2017). But research that connects the reproduction of households and communities with processes and mechanisms of financialization, and the forms of de- and reregulation that enable them, remains at the margins of economic geography.

So what is at stake for economic geography as a field in which the implicit consensus is that the domain of social reproduction and forms of paid and unpaid care labour remain secondary, both epistemologically and empirically? In the last part of this chapter I use an example from my own research to briefly illustrate how focusing on the social and economic centrality of care using SRT can generated and move forward an agenda for empirically and theoretically richer geographies of contemporary capitalism.

Seniors' care is one area in which various crises have failed to sustain mainstream attention, including from economic geographers. As Federici argued, debates about how older people should be cared for, by whom, and where, have largely been framed in mainstream policy discourses in relation to alarmist predictions about the costs of demographic ageing that pit younger and older generations against one another in a struggle over scarce state resources. They are almost entirely absent from 'the literature of the radical Left' (2012: 115). At the same time, while feminist economists and feminist geographers (Eaton, 2005; Yeoh and Huang, 2010; Schwiter et al, 2018b; Horton, 2019; Pratt and Johnston, 2021) have analysed labour, care, privatization, financialization, and new spaces and scales of service provision, these analyses have seldom registered in broader debates about geographical political economy.

When we started our comparative project on seniors' care labour markets in Vancouver and Shanghai in 2016, my collaborator Dr Feng Xu and I were interested both in how eldercare labour markets are created, and who is channelled into paid eldercare work. What we found is that the peripheralization of senior's care in political economy and economic geography reflects and reproduces its peripheralization in the realm of politics; its subordination to the logics and discourses of low taxes (especially on the wealthy); privatization and marketization; and the devaluation of workers and their labour (Strauss, 2021; Strauss and Xu, 2021). This is true even as the state at a variety of scales in both Canada and China are forced to contend with urgent demographic transitions. At the same time, health and social care represent both huge (and growing) areas of fiscal responsibility for governments, and sectors of employment. They are also significant domains for expansion and experimentation in financialization and assetization, and intimately connected to processes of urbanization that shape the organization of eldercare infrastructures (and vice versa). In other words, they are domains in which we can see future economies emerging, and yet seniors' care is not treated as 'properly economic'.

Eldercare has traditionally been the responsibility of the family, often although not exclusively women and girls; it is part of social reproduction, but unlike childcare or domestic tasks that reproduce labour power, 'it is deemed to absorb value but not produce it', at least in many Western societies (Federici, 2012: 116). When this labour is waged, jobs are highly feminized and often racialized, including through migration and immigration regimes that produce precarious legal status in many countries. We came to think about eldercare labour itself as a vital social infrastructure.

Theorizing the labour of eldercare workers as a social infrastructure of care makes explicit connections between strategies of capital and the enabling role of the state in extracting profits through intensive and extensive forms of privatization, financialization and rentierization (Christophers, 2019) that blur putatively clear distinctions between productive and reproductive domains. If this theoretical move clarifies and reinforces (as I believe it does) these conceptual and analytical connections, it also aligns with Rosenman et al's (2019) call for agenda setting and future-oriented efforts in economic geography that genuinely confront the politics of knowledge production about the economy. Doing so has implications not only for the richness, vibrancy and relevance of the subfield within and beyond geography, but also for feminist economic geography praxis itself.

Conclusion

Feminist geographers researching the diverse economies *of* capitalism, like Faria and Jones's (2020) study of postcolonial economies of beauty, Katz's (2018: 725) work on the political economy and biopolitics of 'securing childhood', and Mullings's (2021) examination of the links between racialized unfree labour and racialized precarity (see Chapter 2 in this volume), are already setting an agenda that challenges economic geography to account more fully for the myriad ways value – and values – are produced. This has methodological as well as epistemological implications: Karaagac (2020: 6) argues in the context of financialization that 'the everyday is not just a scale for microeconomic approaches to financialization but a stage for informing financialization research with lived experiences' in ways that produce both a fuller understanding of how financialization has transformed contemporary economies, and also where it fails.

Yet for feminists, this project is also a political one, which has implications for feminist economic geography as a knowledge project and community of praxis. One of the findings of the British Columbia case study in our eldercare project was a sense not only of fatigue with the lack of attention to the problems of the care regime there and the downloading of the (social and economic) costs of privatization onto workers and care recipients; it was also a sense of fatigue with the lack of a difference that *knowing and showing those costs* made. One implication is that feminist knowledge production inside the academy is constrained by the institution itself; this is hardly a new or original insight, but it reinforces the need for open and honest discussions about the politics of research that seeks to confirm what our research participants already know, as opposed to the politics of co-creating knowledge that actively and explicitly centres their expertise, including in the realms of theory and policy analysis.

In a footnote in *Sex, Race, and Class* (James, 2012: 52) is scathing about the very idea of 'Marxist political economy', stating that 'Marx negated political economy in theory and the working class negates it in practice'. While likely to make academics bridle, the provocation forces us to confront the idea and position of critique. For feminist economic geographers, does it matter that economic geography incorporates feminist analyses or concepts/ frameworks like social reproduction? The answer varies, depending on one's social location, career stage and degree of security in the academy. Perhaps the more the more pressing question is: does feminist economic geography, and relatedly social reproduction theory, offer a foundation for working towards a more radical politics of care? Possibly. But only if understood not as a unified or singular solution to the epistemological and political problem of the neglect of reproductive labour, but rather as an unfinished experiment, with multiple histories, in what it is possible to imagine.

Notes

[1] The project, 'Workers in the Ageing City: Eldercare Labour Markets in Vancouver and Shanghai', ran from 2016 to 2021 and was supported by an Insights grant from the Social Sciences and Humanities Research Council of Canada.

[2] Boyce Davies (2007: 1–2) describes Jones, a Marxist-Leninist, as 'a popular public figure, an active journalist and public speaker, a close friend of Paul and Eslanda Goode Robeson, a housemate of Lorraine Hansberry, mentored by W.E.B. Du Bois … a close friend of Amy Ashwood Garvey, [and] a female political and intellectual equivalent of C.L.R. James' who nevertheless remains largely invisible in both feminist and left theory. She is better known in England, where she lived after being deported from the US in 1955.

[3] These numbers are based on a Web of Knowledge search in May 2021 on the term 'social reproduction'. The same search revealed that fewer than 40 papers were published on the topic in 2002 across all disciplines, rising to more than 200 a year from 2018 onwards.

References

Bair, J. (2015) 'Gendered Commodity Chains: Seeing Women's Work and Households in Global Production, edited by Wilma Dunaway' [review], *Economic Geography*, 91(1): 109–11.

Bakker, I. and Silvey, R. (eds) (2008) *Beyond States and Markets: The Challenges of Social Reproduction*, Abingdon: Routledge.

Barnes, T.J. and Sheppard, E. (2010) '"Nothing includes everything": towards engaged pluralism in Anglophone economic geography', *Progress in Human Geography*, 34(2): 193–214.

Boyce Davies, C. (2007) *Left of Karl Marx: The Political Life of Black Communist Claudia Jones*, Durham, NC: Duke University Press.

Boyer, K., Dermott, E., James, A. and MacLeavy, J. (2017) 'Regendering care in the aftermath of recession?', *Dialogues in Human Geography*, 7(1): 56–73.

Christophers, B. (2019) 'The rentierization of the United Kingdom economy', *Environment and Planning A: Economy and Space*, ahead of print. Available from: https://doi.org/10.1177/0308518X19873007 [Accessed 30 June 2023].

Christopherson, S., Martin, R. and Pollard, J. (2013) 'Financialisation: roots and repercussions', *Cambridge Journal of Regions Economy and Society*, 6(3): 351–7.

Dalla Costa, M. and James, S. (eds) (1973) *The Power of Women and the Subversion of the Community* (2nd edn), Bristol: Falling Wall Press.

Davis, A.Y. (1981) *Women, Race, and Class*, New York: Random House.

Eaton, S.C. (2005) 'Eldercare in the United States: inadequate, inequitable, but not a lost cause', *Feminist Economics*, 11(2): 37–51.

England, K. and Dyck, I. (2012) 'Migrant workers in home care: routes, responsibilities, and respect', *Annals of the Association of American Geographers*, 102(5): 1076–83.

Faria, C.V. and Jones, H. (2020) 'A Darling® of the beauty trade: race, care, and the imperial debris of synthetic hair', *Cultural Geographies*, 27(1): 85–99.

Federici, S. (2012) *Revolution at Point Zero: Housework, Reproduction, and Feminist Struggle*, Oakland, CA: PM Press.

Fraser, N. (2014) 'Behind Marx's hidden abode: for an expanded conception of capitalism', *New Left Review*, 86: 55–72.

Government of Canada (2021) 'Budget 2021: supporting women – backgrounder', Department of Finance, 19 April. Available from: https://www.canada.ca/en/department-finance/news/2021/04/budget-2021-supporting-women.html [Accessed 30 June 2023].

Grindsted, TS. (2016) 'Geographies of high frequency trading: algorithmic capitalism and its contradictory elements', *Geoforum*, 68: 25–8.

Hanieh, A. (2020) 'New geographies of financial power: global Islamic finance and the Gulf', *Third World Quarterly*, 41(3): 525–46.

Horton, A. (2019) 'Financialization and non-disposable women: real estate, debt and labour in UK care homes', *Environment and Planning A: Economy and Space*, 54(1): 144–59.

James, S. (2012) *Sex, Race, and Class: The Perspective of Winning – A Selection of Writings, 1952–2011*, Oakland, CA: PM Press.

Jones, C. (1949) An End to the Neglect of the Problems of the Negro Woman!, New York: National Women's Commission, CPUSA. Available from: https://abolitionnotes.org/claudia-jones/neglect [Accessed 30 June 2023].

Karaagac, E.A. (2020) 'The financialization of everyday life: caring for debts', *Geography Compass*, 14(11): art e12541. Available from: https://doi.org/10.1111/gec3.12541 [Accessed 30 June 2023].

Katz, C. (2004) *Growing Up Global: Economic Restructuring and Children's Everyday Lives*, Minneapolis: University of Minnesota Press.

Katz, C. (2018) 'The angel of geography: superman, tiger mother, aspiration management, and the child as waste', *Progress in Human Geography*, 42(5): 723–40.

Kelly, P.F. (2009) 'From global production networks to global reproduction networks: households, migration, and regional development in Cavite, the Philippines', *Regional Studies*, 43(3): 449–61.

Knox-Hayes, J. (2013) 'The spatial and temporal dynamics of value in financialization: analysis of the infrastructure of carbon markets', *Geoforum*, 50: 117–28.

Kofman, E. (2012) 'Rethinking care through social reproduction: articulating circuits of migration', *Social Politics*, 19(1): 142–62.

Kofman, E. and Raghuram, P. (2012) 'Women, migration, and care: explorations of diversity and dynamism in the Global South', *Social Politics*, 19(3): 408–32.

Krupar, S. and Sadural, A. (2022) 'COVID "death pits": US nursing homes, racial capitalism, and the urgency of antiracist eldercare', *Environment and Planning C: Politics and Space*, 40(5): 1106–29.

Lai, P.Y.K. and Pan, F. (2021) 'Brexit and shifting geographies of financial centres in Asia', *Geoforum*, 125: 201–2.

Mahon, R. (2006) 'Of scalar hierarchies and welfare redesign: child care in three Canadian cities', *Transactions of the Institute of British Geographers*, 31(4): 452–66.

McDowell, L. (2003) 'Cultures of labour – work, employment, identity and economic transformations', in K. Anderson, M. Domosh, S. Pile and N. Thrift (eds) *Handbook of Cultural Geography*, London: Sage, pp 98–115.

McDowell, L. (2017) 'Youth, children and families in austere times: change, politics and a new gender contract', *Area*, 49(3): 311–16.

Meehan, K. and Strauss, K. (eds) (2015) *Precarious Worlds: Contested Geographies of Social Reproduction*, Athens: University of Georgia Press.

Mezzadri, A. (2021) 'A value theory of inclusion: informal labour, the homeworker, and the social reproduction of value', *Antipode*, 53(4): 1186–205.

Mies, M. (2014) *Patriarchy and Accumulation on a World Scale: Women in the International Division of Labour* (3rd edn), London: Zed Books.

Miraftab, F. (2011) 'Faraway intimate development: global restructuring of social reproduction', *Journal of Planning Education and Research*, 31(4): 392–405.

Mitchell, K., Marston, S.A. and Katz, C. (eds) (2004) *Life's Work: Geographies of Social Reproduction*, Malden, MA: Blackwell.

Molinari, N. and Pratt, G. (2021) 'Seniors' long-term care in Canada: a continuum of soft to brutal privatisation', *Antipode*, 55(4): 1089–109.

Mullings, B. (2005) 'Women rule? Globalization and the feminization of managerial and professional workspaces in the Caribbean', *Gender Place & Culture*, 12(1): 1–27.

Mullings, B. (2021) 'Caliban, social reproduction and our future yet to come', *Geoforum*, 118: 150–8.

Nagar, R., Lawson, V., McDowell, L. and Hanson, S. (2002) 'Locating globalization: feminist (re)readings of the subjects and spaces of globalization', *Economic Geography*, 78(3): 257–84.

Neely, A.H. and Lopez, P.J. (2022) 'Toward healthier futures in post-pandemic times: political ecology, racial capitalism, and Black feminist approaches to care', *Geography Compass*, 16(2): art e12609. Available from: https://doi.org/10.1111/gec3.12609 [Accessed 30 June 2023].

Peck, J. (1996) *Work Place: The Social Regulation of Labor Markets*, London: Guilford Press.

Pimlott-Wilson, H. (2015) 'Parental responsibility for paid employment and social reproduction: children's experiences in middle-class and working-class households in England', *Environment and Planning A: Economy and Space*, 47(9): 1892–906.

Pollard, J. (2013) 'Gendering capital: financial crisis, financialization and (an agenda for) economic geography', *Progress in Human Geography*, 37(3): 403–23.

Potts, S. (2017) 'Deep finance: sovereign debt crises and the secondary market "fix"', *Economy and Society*, 46(3/4): 452–75.

Pratt, G. (1999) 'From registered nurse to registered nanny: discursive geographics of Filipina domestic workers in Vancouver, BC', *Economic Geography*, 75(3): 215–36.

Pratt, G. and Johnston, C. (2021) 'Dementia, infrastructural failure, and new relations of transnational care in Thailand', *Transactions of the Institute of British Geographers*, 46(3): 526–39.

Rao, S. (2021) 'Beyond the coronavirus: understanding crises of social reproduction', *Global Labour Journal*, 12(1): 39–53.

Rosenman, E., Loomis, J. and Kay, K. (2019) 'Diversity, representation, and the limits of engaged pluralism in (economic) geography', *Progress in Human Geography*, 44(3): 510–33.

Ruwanpura, K.N. (2013) 'It's the (household) economy, stupid! Pension reform, collective resistance and the reproductive sphere in Sri Lanka', in J. Elias and S.J. Gunawardana (eds) *The Global Political Economy of the Household in Asia*, Basingstoke: Palgrave Macmillan, pp 145–61.

Schwiter, K., Berndt, C. and Truong, J. (2018a) 'Neoliberal austerity and the marketisation of elderly care', *Social & Cultural Geography*, 19(3): 379–99.

Schwiter, K., Strauss, K. and England, K. (2018b) 'At home with the boss: migrant live-in caregivers, social reproduction and constrained agency in the UK, Canada, Austria and Switzerland', *Transactions of the Institute of British Geographers*, 44(3): 462–76.

Strauss, K. (2021) 'Beyond crisis? Using rent theory to understand the restructuring of publicly funded seniors' care in British Columbia, Canada', *Environment and Planning A: Economy and Space*, ahead of print. Available from: https://doi.org/10.1177/0308518X20983152 [Accessed 30 June 2023].

Strauss, K. and Xu, F. (2021) 'What we talk about when we talk about austerity: social policy, public management and politics of eldercare funding in Canada and China', in D. Baines and I. Cunningham (eds) *Working in the Context of Austerity: Challenges and Struggles*, Bristol: Bristol University Press, pp 131–50.

The Economist (2021) 'The pandemic has exposed a crisis in Canada's care homes', The Economist, 23 January. Available from: https://www.econom ist.com/the-americas/2021/01/23/the-pandemic-has-exposed-a-crisis-in-canadas-care-homes [Accessed 30 June 2023].

Weeks, K. (2011) *The Problem with Work: Feminism, Marxism, Antiwork Politics, and Postwork Imaginaries*, Durham, NC: Duke University Press.

Werner, M., Strauss, K., Parker, B., Orzeck, R., Derickson, K. and Bonds, A. (2017) 'Feminist political economy in geography: why now, what is different, and what for?', *Geoforum*, 79: 1–4.

Winders, J. and Smith, B.E. (2019) 'Social reproduction and capitalist production: a genealogy of dominant imaginaries', *Progress in Human Geography*, 43(5): 871–89.

Wojcik, D. (2021) 'Financial geography II: The impacts of FinTech–Financial sector and centres, regulation and stability, inclusion and governance', *Progress in Human Geography*, 45(4): 878–89.

Worth, N. (2018) 'Mothers, daughters, and learning to labour: framing work through gender and generation', *Canadian Geographer/Le Géographe canadien*, 62(4): 551–61.

Yeoh, B.S.A. and Huang, S. (2010) 'Foreign domestic workers and home-based care for elders in Singapore', *Journal of Aging & Social Policy*, 22(1): 69–88.

25

The Future of Creative Industries and Labour

Taylor Brydges

Introduction

When asked in early 2020 to write about the future of creative industries and labour, it would have been quite difficult to predict what lay ahead. Like so many other sectors of the economy, the creative industries have been greatly impacted by COVID-19 (Banks, 2020; Comunian and England, 2020; Florida and Seman, 2020). Described as a 'calamity on top of a crisis' (Meyrick, 2020), the COVID-19 pandemic has shed light on many of the structural tensions that define the contemporary nature of work in creative industries (Banks, 2020; Comunian and England, 2020; Eikhof, 2020). In particular, the chapter focuses on contemporary inequalities in creative labour. With sites of creative production and consumption moving in and out of lockdown, estimated job losses due to COVID-19 range from nearly one third of all creative economy jobs in the US (Florida and Seman, 2020) to three quarters of creative and performing arts jobs in Australia (Coates et al, 2020).

It is a unique – and indeed, challenging – time to reflect upon the nature of work in creative industries and propose an agenda for moving forward. Yet, in order to think about where we might be going, we also need to know where we've been. To that end, this chapter is structured in three parts. First, I begin by reviewing the core tenets of creative economy theory in economic geography, before introducing the important critique of feminist economic geographers who have laid the foundation for critical study of labour in creative industries. Here, contemporary inequalities in creative labour are explored with a focus on the importance of intersectionality in driving these experiences. Building on this, and in light of the ongoing impact of

COVID-19 on creative industries, I share new research on the evolving nature of work in the creative industries during the pandemic through a case study of the Australian fashion industry. The chapter concludes by providing a number of potential avenues for future research.

An introduction to the study of creative industries

With the cultural turn in geography and the social sciences more broadly, there has been significant and growing attention paid to the cultural and creative industries, bringing with it a range of debates and studies of production, consumption, aesthetics, representation, identities and more (compare Aitken and Valentine, 2006; Leslie, 2012). Here, studies of creative industries have explored a number of themes, including the economic and cultural contributions of the workers in a range of fields (including the arts, advertising, fashion, music, publishing and video games) and the role of these industries in the transition from a manufacturing to post-industrial or knowledge economy in cities and countries around the world (Florida, 2002; Power and Scott, 2004; Hracs et al, 2022).

Popular books such as *The Creative City* (Landry, 2000) and *The Rise of the Creative Class* (Florida, 2002) were central in spurring academic debates pertaining to the creative economy and creative industries (Rantisi et al, 2006; Leslie and Catungal, 2012). A concept with tremendous policy mobility (Flew and Cunningham, 2013), the foundation of much of this work is an examination of the growing role of human creativity in fuelling economic growth and innovation in the transition from industrial to post-industrial or knowledge-based economies (Florida, 2002).

Discourses of creativity are not without critique. For example, it has been argued that the valorization of creativity, implemented through 'one-size-fits-all' policy approaches built upon competition, gentrification and inequality (Catungal et al, 2009). Here, a common theme is an exploration of consequences of urban economic development policies – built upon exclusionary conceptualizations of creativity and the creative economy (Gibson and Kong, 2005) – designed to attract and retain 'talent', often at the expense of existing residents and communities.

Moreover, in unpacking what is meant by concepts such as creativity or talent, the methodological underpinnings of much of this work (much of which relied on large quantitative studies) have also been challenged for a lack of conceptual clarity (Markusen et al, 2008). A key critique of much of the literature on creative industries and labour, which will be expanded upon in the next section, is that the commonly theorized creative worker underpinning much of this research is 'white, middle-class, male and urban' (Alacovska and Gill, 2019: 196). Thus, critical approaches to the study of creative industries and the creative economy have advocated for the need to move beyond these exclusionary theoretical foundations and instead adopt a 'complex and relational' understanding of creativity (Gibson and Kong, 2005; de Dios and Kong, 2020).

Over the last 20 years, studies of creative industries have taken up this call and evolved from research demonstrating how that creative work is distinct from other sectors of the economy to research looking *within* creative industries – such as music (Hracs, 2012; Watson, 2013), fashion (McRobbie, 1998, 2016; Leslie and Brail, 2011), film and TV (Swords and Wray, 2010; Johns and Swords, 2020), new media (Gill, 2002; Warren, 2018), design (Reimer, 2016), video games (Izushi and Aoyama, 2006; Johns, 2006) and more – to see how sector specific dynamics shape the nature of work in creative industries in different industries and geographic contexts.

In particular, this growing body of research has called into question just how 'cool, creative and egalitarian' working in a creative industry really is (Gill, 2002). While the creative economy promised to usher in a new era defined by a meritocratic no-collar workplace (Florida, 2002), it has since been demonstrated that creative work is in fact highly inequitable, precarious and insecure (Christopherson, 2008; Hesmondhalgh and Baker, 2010) (see also Chapters 3 and 16 in this volume). As Banks and Milestone argue, 'discourse(s) of flexibility and creative freedom has been allowed to mask some fundamental inequalities and discriminatory practices' (2011: 73).

As creative work has increasingly become defined by a range non-standard employment relations, such as freelance, contract or entrepreneurial ways of working (McRobbie, 1998, 2016; Stokes, 2017; Brydges and Hracs, 2019a), this has had a number of implications for creating entry barriers to, and labour dynamics within, creative industries. While working in a creative industry may provide the opportunity for creative expression and flexibility, it increasingly comes at the cost of entrepreneurial self-management, which further contributes to the precariousness and extensification of work (Bain and MacLean, 2013; Brydges and Hracs, 2019a).

From the home (Luckman, 2013) to the studio (Sjöholm, 2014) to the school gate (Ekinsmyth, 2011) and seemingly everywhere in between, spaces of work and leisure are increasingly entangled. A key consequence of this is new and changing configurations and spatialities of work whereby the private and professional lives seemingly become one (Brydges and Sjöholm, 2019). For example, through an in-depth case of a personal style blogger over nearly a decade, Brydges and Sjöholm (2019) explored the evolution of a blog from one built upon 'outfit-of-the-day' posts created in anonymous public spaces to one which evolved over time to include food, fitness, home renovations and even the blogger's birth story. This is indicative of the 'very complicated version of freedom' described by Hesmondhalgh and Baker (2010) whereby creative freedom and the commodification of the self are in seemingly constant negotiation.

Yet, in the face of precarity, individuals still decide to make their livelihood in the creative economy. The appeal of working in a creative industry where one has the opportunity to 'do what you love' (Arvidsson et al, 2010; Brydges and Hracs, 2019a) remains an important motivating factor for many creative workers. It means for many creative workers that they are likely to be hesitant to leave, no matter how challenging things get (Brydges and Hracs, 2019b). However, here it is important to point out that, crucially, it has been argued that experiences of work in creative industries are highly uneven, shaped by the intersectionality of workers (Valentine, 2007; Stokes, 2017; Brydges and Hracs, 2019a). The potential risks and rewards of creative work are experienced very differently by different creative workers based on a range of deeply personal factors.

A feminist economic geography approach to the study of creative work

In this context, feminist (economic) geographers have taken up the challenge of theorizing intersectionality (Valentine, 2007). Building on Crenshaw's (1991) pioneering work, the concept seeks to 'understand the connections between multiple axes of oppression and exclusion' acknowledging that these constitute distinct experiences and subjectivities' (Gill, 2014: 510). Creative work is often seen as gender neutral but in reality, it is often based upon an inherently 'masculinist subject' (Reimer, 2016). Despite the fact that identity markers shape individual experiences of creative work, a narrow conceptualization of the creative worker has come to serve as the foundation of academic knowledge of all creative workers, resulting in the universalization of what is actually a very particular experience.

Here, there is a growing body of research which advocating for an intersectional approach to the study of creative work, shedding light on individual's experiences in various industries (Reimer, 2009, 2016; Leslie and Catungal, 2012; Idriss, 2016; Worth, 2016a, 2016b; Warren, 2018; Brydges and Hracs, 2019a; see also Chapter 18 in this volume). This work highlights that models of production underpinning creative industries reinforce social inequalities, and workers experience work in very different ways, even within the same industry and city (Leslie and Brail, 2011; Eikhof and Warhurst, 2013; Rantisi, 2014; Reimer, 2016; Stokes, 2017; Brydges and Hracs, 2019b).

However, we also see examples of workers challenging the exclusionary nature of many creative industries. Researchers must embrace this complexity to account for the diversity of experiences of labour within creative industries, whether that be Warren's (2018) research exploring how, in the face of widespread discrimination, Muslim bloggers, through their use of digital technologies and social media, have constructed new spaces of work, community and activism, or Idriss's (2016) work exploring how Arab-Australian artists challenge their 'marginal' position in the Australian art world by using their creativity in strategic ways. Thus, researchers must embrace this complexity to account for the diversity of experiences of labour within creative industries.

Experiences studying the evolving nature of work in creative industries during COVID-19

In my own work on the fashion industry, I have sought to explore a number of these themes. The fashion industry is an exemplifier of many of the key tensions that define creative work. It is an industry defined by a handful of superstar creative cities (London, Paris, Milan, New York) that hold tremendous power and continue to act as global talent magnets (Larner and Molloy, 2009). As such, the industry typically demands a tremendous amount of mobility on behalf of those who want to work for a leading fashion house (Brydges and Hracs, 2019b). The alternative is to carve out an alternative career path that is more likely to offer flexible configurations of work but is also more likely to be in a smaller/independent and highly localized business (Brydges and Hracs, 2019b).

Fashion is also an industry that despite notoriously precarious working conditions, continues to attract workers who are drawn to it for the opportunity to work in an industry they are passionate about (Arvidsson et al, 2010; Brydges and Hracs, 2019a). Moreover, a successful, or even stable, career in the fashion industry is no guarantee, particularly for women. Research has shown that even though the fashion industry is a highly feminized industry across supply chains, women experience the 'glass runway' where opportunities to take leading roles in the industry are few and far between and for the few who do make it, their accomplishments are rarely recognized (Stokes, 2015).

Like other creative industries, fashion is constantly evolving, with experiences of work varying due to both internal and external shocks, one of which is the COVID-19 pandemic. In early 2020, with colleagues from the University of Technology Sydney and University of Sydney, we began a project on the fashion industry in Australia. While conducting interviews with fashion designers (ranging from independent fashion designers to the head designers of brands with sales revenue upwards of AU$5 million, all of whom were female) we found that experiences of work varied significantly across the sample, shaped by factors including geography, industry segment, number of years in business, age, family status and more, all of which affected how fashion designers could adapt to the changing circumstances brought on by the COVID-19 pandemic. (For a broader overview of this work, see Brydges et al, 2021.)

The fashion designers we interviewed have managed the effects of a public health crisis on their professional and personal lives. For example, the early impact of the pandemic on creative work appeared for some to be reinforcing key tensions associated with creative work, such as the need to balance creative and professional, entrepreneurial tasks, including designing new collections to meet evolving consumer demands, navigating supply chain delays both domestically (such as the impact of localized lockdowns on garment manufacturing) and abroad (particularly relating to the import of materials, shipping and distribution) (Brydges and Hracs, 2019a; Brydges et al, 2021).

During interviews, a common theme was concern for worker well-being across their supply chains. Fashion designers felt personally responsibility for the many jobs and livelihoods dependent on their response to the crisis and their ability to stay in business despite highly uncertain circumstances. Juggling the administration of applications for COVID-19-response employee assistance programmes in order to help their business remain financially viable further added to the myriad tasks faced by designers at this time. These feelings were compounded by concerns for family and personal health, as well as the stress and uncertainties caused by state and/or national border lockdowns, stay-at-home orders, school closures and more.

We also found differences in experiences of managing new facets of the extensification of work in relation to the opportunities and challenges of working from home. For example, for some designers we interviewed, working remotely offered a reprieve from daily commutes and meetings as well as the opportunity to work from regional centres rather than in one of Australia's major fashion cities of Melbourne and Sydney. For others, this time was defined by the challenges of working from home while managing the home-schooling of young children and/or childcare responsibilities. Indeed, these are dynamics that are not only shaped by age and family status but by gender as well. For example, it was found that gender disparities in responsibilities for childcare in Australian households were only amplified during the pandemic, resulting in a disproportionate burden on women (Johnston et al, 2020).

And while not discounting the significant stressors that workers have experienced during this time, we were also surprised at the amount of optimism that fashion designers held for the future. For instance, a number of designers described the time as a 'reset' for the industry that allowed them to rethink business models and their previous ways of working. As one designer told us,

'Once the panic subsided and things started to settle down, there have been some good changes. It has given us the chance to reset. We've shortened our working hours, adapted our fashion calendar and become more responsive. We're a smaller and more agile business. I had been thinking of making some changes but I was concerned my retailers and customers would be reluctant. But because of what has happened, they are more accepting now.'

Interestingly, despite operating in a broader climate of economic uncertainty, we also found examples of fashion design entrepreneurs continuing to enter the industry and start new businesses during this time. Businesses that were in the works pre-pandemic were still launched and while understandably nervous, the designers we interviewed were still incredibly excited and hopeful about the future. This is another example of experiences of creative labour varying significantly.

Although there have been significant questions regarding the Australian government's support of creative industries during the pandemic more broadly (compare Caust, 2020), there have also been new, and indeed positive, conversations regarding the role of the fashion industry in Australia, from shop local campaigns to renewed calls for investment in domestic manufacturing. Many of the designers we interviewed reported feeling more connected to their local fashion community. For example:

'As an industry, we've come together. We're talking about the issues and how we're going to move forward and what we can do to support each other. Obviously, everyone's got their own DNA and their own supply chain, but I think for the first time. I really felt a sense of, like, we're actually in it together.'

These are themes that will need to be revisited in subsequent follow-up studies as the impact of the pandemic continues to be felt and experiences of work once again evolve. For example, will the fashion industry continue to concentrate in the major cities of Sydney and Melbourne, or will the entrenchment of home-based work support the development and expansion of fashion design businesses in smaller creative cities such as Brisbane and Adelaide? How will this impact the insertion of Australian fashion design businesses within the global hierarchy of fashion cities? What will the implications of changing spaces of work be, not only for career opportunities but for the pursuit of work–life balance and the management of stress, precarity and loneliness experienced by fashion designers?

The future of creative industries and labour: where do we go from here?

As we face economic uncertainty, feminist economic geographers offer insights for advancing the study of creative industries and labour. First, more research is needed to examine the nature of work in different creative sectors, using comparative case studies to highlight variations in experiences across industries and locations. For example, to challenge the Western bias of creative industries research, researchers such as Comunian, England and Hracs have undertaken collaborative research based on their Creative Industries in Africa network (Comunian and England, 2020; Comunian et al, 2021; England et al, 2021). Other recent work, such as Khan's (2019) interrogation of discourses of creativity in the Bangladeshi fashion industry and Steedman's (2019) and Alacovska et al's (2021) expansion of our conceptualization of hustling as a creative practice through their studies of filmmakers in Kenya and Ghana, also move the field beyond this bias.

Second, to move beyond dominant theories of the middle-class male creative worker, intersectional research is needed, recognizing the diverse identity markers shaping personal experiences in creative work. This requires acknowledging the various factors that make this work appealing and how creative workers manage precarity. As the impact of COVID-19 on creative industries continues, it is crucial to address inequalities and advocate for a more inclusive approach that values workers' lived experiences.

Third, research rooted in an intersectional approach may have important policy implications. As past downturns have shown, creative industries are often linked to economic recovery, and history may repeat itself. Policy must adopt a sectoral approach that recognizes the varied impact of the pandemic on different creative industries (Johns and Swords, 2020), while acknowledging the intersectionality of factors such as class, skill, gender, ethnicity, and more (Carey et al, 2020). Failure to do so risks reinforcing existing inequalities and exacerbating them (Banks, 2020), posing a threat to inclusion and workforce diversity (Eikhof, 2020). Therefore, policy must be informed by research driven by a feminist, intersectional approach that accounts for the diversity of individuals and experiences in the creative economy.

Fourth, studying creative industries should consider their implications for defining agendas such as the UN Sustainable Development Goals (United Nations, 2018). The UN Sustainable Development Goals Fund (UNSDGF, nd) recognized the importance of creative industries in achieving sustainable development goals, including Goal 8: Decent Work and Economic Growth. The SDGF supported initiatives to include creative industries in sustainable development discourse, acknowledging the cultural and economic benefits they bring. Moreover, 2021 was declared by the UN Conference on Trade and Development (UNCTAD, 2021) as the International Year of Creative Economy for Sustainable Development, highlighting the need to move beyond Western-centric accounts and to deepen connections with sustainable development fields.

In conclusion, the field of economic geography risks losing relevance if it fails to adopt a more intersectional approach. The dominant conceptualization of creative labour as performed by a White, highly paid, male body must be reimagined, and feminist economic geographers are well placed to lead the way in addressing this issue. It is crucial to recognize that creative work is experienced differently by people with different identities, and adopting an intersectional approach is fundamental to the advancement of the field.

References

Aitken, S. and Valentine, G. (2006) *Approaches to Human Geography*, London: Sage.

Alacovska, A. and Gill, R. (2019) 'De-westernizing creative labour studies: the informality of creative work from an ex-centric perspective', *International Journal of Cultural Studies*, 22(2): 195–212.

Alacovska, A., Langevang, T. and Steedman, R. (2021) 'The work of hope: spiritualizing, hustling and waiting in the creative industries in Ghana', *Environment and Planning A: Economy and Space*, 53(4): 619–37.

Arvidsson, A., Malossi, G. and Naro, S. (2010) 'Passionate work? Labour conditions in the Milan fashion industry', *Journal for Cultural Research*, 14(3): 295–309.

Bain, A. and McLean, H. (2013) 'The artistic precariat', *Cambridge Journal of Regions, Economy and Society*, 6(1): 93–111.

Banks, M. (2020) 'The work of culture and C-19', *European Journal of Cultural Studies*, 23(4): 648–54.

Banks, M. and Milestone, K. (2011) 'Individualization, gender and cultural work', *Gender, Work & Organization*, 18(1): 73–89.

Brydges, T. and Hracs, B.J. (2019a) 'What motivates millennials? How intersectionality shapes the working lives of female entrepreneurs in Canada's fashion industry', *Gender, Place & Culture*, 26(4): 510–32.

Brydges, T. and Hracs, B.J. (2019b) 'The locational choices and interregional mobilities of creative entrepreneurs within Canada's fashion system', *Regional Studies*, 53(4): 517–27.

Brydges, T. and Sjöholm, J. (2019) 'Becoming a personal style blogger: changing configurations and spatialities of aesthetic labour in the fashion industry. *International Journal of Cultural Studies*, 22(1): 119–39.

Brydges, T., Heinze, L. and Retamal, M. (2021) 'Changing geographies of fashion during COVID-19: the Australian case', *Geographical Research*, 59(2): 206–16.

Carey, H., Florisson, R., O'Brien, D. and Lee, N. (2020) *Getting In and Getting On: Class, Participation and Job Quality in the UK Creative Industries*, Policy Review Series: Class in the Creative Industries Paper No. 01, London: Creative Industry Policy and Evidence Centre. Available from: https://pec.ac.uk/research-reports/getting-in-and-getting-on-class-participation-and-job-quality-in-the-uks-creative-industries [Accessed 1 July 2023].

Catungal, J.P., Leslie, D. and Hii, Y. (2009) 'Geographies of displacement in the creative city: the case of Liberty Village, Toronto', *Urban Studies*, 46(5/6): 1095–14.

Caust, J. (2020) 'Coronavirus: 3 in 4 Australians employed in the creative and performing arts could lose their jobs', The Conversation, 20 April. Available from: http://theconversation.com/coronavirus-3-in-4-australi ans-employed-in-the-creative-and-performing-arts-could-lose-their-jobs-136505 [Accessed 1 July 2023].

Christopherson, S. (2008) 'Beyond the self-expressive creative worker an industry perspective on entertainment media', *Theory, Culture & Society*, 25(7/8): 73–95.

Coates, B., Cowgill, M., Chen, T. and Mackey, W. (2020) *Shutdown: Estimating the COVID-19 Employment Shock*, Carlton, VIC: Grattan Institute. Available from: https://grattan.edu.au/wp-content/uploads/2020/04/Shutdown-estimating-the-COVID-19-employment-shock-Grattan-Institute.pdf [Accessed 1 July 2023].

Comunian, R. and England, L. (2020) 'Creative and cultural work without filters: Covid-19 and exposed precarity in the creative economy', *Cultural Trends*, 29(2): 112–28.

Comunian, R., Hracs, B.J. and England, L. (eds) (2021) *Higher Education and Policy for Creative Economies in Africa: Developing Creative Economies*, Abingdon: Routledge.

de Dios, A. and Kong, L. (eds) (2020) *Handbook on the Geographies of Creativity*, Cheltenham: Edward Elgar.

Eikhof, D.R. (2020) 'COVID-19, inclusion and workforce diversity in the cultural economy: what now, what next?', *Cultural Trends*, 29(3): 234–50.

Eikhof, D.R. and Warhurst, C. (2013) 'The promised land? Why social inequalities are systemic in the creative industries', *Employee Relations*, 35(5): 495–508.

Ekinsmyth, C. (2011) 'Challenging the boundaries of entrepreneurship: the spatialities and practices of UK "mumpreneurs"', *Geoforum*, 42(1): 104–14.

England, L., Ikpe, E., Comunian, R. and Kabir, A.J. (2021) 'Africa fashion futures: creative economies, global networks and local development', *Geography Compass*, 15(9): art e12589. Available from: https://doi.org/ 10.1111/gec3.12589 [Accessed 1 July 2023].

Flew, T. and Cunningham, S. (2013) 'Creative industries after the first decade of debate', in *Creative Industries and Urban Development*, Routledge, pp 68–78.

Florida, R. (2002) *The Rise of the Creative Class: And How It's Transforming Work, Leisure, Community and Everyday Life*, New York: Basic Books.

Florida, R. and Seman, M. (2020) Lost Art: Measuring COVID-19's Devastating Impact on America's Creative Economy, Washington, DC: Metropolitan Policy Program Brookings.

Gibson, C. and Kong, L. (2005) 'Cultural economy: a critical review', *Progress in Human Geography*, 29(5): 541–61.

Gill, R. (2002) 'Cool, creative and egalitarian? Exploring gender in project-based new media work in Euro', *Information, Communication & Society*, 5(1): 70–89.

Gill, R. (2014) 'Unspeakable inequalities: post feminism, entrepreneurial subjectivity, and the repudiation of sexism among cultural workers', *Social Politics*, 21(4): 509–28.

Hesmondhalgh, D. and Baker, S. (2010) '"A very complicated version of freedom": conditions and experiences of creative labour in three cultural industries', *Poetics*, 38(1): 4–20.

Hracs, B.J. (2012) 'A creative industry in transition: the rise of digitally driven independent music production', *Growth and Change*, 43(3): 442–61.

Hracs, B.J., Brydges, T., Haisch, T., Hauge, A., Jansson, J. and Sjöholm, J. (eds) (2022) *Culture, Creativity and Economy: Collaborative Practices, Value Creation and Spaces of Creativity*, Abingdon: Routledge.

Idriss, S. (2016) 'Racialisation in the creative industries and the Arab-Australian multicultural artist', *Journal of Intercultural Studies*, 37(4): 406–20.

Izushi, H. and Aoyama, Y. (2006) 'Industry evolution and cross-sectoral skill transfers: a comparative analysis of the video game industry in Japan, the United States, and the United Kingdom', *Environment and Planning A: Economy and Space*, 38(10): 1843–61.

Johns, J. (2006) 'Video games production networks: value capture, power relations and embeddedness', *Journal of Economic Geography*, 6(2): 151–80.

Johns, J. and Swords, J. (2020) 'The impact of COVID-19 on TV freelancers', Sign: Screen Industries Growth Network, 3 August. Available from: https://screen-network.org.uk/the-impact-of-covid-19-on-tv-freelancers/ [Accessed 1 July 2023].

Johnston, R.M., Sheluchin, A. and van der Linden, C. (2020) 'Evidence of exacerbated gender inequality in child care obligations in Canada and Australia during the COVID-19 pandemic', *Politics & Gender*, 16(4): 1131–41.

Khan, R. (2019) '"Be creative" in Bangladesh? Mobility, empowerment and precarity in ethical fashion enterprise', *Cultural Studies*, 33(6): 1029–49.

Landry, C. (2000) *The Creative City: A Toolkit for Urban Innovators*, London: Earthscan.

Larner, W. and Molloy, M. (2009) 'Globalization, the "new economy" and working women: theorizing from the New Zealand designer fashion industry', *Feminist Theory*, 10(1): 35–59.

Leslie, D. (2012) 'Gender, commodity chains and everyday life', in B. Warf (ed), *Encounters and Engagements between Economic and Cultural Geography*, Dordrecht: Springer, pp 65–78.

Leslie, D. and Brail, S. (2011) 'The productive role of "quality of place": a case study of fashion designers in Toronto', *Environment and Planning A: Economy and Space*, 43(12): 2900–17.

Leslie, D. and Catungal, J.P. (2012) 'Social justice and the creative city: class, gender and racial inequalities', *Geography Compass*, 6(3): 111–22.

Luckman, S. (2013) 'The aura of the analogue in a digital age: women's crafts, creative markets and home-based labour after Etsy', *Cultural Studies Review*, 19(1): 249–70.

Markusen, A., Wassall, G.H., DeNatale, D. and Cohen, R. (2008) 'Defining the creative economy: industry and occupational approaches', *Economic Development Quarterly*, 22(1): 24–45.

McRobbie, A. (1998) *British Fashion Design: Rag Trade or Image Industry?*, London: Routledge.

McRobbie, A. (2016). *Be Creative: Making a Living in the New Culture Industries*, Cambridge: Polity Press.

Meyrick, J. (2020) 'As we turn to creativity in isolation, the coronavirus is a calamity on top of an arts crisis', The Conversation, 27 March. Available from: http://theconversation.com/as-we-turn-to-creativity-in-isolation-the-coronavirus-is-a-calamity-on-top-of-an-arts-crisis-134230 [Accessed 1 July 2023].

Power, D. and Scott, A.J. (eds) (2004) *Cultural Industries and the Production of Culture*, Abingdon: Routledge.

Rantisi, N.M. (2014) 'Gendering fashion, fashioning fur: on the (re) production of a gendered labor market within a craft industry in transition', *Environment and Planning D: Society and Space*, 32(2): 223–39.

Rantisi, N.M., Leslie, D. and Christopherson, S. (2006) 'Placing the creative economy: scale, politics, and the material', *Environment and Planning A: Economy and Space*, 38(10): 1789–97.

Reimer, S. (2009) 'Geographies of production II: fashion, creativity and fragmented labour', *Progress in Human Geography*, 33(1): 65–73.

Reimer, S. (2016). ' "It's just a very male industry": gender and work in UK design agencies', *Gender, Place & Culture*, 23(7): 1033–46.

Sjöholm, J. (2014) 'The art studio as archive: tracing the geography of artistic potentiality, progress and production', *Cultural Geographies*, 21(3): 505–14.

Steedman, R. (2019) 'Nairobi-based middle class filmmakers and the production and circulation of transnational cinema', *Poetics*, 75: art 101333. Available from: https://doi.org/10.1016/j.poetic.2018.11.002 [Accessed 1 July 2023].

Stokes, A. (2015) 'The glass runway: how gender and sexuality shape the spotlight in fashion design', *Gender & Society*, 29(2): 219–43.

Stokes, A. (2017) 'Fashioning gender: the gendered organization of cultural work', *Social Currents*, 4(6): 518–34.

Swords, J. and Wray, F. (2010) 'The connectivity of the creative industries in North East England: the problems of physical and relational distance', *Local Economy*, 25(4): 305–18.

United Nations (2018) 'The 17 United Nations Sustainable Development Goals', United Nations. Available from: https://sdgs.un.org/goals [Accessed 1 July 2023].

UNCTAD (United Nations Conference on Trade and Development) (2021) 'International Year of Creative Economy for Sustainable Development, 2021', UNCTAD. Available from: https://unctad.org/topic/trade-analy sis/creative-economy-programme/2021-year-of-the-creative-economy [Accessed 1 July 2023].

UNSDGF (United Nations Sustainable Development Goals Fund) (nd) Creative Industries and Sustainable Development. Available from: https:// www.sdgfund.org/creative-industries-and-sustainable-development [Accessed 1 July 2023].

Valentine, G. (2007) 'Theorizing and researching intersectionality: a challenge for feminist geography', *Professional Geographer*, 59(1): 10–21.

Warren, S. (2018) 'Placing faith in creative labour: Muslim women and digital media work in Britain', *Geoforum*, 97: 1–9.

Watson, A. (2013) '"Running a studio's a silly business": work and employment in the contemporary recording studio sector', *Area*, 45(3): 330–6.

Worth, N. (2016a) 'Feeling precarious: millennial women and work', *Environment and Planning D: Society and Space*, 34(4): 601–16.

Worth, N. (2016b) 'Who we are at work: millennial women, everyday inequalities and insecure work', *Gender, Place & Culture*, 23(9): 1302–14.

26

Future Finance

Sabine Dörry

Introduction

Financialization, aptly portrayed as a geographically non-neutral process and defined as a political project and 'process of cultural and economic transformation' (Christopherson et al, 2013: 352), has fundamentally changed our societies, especially the way we 'value' (attach a price tag to) things (for example, nature) and services (such as education, care for the elderly) (Christophers et al, 2017). The consequences of financialization have been diligently well documented through multiple manifestations as it drives inequality within our economies and societies. Important examples include the increasing financialization of care homes via ownership structures (Horton, 2022), the securitization of climate change–related catastrophe risk (Johnson, 2014) in the larger processes of clean energy transition (Knuth, 2018, Liu and Lai, 2021) and the rising assetization of public infrastructure (Kass et al, 2019; Deruytter et al, 2022). Further contributions provide valuable insights into the deepening impacts of financial exclusion on individuals trapped in long-term poverty (Loomis, 2018; Rosenman, 2019) and of households' over-indebtedness on physical, mental and social well-being aided by gendered labour structures (Natarajan and Brickell, 2022) and racial capitalism (Ponder, 2021). Extensive changes in large-scale infrastructure financing (Liu and Dixon, 2022) and broader ramifications of fiscal deficiencies in urban areas (Tapp and Kay, 2019) complement these far-reaching changes across the micro- and meso-levels.

What is less well understood is how, why and where financial dominance is created and designed in the first place, and how particular places are able to subject other places to the control of financial metrics, motives and rationales. Indeed, finance has evolved from its traditionally intermediary role, although economic textbooks still speak, for example, of bank lending to 'productive' investments whereas in reality, loans for 'unproductive' transactions have become the norm (Ryan-Collins et al, 2017). The latter channels capital from companies to their shareholders and to real estate markets where it does not create jobs and value but rather inflates asset prices with repercussions on firms, households, the (built) environment and more generally, societies' values and behaviour (for example, Hall and Leyshon, 2013; Lai, 2013; Heeg, 2016; Fields, 2017; Froud et al, 2017). In short, finance has evolved into a growth industry in its own right where key financial practices and motives embody and mediate financialized logics across places and space. The 'superprofits in finance and simultaneous massive unemployment in most Global North economies' (Sassen, 2019: 10) expose how unevenly financial instruments and practices connect social systems and their geographies with one another; thereby deepening social and spatial inequalities and largely undermining the noble promise and foundation that (financial) economics can improve the lives of the many (Shiller, 2012).

This chapter places finance as a fully fledged industry at the centre of economic-geographical analyses (Pike and Pollard, 2010) in order to understand how finance is organized across space and place, how geographies of (super)profits are created and manipulated and where complex financial products are produced (Dörry, 2015). In this chapter, we therefore focus on a production-oriented analytical approach to finance that has not yet realized its full potential. The 'finance curse' (Shaxson, 2018), a demonstration of how too much global finance makes us all poorer, has seen finance developing into a force in its own right with its own interest, power and agency. New technologies for finance (FinTech) but also rising pressures on financial institutions to finance sustainable projects fundamentally challenges the industry's current character. We thus ask whether and how future finance can be (better) employed for the benefit of society as a whole rather than feeding its merely self-serving character, which imposes exploding social and environmental costs.

Thus, the next section provides a brief overview of *productive* finance that sees a current revival in our environment of multiple crises. The subsequent section contrasts it by illustrating how *unproductive* financial practices act as a powerful engine for financialization. I then summarize how new approaches could help grasp currently emerging financial geographies in the hope of challenging the pervasive nature of financialization logics. The chapter concludes with critical remarks on future finance.

Geographies of productive finance

Theory states that finance is indispensable to innovation and economic growth, and economic growth is the basis for social welfare creation in many Western democracies. Banking/financing used to be simple: banks would mediate savings and lending to help lubricate the wheels of the productive real economy. According to the textbooks (Greenbaum et al, 2019; Mishkin, 2022), the greater the efficiency of capital exchange through financial intermediaries, the higher the productivity gains for the economy as a whole will be.

Private commercial banks, however, do not just allocate capital; private commercial banks *create* money (Bundesbank, 2017). The process of credit creation is distinctly spatial (Klagge et al, 2017): as a rule, the fewer banks there are within a country, the larger the individual banks will be. Large banks tend to finance large-scale projects that are geographically located in only a select few cities and centres. Bank-based (local banking, for example Germany, Italy, Poland) and market-based (large-scale banking, for example the UK) systems thus have important spatial consequences (Pratt, 1998). Over time, realizable economies of scale for large banks lead to negative economies of scale for regional and SME (small and medium enterprises) development: the larger a bank is, the less interested it is in small loans demanded by businesses and households in a region (Pratt, 1998). For example, in Germany, almost 2,000 small (mainly savings) banks in all regions account for 70 per cent of bank deposits. By comparison, British banks prefer to make large loans to projects in urban centres and traditionally account for only 13 per cent of bank deposits. The many local banks in Germany are legally subject to the regional principle that prevents them from fleeing their possibly unattractive location and lending to distant large-scale projects. With centralized back-office activities, however, these banks can achieve some administrative economies of scale and remain competitive – key for the spatially even distribution of economic activity, income, wealth equality and overall stability (Flögel and Gärtner, 2018).

These examples represent a wider discussion related to centralized versus decentralized banking and financial systems as well as their respective benefits. While the few large German banks – like their UK counterparts – have significantly reduced their lending since 2008 to less than 15 per cent of their usable capital to productive new businesses, the dominant small local banks increased their lending to SMEs. Crucially, the debate of centralizing or decentralizing national financial systems is currently resurfacing as a way to create economically and socially just and sustainable regional economies (Lange et al, 2021). Some observers consider sustainable banking and 'sustainability banks' key to providing access to patient capital for economic activity bound to regional sourcing and value capture (Hobson, 2016). This includes new forms of and better access to capital for building more diverse economies and economic activity that is still little valued and invisible to most (Gibson-Graham, 2008; see also Chapters 4 and 21 in this volume). The next section contrasts the principles of productive finance with those considered unproductive and suggests analytical ways to unpack their practices and geographies.

Geographies of 'unproductive' finance

Towards financialization 2.0

Financial rent and revenue have become an end in itself, and a plethora of financial practices designed exclusively for rent and revenue extraction have left the economic system 'sabotaged' for short-term gains and excess profits (Nesvetailova and Palan, 2020), be it through:

- coding capital in law to shield private wealth (Pistor, 2019)
- capitalizing on steady income streams from creating economic monopoly (Christophers, 2020)
- assetizing all kinds of interests, skills and nature (Christophers et al, 2017; Langley, 2021)
- forming too-big-to-fail banks with deliberately inflated balance sheets (Ioannou et al, 2019) or
- deregulating finance to transform economies and cause hazardous financial expansion (Krippner, 2011; Karwowski, 2019).

Traditionally, once a bank issued a loan, it held it on its balance sheet until maturity. Issuing loans, though, comes with the risk of borrowers defaulting, and banks need to fund that risk with equity. The erosion of the traditional US banking model since the 1980s made financing loans via securitization more profitable than equity-based financing, leading to a massive take-off of an entire securitization industry. Securitization transforms otherwise illiquid financial assets into tradeable capital market securities. To illustrate, it pools masses of bank loans together and trades them as asset-backed securities on the capital markets. Today, outstanding securitized assets, for example mortgages, credit cards, cars and student loans, have exceeded the size of all outstanding marketable US Treasury securities, and credit derivatives with no link to underlying assets are thriving as credit-risk trading across the globe provides lucrative premiums.

Whether securitization has been a blessing (via hedging, risk allocation and so forth) or a curse (speculation, originators' release from risk reliability and so on) cannot be answered unequivocally. Securitization, however, has fundamentally transformed the practices of lending and therefore also its geographies. It conveniently helped banks circumvent huge credit risks in their own books while creating new – systemic – risks instead (Tooze, 2018). In 2016, more than 80 per cent of global capital – roughly US$69.1 trillion of total global assets under management – did *not* go into financing productive economic activity but instead channelled to speculative asset inflating and extractive financial activity (Nesvetailova and Palan, 2020). A continuous logic of financial capitalism's long-standing trend is to depend on the creation of ever new asset streams (Christophers, 2020), and one entry point to understanding their creation is via law and legal practice. Law is designed for a specific purpose that is often based on ideological determination. Law can change over time, but its imprint echoes the past and 'provides the core infrastructure for the structuration of social exchanges and the integration of society' (Kjaer, 2020: 25). Law has thus a particular form through which expectations are stabilized and where property and property rights constitute ordering mechanisms in economic and financial geographies (Haila, 2016; Knuth and Potts, 2016).

Recently, new practices have emerged that seek to *fractionalize* property rights of illiquid assets such as real property, vintage cars, fine art or the like (Dörry and Hesse, 2022). This practice translates an existing non-financial asset like a house into a financial asset by *dividing* its ownership to only parts of the house. Fractionalization practices promise to make assets marketable and thus formerly illiquid markets liquid. Rather than creating new value, however, these legal practices generate new sources of value extraction – a practice we may call financialization 2.0. Although proponents of legal fractionalizing techniques stress their democratic character by providing access to assets normally outside the financial reach of the average household, the intrinsic links of law with the expansion of financialization and finance's ongoing search for fresh revenue streams suggest otherwise; it requires further research.

The importance of law and legal practice

Just like lending practices, investment practices increased in importance with the rise of *money manager capitalism* that imposed 'a new layer of intermediation ... into the financial structure' (Minsky, 1996: 363). The global expansion of Euromarkets since the 1950s, and the associated deepening of financialization, contributed to a massive credit boom and a gigantic increase in private wealth (Minsky, 1996). It heralded the age of a thriving asset management industry (for example, pension fund capitalism; Clark, 2000). Asset managers, the new direct owners of a large proportion of financial instruments who traditionally combined dividends, interest and appreciation in per share value, soon shifted more boldly to strategies of wealth shielding and tax engineering as equally important goals (Minsky, 1996). A key financial practice that essentially involves both geography and legal practices is arbitrage creation. Arbitrage aids the global manipulation of the geographies of superprofits and relies on the exploitation of *difference*, for example in price, time and between jurisdictions. While economists have extensively discussed arbitrage between rates that in principle should be the same (but are not), spatial arbitrage relies on different territorialities of law that is increasingly artificial in nature (Marian, 2017). While such global profit shifting strategies harm states and societies, states paradoxically support such practices.

To illustrate this point, complex financial arrangements, for example funds-of-funds or feeder funds, are essentially *multi*national corporations (MNCs). They have adapted MNCs' principle to be '*not* a single *legal entity*, but rather a group of corporations throughout the world sharing *a single* underlying *economic unity*' (Palan, 2002: 170, emphasis added). Importantly, the *legal design* of a financial vehicle's organizational structure defines its efficiency and economic success. Over time, the socially constructed phenomenon of a *divided* fiscal subject and a *whole* real subject became a key principle in mediating capital flows between offshore and onshore jurisdictions. The legally fractured, complex financial MNC learned to capitalize on this fiction of fragmentation and went jurisdiction shopping (Roberts, 1994). In short, the legal design of (complex) financial vehicles permits and restricts their financial and fiscal operations; it puts commercial law(yers) as well as the role(s) of the state in the spotlight when engaging with enabling financialization practices. It further suggests resuming in–depth studies into financial professions and professionals (Hall and Appleyard, 2009), which also includes linking the role, expertise and agency of 'transnational professionals' (Harrington and Seabrooke, 2020) and elites (McDowell, 1998) from banking and finance, law, auditing and other business services to these practices (see Chapter 6 in this volume).

States have competed by promoting their sovereign rights, and offshore centres have provided the important legal platform to globalize financial services. This legacy and early recipe for economic success of offshore financial centres echo still today. Not only have more governments recently joined this global game, but the overall growth and concentration of the financial sector has stabilized the 'hierarchy' of international financial centres (IFCs; Poon, 2003) with leading IFCs growing faster than the rest and the overall number of IFCs increasing (Sassen, 2019; see also Chapters 5 and 10 in this volume). Complex financial arrangements have perfected leverage (debt-based) financing and speculative profit-making. These examples demonstrate the need and urgency for a better comprehension of the coevolution of legal practice with the territorialities of law (Dörry, 2022), thereby increasingly producing inseparable links between enabling financialized practices and the creation of law biased in its benefits towards selected social groups.

Future finance

We can summarize, first, that the *business* of finance is in most aspects not very different from other businesses, neither in its search for high (and fast) profits (Nesvetailova and Palan, 2020) nor its distinct spatial patterns (Blažek et al, 2021). While geographers have provided empirically rich and detailed structural insights, there is the need to better know what shapes and holds these financial networks together. To better understand these financial dynamics, a closer reading of legal and economic practices across scales is required.

Second, the discussion on financial intermediation showed that *context* crucially determines the legacy of banking and financial systems (Alamá and Tortosa-Ausina, 2012). Context needs to inform and complement financial economic studies with narrower foci. While such an approach takes into account the varieties of capitalism, we also suggest combining the holistic research of system evolution with forensic exploration of specific financial *practices*, for example lending, investing, securitization and the more recent fractionalization of property rights.

Third, finance is *not a monolithic block* but a variety of subindustries. Each comes with its own vested interests, specific infrastructures and regulations. The importance attributed to financial subsectors can shift over time, evidenced, for example, by the relative post-crisis decline of investment banking as compared to the growing asset management industry. This can correspondingly shift dynamics between different IFCs, which specialize in certain activities. Aligned with the evolution of financial capitalism (Strange, 1998) and ongoing competition between IFCs, states have not only adapted and augmented commercial law to attract financial business but also changed the very principles of financial regulation (Westermeier, 2018).

Fourth, *the state* and the aforementioned institutional elements, which are usually 'exogenous factors' to standard economic models, are in fact essential shapers of financial geographies that, as evident in this chapter, need more analytical attention. The increased (spatial) concentration of financial power and private wealth further raises questions of law and governance for future finance including issues of social cohesion, accountability and democracy.

As we look to the future of finance from the perspective of its production, three aspects are significant: the rise of China, new technologies and global finance, and sustainable finance. China's rise as a new geopolitical power is already obvious in the global financial markets. New forms of political economies grounded in distinct financial practices and principles notably different from financialized Western models (Töpfer, 2018; Hall, 2017) have emerged and started to influence global financial geographies. New geopolitical agency has been attributed to and through financial infrastructure including via Chinese state-owned exchanges (Petry, 2020), internationalization strategies of Chinese state-owned banks (Balmas and Dörry, 2023) or its renminbi currency (Kaltenbrunner and Lysandrou, 2017). Whether and how China defies financialization that underpins much of the current global financial order remains to be seen (Dal Maso, 2019). It is surely an important avenue for future research.

Global financial infrastructures such as SWIFT and correspondent banking are new centres of what some scholars summarize as geopolitical financial warfare, with US security sanctions executed through global payments infrastructure (de Goede, 2021) having repercussions on the geoeconomics of finance. The financial infrastructure itself, but also tech-induced organizational and power shifts in finance, call for more analytical attention (Gabor and Brooks, 2017; Lai and Samers, 2021). Emerging questions revolve around information as the fundamental element that once allowed the geographical expansion of banking (Robinson et al, 2023). This is increasingly challenged by rapidly developing (public and private) cryptocurrencies and their virtual spaces (Kuehnlenz et al, 2023), which in turn can affect the stability of finance as a spatial, functional, social system. While FinTech had initially been hailed as a democratic game changer and disruptor to a powerful industry that serves mostly itself, for example through platformization from crowdfunding platforms (Langley, 2021), empirical observations to date suggest that new technology may not change the underlying financialization logic but rather invite its perpetuation (Gabor and Brooks, 2017).

Current debates on green finance and sustainable investing are fierce (Knox-Hayes, 2017; van der Ploeg and Rezai, 2020) and shaped by the search for alternative ways of investing large volumes of capital to provide economic returns while abiding by high social and ecological standards (Dörry and Schulz, 2018). Financial institutions increasingly align their investments and financing; new 'sustainable' IFCs position themselves to benefit from opportunities through rebranding their core activities and the creation of new institutional environments for sustainable finance. In managing this transition, a balance needs to be struck between the various vested interests and the inertia (of social systems) on the one hand, and the need and inherent urgency of these transitions on the other. Fundamental conflicts revolve around economies' addiction to growth (Kallis, 2019) and altered financial and investment needs for parts of the economy that increasingly turn to approaches with a strong public welfare orientation, for example, circular economies (Hobson, 2016), and a reimagination of public finance (August et al, 2022). Further, little light has been shed on the deeply conflicted nature of institutional logics and the motivations of investors and investments. This is clearly problematic as this chapter's discussion showed. Put bluntly, the transition towards sustainability in its true meaning would challenge the very foundations of large parts of the financial system under the 'finance curse'. Further probing these socio-spatial arrangements defined by a range of interests, practices and agency is a vital avenue for research.

Conclusion

Where does this leave future finance? Finance is an essential, powerful social institution with numerous links to other social systems. Agency and practices mediate interpretative cultures between places. IFCs offer complex environments that have nurtured such interpretative cultures and can mediate between national cultures and newly set global standards and norms (Sassen, 2008). Holistic–integrative concepts coupled with forensic analysis (Proskurovska and Dörry, 2022) help to qualify and better understand contextualized financial practices as a way forward in unpacking financial systems across place and scale. Such an endeavour calls for truly interdisciplinary engagement and collaboration, which needs to avoid the trap of developing siloed disciplinary bodies of knowledge. The importance of the interdisciplinary nature of this undertaking is indicated by referenced work from women scholars with backgrounds across the social sciences of which geography is but one important cornerstone. Future finance not only ought to help make finance more sustainable and useful for our societies but also encourage and invite more women scholars to further define and enrich this growing field. Alas, the future is now.

Acknowledgements
I am indebted to Gary Dymski who helped me structure my thoughts and reiterated the importance of Minsky's arguments to the debate in financial geographies. Christian Schulz provided valuable critical feedback from which this chapter has benefited greatly. All errors, however, remain mine alone.

References
Alamá, L. and Tortosa-Ausina, E. (2012) 'Bank branch geographic location patterns in Spain: some implications for financial exclusion', *Growth and Change*, 43(3): 505–43.

August, M., Cohen, D., Danyluk, M., Kass, A., Ponder, C. and Rosenman, E. (2022) 'Reimagining geographies of public finance', *Progress in Human Geography*, 46(2): 527–48.

Balmas, P. and Dörry, S. (2023) 'Chinese bank networks in Europe: FDI-oriented by legal and strategic design', *Eurasian Geography and Economics*, ahead of print. Available from: https://doi.org/10.1080/15387216.2023.2182805 [Accessed 1 July 2023].

Blažek, J., Bělohradský, A. and Holická, Z. (2021) 'The role of tier, ownership and size of companies in value creation and capture', *European Planning Studies*, 29(11): 2101–20.

Bundesbank (2017) 'How money is created', Deutsche Bundesbank, 25 April. Available from: https://www.bundesbank.de/en/tasks/topics/how-money-is-created-667392 [Accessed 1 July 2023].

Christophers, B. (2020) *Rentier Capitalism: Who Owns the Economy, and Who Pays for It?*, London: Verso.

Christophers, B., Leyshon, A. and Mann, G. (eds) (2017) *Money and Finance After the Crisis: Critical Thinking for Uncertain Times*, Hoboken, NJ: Wiley.

Christopherson, S., Martin, R. and Pollard, J. (2013) 'Financialisation: roots and repercussions', *Cambridge Journal of Regions, Economy and Society*, 6(3): 351–7.

Clark, G.L. (2000) *Pension Fund Capitalism*, Oxford: Oxford University Press.

Dal Maso, G. (2019) 'The financial crisis and a crisis of expertise: a Chinese genealogy of neoliberalism', *Historical Materialism*, 27(4): 67–98.

de Goede, M. (2021) 'Finance/security infrastructures', *Review of International Political Economy*, 28(2): 351–68.

Deruytter, L., Juwet, G. and Bassens, D. (2022) 'Why do state-owned utilities become subject to financial logics? The case of energy distribution in Flanders', *Competition & Change*, 26(2): 266–88.

Dörry, S. (2015) 'Strategic nodes in investment fund global production networks: the example of the financial centre Luxembourg', *Journal of Economic Geography*, 15(4): 797–814.

Dörry, S. (2022) 'The dark side of innovation in financial centres: legal designs and territorialities of law', *Regional Studies*, ahead of print. Available from: https://doi.org/10.1080/00343404.2022.2107629 [Accessed 1 July 2023].

Dörry, S. and Hesse, M. (2022) 'Zones and zoning: linking the geographies of freeports with ArtTech and finance', *Geoforum*, 134: 165–72.

Dörry, S. and Schulz, C. (2018) 'Green financing, interrupted: potential directions for sustainable finance in Luxembourg', *Local Environment*, 23(7): 717–33.

Fields, D. (2017) 'Unwilling subjects of financialization', *International Journal of Urban and Regional Research*, 41(4): 588–603.

Flögel, F. and Gärtner, S. (2018) *The Banking Systems of Germany, the UK and Spain from a Spatial Perspective: Lessons Learned and What Is to be Done?*, IAT Discussion Paper18/01A, Gelsenkirchen: Institut Arbeit und Technik (IAT). Available from: https://www.iat.eu/discussionpapers/download/IAT_Discussion_Paper_18_01A.pdf [Accessed 1 July 2023].

Froud, J., Johal, S., Moran, M. and Williams, K. (2017) 'Outsourcing the state: new sources of elite power', *Theory, Culture & Society*, 34(5/6): 77–101.

Gabor, D. and Brooks, S. (2017) 'The digital revolution in financial inclusion: international development in the fintech era', *New Political Economy*, 22(4): 423–36.

Gibson-Graham, J.K. (2008) 'Diverse economies: performative practices for "other worlds"', *Progress in Human Geography*, 32(5): 613–32.

Greenbaum, S.I., Thakor, A.V. and Boot, A.W.A. (eds) (2019) *Contemporary Financial Intermediation* (4th edn), London: Academic Press.

Haila, A. (2016) *Urban Land Rent: Singapore as a Property State*, Chichester: Wiley.

Hall, S. (2017) 'Rethinking international financial centres through the politics of territory: renminbi internationalisation in London's financial district', *Transactions of the Institute of British Geographers*, 42(4): 489–502.

Hall, S. and Appleyard, L. (2009) '"City of London, city of learning"? Placing business education within the geographies of finance', *Journal of Economic Geography*, 9(5): 597–617.

Hall, S. and Leyshon, A. (2013) 'Editorial: financialization, space and place', *Regional Studies*, 47(6): 831–3.

Harrington, B. and Seabrooke, L. (2020) 'Transnational professionals', *Annual Review of Sociology*, 46: 399–417.

Heeg, S. (2016) 'Building for urban success? Project development and social exclusivity in Germany: Frankfurt/Main as a case study', in A. Lehavi (ed) *Private Communities and Urban Governance: Theoretical and Comparative Perspectives*, Cham: Springer, pp 151–64.

Hobson, K. (2016) 'Closing the loop or squaring the circle? Locating generative spaces for the circular economy', *Progress in Human Geography*, 40(1): 88–104.

Horton, A. (2022) 'Financialization and non-disposable women: real estate, debt and labour in UK care homes', *Environment and Planning A: Economy and Space*, 54(1): 144–59.

Ioannou, S., Wójcik, D. and Dymski, G. (2019) 'Too-big-to-fail: why megabanks have not become smaller since the global financial crisis?', *Review of Political Economy*, 31(3): 356–81.

Johnson, L. (2014) 'Geographies of securitized catastrophe risk and the implications of climate change', *Economic Geography*, 90(2): 155–85.

Kallis, G. (2019) *Limits: Why Malthus Was Wrong and Why Environmentalists Should Care*, Stanford, CA: Stanford University Press.

Kaltenbrunner, A. and Lysandrou, P. (2017) 'The US dollar's continuing hegemony as an international currency: a double-matrix analysis', *Development and Change*, 48(4): 663–91.

Karwowski, E. (2019) 'Towards (de-)financialisation: the role of the state', *Cambridge Journal of Economics*, 43(4): 1001–27.

Kass, A., Luby, M.J. and Weber, R. (2019) 'Taking a risk: explaining the use of complex debt finance by the Chicago public schools', *Urban Affairs Review*, 55(4): 1035–69.

Kjaer, P.F. (2020) 'The law of political economy: an introduction', in P.F. Kjaer (ed) *The Law of Political Economy: Transformation in the Function of Law*, Cambridge: Cambridge University Press, pp 1–30.

Klagge, B., Martin, R. and Sunley, P. (2017) 'The spatial structure of the financial system and the funding of regional business: a comparison of Britain and Germany', in R. Martin and J. Pollard (eds) *Handbook on the Geographies of Money and Finance*, Cheltenham: Edward Elgar, pp 125–55.

Knox-Hayes, J. (2017) 'Alternative circuits of capital: parallel economies of environmental finance', in R. Martin and J. Pollard (eds) *Handbook on the Geographies of Money and Finance*, Cheltenham: Edward Elgar, pp 499–517.

Knuth, S. (2018) ' "Breakthroughs" for a green economy? Financialization and clean energy transition', *Energy Research & Social Science*, 41: 220–9.

Knuth, S. and Potts, S. (2016) 'Legal geographies of finance: editors' introduction', *Environment and Planning A: Economy and Space*, 48(3): 458–64.

Krippner, G.R. (2011) *Capitalizing on Crisis: The Political Origins of the Rise of Finance*, Cambridge, MA: Harvard University Press.

Kuehnlenz, S., Orsi, B. and Kaltenbrunner, A. (2023) 'Central bank digital currencies and the international payment system: the demise of the US dollar?', *Research in International Business and Finance*, 64: art 101834. Available from: https://doi.org/10.1016/j.ribaf.2022.101834 [Accessed 1 July 2023].

Lai, K.P.Y. (2013) 'The Lehman Minibonds crisis and financialisation of investor subjects in Singapore', *Area*, 45(3): 273–82.

Lai, K.P.Y. and Samers, M. (2021) 'Towards an economic geography of FinTech', *Progress in Human Geography*, 45(4): 720–39.

Lange, B., Hülz, M., Schmid, B. and Schulz, C. (eds) (2021) *Post-Growth Geographies: Spatial Relations of Diverse and Alternative Economies*, Bielefeld: transcript.

Langley, P. (2021) 'Assets and assetization in financialized capitalism', *Review of International Political Economy*, 28(2): 382–93.

Liu, F.H. and Lai, K.P.Y. (2021) 'Ecologies of green finance: green *sukuk* and development of green Islamic finance in Malaysia', *Environment and Planning A: Economy and Space*, 53(8): 1896–914.

Liu, I.T. and Dixon, A.D. (2022) 'What does the state do in China's state-led infrastructure financialisation?', *Journal of Economic Geography*, 22(5): 963–88.

Loomis, J.M. (2018) 'Rescaling and reframing poverty: financial coaching and the pedagogical spaces of financial inclusion in Boston, Massachusetts', *Geoforum*, 95: 143–52.

Marian, O.Y. (2017) 'The state administration of international tax avoidance', *Harvard Business Law Review*, 7: 1–65.

McDowell, L. (1998) 'Elites in the City of London: some methodological considerations', *Environment and Planning A: Economy and Space*, 30(12): 2133–46.

Minsky, H.P. (1996) 'Uncertainty and the institutional structure of capitalist economies', *Journal of Economic Issues*, 30(2): 357–68.

Mishkin, F.S. (2022) *The Economics of Money, Banking and Financial Markets* (13th edn), Harlow: Pearson Education.

Natarajan, N. and Brickell, K. (2022) 'Credit, land and survival work in rural Cambodia: rethinking rural autonomy through a feminist lens', *Journal of Agrarian Change*, 22(3): 473–88.

Nesvetailova, A. and Palan, R. (2020) *Sabotage: The Business of Finance*, London: Allen Lane.

Palan, R. (2002) 'Tax havens and the commercialization of state sovereignty', *International Organization*, 56(1): 151–76.

Petry, J. (2020) 'Financialization with Chinese characteristics? Exchanges, control and capital markets in authoritarian capitalism', *Economy and Society*, 49(2): 213–38.

Pike, A. and Pollard, J. (2010) 'Economic geographies of financialization', *Economic Geography*, 86(1): 29–52.

Pistor, K. (2019) *The Code of Capital: How the Law Creates Wealth and Inequality*, Princeton, NJ: Princeton University Press.

Ponder, C.S. (2021) 'Spatializing the municipal bond market: urban resilience under racial capitalism', *Annals of the American Association of Geographers*, 111(7): 2112–29.

Poon, J.P.H. (2003) 'Hierarchical tendencies of capital markets among international financial centers', *Growth and Change*, 34(2): 135–56.

Pratt, D.J. (1998) 'Re-placing money: the evolution of branch banking in Britain', *Environment and Planning A: Economy and Space*, 30(12): 2211–26.

Proskurovska, A. and Dörry, S. (2022) 'The blockchain challenge for Sweden's housing and mortgage markets', *Environment and Planning A: Economy and Space*, 54(8): 1569–85.

Roberts, S. (1994) 'Fictitious capital, fictitious spaces: the geography of offshore financial centres', in S. Corbridge, R. Martin and N. Thrift (eds) *Money, Power and Space*, Oxford: Blackwell, pp 91–115.

Robinson, G., Dörry, S. and Derudder, B. (2023) 'Global networks of money and information at the crossroads: correspondent banking and SWIFT', *Global Networks*, 23(2): 478–93.

Rosenman, E. (2019) 'The geographies of social finance: poverty regulation through the "invisible heart" of markets', *Progress in Human Geography*, 43(1): 141–62.

Ryan-Collins, R., Greenham, T., Werner, R. and Jackson, A. (2017) *Where Does Money Come From?*, London: New Economics Foundation.

Sassen, S. (2008) *Territory, Authority, Rights: From Medieval to Global Assemblages*, Princeton, NJ: Princeton University Press.

Sassen, S. (2019) *Cities in a World Economy*, Thousand Oaks, CA: Sage.

Shaxson, N. (2018) *The Finance Curse*, London: Vintage.

Shiller, R.J. (2012) *Finance and the Good Society*, Princeton, NJ: Princeton University Press.

Strange, S. (1998) *Mad Money. When Markets Outgrow Governments*, Ann Arbor: University of Michigan Press.

Tapp, R. and Kay, K. (2019) 'Fiscal geographies: "placing" taxation in urban geography', *Urban Geography*, 40(4): 573–81.

Tooze, A. (2018) *Crashed: How a Decade of Financial Crises Changed the World*, New York: Viking.

Töpfer, L.-M. (2018) 'China's integration into the global financial system: toward a state-led conception of global financial networks', *Dialogues in Human Geography*, 8(3): 251–71.

van der Ploeg, F. and Rezai, A. (2020) 'Stranded assets in the transition to a carbon-free economy', *Annual Review of Resource Economics*, 12: 281–98.

Westermeier, C. (2018) 'The Bank of International Settlements as a think tank for financial policy-making', *Policy and Society*, 37(2): 170–87.

27

Disasters and Recovery: Postcolonializing Economic Geography

Gemma Sou

Introduction

With the frequent occurrence of disasters in the world, research has greater understanding of disasters, including their cause and how to reduce their impacts and expedite recovery. When disasters first began to be studied in the 1950s, they were typically viewed as naturally occurring events that were the product of the magnitude of an earthquake, the ferocity of a hurricane, the infectiousness of a disease or the rise of the sea level, for example. However, understanding of hazards has expanded to include conflicts, price fluctuations and financial crises. Moreover, research across the social sciences has revealed that disasters are far from a naturally occurring phenomenon. Rather, disasters occur where a vulnerable population is exposed to a hazard (Hewitt, 1995). Thus, vulnerability is the link between the onset of a hazard and a disaster occurring. Vulnerability is highly contested, but it generally refers to 'the capacity to anticipate, cope with, resist and recover from the impact of a hazard' (Wisner et al, 2004: 11).

Given the multidimensional nature of vulnerability, the study of disasters speaks across the social sciences. However, disasters are particularly relevant to economic geography given how the political economy of a country directly impacts the capacity of people to mitigate, prepare, respond and recover from disasters (Neumayer et al, 2014). In this chapter I set out to show how economic geographies can encompass a postcolonial approach to explore both the cause of disasters, that is, the production of vulnerability, and how disaster-affected people respond to disasters during their everyday lives. Postcolonial theory allows one to recognize how the causes of disasters have deep roots in the placation, exploitation and colonization of marginalized peoples (see Chapter 23 in this volume). This approach also shifts our gaze 'down' to shed light on the agency of disaster-affected people to intuitively engage in acts of resilience that can represent political anti-colonial acts of resistance that aim to rupture the status quo by providing different forms of societal and economic organization. Finally, by adopting a postcolonial approach, I argue one can observe how grassroots definitions and forms of resilience do not fit neatly with state-centric conceptualizations of resilience.

The chapter begins with a discussion of how economic geographers might draw on postcolonial theory to explore disasters. Here, I focus on how postcolonial theory can bring a more solid historicization of vulnerability and better understanding of the (unequal) state–citizen power relations that produce vulnerability. I also argue that a postcolonial approach provides an opportunity to highlight the political agency of marginalized groups, which challenges orientalist ideas about disaster-affected people that implicitly circulate in economic geography scholarship on disasters. Finally, I suggest that adopting a postcolonial methodology allows researchers to move beyond reductive economic measurements of recovery and towards imagining alternative futures that can address the processes that create vulnerability to disasters. Following this I draw on empirical data from a one-year study that explored how low-income Puerto Rican families recovered from the impacts of Hurricane Maria in 2017 to demonstrate these ideas.

Postcolonializing economic geography research on disasters

Economic geography has not typically explored disaster and disaster recovery. Where economic geographers have engaged with recovery, they have emphasized the role of the state and tended to gauge whether or not a society has recovered by focusing on statistical indicators such as GDP (for example, Chang, 2010). However, focus on measuring the recovery of the state obscures how disaster-affected people – who are on the frontline of disasters – play a significant role in how and when recovery takes place (Sou et al, 2021). Second, measuring recovery through economic models literally and figuratively opens up a space to expand and capture opportunities for economic growth (Oliver-Smith, 2015). Thus, recovery becomes framed as opportunities to build back better in ways that support economic productivity and growth to prop up the capitalist system (Klein, 2018). However, in this chapter I build on existing writing on postcolonial approaches in economic geography (for example, Robinson, 2003; McCall, 2005; Pollard and Samers, 2007; Pollard et al, 2009; Roy, 2016) to suggest that applying a postcolonial perspective to explore disaster recovery opens up space for economic geographers to identify how recovery is not merely an opportunity for the economic growth of the state, but also represents a space where alternative and transformative forms of societal and economic organization emerge within disaster-affected populations (Cretney, 2017).

Mainstream understandings of disaster vulnerability are based on conservative and ahistorical imaginaries of how and why lower- and middle-income countries have come to be some of the most disaster-prone countries in the world. Hewitt (1995) suggests that in the analysis of disasters there are excluded perspectives which include paying attention to the relationship between history, power and vulnerability to hazards. This includes economic geographers who largely neglect or poorly understand how disasters across the world have roots in historical and ongoing colonialism (Lewis, 2012). By erasing the role that colonialism plays in shaping vulnerability, disasters are implicitly framed as singularities that are disconnected from long-term processes (Rivera, 2022). Anthony Oliver-Smith's research highlighted how disasters are manifestations of historical vulnerabilities that are produced at the intersection of environment and society, and which cannot be disentangled from systemic power structures (1996). Anthony Carrigan (2015) called for disaster scholars to draw on postcolonial theory to understand disasters. At its simplest level, postcolonial theory posits that the historical experience of colonialism has continuing impacts on the political, economic and social development of both the former colonizer and colonized. Postcolonial approaches inspire analysis not just of the iniquities of capitalism but also of other forms of oppression such as patriarchy, neocolonialism and racism (McCall, 2005), which intersect to shape the identities and life chances of diverse groups of people. Indeed, postcolonial theory does not simply refer to a periodization but is a methodology that allows one to unsettle Western structures of knowledge and power. It is a critical approach that reveals the (neo)colonial power relations on both structural and ideological levels (Roy, 2016), which is particularly insightful for analysing both the cause of disasters and the experiences of disaster-affected people.

When the temporal analysis of economic life is broadened to include colonialism, the legacies of colonialism are shown to be deeply related to vulnerability. For example, former colonies of European powers are some of the most indebted countries in the world – a debt that limits their ability to build disaster resilience (Bishop and Payne, 2012). The resource extraction of many former colonies fuelled the industrialization of Western countries, which created the emissions that contribute to climate change, which disproportionately impacts former colonies (Bankoff, 2004). Yet, postcolonial theory is not solely concerned with the legacies of colonial processes that took place before countries became independent. Postcolonial theory seeks to identify unequal power relations that produce the marginalization and continued colonization of communities. For example, many small island developing states that were former colonies were economically structured towards sectors that are highly impacted by climate change – tourism, agriculture and fishing. This is not a natural consequence of physical geography; rather, many island colonies were forced to restructure towards these sectors, and in line with neoliberal development models (Sealey Huggins, 2017: 2445). Rivera (2022) also proposes that poor pre-disaster and post-disaster planning is leveraged to deepen coloniality by displacing and disenfranchising marginalized communities; a process she terms 'disaster colonialism'. A postcolonial approach also criticizes any calls for a 'return to normalcy' or 'bouncing back' after disasters as inherently conservative because it only serves to entrench the vulnerabilities that pre-existed the disaster. Recovering societies to pre-disaster conditions also stifles discussions about rethinking alternative ways of structuring societies to unsettle the colonialism that exacerbates disaster vulnerability (Veland et al, 2013).

Neglecting how colonization shapes disaster risk tacitly represents disasters as removed and unaffected by historical and contemporary processes of colonial power. Such a limited analysis fails to appreciate why people need to be resilient in the first place. Overlooking the role of colonialism also depoliticizes the cause of disasters, implicitly suggesting that disasters can be avoided through technocratic programmes that reduce, avoid or eliminate hazards, rather than through the reformation of society to reduce the vulnerability of marginalized communities. Second, the erasure of colonialism shifts attention away from the role that colonial powers play(ed) in shaping vulnerability, thereby negating rather than fostering responsibility to address contemporary vulnerabilities.

I argue that acknowledging colonialism, and the associated asymmetrical power relations that shape vulnerability and necessitate resilience provides a potential opportunity to reinterpret resilient behaviours as resistance, including those of a monetary form. Examples of political forms of resistance are not easily seen from a top-down or state-centric view. Therefore, I suggest that it is important to explore resilience 'from below' as a method or strategy used intuitively by disaster-affected populations. At this scale it becomes possible to expose the many grassroots forms of resilience that are taking place and to unearth how people's definitions of resilience do not reflect state-centric conceptualizations of resilience.

Coming back to my key argument, postcolonial theory also aims to provide a basis for resistance and to change colonial narratives and relationships. These colonial narratives were identified and critically discussed in Edward Said's seminal work, *Orientalism* (1978). In this groundbreaking work he laid out how Europe produced colonial discursive constructs of the Orient (by which he meant not just the Middle East but all colonized geographies) as passive, backward, uncivilized, exotic and irrational, for example. These discourses essentialized and homogenized the colonized world as the 'Other' and enabled colonial powers to maintain power and control over their colonies (Wolff, 1970). Postcolonial scholars seek to reject orientalist frames of reference and are concerned with investigating the agency, experiences and the heterogeneity of 'colonized' subjects, typically using methodologies that centre on the voices, stories, histories and cultural experiences of colonized people.

Postcolonial theory's concern with challenging colonial myths is particularly beneficial for the study of disasters because it forces a shift in gaze 'down' to centre on disaster-affected people's voices and experiences. Focus here opens the opportunity to identify the agency of marginalized people to mitigate, prepare for, respond to or recover from disasters. Highlighting the capacity of disaster-affected people provides a counter-narrative to essentialist ideas that people are helpless victims who must passively wait for the state to intervene on their behalf – an idea that implicitly circulates in economic geography research that measures recovery economically and as something that the state principally does (Chang, 2010). A postcolonial approach demands that we analyse how states express their power in ways that (re)produce the vulnerability of citizens and undermine people's capacity to be resilient. Postcolonial theory rejects notions that citizens are passively acted *on* by the state. Rather, citizens can use their creativity to resist their colonization in ways that may lessen their vulnerability to hazards (Jefferess, 2016).

In the following section, I draw on my own research in Puerto Rico to illustrate how economic geography would benefit from postcolonial theory to understand disasters.

Resisting dependence in disaster contexts: insights from Puerto Rico

In 2017 and 2018 I investigated how low-income Puerto Rican families recovered from the impacts of Hurricane Maria, which devastated the Caribbean Island in September 2017 (see Sou et al, 2021). The case site was Ingenio – a low-lying and low-income community in Toa Baja municipality, 13.5 km from the capital, San Juan. Puerto Rico is an unincorporated territory of the US, and as US citizens Puerto Ricans are entitled to federal recovery support. Yet, the US federal government's response was slow, inadequate and laden with derisive discourse about Puerto Rico. The effects of the storm are best understood as the compounded results of five centuries of colonialism (first Spain and then the US from 1898) and a history of structural vulnerability and forced dependency that created widespread poverty and unemployment, and decrepit infrastructure, which enabled Maria to have such devastating impacts (Bonilla, 2020a). After Hurricane Maria, the US government focused on 'bouncing back' to 'normality'. Yet, calling for a return to 'normalcy' ultimately aims to uphold existing social inequities within Puerto Rico and between Puerto Rico and the US. Such a conservative view of disaster recovery undermines any discussion about radically rethinking economic, environmental and social relations in ways that unsettle the colonization of Puerto Rico and its citizens. However, this section will discuss how Ingenio residents – and Puerto Ricans more generally – spontaneously engaged in grassroots strategies that increased their resilience *and* challenged US control over their everyday lives following Hurricane Maria.

US colonial policies, and practices imposed by the US, have diluted national Puerto Rican sovereignty. 'Sovereignty' here not only refers to Puerto Ricans' ability to make their own decisions regarding the future of the island, but also over their everyday lives. US policy has focused on extracting Puerto Rico's natural and renewable resources, which has been labelled environmental colonialism. For example, the selling of Puerto Rican land to private interests and stripping farmers of their livelihoods has resulted in widespread environmental degradation and toxic wastes polluting Puerto Rican air, water and soil. US policy favours and encourages private investors and corporations to buy up land to create businesses (Klein, 2018). Failing and precarious produce crops in Puerto Rico have primarily been used for trade instead of domestic consumption. As such, most Puerto Ricans do not have access to the foods grown on the island but, instead, depend on substandard consumables provided by the US government (Carro-Figueroa, 2002).

Since the 1950s Puerto Rico has been highly dependent on the US for goods: 85 per cent is imported from the US (Garriga-López, 2019). Imported goods must arrive on ships from the US with US crews – a process agreed under the Merchant Marine Act of 1920, also known as the Jones Act. This Act undermines international trade competition, making commodities slow to arrive, limited in availability and often higher priced than in the mainland US. The dependency on importing food from the US trickles down and restricts the self-determination of ordinary Puerto Ricans to determine their diets and access to nutritious and affordable consumables (Ginzburg, 2022). Puerto Ricans often consume pre-packaged canned, frozen or preserved foods, that are not truly fresh and have high pesticide content (García-López, 2018). Consumption of locally produced staples such as root vegetables dropped from 56 per cent in the 1980s, to 33 per cent in the 1990s (Diaz and Hunsberger, 2018). US policy also overtaxes fresh produce and high poverty rates results in people prioritizing paying bills before healthy food (Ginzburg, 2022). This helps explain why only 14.5 per cent of Puerto Rican adults consume five fruits and vegetables daily. This shift in consumption patterns also cemented supermarkets as sites of food transactions (see Chapters 14 and 28 in this volume).

For the initial six weeks after the hurricane, families' access to consumables depleted rapidly for three reasons. Puerto Rico's lack of food reserves, the island's import dependency on the US, and the federal government's focus on importing disaster aid rather than routine consumables (Sou and Webber, 2019). Thus, the Puerto Rican population – including many families in Ingenio – became highly reliant on relief aid, which they complained was "bland", unvaried and was far below nutritional standards. Many boxes of relief aid, which were "full of chips and candy" and canned vegetables that were "salty" and "unhealthy". Between six weeks and six months after the hurricane, food began to be imported, but at a lower rate than pre-hurricane standards, given the precedence placed on materials needed to reconstruct homes (Kim and Bui, 2019). Local food retailers responded by increasing prices to mitigate their losses. On average, the cost of everyday food items rose by 35 per cent between Months 2 and 8 after the hurricane, which is significant given how the Jones Act already inflated commodity prices prior to the hurricane. Higher-income families were better able to afford the inflated prices than their lower-income neighbours. However, residents did not passively wait for food prices to return to normal. Neighbourhood residents – and thousands of Puerto Ricans across the island – responded to the lack of fresh produce and began growing their own. Within Ingenio a group of seven women from across four families spontaneously collectivized and began growing their own vegetables and raising chickens.

'A group of us have started growing our own vegetables. Some peas, okra and green beans. We have some chickens too. Now, we are seven from different families, and it's going very good. It's in the garden of one of the houses that was abandoned after Maria – we know they are not coming back.' (34-year-old woman)

The vegetables and eggs were shared out based on "how many people [are] in the family". The produce was not enough to replace reliance on retailed produce as one of the women explained, "between us it is not a lot, but it makes a difference … it can make the dinner a little better". However, it supplemented their family's diet with renewable and nutritious ingredients and fresh produce, which they valued after relying heavily on relief aid for the initial months. The women, all mothers, aged between 25 and 48 and from lower-income families were friends prior to the hurricane, and they drew on this social capital to establish the garden. I identify three reasons why women and not men initiated the garden. First, the women spent more time in Ingenio because they ran home-based businesses and/or were responsible for domestic duties given the gendered divisions of labour, reproduction and heteronormativity across Puerto Rico. Second, as the women were responsible for food preparation and cooking, they were more aware and affected by the decline in food quality than men. Third, the women had knowledge of the vegetables native to Puerto Rico and/or which grew well, which reflects how traditional ecological knowledge is often gendered (Turner et al, 2022).

The garden ensured families had access to food that could maintain their health and nutrition so that family members could continue to engage in income-earning opportunities and other recovery activities. The women's initiative also helped families to offset their expenditure so that they could invest more in housing reconstruction (Steenbergen et al, 2020). From this analytical perspective, the women's garden represents a creative economic strategy to adapt to, mitigate and recover from the impacts of the hurricane. However, to only interpret the garden according to notions of economic resilience obscures the inherently political nature of the garden. Adopting a postcolonial analysis and situating the garden within the ongoing US colonialism can reframe the women's initiative as an inherently political activity. The women's actions represent an attempt to reclaim abandoned land to take back some control of their food supply, diet, culinary experience and tastescapes. (For further discussion about how the women aimed to take some control over their diet see Sou and Webber, 2023.) Their initiative has an implicit resistance mandate that aims to decolonize their food supply and resist the US's domination of their access to and experiences of food. The women challenged the status quo as colonized subjects by seeking greater self-determination to make decisions that are independent of the systems, laws and policies imposed by the US (Penehira et al, 2014). The emphasis on establishing locally owned and renewable food supply also has clear ties with struggles for environmental justice, which centre on notions of autonomy, direct democracy and sustainability (Atiles-Osoria, 2014).

Food sovereignty is broadly defined as the right of peoples to healthy and culturally appropriate food produced through ecologically sound and sustainable methods, and their right to define their own food and agriculture systems. Within Puerto Rico, the food sovereignty movement pre-existed Hurricane Maria, but broadened its grassroots participation in the aftermath (Garriga-López, 2019). The movement supports food sovereignty through shared resources, exchange of labour and knowledge, and food in all its forms. These grassroots initiatives often have a clear political mandate, aligning themselves with the *independentista* (pro-independence) and anti-colonial movements (Roberto, 2019). In establishing the garden initiative, the women in Ingenio tacitly became part of this larger political movement. Although none of the women framed their garden as politically motivated and I cannot say if they were even aware of the food sovereignty movement, their initiative still reflects an intention to develop a sense of sovereignty over their access to food and diet. If one only interprets the garden through its ability to facilitate economic recovery, the political significance of the women's initiative will be missed. Specifically, we miss how the garden represents the women's attempts to challenge US policies that control their access to nutritious and affordable food before and after the hurricane. Thus, I argue that the garden symbolizes a grassroots form of resistance to undermine the US colonization of the women's diets. Thus, the Puerto Rico case speaks directly to postcolonial geographers such as Lee (2006) and

Pollard et al (2009) who argue that postcolonial economic geography allows geographers to shift away from ideas that the economy is simply a question of material success. Rather, postcolonial approaches allow one to reflect on economic practices and outcomes that unsettle mainstream interpretations of economic practices and recognize the performance of other values such as sovereignty, autonomy and feminism come if one looks to women's practices in post-disaster Puerto Rico.

The women's initiative reveals a feminization of resistance, whereby the nature, meaning and subjects of political resistance are reconfigured and reimagined. That is, resistance enacted by women challenges the dominant masculinist conceptualizations of political and social transformation which excludes women and all that is represented by femininity and women's bodies (see Chapter 27 in this volume). Recognition of women's role in resistance is crucial to avoid reproducing and reifying the historical masking and delegitimization of women's role at the heart of revolutionary and popular struggle. This is significant in Puerto Rico, where anti-colonialism has often been framed through a patriarchal perspective in which women's role has typically been limited to guardians of Puerto Rican culture as they bring citizens into the world (Briggs, 2003).

Conclusion

In this chapter, my aim was to draw on the Puerto Rico case study to demonstrate how economic geographers will benefit from adopting a postcolonial approach to studying disasters. First, analyses of vulnerability will be widened to incorporate how historical and ongoing colonial processes shape vulnerability, which challenges the ahistorical and apolitical perspectives that characterize most economic geography understandings of disasters. Second, and relatedly, postcolonial theory allows us to understand state–citizen relations in disaster contexts – not simply how the state wields its power to produce citizens' vulnerability, but also how citizens respond to the state as active political agents to increase their resilience. Third, by situating disaster-affected people's responses to disasters within colonial processes we can reframe strategies of grassroots resilience as anti-colonial acts of resistance. Although people may not be acting with conscious political intent, they tacitly aim to reclaim sovereignty over their everyday lives (Scott, 1985). Overlooking acts of resistance that do not have legitimate or 'appropriate' intentions will prevent conversations about the transformational potential of such acts (de Certeau, 1984). Reclaiming the political nature of resilience will allow economic geographers to demonstrate how resilience and resistance are complimentary, rather than competitive and mutually exclusive. I recognize that there are situations where the two concepts are irreconcilable and where resilience is the only means of survival and resistance is impossible. However, I am arguing for an analysis of grassroots resilience that incorporates political and historical contexts.

Current geographies of economic knowledge are limited because they fail to prioritize case studies that unsettle the interpretations of economic practices elsewhere, reflecting varying motivations and values (Robinson, 2003). Rather, focus on Puerto Rico highlights how a postcolonial economic geography centres and reflects on economic outcomes and practices that contradict mainstream and 'logical' interpretations of economic practices (Pollard and Samers, 2007). Moreover, the postcolonial approach centres on unearthing the experiences, voices and agency of marginalized groups, which can challenge orientalist notions of colonized subjects as passive or backward for example. This requires exploring experiences of disasters 'from below'. In Puerto Rico this approach allowed me to unearth how anti-colonial struggles are not separate from motherhood, family and the domestic space, which challenges the patriarchal and masculinist perceptions of resistance and anti-colonial struggles that dominate resistance scholarship. By shifting our analytical gaze down, we can recognize how grassroots act of resilience are widespread and that state-centric conceptualizations of resilience do not fit neatly with how marginalized people understand and intuitively enact resilience themselves. With this knowledge we are better positioned to design programmes that can support grassroots resilience.

In sum, postcolonial thinking opens an exciting potential for economic geographers to reinterpret and reimagine disasters in ways that move beyond recovery as a quantitative measurement of economic health. Postcolonial theory offers a solid historicization of contexts and how the need to adapt and be resilient among marginalized people across the world has its origins in their placation, exploitation and colonization. Future economic geography research would benefit greatly from postcolonial thinking as it opens space to unearth the grassroots and subtle ways that disaster-affected people aim to forge different forms of societal and economic organization. Moreover, adopting a postcolonial methodology in disaster contexts is not merely about understanding how a society recovers, it is also about thinking critically and imaginatively about alternative futures that take seek to address the structures that (re)produce the vulnerabilities which predicate disasters in society (Bonilla, 2020b). Thus, postcolonial theory can provide economic geographers with the conceptual framing to normatively reimagine what recovery and society could look like.

Acknowledgements

Parts of this chapter were originally published as an article under a Creative Commons licence in *The Geographical Journal* (see Sou, 2022).

References

Atiles-Osoria, J.M. (2014) 'Environmental colonialism, criminalization and resistance: Puerto Rican mobilizations for environmental justice in the 21st century', K. Bennett (trans), *RCCS Annual Review*, 6. Available from: https://doi.org/10.4000/rccsar.524 [Accessed 2 July 2023].

Bankoff, G. (2004) 'The historical geography of disaster: "vulnerability" and "local knowledge" in Western discourse', in G. Bankoff, G. Frerks and D. Hilhorst (eds) *Mapping Vulnerability: Disasters, Development and People*, London: Earthscan, pp 25–36.

Bishop, M.L. and Payne, A. (2012) 'Climate change and the future of Caribbean development', *Journal of Development Studies*, 48(10): 1536–53.

Bonilla, Y. (2020a) 'The coloniality of disaster: race, empire, and the temporal logics of emergency in Puerto Rico, USA', *Political Geography*, 78: art 102181. Available from: https://doi.org/10.1016/j.polgeo.2020.102 181 [Accessed 2 July 2023].

Bonilla, Y. (2020b) 'Postdisaster futures: hopeful pessimism, imperial ruination, and *La futura cuir*', *Small Axe*, 24(2): 147–62.

Briggs, L. (2003) *Reproducing Empire: Race, Sex, and Science and U.S. Imperialism in Puerto Rico*, Berkeley: University of California Press.

Carrigan, A. (2015) 'Towards a postcolonial disaster studies', in E. DeLoughrey, J. Didur and A. Carrigan (eds) *Global Ecologies and the Environmental Humanities: Postcolonial Approaches*, New York: Routledge, pp 117–39.

Carro-Figueroa, V. (2002) 'Agricultural decline and food import dependency in Puerto Rico: a historical perspective on the outcomes of postwar farm and food policies', *Caribbean Studies*, 30(2): 77–107.

Chang, S.E. (2010) 'Urban disaster recovery: a measurement framework and its application to the 1995 Kobe earthquake', *Disasters*, 34(2): 303–27.

Cretney, R.M. (2017) 'Towards a critical geography of disaster recovery politics: perspectives on crisis and hope', *Geography Compass*, 11(1): art e12302. Available from: https://doi.org/10.1111/gec3.12302 [Accessed 2 July 2023].

de Certeau, M. (1984) *The Practice of Everyday Life*, S. Randall (trans), Berkeley: University of California Press.

Diaz, I.I. and Hunsberger, C. (2018) 'Can agroecological coffee be part of a food sovereignty strategy in Puerto Rico?', *Geoforum*, 97: 84–94.

García-López, G.A. (2018) 'The multiple layers of environmental injustice in contexts of (un) natural disasters: the case of Puerto Rico post-Hurricane Maria', *Environmental Justice*, 11(3): 101–8.

Garriga-López, A. (2019) 'Puerto Rico: the future in question', *Shima*, 13(2): 174–92.

Ginzburg, S.L. (2022) 'Colonial comida: the colonization of food insecurity in Puerto Rico', *Food, Culture & Society*, 25(1): 18–31.

Hewitt, K. (1995) 'Sustainable disasters? Perspectives and powers in the discourse of calamity', in J. Crush (ed) Power of Development, London: Routledge, pp 115–29.

Jefferess, D. (2016) '6 Cosmopolitan appropriation or learning?', *Globalization and Global Citizenship: Interdisciplinary Approaches*, 87.

Kim, K. and Bui, L. (2019) 'Learning from Hurricane Maria: island ports and supply chain resilience', *International Journal of Disaster Risk Reduction*, 39: art 101244. Available from: https://doi.org/10.1016/j.ijdrr.2019.101 244 [Accessed 2 July 2023].

Klein, N. (2018) *The Battle for Paradise: Puerto Rico Takes on the Disaster*, Chicago: Haymarket Books.

Lee, R. (2006) 'The ordinary economy: tangled up in values and geography', *Transactions of the Institute of British Geography*, 31(4): 413–32.

Lewis, J. (2012) 'The good, the bad and the ugly: disaster risk reduction (DRR) versus disaster risk creation (DRC)', *PLoS Currents*, 4: art e4f8d4eaec6af8. Available from: https://doi.org/10.1371/4f8d4eaec6af8 [Accessed 2 July 2023].

McCall, L. (2005) 'The complexity of intersectionality', *Signs*, 30(3): 1771–800.

Neumayer, E., Plümper, T. and Barthel, F. (2014) 'The political economy of natural disaster damage', *Global Environmental Change*, 24: 8–19.

Oliver-Smith, A. (1996) 'Anthropological research on hazards and disasters', *Annual Review of Anthropology*, 25: 303–28.

Oliver-Smith, A. (2015) 'Conversations in catastrophe: neoliberalism and the cultural construction of disaster risk', in F. Krüger, G. Bankoff, T. Cannon, B. Orlowski and E.L.F. Schipper (eds) *Cultures and Disasters: Understanding Cultural Framings in Disaster Risk Reduction*, Abingdon: Routledge, pp 37–52.

Penehira, M., Green, A., Smith, L.T. and Aspin, C. (2014) 'Māori and Indigenous views on R and R: resistance and resilience', *Mai*, 3(2): 96–110.

Pollard, J. and Samers, M. (2007) 'Islamic banking and finance and postcolonial political economy: decentring economic geography', *Transactions of the Institute of British Geographers*, 32(3): 313–30.

Pollard, J., McEwan, C., Laurie, N. and Stenning, A. (2009) 'Economic geography under postcolonial scrutiny', *Transactions of the Institute of British Geographers*, 34(2): 137–42.

Rivera, D.Z. (2022) 'Disaster colonialism: a commentary on disasters beyond singular events to structural violence', *International Journal of Urban and Regional Research*, 46(1): 126–35.

Roberto, G. (2019) 'Community kitchens: an emerging movement?', in Y. Bonilla and M. LeBrón (eds) *Aftershocks of Disaster: Puerto Rico Before and After the Storm*, Chicago: Haymarket Books, pp 309–18.

Robinson, J. (2003) 'Postcolonialising geography: tactics and pitfalls', *Singapore Journal of Tropical Geography*, 24(3): 273–89.

Roy, A. (2016) 'Who's afraid of postcolonial theory?', *International Journal of Urban and Regional Research*, 40(1): 200–9.

Said, E. (1978) *Orientalism*, New York: Pantheon.

Scott, J.C. (1985) *Weapons of the Weak: Everyday Forms Of Peasant Resistance*, New Haven, CT: Yale University Press.

Sealey-Huggins, L. (2017) '"1.5° C to stay alive": climate change, imperialism and justice for the Caribbean', *Third World Quarterly*, 38(11): 2444–63.

Sou, G. (2022). 'Reframing resilience as resistance: situating disaster recovery within colonialism', *The Geographical Journal*, 188(1): 14–27.

Sou, G. and Webber, R. (2019) 'Disruption and recovery of intangible resources during environmental crises', *Geoforum*, 106: 182–92.

Sou, G. and Webber, R. (2023) 'Un/making the "sensory home": tastes, smells and sounds during disasters', *Social & Cultural Geography*, 24(6): 949–67.

Sou, G., Shaw, D. and Aponte-Gonzalez, F. (2021) 'A multidimensional framework for disaster recovery', *World Development*, 144: art 105489. Available from: https://doi.org/10.1016/j.worlddev.2021.105489 [Accessed 2 July 2023].

Steenbergen, D.J., Neihapi, P.T., Koran, D., Sami, A., Malverus, V., Ephraim, R. and Andrew, N. (2020) 'COVID-19 restrictions amidst cyclones and volcanoes: a rapid assessment of early impacts on livelihoods and food security in coastal communities in Vanuatu', *Marine Policy*, 121: art 104199. Available from: https://doi.org/10.1016/j.marpol.2020.104199 [Accessed 2 July 2023].

Turner, K.L., Idrobo, C.J., Desmarais, A.A. and Peredo, A.M. (2022) 'Food sovereignty, gender and everyday practice: the role of Afro-Colombian women in sustaining localised food systems', *Journal of Peasant Studies*, 49(2): 402–28.

Veland, S., Howitt, R., Dominey-Howes, D., Thomalla, F. and Houston, D. (2013) 'Procedural vulnerability: understanding environmental change in a remote Indigenous community', *Global Environmental Change*, 23(1): 314–26.

Wisner, B., Blaikie, P., Cannon, T. and Davis, I. (2004) *At Risk: Natural Hazards, People's Vulnerability, and Disasters* (2nd edn), Abingdon: Routledge.

Wolff, R.D. (1970) 'Economic aspects of British colonialism in Kenya, 1895 to 1930', *Journal of Economic History*, 30(1): 273–7.

28

Retail Market Futures: Retail Geographies from and for the Margins

Myfanwy Taylor and Sara González

Introduction

This chapter argues that by engaging with feminist and postcolonial perspectives and collaborative methods, retail geographies can be a powerful and critical subdiscipline to challenge dominant understandings of economic and urban development. Drawing on our research on UK traditional retail markets – markets selling a wide range of relatively low-cost food, other goods and services to predominately low-income communities – we outline a new trajectory for retail geographies from and for the margins, contributing to socially just and inclusive urban and retail policy agendas.

Markets are indoor or outdoor spaces where people gather to sell and buy a variety of products and services. They are one of the oldest forms of exchange and trade found all over the world serving millions of people and are often operated by public authorities. Despite markets being all about locally situated economic interaction, economic geography and mainstream retail or economics research has paid little attention to them although there is recent interest from urban scholars (Seale, 2016; González, 2018; Van Melik and Sezen, forthcoming).

Outside the academy, markets are caught up in complex and contradictory tendencies: sometimes neglected, actively dismantled or evicted by authorities but at the same time celebrated as 'authentic' destinations (González, 2020). In the UK, where both authors are based, markets account for a small proportion of the grocery shopping and tend to be seen in decline, their future cast narrowly as redeveloped shopping destinations for higher-income consumers (Taylor et al, 2019). The marginalization and redevelopment of markets has a major impact on the low-income, elderly, migrant and ethnically diverse communities they serve (see also Chapter 21 in this volume).

Our collaborative research project, Markets4People,[1] challenges these views and reframes markets as inclusive community spaces making visible the multiple benefits they generate for low-income, minoritized and disadvantaged groups, pointing to an alternative policy agenda based on valuing and supporting these functions. Drawing on our research, this chapter calls for retail geographers to contribute to more socially just and inclusive retail policy agendas by collaborating with those who make, use and value markets and other marginalized retail spaces (compare also Chapters 11, 14 and 20 in this volume).

Mainstream retail research and its margins

Retailing remains a marginalized and fragmented area of research in a field dominated by a focus on economic globalization, manufacturing and advanced producer services (Evans, 2011; Coe and Wrigley, 2018). However, as Wrigley and Lowe argue, it is precisely the position of retailing between production and consumption that makes it a generative focus for research, requiring the 'constant shattering' of the 'arbitrary categories' of economy and culture ([1998] 2014: 3; see also Wrigley and Lowe, 1996; Coe and Wrigley, 2018).

Mainstream retail research tends to assume the increasing power and dominance of supermarkets, chain retailers and shopping centres (malls) particularly in the US and UK (Evans, 2011; Faria and Whitesell, 2021; Frimpong Boamah et al, 2020). The key underpinning theories (for example, retail life cycle; central-place theory; wheel of retailing; scrambled merchandising) are based on a singular, Western model of development from 'traditional' to 'modern' retailing (Evans, 2011), geographically expanding from Europe and North America (Reardon and Hopkins, 2006). This research sees supermarketization as a natural consequence of modernization and urbanization, framing countries with fewer supermarkets as 'lagging'. However, it overestimates supermarketization, which is not complete in the Global North and South where independent retailers, markets and/or informal street traders play important economic and social roles, especially for low-income communities and for fresh produce (Evans, 2011; Coe and Wrigley, 2018; GRAIN, 2018; Frimpong Boamah et al, 2020; Ray et al, 2020).

Location planning, an important area of retail geography, has focused overwhelmingly on major supermarkets who have the capital to invest in computing infrastructure and data collection, resulting in a 'dialectical' relationship between universities and food major retailers (Wood and Browne,

2006: 234; Alexander et al, 2008). However, there are opportunities to focus elsewhere. A body of research on charity shops, social supermarkets and small independent chains shows that their location decisions are based instead on local knowledge, site visits, intuition, personal requirements and other factors (Alexander et al, 2008; Lienbacher et al, 2020) and demonstrates that academic retail geography can support more diverse retailers.

A similar critical reorientation is underway on the edges of mainstream retail geography research on 'food deserts'. Nearly two decades of research has drawn attention to spatial food injustice but has been criticized for being 'stigmatizing, inaccurate, and insufficient to characterize entrenched structural inequalities' (De Master and Daniels, 2019: 241; see also Shannon, 2014; Brinkley et al, 2017). The focus on access to supermarkets as the defining characteristic of food deserts creates a 'neatly bounded' problem, 'solved by creating new food retail where none exists' (Shannon, 2014: 258). This perspective fails to see the complexity of people's lives and the existence of alternative forms of food provisioning, promoting a market-based solution (Agyeman and McEntee, 2014; Battersby, 2019). Critical retail geographers and food justice scholars have used participatory mapping and radical cartography to reveal the importance of small grocery stores, street food, markets, community gardens and kitchens as sources of healthy and affordable food in low-income neighbourhoods (Raja et al, 2008; De Master and Daniels, 2019).

The 'new retail geography' advanced by Wrigley and Lowe in the 1990s expanded the narrow focus of mainstream retail research, bringing critical attention to the role of global retail capital in driving retail change as well as the specific role of retail capital within capitalism (1996; [1998] 2014; see also Ducatel and Blomley, 1990). While global retail capital is a major factor driving changes in cities and in the retail landscape, it is also resisted and reshaped by various actors across many geographies (Hughes et al, 2013; Faria and Whitesell, 2021). Such resistance has received little academic attention, however, even where it has been successful (for example, the Tescopoly and Make Amazon Pay campaigns; Simms, 2007; Shaw, 2012; GRAIN, 2018; Carlile, 2021).

Wrigley and Lowe's new retail geography emphasized 'the cultural geographies of consumption spaces and places' ([1998] 2014: 14), making space for research on independent businesses, marketplaces and other forms of retailing. However this frame of thinking continues to view these forms of retailing as marginal or alternative, animated more by social than economic values. Marketplaces or car boot sales tend to be 'othered' ([1998] 2014: 14; Crewe and Gregson, 1998) ultimately limiting a more diverse view of retail geographies. Economic geographers researching alternative trading and exchange spaces have also encountered this issue, taking 'the mainstream' as the measure to define and research alternatives (Crewe et al, 2003; Hughes, 2007).

This marginalization relates to wider understandings of value in the economy. One powerful example is the lack of attention given to the informal economy, even though it employs 61 per cent of the world's workers (ILO, 2018). Informal street traders make up a significant proportion of the retail sector in many African cities, for example, but are often seen as 'premodern' and thus excluded from or removed by urban development plans (Skinner, 2008). That many informal workers and street traders are women contributes to the erosion of their labour as shown by feminist thinkers (Mezzadri, 2019). Colonial regimes of planning and modernization are also implicated, as Faria and colleagues (2021) demonstrate in relation to women traders in Uganda. Class-based discrimination plays a role too, for example in the devaluing of so-called 'failing' high streets which remain important to working-class communities in the UK (Hubbard, 2017). A growing body of research on retail gentrification has examined how ideas and discourses of decline are mobilized by local state actors and developers to pursue regeneration and development plans which displace retailers serving low-income communities (Zukin et al, 2009; González and Waley, 2013; Román-Velázquez, 2014; Hubbard, 2017; Faria and Whitesell, 2021). Parallels can be drawn with the co-option and reconstitution of LGBTQIA+ neighbourhoods into mainstream consumption spaces, driving out LGBTQIA+ people and activities that do not serve neoliberal (and heteronormative) urban policy agendas (Gorman-Murray and Nash, 2017).

New work from feminist and postcolonial urban perspectives such as Faria and Whitesell's (2021) exploration of women traders in Kampala or Hall and colleagues' (2017; Hall et al, 2021) research on transaction economies built by migrant retailers on disadvantaged UK high streets demonstrates the potential of retail geography, echoing the wider shift within the wider economic geography discipline (for example, Pollard et al, 2011). By engaging with migrant retailers and traders on their own terms, rather than as marginal or alternative 'others' this chapter uses our research on UK marketplaces to demonstrate how critical research on the retail margins can inform socially just retail policy agendas.

The marginalization of markets

Markets are productive spaces to advance retail research from and for the margins as show by the work of sociologists and anthropologists who have paid significant attention to their role as social and public spaces, where exchange is socially embedded and transactions overspill the narrow frame of 'the economic' (Stillerman, 2006; Watson and Studdert, 2006).

In the UK, the term 'traditional' is used to distinguish marketplaces from 'modern' supermarkets and farmers and specialist markets generally aimed at higher-income communities. This label marks them out as premodern and associates them with a nostalgic past, implying they need to transform and evolve to more 'modern' retail formats and a different profile of traders and customers in order to survive. This linear path of transformation reflects the singular understanding of modernity and development that informs understandings of retail change and evolution more generally.

A broader and critical analysis of markets' history and political economy puts in context this limited narrative. Outdoor markets started to decline in the UK by the 16th or 17th century and street trading was persecuted and banned by the 19th century to make way for a more bourgeois use of public space (Schmiechen and Carls, 1999; Jones, 2016). The covered market hall was the elite's response, becoming by the end of the 19th century one of the most important features of British towns and cities. Into the 20th century, modernist post-war planning, suburbanization, the arrival of supermarkets and local authorities' increasing disregard for the public role of markets placed them under significant pressure (Schmiechen and Carls, 1999). The market hall was marginalized, becoming a 'working class department store' (Schmiechen and Carls, 1999: 193).

More recently, this decline and marginalization has been linked to local authority–run markets, considered the most 'traditional' in the sector, with farmers markets and events and street food traders in private markets doing better (House of Commons Communities and Local Government Committee, 2009; Zasada, 2009; Oldershaw, 2012; Mayor of London and the Local Enterprise for London, 2017; Savage and Wolstenholme, 2018). Still, it is hard to draw a trend about a linear decline as markets evolve in unique ways in different places (Smith, 2011; Smith et al, 2014). There has also been a lack of tools to reveal markets' variegated functions and positive impacts (Bua et al, 2018).

Despite the mixed evidence for decline, this narrative is embedded in and mobilized by key organizations in the UK markets sector through publications, events and social media. This framing of decline has put pressure on markets to move from the more 'generalist' format selling essential goods such as fresh food or household products that attract lower-income and older customers, towards specialist formats aimed at higher-income customers. Markets that have 'turned themselves around' with street food markets and food halls are highlighted as models, particularly by a small number of private companies offering market redevelopment services. A similar trend is dominant internationally with markets oriented at visitors and tourists selling prepared food or souvenirs becoming models for renewal and redevelopment (Salinas Arreortúa and Cordero Gómez del Campo, 2018).

This marginalization and redevelopment of traditional retail markets has a major impact on the low-income, elderly, migrant and ethnically diverse communities they serve. As in the case of so-called 'failing' high streets (Hubbard, 2017), these impacts are rarely, if ever, taken into account. Partly this disregard reflects the discrimination that market users face as women, elderly people, people with long-term health issues or disabilities, migrants and/or people of colour. These ideas and processes are being increasing contested by market traders, customers and their supporters and allies and the threat of redevelopment has mobilized broad-based campaigns across the UK (González and Dawson, 2015). These groups face challenges in organizing and representing themselves across various marginalized communities with limited resources, necessitating skills and capacities for working across difference (Taylor, 2020; Hall, 2021).

Critical retail and economic geographers can challenge this narrow framing and the policy response it inspires by questioning the power of corporate capital and contextualizing markets within a neoliberal project. This critical approach must also consider a long-term erosion of the public sphere and the neglect of municipal services and budgets. This has led to long-term underinvestment in local authority–run markets as well as a search to privatize the ownership and management of markets (ROI Team, 2018; Savage and Wolstenholme, 2018) and embark on redevelopment schemes. While these issues are explored in the small but growing body of critical research on retail gentrification referenced earlier, they have yet to influence wider retail research. As such, retail geography remains overwhelmingly informed by a linear, colonial and modernist understanding of economic development, ignoring key questions of power and contestation. There is also more to do to move beyond critique of neoliberalism and global retail capital to advance propositions for more socially just and sustainable retail agendas. Drawing on our own Markets4People research, we propose that retail geographers take inspiration from feminist and postcolonial approaches and engage with diverse retail spaces and practices on their own terms.

Markets for people

The Markets4People research project pursued several strategies to counter the marginalization of UK traditional retail markets in academic and policy discourses. We carried out around 50 interviews with key actors in the markets sector, critically engaging with the framing of traditional retail markets in decline. The majority of project resources were focused not on critique of the current dominant narrative but rather on developing and mobilizing a new frame of reference. Taking inspiration from feminist and postcolonial approaches, our research design centred the voices of market users who tend to be women and from low-income, migrant, Black and ethnic minority (BME) communities (Watson and Studdert, 2006; González and Waley, 2013; Cross River Partnership, 2014). These market users are often regarded as undesirable because their lesser spending power and 'economic' value than younger and wealthier potential customers and hence are not the main focus of surveys and consultations.

The Markets4People project challenged the marginalization of these groups through a representative survey of 1,500 market users of three large successful traditional retail markets. Quotas for gender, ethnicity and age were set using the best available data. As one case study, Queen's Market in East London, was particularly important to local Asian communities, we offered translation and interpretation of the survey in Bengali, Gujarati and Urdu, reaching Asian women who would not normally take part in research or consultations. This method was complemented with six user focus groups, focusing on specific usually marginalized groups that derive the most benefit from markets. While the project was challenged for its insistence on foregrounding the perspectives of current market users, we persisted with this research strategy to show how under-represented groups experience and benefit from markets.

We also pursued an interdisciplinary approach to challenge and work across the divides described earlier. While our own expertise is qualitative research, we worked with colleagues to generate statistics communicating markets' social and cultural importance that could speak more directly to the policy and mainstream retail geography debates (Newing et al, 2023). We also questioned and 'troubled' some of the quantitative tools used in the retail sector and mainstream retail geography such as catchment analysis, reporting the 'over-recruitment' of older or low-income groups as a positive feature of our case study markets (González et al, 2021; Taylor et al, 2021; Waley et al, 2021). We have also made our data available via the Consumer Data Research Centre, to address the marginalization of markets within future retail and consumer research.

Finally, we pursued a collaborative, policy-oriented and activist approach to the project to maximize its impact. This approach was informed by our wider involvement in trader- and community-led campaigns to safeguard markets and advance socially just improvement and redevelopment schemes. We included co-investigators from a national market trader body and a think tank and formed a steering group with diverse members including community groups and the national body for market operators, offering new opportunities for exchange and dialogue. As market traders and operators already have well-developed organizations and networks at national and regional level, we used project resources to bring together market campaigners across the UK in workshops and to organize their own conference on London street markets (González, 2019). These efforts helped to ensure that users and community campaigners' voices were as important as trader and operator voices in the project.

This strategy generated firm evidence that the most disadvantaged groups are the ones that rely most heavily on markets for affordable provisioning and engage in more frequent and meaningful social interaction (González et al, 2021; Taylor et al, 2021; Waley et al, 2021). For example, the oldest and those from less affluent backgrounds and neighbourhoods made up the biggest part of the customer base and visited most often. Older, disabled, unemployed and lower-income groups were also most likely to feel less lonely when they visit markets. In focus groups, we heard how people valued markets for being able to buy affordable and quality produce and how they generated relationships of trust and care with traders and other users. We heard about an ethic of care in markets where older and disabled customers felt safe.

These data enabled us to reframe traditional retail markets, providing a new positive vision from the perspective of market users themselves. Seen from this perspective, markets' wide-ranging benefits makes visible their role as community hubs for inclusive economies and repositions them as spaces of potential and possibility. We have published handbooks (Taylor et al, 2022a, 2022b) sharing best practices that align to this vision and this is opening productive conversations with interested local authority market operators.

Conclusion

This chapter has discussed the contribution of academic research to the marginalization of forms of retailing particularly important to women, low-income groups, migrants and people of colour globally: informal and street trade, marketplaces and other small retailers. It has shown how the idea of a singular, Western model of development has led academic research to overestimate supermarketization and the dominance of global retail capital, obscuring the continued importance of small retailers as well as the contested nature of retail change across the Global North and South. Absences and silences in academic research on retailing and consumption reflects the wider devaluation of women's labour, working-class cultures and racialized peoples within contemporary economies and societies.

Our Markets4People research has critically questioned the decline of marginal retail spaces such as traditional markets, evidencing the crucial role they play for disadvantaged groups. This approach has taken inspiration from postcolonial and feminist engagements with informal and street trade (Faria and Whitesell, 2021; Faria et al, 2021) and migrant retailers (Hall, 2021; Hall et al, 2017). These scholars not only trace the colonial and racist logics that marginalize and threaten retailers but also produce new accounts of their importance and value and engage with their collective efforts to secure their livelihoods. In these accounts, retail change may be oppressive and violent, but it is not assured or uncontested. Such a perspective repositions retail spaces at the margins as spaces of possibility, rich with importance to marginalized communities to be protected and nurtured through socially just retail policy agendas.

Our proposal for a repurposed retail geography is in line with wider efforts to secure socially just and sustainable ways of living. Sitting at the intersection between production and consumption, retailing offers generative possibilities for researchers to challenge and work across divides between the economy and society/culture, producing new understandings of value beyond the confines of 'the market' or 'capitalism'. In a similar way, struggles to defend valued retail spaces offer opportunities to explore the potential and limits of urban movements involving an unusually wide range of economic and social actors. Crucially, researching retail from and for the margins can inform new considerations about the role and contribution of hitherto marginalized retailers to wider movements for urban social justice and economic democracy. Our own research suggests that feminist, postcolonial and collaborative research approaches will be particularly important in building knowledge, proposals and networks to support more socially just and sustainable retail geographies and policy agendas.

Acknowledgements

This chapter is based on research that was funded by a UK Research and Innovation Grant. Grant reference number ES/P010547/1. The data from this research is available here: https://data.cdrc.ac.uk/dataset/traditional-retail-markets-community-value-survey-data.

Note

[1] https://trmcommunityvalue.leeds.ac.uk/

References

Agyeman, J. and McEntee, J. (2014) 'Moving the field of food justice forward through the lens of urban political ecology', *Geography Compass*, 8(3): 211–20.

Alexander, A., Cryer, D. and Wood, S. (2008) 'Location planning in charity retail', *International Journal of Retail & Distribution Management*, 36(7): 536–50.

Battersby, J. (2019) 'The food desert as a concept and policy tool in African cities: an opportunity and a risk', *Sustainability*, 11(2): art 458. Available from: https://doi.org/10.3390/su11020458 [Accessed 3 July 2023].

Brinkley, C., Raj, S. and Horst, M. (2017) 'Culturing food deserts: recognizing the power of community-based solutions', *Built Environment*, 43(3): 328–42.

Bua, A., Taylor, M. and González, S. (2018) *Measuring the Value of Traditional Retail Markets: Towards a Holistic Approach*, London: New Economics Foundation. Available from: https://neweconomics.org/uploads/files/retail-markets.pdf [Accessed 3 July 2023].

Carlile, C. (2021) 'Shopping without Amazon', *Ethical Consumer*, 15 June.

Coe, N.M. and Wrigley, N. (2018) 'Towards new economic geographies of retail globalization', in G.L. Clark, M.P. Feldman, M.S. Gertler and D. Wójcik (eds) *The New Oxford Handbook of Economic Geography*, Oxford: Oxford University Press, pp 427–47.

Crewe, L. and Gregson, N. (1998) 'Tales of the unexpected: exploring car boot sales as marginal spaces of contemporary consumption', *Transactions of the Institute of British Geographers*, 23(1): 39–53.

Crewe, L., Gregson, N. and Brooks, K. (2003) 'Alternative retail spaces', in A. Leyshon, R. Lee and C.C. Williams (eds) *Alternative Economic Spaces*, London: Sage, pp 74–106.

Cross River Partnership (2014) *Sustainable Urban Markets: An Action Plan for London*, London: Cross River Partnership.

De Master, K.T. and Daniels, J. (2019) 'Desert wonderings: reimagining food access mapping', *Agriculture and Human Values*, 36(2): 241–56.

Ducatel, K. and Blomley, N. (1990) 'Rethinking retail capital', *International Journal of Urban and Regional Research*, 14(2): 207–27.

Evans, J.R. (2011) 'Retailing in perspective: the past is a prologue to the future', *International Review of Retail, Distribution and Consumer Research*, 21(1): 1–31.

Faria, C. and Whitesell, D. (2021) 'Global retail capital and urban futures: feminist postcolonial perspectives', *Geography Compass*, 15(1): e12551.

Faria, C., Katushabe, J., Kyotowadde, C. and Whitesell, D. (2021) '"You rise up … they burn you again": market fires and the urban intimacies of disaster colonialism', *Transactions of the Institute of British Geographers*, 46(1): 87–101.

Frimpong Boamah, E., Amoako, C. and Kuffuor Asenso, B. (2020) 'Spaces of market politics: retailscapes and modernist planning imaginaries in African cities', *Applied Geography*, 123: art 102265. Available from: https://doi.org/10.1016/j.apgeog.2020.102265 [Accessed 3 July 2023].

González, S. (2019) 'Urban motley geographies or "geografías urbanas abigarradas"', *Dialogues in Human Geography*, 9(3): 341–43.

González, S. (2019) 'The Future of London's Street Markets conference', Markets4People, 19 July. Available from: https://trmcommunityvalue.leeds.ac.uk/the-future-of-londons-street-markets-conference/ [Accessed 20 January 2022].

González S. (2020) 'Contested marketplaces: Retail spaces at the global urban margin', *Progress in Human Geography*, 44(5): 877–97.

González, S. and Dawson, D. (2015) *Traditional Markets Under Threat: Why It's Happening and What Traders and Customers Can Do*. Available from: https://antipodeonline.org/wp-content/uploads/2015/10/traditional-markets-under-threat.pdf [Accessed 20 January 2022].

González, S. and Waley, P. (2013) 'Traditional retail markets: the new gentrification frontier?', *Antipode*, 45(4): 965–83.

González, S., Taylor, M., Newing, A., Buckner, L. and Wilkinson, R. (2021) Grainger Market: *A* Community Asset at the *H*eart of Newcastle upon Tyne. Available from: https://trmcommunityvalue.leeds.ac.uk/wp-content/uploads/sites/36/2021/06/210602-M4P-Grainger-FINAL.pdf [Accessed 15 July 2021].

Gormon-Murray, A. and Nash, C. (2017) 'Transformations in LGBT consumer landscapes and leisure spaces in the neoliberal city', *Urban Studies*, 54(3): 786–805.

GRAIN (2018) 'Supermarkets out of Africa! Food systems across the continent are doing just fine without them', GRAIN, 8 November. Available from: https://grain.org/en/article/6042-supermarkets-out-of-afr ica-food-systems-across-the-continent-are-doing-just-fine-without-them [Accessed 17 May 2021].

Hall, S.M. (2021) *The Migrant's Paradox: Street Livelihoods and Marginal Citizenship in Britain*, Minneapolis: University of Minnesota Press.

Hall, S.M., King, J. and Finlay, R. (2017) 'Migrant infrastructure: transaction economies in Birmingham and Leicester, UK', *Urban Studies*, 54(6): 1311–27.

House of Commons Communities and Local Government Committee (2009) *Market Failure? Can the Traditional Market Survive?*, HC 308-II, London: Stationery Office.

Hubbard, P. (2017) *The Battle for the High Street: Retail Gentrification, Class and Disgust*, London: Palgrave Macmillan.

Hughes, A. (2007) 'Geographies of exchange and circulation: alternative trading spaces', *Progress in Human Geography*, 29(4): 496–504.

Hughes, A., McEwan, C. and Bek, D. (2013) 'Retailers, supply networks and changing articulations of ethicality: lessons from Flower Valley in South Africa', *Journal of Economic Geography*, 13(2): 211–30.

ILO (International Labour Organization) (2018) *Women and Men in the Informal Economy: A Statistical Picture* (3rd edn), Geneva: ILO.

Jones, P.T.A. (2016) 'Redressing reform narratives: Victorian London's street markets and the informal supply lines of urban modernity', *London Journal*, 41(1): 60–81.

Lienbacher, E., Koschinsky, J., Holweg, C. and Vallaster, C. (2020) 'Spatial decision support for social hybrid organizations: siting new social supermarkets in Austria', *International Journal of Retail & Distribution Management*, 49(7): 999–1024.

Mayor of London and the Local Enterprise Partnership for London (2017) Understanding London's Markets, London: Greater London Authority. Available from: https://www.london.gov.uk/sites/default/files/gla_mar kets_report_web.pdf [Accessed 3 July 2023].

Mezzadri, A. (2019) 'On the value of social reproduction: informal labour, the majority world and the need for inclusive theories and politics', *Radical Philosophy*, 2(4): 33–41.

Newing, A., Clarke, G., Taylor, M., González, S., Buckner, L. and Wilkinson, R. (2023) 'The role of traditional retail markets in addressing urban food deserts', *International Review of Retail, Distribution and Consumer Research*, ahead of print. Available from: https://doi.org/10.1080/09593 969.2023.2198251 [Accessed 3 July 2023].

Oldershaw, J. (2012) *Retail Markets in the UK: A Review of Recent Research*, Barnsley: National Market Traders Federation. Available from: https://www.nmtf.co.uk/wp-content/uploads/2017/02/Retail-Markets-in-the-UK-NTMF-2012.pdf [Accessed 3 July 2023].

Pollard, J., McEwan, C. and Hughes, A. (2011) *Postcolonial Economies*, London: Zed Books.

Raja, S., Ma, C. and Yadav, P. (2008) 'Beyond food deserts: measuring and mapping racial disparities in neighborhood food environments', *Journal of Planning Education and Research*, 27(4): 469–82.

Ray, N., Clarke, G. and Waley, P. (2020) 'The rise of corporate retailing and the impacts on small-scale retailing: the survival strategies of Kirana stores and informal street vendors in Durgapur, India', *Singapore Journal of Tropical Geography*, 41(2): 269–83.

Reardon, T. and Hopkins, R. (2006) 'The supermarket revolution in developing countries: policies to address emerging tensions among supermarkets, suppliers and traditional retailers', *European Journal of Development Research*, 18(4): 522–45.

ROI Team (2018) 'Management Options Revisited: Review for Nabma Conference by ROI Team September', in *NABMA Conference*, Stratford Upon Avon.

Román-Velázquez, P. (2014) 'Claiming a place in the global city: urban regeneration and Latin American spaces in London', *Political Economy of Technology, Information and Culture Journal*, 16(1): 68–83.

Salinas Arreortúa, L.A. and Cordero Gómez del Campo, L. de L. (2018) 'Gourmet markets as a commercial gentrification model: the cases of Mexico City and Madrid', in S. González (ed) *Contested Markets, Contested Cities: Gentrification and Urban Justice in Retail Spaces*, Abingdon: Routledge, pp 86–98.

Savage, C. and Wolstenholme, C. (2018) 'Mission for Markets. Survey Results 2017–18', paper presented at 2018 NABMA Annual Conference, Stratford Upon Avon, 16–18 September. Available from: https://www.miss ion4markets.uk/survey/17-18.html [Accessed 3 July 2023].

Schmiechen, J. and Carls, K. (1999) *The British Market Hall: A Social and Architectural History*, New Haven, CT: Yale University Press.

Seale, K. (2016) *Markets, Places, Cities*, Abingdon: Routledge.

Sezer, C. and van Melik, R. (2023) *Marketplaces: Movements, Representations and Practices*, Oxon: Routledge.

Shaw, H.J. (2012) 'CSR, SMEs and food retailing: the advantages of being a lesser good', *Journal of Business and Retail Management Research*, 6(2): 15–25.

Shannon, J. (2014) 'Food deserts: governing obesity in the neoliberal city', *Progress in Human Geography*, 38(2): 248–66.

Simms, A. (2007) *Tescopoly: How One Shop Came Out on Top and Why it Matters*, London: Constable & Robinson.

Skinner, C. (2008) 'The struggle for the streets: processes of exclusion and inclusion of street traders in Durban, South Africa', *Development Southern Africa*, 25(2): 227–42.

Smith, J. (2011) The Everyday Life of Food: The Cultural Economy of the Traditional Food Market in England. PhD thesis submitted to the University of Gloucestershire. Available from: https://eprints.glos.ac.uk/3261/ [Accessed 3 July 2023].

Smith, J., May, D. and Ilbery, D. (2014) 'The traditional food market and place: new insights into fresh food provisioning in England', *Area*, 46(2): 122–8.

Stillerman, J. (2006) 'Private, parochial, and public realms in Santiago, Chile's retail sector', *City & Community*, 5(3): 293–317.

Taylor, M. (2020) 'The role of traders and small businesses in urban social movements: the case of London's workspace struggles', *International Journal of Urban and Regional Research*, 44(6): 1041–56.

Taylor, M., González, S. and Northrop, F. (2019) 'Building community markets', *STIR: The Magazine for the New Economy*, 26.

Taylor, M., González, S., Waley, P. and Wilkinson, R. (2022a) *Developing Markets as Community Hubs for Inclusive Economies: A Best Practice Handbook for Market Operators*, Leeds: Markets4People, University of Leeds. Available from: https://trmcommunityvalue.leeds.ac.uk/wp-content/uploads/sites/36/2022/04/220408-HB1-final-version_RW_ONLINE.pdf [Accessed 7 April 2023].

Taylor, M., Northrop, F., Kiberd, E., Phagoora, J., Scurrah, E., Power, H., González, S., Waley, P. and Wilkinson, R. (2022b) Trader- *and Community-Run Markets: A Practical Guide to Setting Up, Running Your Market and Accessing Support*, Leeds: Markets4People, University of Leeds. Available from: https://trmcommunityvalue.leeds.ac.uk/wp-content/uploads/sites/36/2023/01/230126_TandC_run_Markets_FINAL-1.pdf [Accessed 7 April 2023].

Taylor, M., Watson, S., González, S., Newing, A. and Wilkinson, R. (2021) *Queen's Market: A Successful and Specialised Market Serving Diverse Communities in Newham and Beyond*, Leeds: Markets4People, University of Leeds. Available from: https://trmcommunityvalue.leeds.ac.uk/wp-content/uploads/sites/36/2021/06/210531-M4P-Queens-FINAL.pdf [Accessed 20 January 2022].

Waley, P., Taylor, M., González, S., Newing, A., Buckner, L. and Wilkinson, R. (2021) *Bury Market: Shopping Destination and Community Hub*, Leeds: Markets4People, University of Leeds. Available from: https://trmcommunityvalue.leeds.ac.uk/wp-content/uploads/sites/36/2021/06/210531-M4P-Bury-FINAL.pdf [Accessed 20 January 2022].

Watson, S. and Studdert, D. (2006) *Markets as Sites for Social Interaction: Spaces of Diversity*, York: Joseph Rowntree Foundation.

Wood, S. and Browne, S. (2006) 'Convenience store location planning and forecasting: a practical research agenda', *International Journal of Retail & Distribution Management*, 35(4): 233–55.

Wrigley, N. and Lowe, M. (1996) *Retailing, Consumption and Capital: Towards the New Retail Geography*, Harlow: Longman.

Wrigley, N. and Lowe, M. ([1998] 2014) *Reading Retail: A Geographical Perspective on Retailing and Consumption Spaces*, Abingdon: Routledge.

Zasada, K. (2009) *Markets 21: A Policy and Research Review of UK Retail and Wholesale Markets in the 21st Century*. The Retail Markets Alliance.

Zukin, S., Trujillo, V., Frase, P., Jackson, D., Recuber, T. and Walker, A. (2009) 'New retail capital and neighborhood change: boutiques and gentrification in New York City', *City & Community*, 8(1): 47–64.

29

Resources and Extraction

Julie Ann de los Reyes

Introduction

Ongoing efforts to avert climate change have brought to the fore the complexities of a societal shift to a low-carbon future. The extraction of fossil fuel resources has been instrumental in profound increases in productivity and economic growth but have also largely contributed to anthropogenic climate change. The enforcement of the Paris Agreement and subsequent pledges of net-zero emissions in key industrialized economies have created a momentum for rebasing the energy system from traditional fossil fuels towards renewable sources. This requires rendering 'unburnable' part of the existing fossil fuel reserves (McGlade and Ekins, 2015) and mobilizing technologies and resources such as solar, wind, biomass and 'critical minerals' in socially useful and economically viable ways.

This chapter looks at the significance of these transformations for economic geographical research using examples from, and insights on, the Asia Pacific – a region that is experiencing dramatic societal transformations in the context of decarbonization, but also one that remains on the fringes of the subdiscipline. This is a serious lacuna given its significance for energy transition: it accounts for half of global carbon emissions and is home to some of the largest fossil fuel producers, consumers and funders in the world. It is also an important geography for renewable energy, given its role in the development and supply of low-carbon resources and technologies (Cao et al, 2018). I first reflect on the relatively recent work on the geographies of energy transition within economic geography, highlighting limitations in its engagement with geographies outside of a few 'core' countries and the implications of this spatial bias. I then consider what a more geographically inclusive research agenda might have to offer in understanding the dynamics of energy transition, particularly its spatial and resource constitution and financing. Economic geography research on energy and resources touches on long-running themes within the subdiscipline but also opens new avenues for exploration that could help expand its geographical reach and address existing inadequacies.

Transition beyond the core

Economic geography has historically made important contributions studying the role of resources such as coal, oil and gas in economic growth, resource-led development, and the spatial organization of industries (Roepke, 1955; McNee, 1958) – core themes within the subdiscipline. At the turn of the century however, growing concerns on the impacts of these industries, and extractive activities in general, on the natural environment led to strengthened calls for a more explicitly 'environmental' focus for economic geographical research (Gibbs, 2006; Hayter, 2008; Radcliffe et al, 2010). Research during this period has paid greater attention to how dominant modes of economic development have largely contributed to and accelerated resource extraction, environmental degradation and global warming (Johnson, 2014; Knox-Hayes, 2016; de los Reyes, 2017); the financial logics that underpin climate solutions and the management of environmental ills (Knuth, 2017; Bracking, 2019); and explorations of alternative economies and systemic changes that go beyond the techno-fixes, or socio-ecological fixes of the 'green economy' and sustainable development agenda (Bina, 2013; Gibson-Graham et al, 2019). Evident in this new crop of environmentally oriented research is a recognition of the growing urgency of socio-environmental crises, and the need for economic geography to critically engage and advocate solutions as a matter of ethical concern (Gibson-Graham et al, 2019).

Since the early 2010s, research on the economy–energy resource interface within economic geography has expanded, which helped bring greater visibility to the socio-material and socio-spatial implications of a low-carbon transition (Zimmerer, 2011; Gailing et al, 2020). It is now widely recognized that the dramatic decline in the consumption – and (some would argue) production (McGlade and Ekins, 2015; Le Billon and Kristoffersen, 2020) – of fossil fuel resources necessitated by a low-carbon shift would have manifold consequences for current patterns and scales of economic and social activity (Bridge et al, 2013; Miller and McGregor, 2020). Economic geographers have been at the forefront of debates in social science research on energy and have made significant strides at advancing a more spatially sensitive framework for studying transition by foregrounding how cultural, social, political and economic arrangements in particular settings shape (and are shaped by) this process (McEwan, 2017; Bustos-Gallardo et al, 2021).

Despite the emphasis on the role of space however, a critical weakness lies in the geographical constitution of the knowledge produced on energy transition within economic geography and social science research on energy in general. As Bridge (2018: 16) notes, much of what is known 'emerged from a close engagement with energy systems and processes of change in a relatively small number of national crucibles', notably from liberal economies in (Northern) Europe and the US. The limitations of this geographical focus are increasingly becoming evident as new studies emerge from outside of these core countries, leading to a questioning of the applicability and transferability of existing theories and models. This is especially pronounced when analysing non-market-based economies, where the opportunities for a shift in the production and consumption of fossil fuels depend not on market actors or price signals as found in the West, but on broader shifts in development priorities and goals (see Mathews and Tan, 2015). The relative neglect of marginal and/or less affluent regions of the global economy in transition studies further means that existing framings of the energy challenge are ill-suited at grasping the variegated experiences, meanings and logics attached to an energy shift elsewhere (Sarrica et al, 2018; Huang et al, 2021). As Huang et al (2021: 901) have argued, understanding the 'epistemological and philosophical traditions' found in particular societies is necessary if scholars are to interpret place-based dynamics accurately.

A challenge, and opportunity, for economic geography then is to take its spatial commitments seriously by expanding its geographical focus to make visible the distinctive energy trajectories currently at play and the place-specific barriers (or openings) that may exist that inhibit (or facilitate) the shift to renewable sources. Even within the Asia Pacific, it should be said, these are highly diverse. Here, prior work by economic geography scholars on the region on transnationalism, state–capital–labour relations, and networks are instructive and give a sense of some of the peculiarities that exist. Studies on ethnic Chinese firms, for example, have highlighted the salience of guanxi, or networked relationships in determining the direction, stability and (re)location of firms' business operations (Tan and Yeung, 2000; Jou et al, 2004). Sociocultural connections are found to exert an influential role in business activities and are not mainly driven by economic considerations (profit maximization) or deterred by market risks. A more spatially extensive, and inclusive, research agenda in this regard has the potential to enrich our understanding of the 'conditions of possibility' of different energy trajectories, as well as challenge some of the frameworks that scholars apply that, too often, are perceived as universal.

Beyond encounters with spatial difference, studying processes of change outside of industrialized economies is also fertile ground for drawing out the socio-spatial differentiations and uneven forms of development that might arise with decarbonization. How space is remade as a consequence of the transition process, and the extent to which this reinforces core–periphery relations or create new societal divides are crucial lines of inquiry, with implications for the organization of the global economy. Economic geographers, I argue, are well equipped to tease out the interconnections and uneven outcomes from such processes that are otherwise lost with a more explicit focus on transition in a few core countries. I expound on these points in the following sections by showing how economic geography could contribute to emerging work on the material foundations of low-carbon transitions and the role of finance through an expanded geographical remit.

The material foundations of a low-carbon transition

Decarbonization entails the enrollment of a new range of raw materials, with distinct power densities, geographical occurrences and spatial requisites. While previous transitions have been marked by a progressive move to higher density sources, a distinctive feature of the current transition is its reliance on resources that have lower power densities than its predecessors (Smil, 2015). The distribution, stability and geographical possibilities of renewable sources are also significantly different from fossil fuels. Resources such as wind and solar rely on natural conditions to generate electricity, are variable in output and are not geographically concentrated. These characteristics are significant since they imply fundamentally different arrangements to source and harness alternative forms of energy across space (Kama, 2020; Bustos-Gallardo et al, 2021). This points to the need for economic geographical research to take a more encompassing approach in order to understand the different challenges and responses to transition and the differing impacts this has had across geographies.

For carbon-intensive but resource-poor economies in the Asia Pacific, the push to shift to low-carbon sources revitalizes concerns surrounding the security of future energy supplies to meet domestic energy needs. The economies of Japan, Singapore and South Korea have been built on raw materials access overseas (Bunker and Ciccantell, 2007) and nearly all of their energy needs depend on imported fossil fuels. Decarbonization privileges, in contrast, the development of indigenous supplies. Solar, wind and run-of-river must be deployed closer to sites of consumption and located in areas where the production potential is highest, that is, where the natural resource is (most) available. These locations are often remote, thus drawing in spaces that have previously not been part of the energy landscape. The revaluation of energy carriers such as hydrogen, as the low carbon 'fuel of the future' (Trencher and van der Heijden, 2019: 210), is also reconfiguring supply chains and bringing into orbit resources such as lignite, that were considered too low-grade, unstable (for example, to transport), or inefficient to burn, but which are now prized for their hydrogen potential (Hancock and Ralph, 2021; and see Figure 29.1).

Figure 29.1: Kawasaki Heavy Industries' (KHI) shipyard in Kobe port, Japan

Note: KHI built the world's first liquefied hydrogen carrier, *Suiso Frontier*, as part of a pilot project demonstrating the feasibility of sourcing and transporting hydrogen produced from lignite from Latrobe Valley, Australia by sea.

Source: Author's photo

The low-carbon economy, in this sense, is constitutive of new territories and is premised on the creation of a new resource periphery. This makes access to and control of these new spaces a strategic concern. 'Green grabbing' – the appropriation of land and resources for environmental purposes – is occurring across a wide range of places globally (Fairhead et al, 2012; Holmes, 2014) fuelling conflict from competing land uses (Borras and Franco, 2012; Yenneti et al, 2016). In the Negros Islands of the Philippines, for example, the combination of growing energy demand, the availability of large tracts of contiguous land, ample solar radiation, lack of formal land titles (for farmers, Indigenous communities), and concentration of land ownership in the hands of sugar barons (a legacy of colonial rule) has created fertile ground for hosting solar projects but has also become a means to evade land redistribution (see Figure 29.2). Economic geography could take a more active role, in this regard, at examining the multi-scalar reconfigurations and patterns of uneven development that are emerging with the low-carbon transition. Insights from work on global production networks, for example, could help illuminate how the material characteristics of low-carbon sources are (re)shaping the organization and geography of supply chains, especially as in most cases the relative distance between energy production and consumption becomes shorter. Extant work within critical geography on materiality

Figure 29.2: One of the leaders of the farmer's federation, Task Force Mapalad, confronts police forces in Negros Occidental

Note: Farmer groups have been pushing for land redistribution for decades in Negros, dubbed the renewable energy capital of the Philippines.

Source: Photo by Jimmy A. Domingo

and the 'matter of nature' (Bakker and Bridge, 2006; Bakker, 2012) could help inform analyses of the geopolitical arrangements and sociotechnical strategies employed to make renewable resources (economically) viable, scalable and (qualify as) renewable. Future research in this area should also be attendant to how the resource periphery is being rescaled and redefined in ways that challenge existing conceptualizations that are predominantly based on notions of long-distance flows of raw materials from typically far-flung spaces of extraction.

Financing the transition

Financing a sustainable energy transition remains an underexplored area in economic geography research, even as there is wide recognition of the vital importance of finance to meet decarbonization goals. The International Energy Agency (2021) estimates that about $4 trillion worth of annual investments by 2030 must be mobilized to reach the 2050 net-zero emissions target – or a threefold growth from its current level. Despite strong interests in aspects of 'carbon finance', such as carbon markets and ecosystem services (Bumpus and Liverman, 2008; Knight, 2011; Knox-Hayes, 2013), only in recent years have economic geographers started to direct their attention to the capital flows sustaining fossil fuel industries (Cojoianu et al, 2021) and the challenges associated with financing low-carbon investments (Bridge et al, 2020). Although analytically attentive to the motives that underpin shifts in the financing of energy projects, these studies have been largely based on the US, UK and EU contexts (which comprise much of the studies in this area within the subdiscipline and other fields) where market forces are the key drivers of change and considerations of price, profit and risk heavily shape investment trajectories.

To date, little is known as to what drives investment and disinvestment trends in non-traditional market economies. This is especially crucial to unpack given the importance of East Asian economies in the financing of fossil-fuel projects. China, Japan and South Korea are among the largest sources of demand for coal, oil and gas, and are actively involved in both upstream (exploration and mining) and downstream (power plant development) operations abroad (Makhijani, 2014; Lee and Woo, 2020). Since 2013, for example, they have been responsible for 95 per cent of the total overseas financing for coal-fired power projects globally (Liu et al. 2021). Ironically, they are also some of the largest funders of renewable projects, especially following recent pledges to support the development of green industries as part of post-pandemic recovery.

The actors involved in the financing of energy projects are highly diverse, with differing motives, investment horizons and return requirements (Hall et al, 2017; Cojoianu et al, 2021). While private sources such as stock markets and banks – the key funding institutions in the West – have their counterparts in the East Asian financial landscape, and the financial centres of Beijing, Shanghai and Tokyo have grown in size and significance in global financial markets since the early 2000s, as economic geographers attest (Zhao et al, 2004; Wang, 2019), state actors and institutions still remain highly influential in 'steering' business activities in these economies (albeit variations exist in terms of degree of intervention and control) particularly in strategic sectors (Yang et al, 2019). States exercise allocative power over energy projects and related investments through state-owned banks and development financial institutions, but also indirectly shape private sector investments through policy support. The dominant business models are also characterized by close integration between typically large and diversified industrial firms, financial institutions and the state, which result in different risk perceptions, and distinct and usually more varied strategies in investing (Bhattacharya and Kojima, 2012; Jiang, 2019; Zhao, 2019). For instance, Japanese general trading companies (sōgō shōsha) that are among the top players in the international coal market have benefited from ready access to credit by financial institutions who 'strongly perceive the support of business activities for Japanese industry as a core responsibility' (Trencher et al, 2020: 10), while state support helps derisk large capital investments required to carry out business activities outside of their home country (Chen et al, 2020; Wijaya, 2022). A fuller understanding, however, is required as to how these differences – place-specific institutional norms and state–market configurations – impact the spatio-temporal profile of energy investments and, importantly, the pace and scale of transition. Indeed, East Asian economies have taken great leaps in energy investments that were deemed 'paradoxical' but which resulted to some of the most remarkable advances in technological development and deployment of renewable energy in recent years (Behling et al, 2015; Zeng et al, 2014).

Research in this area much to do to shed light on the internal deliberations that underpin investment decisions, how the risk/reward ratio of projects is determined, how investment timeframes and returns criteria differ (Zhang et al, 2021; Yang et al, 2019), while being attentive to other categories and forms of valuations that may be particular to these settings. Economic geography scholars studying the region have highlighted the influence of geopolitical ambitions on market dynamics (Klinger, 2018; Gemici and Lai, 2020; Pan et al, 2020) as perhaps best exemplified by the Chinese government's Belt and Road Initiative, which has been pivotal in the funding of energy and infrastructure projects (Lin and Bega, 2021). This raises important questions on how shifts in national development goals could help alter investment practices and trajectories, especially in light of revamped policy commitments by the governments of Japan, China and South Korea to reach net-zero emissions by the mid-21st century. The sizeable financial support for a green recovery suggests an even bigger role for the state in shifting energy investments, but whether this will herald a decisive shift to renewable energy and what considerations will drive public investments is a task for future studies.

Studying the factors that shape energy investments map onto emerging critique within geography on the outsized role of market forces in addressing climate change (Knox-Hayes, 2010, 2013; Christophers, 2022), as well as long-standing critique on the inherent limits – and hegemony – of the capitalist economy (Gibson-Graham, 2008: 615; Harvey, 2018). Transition dynamics in East Asia hint at distinct opportunities and possibilities – but also challenges, attention to which could lead to fuller and more nuanced discussions on how things could be done differently to enable a low–carbon transition. Although the contours of a future energy system are still open-ended, the investment and policy decisions taken by these countries carry particular weight. This makes economic geographical research on the region not only welcome but necessary.

Conclusion

Building on economic geography's sustained interest on 'resources' and emerging research on energy, I considered in this chapter how a low–carbon shift presents new avenues for research, interdisciplinary engagements and challenges to the subdiscipline's empirical and epistemological commitments. The resource requirements of energy transition are now increasingly apparent, and while geographers are taking an active role in shaping the research agenda in this area, there are several lines of inquiry that remain understudied. I highlighted, in particular, the significance of ongoing reconfigurations in the Asia Pacific in light of their potential to broaden existing understandings on the material foundations of a low-carbon transition, and investments and disinvestments patterns associated with this process. While geographers recognize the context specificity and polysemic nature of transition, current frameworks on energy transition have been mainly rooted in the experiences and concerns of a few industrialized, predominantly Western economies, such that 'current transitions thinking does not reflect the geographical plurality that the discipline aspires to' (Huang et al, 2021: 902). Attention to transition dynamics in Asia highlight some of the shortcomings of these frameworks, especially when applied in economies that do not quite fit the market-based mold.

Transition processes in the region carry vast implications for the fossil-fuel-based global economy, given its reliance on, and involvement in, fossil-fuel financing, production and consumption. Economic geography, I argued, is well-placed to contribute to addressing existing knowledge gaps, as well as benefit from engaging with geographies that remain marginal in the discipline. For instance, the resilience and relative strength of fossil fuel, and most especially coal investments in the Asia Pacific region, need to better understood. There is a paucity of research on the actors, interests and concerns that shape investment trajectories in these economies, even more apparent when compared to the fine-grained analyses on Western, market-based ones. Future research should also be devoted to studying the socio-spatial reorganizations and trade-offs arising from a shift to renewable sources, in light of their particular attributes and their implications for the resource periphery. Evidence from countries in South-East Asia vividly demonstrates how the extensive land requirements of resources like solar compete with other land uses, thus generating new (and aggravating old) tensions. Understanding the inequalities and uneven forms of geographical development that might arise from energy transition requires a better engagement with, and potentially a reconceptualization of, the (new) periphery. The uneven pace and scale of decarbonization in different parts of the world highlight the urgency of incorporating – and elevating – the plurality of struggles, experiences and concerns of other societies, and how these are being addressed in diverse ways. Energy transition provides an opening to challenge some of the enduring structural imbalances of the world economy enabled by the fossil-fuel energy system. An economic geography that is plural, inclusive and polyvocal will be better equipped to respond to this challenge.

References

Bakker, K. (2012) 'The "matter of nature" in economic geography', in T.J. Barnes, J. Peck and E. Sheppard (eds) *The Wiley-Blackwell Companion to Economic Geography*, Chichester: Blackwell, pp 104–17.

Bakker, K. and Bridge, G. (2006) 'Material worlds? Resource geographies and the "matter of nature"', *Progress in Human Geography*, 30(1): 5–27.

Behling, N., Williams, M.C. and Managi, S. (2015) 'Fuel cells and the hydrogen revolution: analysis of a strategic plan in Japan', *Economic Analysis and Policy*, 48: 204–21.

Bhattacharya, A. and Kojima, S. (2012) 'Power sector investment risk and renewable energy: a Japanese case study using portfolio risk optimization method', *Energy Policy*, 40: 69–80.

Bina, O. (2013) 'The green economy and sustainable development: an uneasy balance?', *Environment and Planning C: Government and Policy*, 31(6): 1023–47.

Borras, S.M. Jr and Franco, J.C. (2012) 'Global land grabbing and trajectories of agrarian change: a preliminary analysis', *Journal of Agrarian Change*, 12(1): 34–59.

Bracking, S. (2019) 'Financialisation, climate finance, and the calculative challenges of managing environmental change', *Antipode*, 51(3): 709–29.

Bridge, G. (2018) 'The map is not the territory: a sympathetic critique of energy research's spatial turn', *Energy Research & Social Science*, 36: 11–20.

Bridge, G., Bouzarovski, S., Bradshaw, M. and Eyre, N. (2013) 'Geographies of energy transition: space, place and the low-carbon economy', *Energy Policy*, 53: 331–40.

Bridge, G., Bulkeley, H., Langley, P. and van Veelen, B. (2020) 'Pluralizing and problematizing carbon finance', *Progress in Human Geography*, 44(4): 724–42.

Bumpus, A.G. and Liverman, D.M. (2008) 'Accumulation by decarbonization and the governance of carbon offsets', *Economic Geography*, 84(2): 127–55.

Bunker, S.G. and Ciccantell, P.S. (2007) *East Asia and the Global Economy: Japan's Ascent, with Implications for China's Future*, Baltimore, MD: Johns Hopkins University Press.

Bustos-Gallardo, B., Bridge, G. and Prieto, M. (2021) 'Harvesting lithium: water, brine and the industrial dynamics of production in the Salar de Atacama', *Geoforum*, 119: 177–89.

Cao, X., Rajarshi, A. and Tong, J. (2018) 'Technology evolution of China's export of renewable energy products', *International Journal of Environmental Research and Public Health*, 15(8): art 1782. Available from: https://doi.org/10.3390/ijerph15081782 [Accessed 3 July 2023].

Chen, X., Gallagher, K.P. and Mauzerall, D.L. (2020) 'Chinese overseas development financing of electric power generation: a comparative analysis', *One Earth*, 3(4): 491–503.

Christophers, B. (2022) 'Fossilised capital: price and profit in the energy transition', *New Political Economy*, 27(1): 146–59.

Cojoianu, T.F., Ascui, F., Clark, G.L., Hoepner, A.G. and Wójcik, D. (2021) 'Does the fossil fuel divestment movement impact new oil and gas fundraising?', *Journal of Economic Geography*, 21(1): 141–64.

de los Reyes, J.A. (2017) 'Mining shareholder value: institutional shareholders, transnational corporations and the geography of gold mining', *Geoforum*, 84: 251–64.

Fairhead, J., Leach, M. and Scoones, I. (2012) 'Green grabbing: a new appropriation of nature?', *Journal of Peasant Studies*, 39(2): 237–61.

Gailing, L., Bues, A., Kern, K. and Röhring, A. (2020) 'Socio-spatial dimensions in energy transitions: applying the TPSN framework to case studies in Germany', *Environment and Planning A: Economy and Space*, 52(6): 1112–30.

Gemici, K. and Lai, K.P.Y. (2020) 'How "global" are investment banks? An analysis of investment banking networks in Asian equity capital markets', *Regional Studies*, 54(2): 149–61.

Gibbs, D. (2006) 'Prospects for an environmental economic geography: linking ecological modernization and regulationist approaches', *Economic Geography*, 82(2): 193–215.

Gibson-Graham, J.K. (2008) 'Diverse economies: performative practices for "other worlds"', *Progress in Human Geography*, 32(5): 613–32.

Gibson-Graham, J.K., Cameron, J., Healy, S. and McNeill, J. (2019) 'Roepke Lecture in Economic Geography – Economic Geography, Manufacturing, and Ethical Action in the Anthropocene', *Economic Geography*, 95(1): 1–21.

Hall, S., Foxon, T.J. And Bolton, R. (2017) 'Investing in low-carbon transitions: energy finance as an adaptive market', *Climate Policy*, 17(3): 280–98.

Hancock, L. and Ralph, N. (2021) 'A framework for assessing fossil fuel "retrofit" hydrogen exports: security-justice implications of Australia's coal-generated hydrogen exports to Japan', *Energy*, 223: art 119938. Available from: https://doi.org/10.1016/j.energy.2021.119938 [Accessed 3 July 2023].

Harvey, D. (2018) *The Limits to Capital* (new edn), London: Verso.

Hayter, R. (2008) 'Environmental economic geography', *Geography Compass*, 2(3): 831–50.

Holmes, G. (2014) 'What is a land grab? Exploring green grabs, conservation, and private protected areas in southern Chile', *Journal of Peasant Studies*, 41(4): 547–67.

Huang, P., Westman, L. and Castán Broto, V. (2021) 'A culture-led approach to understanding energy transitions in China: the correlative epistemology', *Transactions of the Institute of British Geographers*, 46(4): 900–16.

International Energy Agency (2021) *Net Zero by 2050: A Roadmap for the Global Energy Sector* [Online]. Available from: https://www.iea.org/reports/net-zero-by-2050 [iea.org] [Accessed 18 May 2021].

Jiang, Y. (2019) 'Competitive partners in development financing: China and Japan expanding overseas infrastructure investment', *Pacific Review*, 32(5): 778–808.

Johnson, L. (2014) 'Geographies of securitized catastrophe risk and the implications of climate change', *Economic Geography*, 90(2): 155–85.

Jou, S.-C., Chen, D.-S. and Hsiao, M.H.-H. (2004) 'Re-territorialized guanxi networks: Taiwanese capital in Southeast Asia under the shadow of "Go West"', *Asia Insights*, 3: 17–19.

Kama, K. (2020) 'Resource-making controversies: knowledge, anticipatory politics and economization of unconventional fossil fuels', *Progress in Human Geography*, 44(2): 333–56.

Klinger, J.M. (2018) *Rare Earth Frontiers: From Terrestrial Subsoils to Lunar Landscapes*, Ithaca, NY: Cornell University Press.

Knight, E.R.W. (2011) 'The economic geography of European carbon market trading', *Journal of Economic Geography*, 11(5): 817–41.

Knox-Hayes, J. (2010) 'Constructing carbon market spacetime: climate change and the onset of neo-modernity', *Annals of the Association of American Geographers*, 100(4): 953–62.

Knox-Hayes, J. (2013) 'The spatial and temporal dynamics of value in financialization: analysis of the infrastructure of carbon markets', *Geoforum*, 50: 117–28.

Knox-Hayes, J. (2016) *The Cultures of Markets: The Political Economy of Climate Governance*, Oxford: Oxford University Press.

Knuth, S. (2017) 'Green devaluation: disruption, divestment, and decommodification for a green economy', *Capitalism Nature Socialism*, 28(1): 98–117.

Le Billon, P. and Kristoffersen, B. (2020) 'Just cuts for fossil fuels? Supply-side carbon constraints and energy transition', *Environment and Planning A: Economy and Space*, 52(6): 1072–92.

Lee, J.-H. and Woo, J. (2020) 'Green New Deal policy of South Korea: policy innovation for a sustainability transition', *Sustainability*, 12(23): art 10191. Available from: https://doi.org/10.3390/su122310191 [Accessed 3 July 2023].

Lin, B. and Bega, F. (2021) 'China's Belt & Road Initiative coal power cooperation: transitioning toward low-carbon development', *Energy Policy*, 156: art 112438. Available from: https://doi.org/10.1016/j.enpol.2021.112 438 [Accessed 3 July 2023].

Liu, S., Wang, Y. and Wang, Y. (2021) *South Korea and Japan Will End Overseas Coal Financing. Will China Catch Up?* [Online]. World Resources Institute. Available from: https://www.wri.org/insights/south-korea-and-japan-will-end-overseas-coal-financing-will-china-catch [wri.org] [Accessed 20 July 2021].

Makhijani, S. (2014) Fossil Fuel Exploration Subsidies: Japan, London: ODI and Washington, DC: Oil Change International. Available from: http://cdn-odi-production.s3.amazonaws.com/media/documents/9270.pdf [Accessed 3 July 2023].

Mathews, J.A. and Tan, H. (2015) *China's Renewable Energy Revolution*, Basingstoke: Palgrave Macmillan.

McEwan, C. (2017) 'Spatial processes and politics of renewable energy transition: land, zones and frictions in South Africa', *Political Geography*, 56: 1–12.

McGlade, C. and Ekins, P. (2015) 'The geographical distribution of fossil fuels unused when limiting global warming to 2°C', *Nature*, 517: 187–90.

McNee, R.B. (1958) 'Functional geography of the firm, with an illustrative case study from the petroleum industry', *Economic Geography*, 34(4): 321–37.

Miller, F.P. and McGregor, A. (2020) 'Rescaling political ecology? World regional approaches to climate change in the Asia Pacific', *Progress in Human Geography*, 44(4): 663–82.

Pan, F., Hall, S. and Zhang, H. (2020) 'The spatial dynamics of financial activities in Beijing: agglomeration economies and urban planning', *Urban Geography*, 41(6): 849–64.

Radcliffe, S.A., Watson, E.E., Simmons, I., Fernández-Armesto, F. and Sluyter, A. (2010) 'Environmentalist thinking and/in geography', *Progress in Human Geography*, 34(1): 98–116.

Roepke, H.G. (1955) 'Changing patterns of coal production in the Eastern Interior Field', *Economic Geography*, 31(3): 234–47.

Sarrica, M., Richter, M., Thomas, S., Graham, I. and Mazzara, B.M. (2018) 'Social approaches to energy transition cases in rural Italy, Indonesia and Australia: iterative methodologies and participatory epistemologies', *Energy Research & Social Science*, 45: 287–96.

Smil, V. (2015) *Power Density: A Key to Understanding Energy Sources and Uses*, Cambridge, MA: MIT Press.

Tan, C.-Z. and Yeung, H.W.-C. (2000) 'The regionalization of Chinese business networks: a study of Singaporean firms in Hainan, China', *Professional Geographer*, 52(3): 437–54.

Trencher, G. and van der Heijden, J. (2019) 'Contradictory but also complementary: national and local imaginaries in Japan and Fukushima around transitions to hydrogen and renewables', *Energy Research & Social Science*, 49: 209–18.

Trencher, G., Downie, C., Hasegawa, K. and Asuka, J. (2020) 'Divestment trends in Japan's international coal businesses', *Renewable and Sustainable Energy Reviews*, 124: art 109779. Available from: https://doi.org/10.1016/j.rser.2020.109779 [Accessed 3 July 2023].

Wang, X. (2019) 'The dynamics and governmental policies of Shanghai's international financial center formation: a financial geography perspective', *Professional Geographer*, 71(2): 331–41.

Wijaya, T. (2022) 'Conditioning a stable sustainability fix of "ungreen" infrastructure in Indonesia: transnational alliances, compromise, and state's strategic selectivity', *Pacific Review*, 35(5): 821–52.

Yang, X., He, L., Xia, Y. and Chen, Y. (2019) 'Effect of government subsidies on renewable energy investments: the threshold effect', *Energy Policy*, 132: 156–66.

Yenneti, K., Day, R. and Golubchikov, O. (2016) 'Spatial justice and the land politics of renewables: dispossessing vulnerable communities through solar energy mega-projects', *Geoforum*, 76: 90–9.

Zeng, M., Liu, X., Li, Y. and Peng, L. (2014) 'Review of renewable energy investment and financing in China: status, mode, issues and countermeasures', *Renewable and Sustainable Energy Reviews*, 31: 23–37.

Zhang, K., Wang, Y. and Huang, Z. (2021) 'Do the green credit guidelines affect renewable energy investment? Empirical research from China', *Sustainability*, 13(16): art 9331. Available from: https://doi.org/10.3390/su13169331 [Accessed 3 July 2023].

Zhao, H. (2019) 'China–Japan compete for infrastructure investment in Southeast Asia: geopolitical rivalry or healthy competition?', *Journal of Contemporary China*, 28(118): 558–74.

Zhao, S.X.B., Zhang, L. and Wang, D.T. (2004) 'Determining factors of the development of a national financial center: the case of China', *Geoforum*, 35(5): 577–92.

Zimmerer, K.S. (2011) 'New geographies of energy: introduction to the special issue', *Annals of the Association of American Geographers*, 101(4): 705–11.

30

Workplaces of the Future

Lizzie Richardson

Introduction

The prevalence of home-working for certain sections of the labour force during the COVID-19 pandemic has emphasized with renewed vigour the importance of workplaces in instilling a separation of working activities from other spheres of life. Yet in demonstrating the possibility for alternative spatial arrangements of work, the pandemic has also shown that the 'workplace' is not in any simple sense given, but must be constructed through a range of institutional, technological and individual agents. For scholarship in economic geography, the workplace and its processes of construction have historically been something of a side focus, subsumed into broader concerns of labour geography and even the geographies of capitalism (Herod, 1997). This is not to say that workplaces have not featured in such research, but rather that the primary geographical interest was in the spatial distribution of jobs instead of in the taking place of work. Doreen Massey (1995: 3) set out a canonical challenge to such a perspective, arguing for an interpretation of economic geography in terms of the spatial organization of the relations of production (defined, according to her, 'in the widest sense of term'), so that space was to be understood as 'power-filled social relations' rather than simply 'patterns and distributions of atomized objects' (see Chapter 1 in this volume). Massey's conceptualization of the socio-spatial structures of production can be interpreted to direct attention to workplaces in two ways.

First, foregrounding spatial structures showed how production always involved a co-constitutive relationship between employment and forms of work outside the employment relation, therefore encouraging examination of how work takes place beyond the formal designation of a workplace (McDowell, 1991; see also Chapter 6 in this volume). In particular, a focus on socio-spatial relations could disclose the connections between various forms of social reproduction – that feminists among others have shown are found beyond a formally designated workplace – and the production that they support. Second, it emphasized the importance of understanding change through place, which Massey called 'localities', as contingent articulations of social relations that are constantly being formed and transformed (1995: 333). Therefore, workplaces were not incidental products of spatially uneven economic processes but rather were arrangements through which such inequalities were constructed and played out (Pratt, 2004). In examining the workplace and its future primarily with UK examples in mind, this chapter picks up such concern with the constitutive role of space in understanding processes of production. As Massey illustrated, economic geography gets interesting when space and place are the problem at the start of the analysis, rather than an outcome. Any attempt to understand the future trajectories of the workplace must therefore begin less with designated sites but rather with interrogation of the modes of spatial definition and transformation constituting contemporary geographies of work.

In this regard, it is quite clear that there has been a shift – although by no means universally – from work and its disciplines constituted through spatial enclosure at a specific site, to something frequently more diffuse, less fixed and sometimes even amorphous. The spatial separation of 'work' as paid employment from 'life' – a division that had only ever existed for a limited number of people (disproportionately men) globally – seems to be softening. Acknowledging the importance of recent economic geography scholarship that has examined tendencies in specific workplaces such as discrimination in the digital media sector (Cockayne, 2018), diverse transformations of industry and manufacturing (Schmidt, 2019; Bissell, 2021; Cenere, 2021), and the emergence of co-working spaces (Lorne, 2020; see also Chapter 16 in this volume); this chapter nonetheless develops a different perspective by focusing on the spatial forms of work.

Rather than beginning with a predetermined workplace where work naturally occurs, work processes are understood as integral to, not distinct from, the development of work's spatial forms. The chapter proposes that contingency to spatial form – meaning the absence of a fixed relation between function and location – is central to understanding future workplaces, contingencies that nonetheless result in highly situated geographies with their own forms of (spatial) control even if these are not always produced through the discipline of containment. The chapter outlines three modalities of spatial contingency that arise from work processes that might form focal points for future inquiry in economic geography: *flexibility* in the definition of the workplace, the *coordination* of working arrangements and the *articulation* of infrastructures for work. But before this, the next section examines how the definition of the workplace must be problematized from the outset, showing that attention to the processes defining working space can reveal a more differentiated politics of work.

The problem of the workplace

In common parlance in a country such as the UK, the workplace is generally understood as a fixed location, one that is frequently enshrined as such through regulatory codes and legal requirements. It is a place that is distinct from other sites, spatially enacting a separation of work from alternative forms of activity, and thus encapsulating work discipline as a rhythm that structures social life 'in' and 'out' of working hours. Such an understanding is relatively recent, but one that has nonetheless been foundational to modern social organization in Britain. The containment of paid employment within a discrete workplace materialized the shifting meaning of the term 'work', which with industrial capitalism moved from the basic sense of an activity, effort or achievement, to predominantly denoting a specialization to regular paid employment (Williams, 1976: 335). Work was therefore increasingly understood 'by a definition of its imposed conditions, such as "steady" or timed work, or working for a wage or salary: being hired'. The implication was that 'to be in or out of work' meant 'to be in a definite relationship with some other who had control of the means of productive effort' (Williams, 1976: 335). A distinct workplace was thus a critical – and historically and geographically situated – notion through which the conditions of work – being 'in' work – were imposed, including the discipline of sites such as the factory, that operated variously 'to concentrate; to distribute in space; to order in time' (Deleuze, 1992: 3). This spatial separation, though, is one that has only ever been partial, extended to a small proportion of the world's population, and even then dependent on enrolling the labour of others to support such a division.

First, the creation of a spatially separate site for working activity has relied on gendered and racialized divisions of labour in which spaces of work – albeit frequently unpaid – extend beyond the formal workplace. The fixed function workplace, while the focus of the working-class movement, also relies on and indeed produces spaces such as the home as sites of exploitation of the non-wage labour of 'social reproduction' (Dalla Costa and James, 1972: 10).

Second, a spatially distinct site for work obfuscates the complex social relations composing both working activity and how it takes place. Two examples of this obfuscation will suffice. One is the constitution of social reproduction that itself can perpetuate existing inequalities of class, race and gender, such as when wealthier households pay for care and cleaning work within the domestic space (Glenn, 1992; Pratt, 2012), One person's site of relaxation or leisure might therefore be another person's site of work, and it is associated interests in performances of workplace identity that were the focus of cultural economic geographies of the workplace in the 1990s (McDowell, 1997). The other example is the invisible work of those such as cleaning staff 'out of office hours' to provide the conditions that make the 'real work' possible in office buildings (Wills, 2008). The workplace is thus frequently composed of differentiated types of working activity that are not equally recognized through its definition, so that admission to the workplace is by no means a straightforwardly 'progressive' issue. Thus, uncovering the processes through which spatial definition of work occurs at a given historical moment reveals a more differentiated politics of work. Modes of workplace definition open the historically and geographically situated systems of differentiation through which some activities come to be recognized as work while others do not.

For much of the 20th century in the UK, though, it was possible (although by no means sufficient, as feminist scholarship, for example, has shown) to construct a politics of work around a spatially contained workplace, and thus to at best underplay the significance of such systems of differentiation that normatively produce the workplace. However, towards the end of the 20th century, this consensus concerning the workplace began to be challenged, and it is this that has informed recent feminist economic geographies examining the workplace (Reid-Musson et al, 2020; Cockayne, 2021). Feminist scholarship has in different ways emphasized the growing contingency of working activity across spaces of (re)production. It is to these modalities of spatial contingency and the modulated differentiation of workplaces from other spatial forms that the next section turns.

Future workplaces as spatially contingent

Spatial contingency is central to understanding contemporary working activity, such that a fixed or contained workplace is by no means the most useful starting point for geographies of work. Instead, this section outlines three modalities of spatial contingency for understanding future workplaces. First, workplaces that were previously formally designated and fixed in location now frequently have a flexible spatial definition, notably the office whose nominal working activity can be carried out beyond a specific office building. Second, this flexibility in turn requires greater coordination of working arrangements that produce mobile workspaces such as that of logistics work and logistical media. Third, the coordination necessary to maintain flexible spatial definition itself requires new forms of articulation that is often excluded from formal work definition but nonetheless is an integral infrastructure for work to take place.

Flexible spatial definition

The relationship between work function and work location is no longer as strong as it was, particularly for the activities of knowledge and information work. To carry out a particular task with information and communication technologies does not tie a worker to a specific site in the way that a machine of assembly-line production might do. The gradual digitization of information and the individualized mobility of their associated communication technologies in the latter part of the 20th century has affected all forms of work, but particularly that which is undertaken in the office where the material − paper − attaching workers to that site was slowly undermined, albeit not completely removed. Offices and office work are therefore symptomatic of the way that the definition of 'a workplace' is now frequently spatially flexible, so that its givenness as a fixed site is challenged. However, rather than undermining the importance of geography, such spatial flexibility requires attention to the practices through which workplaces are contingently constructed, creating new geographies of work that have implications for how political demands are made about and through working activity. Sticking with the office example, two broad spatial dynamics of flexibility are observable: the establishment of spaces for work that are dispersed from the office building; and the more or less temporary occupation of the office.

The notion that office work might take place at a distance from the office building − as has become typical for many workers during COVID-19 − has been a familiar one since the 1990s. The 'ever-widening array of high-tech tools' (Perin, 1988: 1) meant that for many professionally and technically trained workers, 'spending every day at the office is beginning to make less and less sense'. Thus even in the late 1980s, there were technologies such as voice mail, electronic conferencing and joint online editing that enabled people to work collaboratively and cooperatively at a distance, so that 'there may be "a place and a time for everything", but the wheres and the whens are no longer as predictable, or as limited, as they once were' (Perin, 1988: 2). The names 'teleworking' and 'telecommuting' emerged to describe these forms of working at distance, which predominantly denoted the creation of an office in the home, but also referred to attempts to develop 'satellite offices' and 'neighbourhood work centres' that enabled the establishment of smaller communities of workers either in suburban areas or in other cities (and even countries) away from a main office.

This dispersal of work from the office to smaller or individually occupied spaces, a tendency which continues today in the 2020s, relies on and indeed produces a form of working control, in which workers internalize the notions of productivity that were previously enacted through workplace disciplines. Although not directly addressing questions of discipline, a range of recent scholarship in economic geography has examined the changing use of office space, critically examining the creativity and 'openness' of co-working (Lorne, 2020), their potential role in community for entrepreneurial workers in urban settings (Avdikos and Kalogeresis, 2017; Merkel, 2019), and the implications for real estate and city planning (Pajević, 2021). Indeed this scholarship on office space has reinstated the 'workplace' and its construction as an area of investigation in economic geography, examining how it shapes spatial organization including forms of temporary concentration of workers that mix social and economic purposes.

It is this social significance of the workplace as a site for congregation, even if – or perhaps exactly because – it is often now only for short periods, which is important for understanding the second dynamic of flexible spatial definition: the temporary occupation of office space. The possibility for workers to undertake office work at other sites has meant less full-time presence in the office, and thus the necessity to support forms of impermanent occupation. While this has occurred on an individual level, for example through co-working offices and co-working spaces more generally, temporary occupation is a broader trend in the real estate industry through the 'space as service' model, in which larger businesses can take out flexible leases on office real estate, where the space itself is made more attractive through the types of hospitality experiences provided (Richardson, 2021). The workplace is thus framed as a consumption choice for workers, as much as a site for businesses, with office space no longer valued quantitatively (in terms of geometric area) but rather for its performative qualities: for the experience it provides. Flexibility does not mean, therefore, that people do not use the office, but rather it implies the creation of more complicated and contingent geographies of work in which the definition of a workplace shifts through varying constellations of use in which the taking place of work can be highly differentiated. This flexible mode of spatial definition illustrated through the contemporary office thus seems to formally decentre work as a constant disciplining rhythm and mode of social stratification (as a distinct occupation – in the sociological sense), thus requiring alternative forms of political claim-making around work that do not centre on a singular worker identity.

Coordination of working arrangements

More sophisticated techniques of spatio-temporal coordination are required by and produced through such flexible definition of workplaces, that allow for more mobile working arrangements. Broadly, there has been a shift from a fixed territorialized site towards the possibility for deterritorialized and mobile coordination. A key purpose of the workplace as a contained site through industrial capitalism was to coordinate production, most obviously in the case of the factory that could improve efficiency and productivity of distributed 'cottage' putting-out systems. The factory as a space, and the associated development of bureaucratic processes to manage production, used location in the workplace as one element in the top-down prescription of coordination through functional specialization in which tasks were broken down into their smallest composite elements so that workers did not have to make decisions concerning their undertaking. The coordination of such tasks was therefore, at least in theory, decided in advance and by those higher up the chain of command in a given workplace. Although fixed location and contained coordination within a workplace remain important, shifts in production processes have resulted in a change to the constitution of coordinating processes in which manufacture is more responsive to (or constitutive of) changing market demands, so that products and services need to be in constant circulation and supply chains contain multiple different actors. Managing but also producing the contingent working arrangements that are necessary to meeting changing market demands therefore requires coordination, which has knock-on effects in supply chains that must be coordinated across a variety of different actors.

Thus coordination is work in and of itself that has its own more or less fixed workplaces, and is also an action that produces or allows for distributed working arrangements. First, sites of coordination – often called 'control centres' – have long been of interest for those studying the role of technologies in workplaces (Luff et al, 2000), including those at logistics hubs such as airports and ports (Gregson et al, 2017). From such locations, the coordination of geographically dispersed actors occurs to achieve a particular step in a given cycle of production or distribution, although not without site-specific frictions. Second, though, technologies of coordination – and processes of decision making concerning work allocation and task definition – are increasingly automated through algorithms – such as those constituting food delivery platforms and thus do not need a distinct physical workplace, but instead distribute working arrangements through handheld mobile devices (Richardson, 2020). These devices are the medium through which a task is delimited and communicated to a worker, who could be anywhere 'on the road'. Real-time geolocational data thus becomes integral to ensuring coordination of these delivery arrangements, through the spatial and temporal delimitation of a task: when and where a pick-up and delivery needs to be made, coordinates which also can change at the last minute. Instantaneous and 'informal' communication about tasks has also therefore become increasingly important, to mitigate such contingencies.

The coordination of work arrangements extends the questions concerning a politics of work that are apparent in the flexible spatial definition of the workplace. In examining logistics, mobile work and platform labour among other areas, economic geography has recently began to address such questions, indicating the frequently individualizing nature of such highly coordination work (Gregson, 2017; Wells et al, 2020). While this coordination potentially produces a greater volume of relations between an individual worker and other actors, this can result in a fragmentation of work-based identities as a variety of different agencies enter working arrangements that lie beyond binary understandings of manager and employee. First, contemporary coordination frequently involves subcontraction and even self-employment, so that many elements are enrolled through modes of organization that exist outside the formal organization. The example of food delivery platforms is again illustrative here, where the delivery workers, who in many cases remain classified as self-employed contractors, are only one element in a distributed working arrangement involving restaurants and customers, that is administered – in theory at least – through an algorithm, a 'non-human agent'. There is, therefore, no formal physical organization to which food delivery workers belong. Second, even within more place-based organizational contexts, the possibilities for rapid coordination of tasks is associated with smaller teams and more ephemeral organizational forms. The rise of 'agile' working is an example of this, in which the orientation and motivation of workers is directed towards short-term project goals through a game-like structure, so that identification and indeed understanding of the overall organizational goals is less clear. Coordination therefore frequently produces more complicated working arrangements, whether in terms of their extensive or intensive forms, which thus poses a challenge for any straightforward claims over work.

Articulation of infrastructure

Enhanced or novel forms of articulation – meaning the effort external to, but necessary for the expression of, work tasks – are required for the coordination of spatially flexible workplaces: from the use of productivity apps for mobile office work to the assembly of supermarket home delivery orders. Articulation involves activities that are integral 'background' for work to take place, so that articulation should in fact be understood as an infrastructure insofar as it patterns the interactions necessary for working activity. Articulation can therefore include activities that are excluded from formal task definition but also involves routinized activities, and so together comprises the 'continuous efforts required to bring together discontinuous elements – of organizations, of professional practices, of technologies – into working configuration' (Suchman, 1996: 407). In this sense then, articulation work has always taken place, as feminist economic geographers have shown (McDowell, 1991) and indeed is indicative of what was frequently the invisible work performed often by women in a variety of formal and informal places for work, including in the design and operation of computers that now are integral to the spatial contingencies of working activities (Light, 1999). Such articulation has often been disregarded or even undiscovered because the emphasis has tended to lie on distribution of rewards, along with the occupational and professional classes through which work is divided, rather than focusing on the activity comprising a given division of labour (Strauss, 1985). Similar to Massey's approach to 'geographies of employment', centring on working activity itself reveals the diversity of work involved in seemingly straightforward notions of 'production', some of which is necessarily 'unproductive', such as much articulation work.

Economic geography has largely left the topic of infrastructure to urban studies (exceptions include O'Neill, 2019; Siemiatycki et al, 2020). However, this should no longer be the case. Given the spatial contingencies to contemporary working activity, the articulation of work infrastructure is now to some degree a proxy for a fixed workplace, insofar as it is what allows work to take place. Thus rather than retaining the term workplace – if this still conjures up an idea of spatial containment – it might be more appropriate to focus analysis on work infrastructures, which as Star (1999) so clearly outlines, primarily become apparent through their articulation or use. A simple example of this are the processes that comprise a place for office work. While in some situations this arrangement can involve a fixed desk, with a desktop computer connected to WLAN (wireless local area network) in a designated office building, many situations are more complicated. It is now possible to turn many spaces into workplaces, thanks to mobile devices and satellite internet connections. These practices of articulating a given space as a place for work may be more or less elaborate – including sometimes simply taking out a laptop in a café – but there are activities which in certain office environments have themselves formed the occupation of 'community manager' who is tasked with creating networks between different actors in the site (Gregg and Lodato, 2018).

In both cases, the articulation of work infrastructure also includes the variety of software that contributes to the working arrangement, and how the laptop or desktop computer interacts with other mobile devices through which 'work' and 'non-work' tasks might be communicated. Building on coordination, then, economic geography of future workplaces could examine the articulation of infrastructure that allows for spatial contingency as a means of considering the diverse agencies comprising spatially diffuse workplaces. Processes of articulation perhaps become a more visible, or at least a more generalized condition, as workers increasingly create and rely on a diffuse set of infrastructural elements that might not be owned or even licensed by their employer (if they are employed), to secure – even if only temporarily – a workplace. Although certainly qualitatively and quantitatively different, the mobile (or stay-at-home) office worker and the food delivery rider must both participate in the articulation of their working arrangements, thus creating the conditions of appearance for work. This means that as much as the spaces of the office 'bleed' in those of home, as Gregg (2011) noted in relation to the intimate attachments of office workers to their work, the erosion of such work–life division is also demanded by the many activities that are required to secure the possibility of work outside of, or without definition through, a 'workplace' or 'work time'.

Conclusion

The definition of the workplace has always been a political issue, serving to systematically differentiate between those activities that count as work and those that do not. Although geography has always been at stake in this definition, it is only more recently that some approaches in the subdiscipline of economic geography have incorporated more relational and differentiated understandings of space that are able to do justice to these politics of definition (Massey, 1995). In economic geography, geographies of labour and capital have tended to be prioritized over questions of how work takes place, and indeed the role of differentiated workplaces inside and outside the employment relation (Gibson-Graham, 1996). Roughly contemporaneously, the increasing prevalence and capacities of digital technologies have altered the constitution of the workplace, demonstrating that the discipline of work is no longer necessarily spatially separate from that of other activities. In combination, this chapter has argued that these conceptual and empirical shifts mean that the economic geographies of the 'workplace of the future' must be comprehended as much through spatial contingencies as through fixities and containment. Thus, rather than focusing on specific sectors, occupations or sites, the chapter has argued for an attention to particular modalities of spatial contingency – flexibility, coordination and articulation – that operate in differentiated ways and produce workplace differentiation. Beginning with the problem of space by understanding how workplaces are spatially contingent is a key question for economic geographies of the workplace of the future.

References

Avdikos, V. and Kalogeresis, A. (2017) 'Socio-economic profile and working conditions of freelancers in co-working spaces and work collectives: evidence from the design sector in Greece', *Area*, 49(1): 35–42.

Bissell, D. (2021) 'Encountering automation: redefining bodies through stories of technological change', *Environment and Planning D: Society and Space*, 39(2): 366–84.

Cenere, S. (2021) 'Making translations, translating Making: actor-networks, spatialities, and forms of Makers' work in Turin', *City*, 25(3/4): 355–75.

Cockayne, D. (2018) 'Underperformative economies: discrimination and gendered ideas of workplace culture in San Francisco's digital media sector', *Environment and Planning A: Economy and Space*, 50(4): 756–72.

Cockayne, D. (2021) 'The feminist economic geographies of working from home and "digital by default" in Canada before, during, and after COVID-19', *Canadian Geographer/Le Géographe canadien*, 65(4): 499–511.

Dalla Costa, M. and James, S. (eds) (1972) *The Power of Women and the Subversion of the Community*, Bristol: Falling Wall Press.

Deleuze, G. (1992) 'Post-script on the societies of control', *October*, 59: 3–7.

Gibson-Graham, J.K. (1996) *The End of Capitalism (As We Knew It): A Feminist Critique of Political Economy*, Minneapolis: University of Minnesota Press.

Glenn, E.N. (1992) 'From servitude to service work: historical continuities in the racial division of paid reproductive labor', *Signs*, 18(1): 1–43.

Gregg, M. (2011) *Work's Intimacy*, Cambridge: Polity Press.

Gregg, M. and Lodato, T. (2018) 'Managing community: co-working, hospitality and the future of work', in B. Röttger-Rössler and J. Slaby (eds) *Affect in Relation: Families, Places, Technologies*, Abingdon: Routledge, pp 175–96.

Gregson, N. (2017) 'Logistics at work: trucks, containers and the friction of circulation in the UK', *Mobilities*, 12(3): 343–64.

Gregson, N., Crang, M. and Antonopoulos, C.N. (2017) 'Holding together logistical worlds: friction, seams and circulation in the emerging "global warehouse"', *Environment and Planning D: Society and Space*, 35(3): 381–98.

Herod, A. (1997) 'From a geography of labor to a labor geography: labor's spatial fix and the geography of capitalism', *Antipode*, 29(1): 1–31.

Light, J.S. (1999) 'When computers were women', *Technology and Culture*, 40(3): 455–83.

Lorne, C. (2020) 'The limits to openness: co-working, design and social innovation in the neoliberal city', *Environment and Planning A: Economy and Space*, 52(4): 747–65.

Luff, P., Hindmarsh, J. and Heath, C. (eds) (2000) *Workplace Studies: Recovering Work Practice and Informing System Design*, Cambridge: Cambridge University Press.

Massey, D. (1995) *Spatial Divisions of Labour: Social Structures and the Geography of Production* (2nd edn), Basingstoke: Macmillan.

McDowell, L. (1991) 'Life without father and Ford: the new gender order of post-Fordism', *Transactions of the Institute of British Geographers*, 16(4): 400–19.

McDowell, L. (1997) *Capital Culture: Gender at Work in the City*, Oxford: Blackwell.

Merkel, J. (2019) '"Freelance isn't free": co-working as a critical urban practice to cope with informality in creative labour markets', *Urban Studies*, 56(3): 526–47.

O'Neill, P. (2019) 'The financialisation of urban infrastructure: a framework of analysis', *Urban Studies*, 56(7): 1304–25.

Pajević, F. (2021) 'The Tetris office: flexwork, real estate and city planning in Silicon Valley North, Canada', *Cities*, 110: art 103060. Available from: https://doi.org/10.1016/j.cities.2020.103060 [Accessed 4 July 2023].

Perin, C. (1988) *The Moral Fabric of the Office: Organizational Habits vs. High-Tech Options for Work Schedule Flexibilities*, MIT Working Paper 2011-88, Cambridge, MA: MIT. Available from: http://dspace.mit.edu/bitstream/handle/1721.1/48477/moralfabricofoff00peri.pdf?sequence=1 [Accessed 4 July 2023].

Pratt, G. (2004) *Working Feminism*, Philadelphia, PA: Temple University Press.

Pratt, G. (2012) *Families Apart: Migrant Mothers and the Conflicts of Labor and Love*, Minneapolis: University of Minnesota Press.

Reid-Musson, E., Cockayne, D., Frederiksen, L. and Worth, N. (2020) 'Feminist economic geography and the future of work', *Environment and Planning A: Economy and Space*, 52(7): 1457–68.

Richardson, L. (2020) 'Platforms, markets, and contingent calculation: the flexible arrangement of the delivered meal', *Antipode*, 52(3): 619–36.

Richardson, L. (2021) 'Coordinating office space: digital technologies and the platformization of work', *Environment and Planning D: Society and Space*, 39(2): 347–65.

Schmidt, S. (2019) 'In the making: Open Creative Labs as an emerging topic in economic geography?', *Geography Compass*, 13(9): art e12463. Available from: https://doi.org/10.1111/gec3.12463 [Accessed 16 June 2023].

Siemiatycki, M., Enright, T. and Valverde, M. (2020) 'The gendered production of infrastructure', *Progress in Human Geography*, 44(2): 297–314.

Star, S.L. (1999) 'The ethnography of infrastructure', *American Behavioral Scientist*, 43(3): 377–91.

Strauss, A. (1985) 'Work and the division of labor', *Sociological Quarterly*, 26(1): 1–19.

Suchman, L. (1996) 'Supporting articulation work', in R. Kling (ed) *Computerization and Controversy: Value Conflicts and Social Choices* (2nd edn), San Francisco, CA: Morgan Kaufmann, pp 407–23.

Wells, K.J., Attoh, K. and Cullen, D. (2020) '"Just-in-Place" labor: driver organizing in the Uber workplace', *Environment and Planning A: Economy and Space*, 53(2): 315–31.

Williams, R. (1976) *Keywords: A Vocabulary of Culture and Society*, Oxford: Oxford University Press.

Wills, J. (2008) 'Making class politics possible: organizing contract cleaners in London', *International Journal of Urban and Regional Research*, 32(2): 305–23.

Postscript: Continuing the Work

Jennifer Johns and Sarah Marie Hall

We have approached this edited collection with an ambitious agenda; to create further space to develop and extend pluralized contemporary economic geographies. This is a task that can only be achieved collectively, and so it is fitting to start our ending by thanking all the contributors to the collection. The work of pluralizing and diversifying is not an equal or shared task, and we are mindful that the labour of doing 'diversity work' often falls to those individuals who are most deeply affected by the problems of privilege and exclusivity. Thus, a collection such as this is more than the sum of its parts, and more than can be seen written on the pages. It represents a collective vision for how to do things differently. In this postscript we take the opportunity to outline what we hope may come from this collection as part of a broader project which brings in you, the readers. This is less of a 'last word' and more of a call to action.

One of the main ways in which we anticipate this book will be adopted is as a teaching resource across multiple disciplines and learning stages. With a wide range of topics and themes, concepts and approaches, from across disciplinary and empirical contexts, the collection offers rich material for teaching pluralistic economic geographies. The chapters are designed to be pithy, accessible and inspiring. As such, they are useful as key readings and introductory texts for foundational undergraduate modules across the social sciences. At the same time, due to the depth and breadth of the contributing chapters, the collection also offers materials for optional courses which explore contemporary economic issues in more detail.

Moreover, with a focus on previous, current and future research agendas, we expect the collection will appeal to students and scholars alike in developing ideas for their own studies (for example, scoping projects, dissertations, funded research). The act of pluralizing any discipline involves active participation and learning, regardless of educational or career stage. Indeed, this collection brings together scholars from a wide range of approaches, perspectives and backgrounds.

Added to this, pluralizing any discipline is a process that requires time and effort. This includes thinking about not just *what* we write about but *how* we write. On this we particularly hope that readers will make use of the reference lists that accompany each chapter, as authors have devoted particular attention to diversifying the sources cited. This is not the only way to pluralize scholarship, of course, but it is one step towards equitable everyday academic practices, including, but not limited to, broadening citations, conference and keynote invitations, and reframing debates away from tried-and-tested approaches.

Finally, there are three ways in which we aspire for the collection to sustain change across economic geographies and for this project to flourish. First, we hope the collection may help to pluralize what might currently be self-described as the current economic geography community – by this we mean those who identify as economic geographers with an interest and investment in the subfield. In this regard we are contributing to change via our upcoming donation of book royalties that will be ringfenced specifically and solely for equality, diversity and inclusion activities. This includes supporting attendance at conferences, events and social activities aligned to the Economic Geography Research Group of the Royal Geographical Society with the Institute of British Geographers, such as travel, registration, childcare and associated costs.

Second, we hope this collection will help to attract more scholars to engage with economic geography and continue our previous ambitions detailed in Chapter 1 to open up the subdiscipline. This involved a reconsideration of what scholarly communities are for and what they can achieve, and what the advantages are (for everyone) of taking a more pluralistic approach. As noted in the introductory chapter, some of the scholars we approached to be involved in the collection did not consider their work as 'economic geography', which we think is a response to how the field is set up from within. With this collection we have tried to challenge these conceptions, and join with those who advocate for more generative, generous scholarship. This can take many forms, such as dialogue with other disciplines, diversity in authorship and an international scope.

Finally, our intentions are to inspire the next generation of scholars working on geographies of the economy. This might include building on the ideas, conceptual frameworks, contextual examples, and methodological approaches that our contributors explore. With each chapter also grounded in empirical insights, readers might be guided in how to also undertake considered research on economies in different contexts, and what can be achieved by adopting a pluralist perspective. This is the principal way in which to ensure this collection represents a meaningful and lasting project. To be continued.

Index

References to figures appear in *italic* type.

Printed and bound by CPI Group (UK) Ltd, Croydon, CR0 4YY

23/04/2025

14661021-0005